Sweet Swan of Avon

Did a Woman Write Shakespeare?

third edition

CW01455686

Well then, must I work
otherwise what I may).

Mary Sidney Herbert, the Countess of Pembroke • 1603

Sweet Swan of Avon

Did a Woman Write Shakespeare?

third edition

Robin P. Williams, Ph.D.

WILTON CIRCLE PRESS
USA

Sweet Swan of Avon: Did a Woman Write Shakespeare? *third edition*
©2019 Robin P. Williams, Ph.D.

Original hardbound published 2006

Library of Congress copyright 2002 in the category
of "original research that reaches a new conclusion":
TXu 1-071-346

WGA registration of screen treatment: 91888

All illustrations © John Tollett
www.MarySidneySociety.org

Wilton Circle Press
7 Sweet Swan Lane
Santa Fe, NM 87508
info@MarySidneySociety.org

Credits
Cover design and production: John Tollett
Portrait of Mary Sidney and of Wilton House: John Tollett
Interior design and production: Robin Williams
Indexer: Robin Williams
Editor: Barbara Riley

Notice of rights
All rights reserved. No part of this publication may be reproduced or transmitted
in any form or by any means, electronic, mechanical, photocopying, recording, any
information storage or retrieval system, or otherwise without permission in writing
from the copyright holder. For information on getting permission for reprints and
excerpts, contact robin@WiltonCircle.com.

The literary paper trail chart by Diana Price is used with permission: *Shakespeare's
Unorthodox Biography, New Evidence of an Authorship Problem,* Diana Price, ©2001
by Diana Price. Reproduced with permission of Greenwood Publishing Group, Inc.,
Westport, CT.

All quotations are from the First Folio, 1623. All line numbers are from *The Complete
Works of Shakespeare, sixth edition,* edited by David Bevington. Bevington's book not
only provides background material, excellent glosses, and thoughtful editing, it has
considerate typography, nice paper, and is the easiest and most pleasant collected works
to read.

For Shakespeare readers, especially reading groups: www.iReadShakespeare.org

Printed and bound in the United States of America.

MARY SIDNEY HERBERT
Countess of Pembroke
1561–1621

WILLIAM SHAKESPEARE
1564–1616

He remains, in fact,
the most anonymous
of our great writers.

Alvin Kernan
Shakespeare, The King's Playwright

In fact, we probably know more
about the daily life of a dinosaur
than we do of the man W. H.
Auden dubbed "The Top Bard."

Norrie Epstein
"Who Wrote Shakespeare"
Living in a Shakespearean World

Contents

Part Three • **The Sonnets**

Part Four • **The Sources**

Part Five • **The Women**

Part Six • The Antagonists

Part Seven • The Publications

Part Eight • The Possibility

Part Nine • The Appendices

Note: *I occasionally repeat information in the book. This is for two reasons: People enter books in different ways and don't always read front to back. Also, there are so many details in this book that I do not expect you to actually remember everything from one chapter to another, so where information is critical for understanding, I repeat it.*

In an effort to reflect the breadth of scholarship around both the Shakespearean canon and Mary Sidney, I quote extensively from published material. This also assures you that I am not speculating or inventing ideas to make my point— I am merely making new connections between people, events, and opinions that are already well established.

I have great cause to give great thanks
Coriolanus

This book has been a long time in the making. I thank the founding members of the Mary Sidney Society and especially the dedicated board of directors for their enduring and endearing support as this project unfolded; Mary Grady for her early editing; Jim'Bo Norrena, Laura Egley Taylor, and Dana Evans for their eager participation on our grand adventure in England, filming a pilgrimage to places where Mary Sidney had been and getting dizzy in roundabouts along the way; Mark Rylance for his warm acceptance and encouragement at Shakespeare's Globe Theatre in London; Claire van Kampen at the Globe Theatre for her invaluable insights into the possible musical work of Mary Sidney, and for her genuine appreciation of this woman; William Leahy at Brunel University in London for helping me get to the next step, and whose trust in me changed my life; for the many friends who have enthusiastically provided great support, especially Elizabeth West, Anna Darrah, Ceryn Schoel, Elizabeth Thornton, Jeanne Bahnson, Joannie Starbuck, Carmen Sheldon, Barbara McNally, Tim Taylor, Reeve Taylor, Ross and Danby Carter, Amy Meilander; Caryl Farkas, Anna Farkas; my mother, Pat Williams, and her friends; my dad, who would have been proud; my sibs Jeff, Shannon, Cliff, and Julie Williams; my uncle Merv Williams and my "Ant Jean" Williams; the First Friday Club and Sundays with Sidney, readers who have spent years reading the plays aloud with me; iReadShakespeare.org and the Mary Sidney Society; Barbara Riley, dear friend and skillful editor who really pulled the book together; Ute, Steven, and Malte Forstat for the elegant German translation; to my incredible kids, Ryan, Jimmy, and Scarlett, who have been unconditionally encouraging, bless their hearts. And the veriest loving thanks to John Tollett, my man of men, my knight in shining technogear.

To JT, my stalwart supporter, who says, "There's more evidence that a spaceship crashed in Roswell than that the man named William Shakespeare wrote those plays."

Who Wrote Shakespeare?

AS EARLY AS THE MID-1700S, experts and amateurs have been debating what may seem like an absurd question—on the order of "Who is buried in Grant's tomb?" The debate has its own title, "The Authorship Question."

It is a surprise to many people that there is even a question of the true authorship of the Shakespearean works. Some adamantly insist there is no question at all. But the query isn't going away. If the arguments for William Shakespeare's authorship were sound, two hundred years' worth of books, articles, debates, and films about the issue would not exist. No one quibbles over who wrote the works attributed to Ben Jonson or Sir Francis Bacon, written in the same era. But because the language and ideas of the Shakespearean plays shape the very patterns of our speech and color our standards of literary excellence worldwide, the Authorship Question is more than a quibble.

Even if you've never seen or read a Shakespeare play in your life and don't intend to, I hope you'll find this presentation to be thought-provoking. I'll explain some of what we know about the author derived from the plays and why William Shakespeare's authorship is a problem. With that in place, I'll introduce you to the documented evidence pertaining to Mary Sidney Herbert, the Countess of Pembroke, and ask you to consider this question:

Might this woman have written the plays and sonnets attributed to the man named William Shakespeare?

The purpose of this book is not to *prove* that Mary Sidney wrote the works attributed to Shakespeare—I only hope to present enough documented evidence to elicit the curiosity of others to pursue further research into this possibility. Most of all, I hope to create an expectation of using *only* documented evidence in future scholarship regarding the Authorship Question.

Robin

Prologue

*To catalogue Shakespeare's largest gifts is almost an absurdity:
where begin, where end? He wrote the best poetry and the best
prose in English, or perhaps in any Western language. That
is inseparable from his cognitive strength; he thought more
comprehensively and originally than any other writer. . . .
he went beyond all precedents (even Chaucer) and invented
the human as we continue to know it.*

Harold Bloom, *Shakespeare: The Invention of the Human,* 1999

THE PLAYS AND SONNETS OF SHAKESPEARE are considered by many to be the most important literary works in the English language; by others, the greatest in any language. Charles Murray in *Human Accomplishment: The Pursuit of Excellence in the Arts and Sciences, 800 B.C. to 1950,* states that, "Of all the giants in all the fields, Shakespeare is the one who seems to leave historians stretching for some way to convey his awesome impact not just on literature but on the modern West." [1]

The importance and influence of this playwright indicates why it is important to know who the author is. People often ask, "Why does it matter who wrote the works? We have the plays themselves." And yes, knowing the author is this white male or that white male might not make such a difference. But if it is a *woman* who towers above the most significant thinkers and creators in the fields of art, literature, science, technology, and philosophy, throughout history and all over the planet—if it is a *woman* who impacted the modern West more than any other human being on earth—then we need to acknowledge that. It could change the world.

The Impact of Shakespeare

THE AUTHOR OF THE PLAYS writes about a wider range of human experience than any other writer before or since. Over a period of fewer than thirty years, the plays explore and present insights into hate, revenge, politics, jealousy, relationships between children and parents, many kinds of love, battles between good and evil, ambition, nature versus nurture, Nature versus Reason, passion, melancholy, old age,

---

1   Charles Murray, *Human Accomplishment: The Pursuit of Excellence in the Arts and Sciences, 800 B.C. to 1950* (New York: HarperCollins Publishers, 2003), 142.

youth, justice, loyalty, marriage, fidelity, perfidy of all sorts, death, philosophy, innocence, wonder, stupidity, war, forgiveness, time, madness, patience, tyranny, guilt, magic, fate, free will, friendships, deception, competition, politics, society, racism—struggles large and small. The playwright doesn't judge, but presents these to us as part and parcel of our humanity—a mirror that simply reflects and illuminates what it is to be human.

THE DEPTH OF THE PLAYS AND SONNETS is astonishing. While the first introduction to the work can be difficult, as many complex things in life can be, the time spent to become familiar with the canon leads to wonder and awe. Each time we read or see a particular play, our appreciation deepens. The first time through a play we often get the gist of the plot, a sense of the language, and we can answer specific questions such as: Why is Romeo melancholy in Act 1? How old is Juliet? To which town did Romeo run away? As we spend more time with a play, we're compelled to look at other questions, such as: Why would the nurse suddenly change her support of Romeo? Why are there so many references to dark and light? And after the whos and whats are out of the way, we start to ponder the deepest questions of love, commitment, revenge, defiance: What does it mean to truly love your daughter or your father? Where should one's allegiance lie? How does this play reflect our present society? Each play presents moral quandaries to which characters must respond, and their reactions force us to regard our own choices.

If it's been said in English, Shakespeare said it better.
Robin P. Williams

THE PLAYWRIGHT USES A VAST RANGE of poetic techniques and rhetorical devices that emphasize and enrich the concepts and human themes explored in the plays, and in the process creates phrases and thoughts that have become settled into our language because of their beauty. The author does not simply pour heart and soul onto the page in a stream of consciousness, but is clearly a classically trained poet who displays a very skilled use of every possible formal device, including anaphora, analepsis, anadiplosis, epistrophe, epanalepsis, hendiadys, synecdoche, isocolon, stichomythia, oxymoron, parison, litote, antanaclasis, ploce, epizeuxis, chiasmus, zeugma, polyptoton, personification, paradox—and many others. Entire books are devoted to Shakespeare's use of classical rhetoric, including the forms of argument.

Of course, many good writers instinctively use a particular technique, unconsciously understanding its inherent effect. But this author's apparently effortless virtuoso use of techniques in poetry and rhetoric, even in the least critically successful of the plays, reveals a master who respects the craft and consciously manipulates the English language to achieve specific emotional responses from the reader or viewer.

THE PLAYWRIGHT EXCELS IN CREATING IMAGES that develop in our minds and are reinforced by not only individual lines, but the stories as a whole. To this end, clusters of particular images appear in the plays. For instance, *Romeo and Juliet* is filled with contrasting visions of dark and light, old and young, hate and love, night and day, death and life—each image strengthening the individual lines while building toward a powerful, cohesive whole.

Hamlet is filled with images of sickness: infection, maggots, weeds, ulcers, disease, and corruption; *Measure for Measure* with justice, balancing, weighing, and comparing; *The Tempest* with master/servant and bondage references, the moon, water, ebbing and flowing, language, dreaming, sleeping, and death. These clusters are treasures of imagery that become richer with repeated readings and viewings.

Provocative and multiple levels of meaning in thousands of lines add to the elegance and depth of the language. For instance:

> *O powerful Love, that in some respects makes a beast a man;*
> *in some other, a man a beast.*
> Falstaff in *The Merry Wives of Windsor*, 5.5.4

Taken *out* of context, the lines are rich in multiple meanings; *in* context, with Falstaff decked in chains and stag horns to meet two married women whom he plans to take advantage of, even more meanings bubble to the surface. It is astonishing how many words and lines in the plays and sonnets resonate with multiple rich, subtle (and not so subtle) meanings—it is one of this writer's greatest gifts.

ON A PERSONAL LEVEL, in every play we are struck by thoughts and ideas that accurately mirror our place in the world at that moment. Rereading the plays at different times in our lives, certain lines might be more or less true for each one of us:

> *Out of my sight, thou dost infect mine eyes.*
> Anne in *Richard 3*, 1.2.151

> *O that my tongue were in the thunder's mouth,*
> *Then with a passion would I shake the world.*
> Constance in *King John*, 3.4.38–39

> *My tongue will tell the anger of my heart,*
> *Or else my heart, concealing it, will break,*
> *And rather than it shall, I will be free,*
> *Even to the uttermost as I please, in words.*
>
> Kate in *The Taming of the Shrew*, 4.3.77–80

> *And whether we shall meet again I know not:*
> *Therefore our everlasting farewell take:*
> *For ever, and for ever, farewell Cassius,*
> *If we do meet again, why we shall smile;*
> *If not, why then, this parting was well made.*
>
> Brutus in *Julius Caesar*, 5.1.118–122

SUCH A WIDE VARIETY OF DISPARATE CHARACTERS, each with a unique voice, has never been equaled by any other writer. There are more than a thousand characters in the collection of plays; more than one hundred are major personalities. Individual character-izations unfold with startling richness and depth through their words and actions.

SPEAKING OF LANGUAGE, not only is this the medium through which the author excels in reaching our hearts, but the language of the plays and sonnets has been a forceful influence for 400 years. The poet had a 30,000-word vocabulary.[2] A college graduate today has a vocabulary of about 10–15,000 words (no wonder we don't understand every line!), and most of us actually use only 3–4,000 of the words we know. This writer contributed about 1,500 new words to the English language, from *addiction* and *assassination* to *wild-goose chase*, *worthless*, and *zany*. Entire phrases have become part of our everyday lives. As Bernard Levin eloquently explains in *The Story of English*:

> If you cannot understand my argument, and declare "It's
> Greek to me," you are quoting Shakespeare; if you claim
> to be more sinned against than sinning, you are quoting
> Shakespeare; if you recall your salad days, you are quoting
> Shakespeare; if you act more in sorrow than in anger, if
> your wish is father to the thought, if your lost property
> has vanished into thin air, you are quoting Shakespeare;

---

2   Robert McCrum, William Cran, Robert MacNeil, *The Story of English*, new and rev. ed. (New York and London: Penguin Books, 1993), 85. Also Jeffrey McQuain and Stanley Malless, *Coined by Shakespeare* (Springfield: Merriam-Webster, Inc., 1998), viii, claim Shakespeare had a vocabulary of 20,000 words.

if you have ever refused to budge an inch or suffered from green-eyed jealousy, if you have played fast and loose, if you have been tongue-tied, a tower of strength, hoodwinked or in a pickle, if you have knitted your brows, made a virtue of necessity, insisted on fair play, slept not one wink, stood on ceremony, danced attendance (on your lord and master), laughed yourself into stitches, had short shrift, cold comfort, or too much of a good thing, if you have seen better days or lived in a fool's paradise—why, be that as it may, the more fool you, for it is a foregone conclusion that you are (as good luck would have it) quoting Shakespeare; if you think it is early days and clear out bag and baggage, if you think it is high time and that that is the long and short of it, if you believe that the game is up and that truth will out even if it involves your own flesh and blood, if you lie low till the crack of doom because you suspect foul play, if you have your teeth set on edge (at one fell swoop) without rhyme or reason, then—to give the devil his due—if the truth were known (for surely you have a tongue in your head) you are quoting Shakespeare; even if you bid me good riddance and send me packing, if you wish I were dead as a door-nail, if you think I am an eyesore, a laughing stock, the devil incarnate, a stony-hearted villain, bloody-minded, or a blinking idiot, then—by Jove! O Lord! Tut, tut! for goodness' sake! what the dickens! but me no buts—it is all one to me, for you are quoting Shakespeare.[3]

What Did the Playwright Value?

Based on close readings of the plays, we can make some educated speculations as to what this author valued.

MUSIC: Every play includes music. There are more than 500 references to music, the depth of which indicates the author is a trained musician.

LITERACY: In every play, there are references to literacy or media (reading, writing, printing, documents, books, etc.), and in most plays

In every man's writings, the character of the writer must lie recorded.
Thomas Carlyle
1795–1881

---

3   Bernard Levin, in *The Story of English*, 81–82. Some of the words and phrases quoted in this statement were not actually created by or used for the first time by Shakespeare, but were popularized through the plays. These include such phrases as: it's Greek to me, play fast and loose, in a pickle, make a virtue of necessity, sleep not one wink, cold comfort, fool's paradise, the long and short of it, your own flesh and blood, teeth set on edge, what the dickens, and give the devil his due. All were used by other authors in print prior to Shakespeare; see *Brush Up Your Shakespeare!*, by Michael Macrone (New York: Harper and Row, 2000), 204–11, and the Oxford English Dictionary.

literate references begin in the very first scene. Letters are exchanged in all but six plays. Intriguingly, there are only four clearly illiterate characters, all male. Even the shepherd girls Phoebe, Mopsa, and Dorcas, are literate. Shakespeare appears to expect literacy.

POLITICAL STATEMENTS: The plays satirize leading political figures and the royal court itself, with its fawning servility and superficiality—an insider's view of the court. The author had a thorough understanding of the feudal aristocracy, its death cries, and the voice of the emerging middle class. "The plays concern themselves with such sensitive issues as the abuse of royal power, political hypocrisy, courtly vanity, monarchical madness, and regicide."[4]

IMAGERY: In Caroline Spurgeon's book, *Shakespeare's Imagery and What It Tells Us*, she categorizes every image in every play.[5] Based on the preponderance of various images, she concludes that the author disliked bad smells and hated war (although none of the imagery suggests a direct knowledge of war or fighting). The author loved the garden and orchard, but did not farm; was a keen observer of birds; knew the names of flowers, weeds, and herbs, as well as their medicinal uses and emotional symbolisms. The author's favorite sport was lawn bowling, second was archery, and had a familiarity with soccer (football) and tennis. Fluent knowledge of alchemy, astrology, and legal terms is evident. The unforced vocabulary of the equestrian, falconer, and hunter suggests lifelong exposure. Although very class-conscious in the human realm, the playwright had more empathy for the down-trodden of every species than did any other writer of the time. While enjoying the occupations of daily indoor life, there is obvious pleasure in nature and the English countryside. Though the images and references to the sea, ships, and seafaring "are generally a landsman's images, a few of them drawn from the management of a ship show that he had some knowledge of technical language and the sailor's craft, which indeed is sufficiently proved in the opening of *The Tempest*."[6]

---

4   Russ McDonald, *The Bedford Companion to Shakespeare* (Boston: Bedford Books, 1996), 25.
5   Caroline Spurgeon, *Shakespeare's Imagery and What It Tells Us* (1935; reprint, Cambridge: Cambridge University Press, 1996).
6   Ibid., 47.

Ms. Spurgeon surmises that the playwright's "interest in and acute observation of cooking operations are very marked all through his work."[7] And "there is clear evidence of his observation of and interest in needlework."[8] The knowledge of medicine, treatment of disease, and actions of medicines on the body became more important as the writer grows older.[9] A dislike of overeating and drunkenness is noticeable.[10] The writer has a remarkable interest in and observation of children and child nature from babyhood.[11] Spurgeon's research makes it clear that "Shakespeare does not rebel against death, but accepts it as a natural process."[12]

You might ask how we can know that the playwright favors particular things, such as particular recreations. For instance, it is often said that the author was an experienced falconer or hawker, yet there is only one short scene about this sport in the entire canon (*2 Henry 4*). But falconry *imagery* is embedded liberally throughout the plays.

FALCONRY: While a writer today might study falconry to describe a hunt or to add color to dialogue, this author was so familiar with the sport that technical terms are integrated into dialogue that has nothing to do with hawking or falconry. For instance, from *Romeo and Juliet*:

> *O for a falconer's voice,*
> *To lure this tassel-gentle back again.*

Juliet in *Romeo and Juliet*, 2.2.159–160

> Juliet wants to be able to call Romeo as loudly as a falconer calls to her hawks. A tassel-gentle (tiercel-gentle) is the peregrine, the noblest of the falcons. The peregrine is also a bird to whom a falconer must make a long-term commitment to train and keep.

The laws of ownership established in the fifteenth century stipulated that certain birds were allocated to certain social ranks, and a person could not hunt with a bird that was allocated to a higher rank. Thus in the quotation above, the writer also indicates the lover's social status—only a person of the upper class is allowed to hunt with a peregrine (a lower class man is allowed to hunt with a kestrel, which catches rodents and bugs.)

---

7   Ibid., 119.
8   Ibid., 124.
9   Ibid., 129.
10 Ibid., 136.
11 Ibid., 137.
12 Ibid., 184.

Or as Juliet says to the Night while waiting for Romeo to arrive to consummate their marriage:

> *Hood my unmann'd blood bating in my cheeks,*
> *with thy black mantle.*
>
> *Romeo and Juliet, 3.2.14–15*

> When a bird is unaccustomed to being handled by a human, it is "unmanned." When a bird is nervous, it "bates," or flutters its wings. When a bird bates, a hood or mantle is placed over its head to calm it down. The mantle refers to the dark cloak of Night that will hide Juliet's blushing face so Romeo won't notice how immodestly she awaits his arrival, but it is also a pun on how a bird mantles, or stands over its kill with its wings wide open to hide it from others.

Romeo calls Juliet his "nyas" (an obsolete term for "eyas," *Romeo and Juliet*, 2.2.167), which is a young hawk taken from its nest in preparation for training.

In *Othello*, however, the Moor says of Desdemona,

> *If I do prove her haggard,*
> *Though that her jesses were my dear heart-strings,*
> *I'd whistle her off, and let her down the wind*
> *To prey at Fortune.*
>
> *Othello, 3.3.276–279*

> A "haggard" is a bird that has been caught as an adult, instead of as a young chick; a haggard is more difficult to train and more likely to leave you. "Jesses" are the straps that fasten around the legs of a trained hawk. To recall a hawk on the wing, you "whistle her off"; when a bird turns "down the wind," she cannot maintain her height and so heads to the ground where the prey is usually caught, either on the ground or on the way down.[13]

LAWN BOWLING: It appears that the author is very fond of bowls, or lawn bowling, because bowling terms appear more often than any other sporting reference and in surprising places:

> *To die, to sleep,*
> *To sleep, perchance to dream, ay there's the rub . . .*
>
> Hamlet in *Hamlet*, 3.1.65–66

> The term "rub" refers to an obstacle or impediment that hinders the bowl (ball) or diverts it from its proper course.

---

13 All of the hawking information is from Emma Ford, *Falconry: Art and Practice*, rev. ed. (London: Blandford, 1995).

A woman's face, with nature's own hand painted,
Hast thou, the master mistress of my passion—

Sonnet 20

> The terms "master" and "mistress" are from the game of bowls
> and refer to the small bowl that is thrown at the beginning of
> the game. It came to mean an object of passionate interest or a
> center of attention.

ALCHEMY was known as "the royal art," and this playwright was an
avid student of metaphysics, based on the abundance of imagery and
ideas in the plays.[14] Alchemy, closely allied with chemistry and
medicine at the time, was a popular study. Queen Elizabeth had her
own personal alchemist.[15] Alchemy, as Carl Jung notes, is "a mystical
system of spiritual growth, an art of personal transformation."[16]
Presentations of transformation in various forms are found throughout the plays.

Numerous images of distillation, specific references to alchemical
materials and paraphernalia, indeed, entire plays and sonnets based
on symbolic death and transmutation with alchemical metaphors,
tools, and practices reveal a scholar's fluency with the material.

Prince Hal discusses the golden crown of a King as a poor substitute
for the true product of alchemy, the elixir of life. Hal says to his father's
crown:

> *The care on thee depending*
> *Hath fed upon the body of my father;*
> *Therefore, thou best of gold art worst of gold.*
> *Other, less fine in carat, is more precious,*
> *Preserving life in medicine portable.*

Prince Hal in 2 Henry 4, 4.5.159–63

> Hal refers specifically to *aurum portable* (portable gold),
> a product of the Paracelsian physician-alchemists.

14 Lyndy Abraham, *A Dictionary of Alchemical Imagery* (Cambridge University
    Press: Cambridge, 1998), 173.
15 Charles Nicholl, *The Chemical Theatre* (The Akadine Press: New York, 1997), 18.
16 Ibid., xii.

Prospero's lines in *The Tempest* are well-known alchemical references to an experiment that is approaching a critical point and has not yet blown up or failed:

> *Now does my project gather to a head:*
> *My charms crack not; my spirits obey . . .*
> Prospero in *The Tempest*, 5.1.1–2

The Tempest is filled with alchemical references as Prospero transforms and restores his world, from the "king being marinated in sea water before he is rescued and taken to dry land" to the wedding of Ferdinand and Miranda that symbolizes the "chemical wedding" of alchemy, death, and regeneration.[17] Even the title word "tempest" is a reference to the alchemical process of removing impurities from the base metal to facilitate its transmutation into gold. These knowledgeable images provide clues to the author's understanding of this spiritual and intellectual art form.

FROM THE PLAYS, an author emerges who seems to have enjoyed various disciplines, sports, and cultural activities as a way of life, possessing a fluency in a broad range of natural interests and pursuits, which in turn encourages the use of technical terms and expressions in complex yet lucid metaphors.

What Did the Playwright Read?

In creating the plays and sonnets, the author drew on a vast breadth of book learning. Scholars have relentlessly dissected every word and line in every play and poem to identify the sources of Shakespeare's plots and references (only four plays have original plots, and even those use existing sources for images and ideas).[18] The results are tremendous: "Geoffrey Bullough's *Narrative and Dramatic Sources of Shakespeare* runs to eight volumes. The sources accumulated for [Ben] Jonson [a contemporary of Shakespeare's] could be contained in one."[19]

---

17 Abraham, *A Dictionary of Alchemical Imagery*, 179.
18 The four plays with original plots are *The Merry Wives of Windsor, A Midsummer Night's Dream, The Tempest,* and *Love's Labor's Lost.*
19 Michael Dobson and Stanley Wells, eds., *The Oxford Companion to Shakespeare* (Oxford: Oxford University Press, 2001), 441.

What scholars have uncovered is that this author read—at the very least—the works listed on the following pages as evidenced by direct plot lines, phrases, or ideas that came from these sources. It is important to know that more than two dozen of these sources did not exist in English translations during Shakespeare's lifetime. According to *The Oxford Companion to Shakespeare,* the playwright "is now generally credited with the ability to read Latin and French, probably Italian and perhaps a little Spanish."[20]

On the following pages is an incomplete list of more than two hundred books the author of the plays is known to have read—a visual representation of the source materials for the plays.[21] Of course, this does not include any books that the poet might have read simply for pleasure.

20 Ibid., 441.
21 Sources are compiled from, among many others:
Geoffrey Bullough, *Narrative and Dramatic Sources of Shakespeare,* vols. 1–8 (London: Routledge and Kegan Paul; New York: Columbia University Press, 1960).
The Riverside Shakespeare, 2nd ed., *The Complete Works* (Boston, New York: Houghton Mifflin Company, 1997).
David Bevington, ed., *The Complete Works of Shakespeare,* 6th ed. (New York: Pearson Longman, 2009).
Stuart Gillespie, *Shakespeare's Books, A Dictionary of Shakespeare's Sources* (London, New York: Continuum, 2004).

Aesop	*Selected Fables*	Appian of Alexandria	*Civil Wars*, translation by W. B., 1578
Anonymous plays	Children's play about friends Titus and Gisippus at court in 1577	Apuleius	*Apologia*, in Latin
			The Golden Ass, in Latin
	Life and Death of Jack Straw, 1593–94		*The Golden Ass*, Adlington's English translation of 1566
	1 Richard II, or Thomas of Woodstock, c. 1592	Ludovico Ariosto	*Orlando Furioso*, translation of Sir John Harington, 1591
Anonymous	*Frederyke of Jennen*, Antwerp in 1518; translated from Dutch in 1520 and 1560	William Averell	*A Marvellous Combat of Contrarieties*, 1588
Anonymous	*Radulphi de Coggeshall Chronicon Anglicanum*, Latin manuscript	John Bale	*King John*, a play begun before 1536 and rewritten in 1538 and 1561
Anonymous	*The Rose of England*	Baldwin, ed.	*A Mirror for Magistrates*, 1559 edition
Anonymous	*The Tragedy of Pyramus and Thisbe*, unpublished manuscript		*A Mirror for Magistrates*, third edition, 1563
Anonymous	*The Rare Triumphs of Love and Fortune*, acted before Queen Elizabeth in 1582	Matteo Bandello	*Novelle (Novella 22)*, 1554, in Italian only AND/OR Belleforest's *Histoires Tragiques*, 1568, the French translation
Anonymous	*The Chronicle History of King Leir*, c. 1590		
Anonymous	*Gl' Ingannati*, 1531, Italian with no translation	Richard Barnfield	*The Affectionate Shepherd*, 1594
			Cynthia, 1595
Anonymous	*Sir Clyomon and Sir Clamydes*, c. 1570	François de Belleforest	*Histoires Tragiques*, 1570
Anonymous	*Caesar and Pompey, or Caesar's Revenge*, c. 1595, pub. 1606–07, performed at Oxford in early 1590s	Lord Berners	anonymous *Huon of Bordeaux*, translated by Lord Berners c. 1533–1542
Anonymous	*The Battle of Agincourt*, c. 1530	Thomas Blenerhasset et alii	*A Mirror for Magistrates*, 1578 edition
Anonymous	*The Jew*, c. 1569~79	Giovanni Boccaccio	*Decameron (Day 2, Tale 9)*, Italian with no English translation (two translations in French)
Anonymous	*The True Tragedy of Richard III*, c. 1591 (or 1594, per Bullough)		
Anonymous	*The History of Titus Andronicus*	Jean Bodin	*Six Books of a Commonweal*, 1606, translation by Richard Knolles
Anonymous	*A Merry Jest of a Shrewd and Curst Wife Lapped in Morel's Skin for her Good Behaviour*, c. 1550	Timothy Bright	*Treatise of Melancholy*, 1586
		Arthur Brooke	*The Tragical History of Romeus and Juliet*, 1562
Anonymous	*The Taming of a Shrew*, 1594	George Buchanan	*Rerum Scoticarum Historia*, 1582, no English translation
Anonymous	*The Troublesome Reign of John, King of England*, two parts, 1591		
Anonymous ms	*Chronicque de la Traison et Mort de Richard Deus*, French manuscript	William Camden	*Remains . . . Concerning Britain*, 1605
		Baldassare Castiglione	*The Courtier*, translation by Sir Thomas Hoby, 1561
Anonymous	*Wakefield Chronicle*, Latin manuscript	William Caxton	*The Ancient History of the Destruction of Troy*, 1473, translation of the French version by Raoul Lefèvre
Anonymous	*Barlaam and Josaphat*, ninth-century Greek, translated into Latin by thirteenth century		
Anonymous	*The Arte of English Poesie*, dubiously attributed to George Puttenham, 1589	Geoffrey Chaucer	"The Knight's Tale"
			"The Miller's Tale"
			"The Legend of Good Women"
Apollonius of Rhodes	*Argonautica*, Greek, 1496, no English translation		*Troilus and Criseyde*
		George Chapman	*Seven Books of the Iliads*, translation of Homer, 1598
Bible	*Geneva Bible*	Henry Chettle	*Troilus and Cressida*, 1599 manuscript plot (with Thomas Dekker)
Chaplain in H5's army	*Henrici Quinti Angliae Regis Gesta*, Latin manuscript		

Cicero	*Ad Herennenium*		Lucius Florus	*Roman Histories*, in Latin
	Marcus Tullius		Emmanuel Forde	*The Famous History of Parismus*, 1598
	Tuscullan Disputations		John Foxe	*Acts and Monuments of Martyrs*, 1570 edition
G. B. Giraldi Cinthio	*Epitia*, 1583, Italian with no translation			*Acts and Monuments of Martyrs*, 1583 edition
	Hecatommithi, 1565 edition, Italian with no translation		Abraham Fraunce	*The Arcadian Rhetoric*, 1588
	Hecatommithi, 1583 edition, Italian with no translation		Jean Froissart	*The Chronicle of England*, Lord Berners' translation of c. 1523–1525
Gasparo Contarini	*The Commonwealth and Government of Venice*, 1599 translation by Lewis Lewkenor		George Gascoigne	*Supposes*, 1566
Sir Thomas Coningsby	*Journal of the Siege of Rouen*, 1591 unpublished manuscript		Geoffrey of Monmouth	*Historia Regum Britanniae*, Latin manuscript
Henry Constable	*Diana*, 1592		Simon Goulart	*Thrésor d' histoires admirables et mémorables*, French, no translation until 1607 by Grimeston, but *Shrew* was written by 1594
	Diana, enlarged edition of 1594			
Thomas Cooper	*Thesaurus Linguae Romanae et Britannicae*, 1573 edition			
Jean Créton	*Histoire du Roy d'Angleterre Richard*, French manuscript only		John Gower	*Confessio Amantis*, 1554 edition
Richard Crompton	*Mansion of Magnanimitie*, 1599		Richard Grafton	*A Chronicle at Large*, 1569
Samuel Daniel	*Delia*, 1592		Saxo Grammaticus	*Historia Danica*, 1180–1208, in Latin
	The First Four Books of the Civil Wars, 1595		Robert Greene	*Planetomachie*, 1585
	Complaint of Rosamond, 1592			*Pandosto: The Triumph of Time*, 1588
	Musophilus, 1599			*The Second Part of Cony-Catching*, 1591
	The Tragedy of Cleopatra, 1599 edition		Jakob Gretser	*Timon: Comoedia Imitata*, 1584, German playwright, no English translation
	Letter from Octavia, 1599			
Sir John Davies	*Nosce Teipsum*, 1599		Edward Hall	*The Union of the Two Noble and Illustre Families of Lancaster and York*, 1548
Thomas & Dudley Digges	*Four Paradoxes, or Politique Discourses*, 1604			
Richard Eden	*History of Travel*, 1577		Nicholas Harpsfield	*The Life of Sir Thomas More*, c. 1557 in ms only during 16th century
Richard Edwards	*Damon and Pithias*, c. 1565		Samuel Harsnett	*Declaration of Egregious Popish Impostures*, 1603
John Eliot	*Ortho-epia Gallica*, 1593			
Thomas Elmham	*Vita et Gesta Henrici Quinti*, erroneously attributed to Elmham; in Latin		Gabriel Harvey	*Pierce's Supererogation*, 1593
				Ciceronianus, 1577, in Latin
Sir Thomas Elyot	*The Governor*, 1531		Heliodorus	*Ethiopian Story*, available in French in 1547; Italian in 1556; in English by Thomas Underwood, 1569
Desiderius Erasmus	*The Praise of Folly*, in Latin			
	The Praise of Folly, translation of Thomas Challoner in 1549		Robert Henryson	*The Testament of Cresseid*, 1532
	A Modest Mean to Marriage, 1568 translation by N. L.		Pontus Heuterus	*De Rebus Burgundicis*, 1584 in Latin (no translation until 1607)
	A Merry Dialogue Declaring the Properties of Shrewd Shrews and Honest Wives, translation of 1557		John Higgins, ed.	*A Mirror for Magistrates*, 1574 edition
				A Mirror for Magistrates, 1587 edition
Giovanni Fiorentino	*Il Pecorone (First story of Fourth day)*, 1558, Italian only		Ralph Holinshed	*The Chronicles of England, Scotland, and Ireland*, second edition, 1587
Edward Forset	*A Comparative Discourse of the Bodies Natural and Politique*, 1606		Homer	*Iliads (Books I–II, VII–XI)*, 1598, translation by George Chapman
Robert Fabyan	*Chronicle*, 1533, first English version			*Achilles' Shield*, 1598
	Chronicle, 1559 edition			

King James I	*Daemonologies*, 1597
	The True Law of Free Monarchies, 1598
	Basilikon Doron, 1599
	A Counterblast to Tobacco, 1604
Sylvester Jourdain	*A Discovery of the Bermudas*, 1610
Richard Knolles	*History of the Turks*, 1603
Thomas Kyd	*The Spanish Tragedy*, play, 1582~89
	Cornelia, 1594
Lewes Lavater	*Of Ghosts and Spirits Walking by Night*, translation of R. H. in 1572
Raoul Lefèvre	*History of Troy*, translated and printed by William Caxton (the first book printed in English in England), 1475
Thomas Legge	*Richardus Tertius*, manuscript of 1579 (Latin tragedy performed at Cambridge)
Gerard Legh	*Accidence of Armory*, 1562
John Leslie	*De Origine, Moribus, et Rebus Gestis Scotorum*, 1578 in Latin
Titus Livy	*The Roman History*; there was an English translation by Philemon Holland, 1600
Thomas Lodge	"Truth's Complaint Over England," in *An Alarum Against Usurers*, 1584
	Rosalynde, 1590
Lucca	*La Prima Parte de le Novelle del Bandello (Novella 22)*, 1554
Lucian	*Timon, or the Misanthrope*, in Greek; or Latin translation by Erasmus, 1506; or Italian translation by Lonigo, 1536; or French translation by Bretin, 1583
John Lydgate	*The Ancient History and Only True Chronicle of the Wars [of Troy]*, 1555 edition, translated by Guido delle Colonne
John Lyly	*Midas*, c. 1589
	Campaspe, c. 1584
	Euphues: The Anatomy of Wit, 1578/9
	Gallathea, 1592
	Endymion: The Man in the Moon, 1591
Thomas Lupton	*Too Good to be True*, 1581
Don Juan Manuel	*El Conde Lucanor*, 1350, in Spanish
Gervase Markham	*How to Choose, Ride, Train, and Diet both Hunting Horses and Running Horses . . . Also a Discourse of Horsemanship*, 1593
Christopher Marlowe	*Hero and Leander* (with George Chapman), 1598
	Jew of Malta, c. 1589, surviving pub. 1633
	Tamburlaine, 1590
	Edward II, c. 1592

John Marston	*The Malcontent*, 1604
Masuccio Salernitano	*Il Novellino (fourteenth story)*, 1476, Italian only
Thomas Moffett	*Of the Silkworms and their Flies*, 1599
Michel Montaigne	*Essays*, original French manuscript
Jorge de Montemayor	*Diana Enamorada*, Spanish original in 1559; French translations in 1578 and 1587
Thomas More	*Dialogue . . . of the Veneration and Worship of Images*, 1529
	The History of King Richard III, unfinished manuscript in 1513; Latin in 1566; English in 1557
Anthony Munday	*Zelauto, or The Fountain of Fame*, 1580
	Fedele and Fortunio, c. 1584 (actually by "M. A."; attributed to Munday)
	John a Kent and John a Cumber
Thomas Nashe	*Have With You to Saffron Walden*, 1596
	Summer's Last Will and Testament, performed 1592, pub. 1600
	Christ's Tears over Jerusalem, 1593
	Terrors of the Night, 1593, 1594
	Lenten Stuffe, 1598–99
	Pierce Penniless, 1592
Ovid	*Metamorphoses*, in Latin
	Metamorphoses, Golding's translations of 1567 and 1575
	Fasti, 1340 translation by John Gower
	Fasti, 1520, in Latin
William Painter	*The Palace of Pleasure*, 1566–67, translation of Boccaccio
Matthew Paris	*Historia Major*, 1571 in Latin
Orlando Pescetti	*Il Cesare*, 1594, Italian
Francesco Petrarch	*Sonnets, Songs, and Triumphs*
Plautus	*Menaechmi*, in Latin; may have known Wm. Warner's translation of 1595
	Amphitruo, in Latin manuscript
Pliny the Elder	*The History of the World*, 1601 translation by Philemon Holland
Plutarch	*Lives of the Noble Grecians and Romans*, North's translation, 1579
	Lives of the Ancient Greeks and Romans, North's translation, 1603
Thomas Preston	*Cambyses*, 1569
George Puttenham	*The Art of English Poesie*, 1589 (the book is anonymous; dubiously attributed to Puttenham)
J. Rathgeb	*Journal*, 1602

Barnaby Riche	*Riche, His Farewell to Military Profession,* 1581	John Stow	*Annals, or a General Chronicle of England,* 1580
	The Adventures of Brusanus, Prince of Hungaria, 1592	Suetonius	*The Lives of the Twelve Caesars*
Clement Robinson et alii	*A Handful of Pleasant Delights,* 1584	Tacitus	*Annales* (Books I and II,) translation of Richard Grenewey, 1598
Richard Robinson	anonymous *Gesta Romanorum* (story 66), translation of Richard Robinson, 1577, 1595	Richard Tarlton	*The Famous Victories of Henry the Fifth,* unpublished manuscript; registered in 1594, but ascribed to Tarlton 1587 or 1588
Samuel Rowley	*When You See Me, You Know Me,* 1604		*News Out of Purgatory,* 1590
Francis Sabie	*The Fisherman's Tale,* 1594	Lawrence Twine	*The Pattern of Painful Adventures,* 1576 and 1607 editions
	Flora's Fortune, 1595	William Tyndale	*The Obedience of a Christian Man,* 1528
Saint Paul	*Acts of the Apostles*		
	Epistle to the Ephesians	Polydore Vergil	*Anglica Historia,* 1534, in Latin
Flaminio Scala	*Flavio Tradito,* Italian manuscript	The Virginia Council	"True Declaration of the Estate of the Colony in Virginia," 1610
Reginald Scot	*Discovery of Witchcraft,* 1584	Juan Luis Vives	*The Office and Duty of an Husband,* translation of 1555
Nicolò Secchi	*L' Interesse,* 1581		
	Gl' Inganni, 1547	R. W.	*The Three Ladies of London,* 1584
Seneca	*Hercules Furens,* Studley translation of 1566 (Bullough says Jasper Heywood translation, 1561)	George Whetstone	*The Rock of Regard,* 1576
			Promos and Cassandra, 1578 (play based on Giraldi Cinthio's *Hecatommithi,* 1565, and Claude Rouillet's *Philanira,* 1556)
	Octavia, Studley translation, 1566		
	Medea, Studley translation, 1566		
	Hippolytus, Studley translation, 1567		*Heptameron of Civil Discourses,* 1582
	Thyestes, Jasper Heywood translation of 1560	George Wilkins (possibly a pseudonym)	*The Painful Adventures of Pericles, Prince of Tyre,* 1608
	Oedipus, translation by Alexander Neville, 1563	Sir Thomas Wilson	*The Art of Rhetoric,* 1553
Mary Sidney	*The Tragedie of Antonie,* 1595	Henry Wotton	*A Courtly Controversy of Cupid's Cautels,* 1578
	A Discourse of Life and Death, 1592	Xenophon	*Opera Varia,* 1495
Philip Sidney	*The Countess of Pembroke's Arcadia,* 1590		
	Astrophil and Stella, 1591	See the following page regarding translations.	
	An Apology for Poetry (A Defense of Poesy), 1595		
	The Lady of May, manuscript		
Robert Sidney	*The Poems of Robert Sidney,* uncirculated manuscript		
Alexander Silvayn	*The Orator,* L. Piot translation, 1596		
Sir John Smith	*Instructions, Observations, and Order Militarie,* 1595		
John Speed	*History of Great Britaine,* 1611		
Edmund Spenser	*Ruins of Rome: By Bellay,* 1591		
	The Shepherd's Calendar, 1579		
	The Faerie Queen, 1590 edition		
	The Faerie Queen, 1596 edition		
William Strachey	"True Repertory of the Wrack and Redemption of Sir Thomas Gates," a letter to the Virginia Company dated July 15, 1610		

The following sources were not in English translations at the time.

French only:

Francois de Belleforest's French translation of Bandello's Italian *Novelle*, titled *Histoires Tragiques,* also in French.

Two eyewitness accounts of Richard 2 in an unpublished French manuscript.

Decameron, Novel 38, by Boccaccio, French and Italian versions.

Italian only:

Il Pecorone (The Dunce), by Ser Giovanni Fiorentino.

Il Novellino, by Masuccio.

Matteo Bandello's *Novelle.*

Gl' Ingannati; anonymous versions were available in Italian, French, Latin, and Spanish.

Epitia, a play, and *Hecatommithi,* a collection of novels, both written by Giraldi Giambattista, known as Cinthio.

Decameron, Day 2, Tale 9, Boccaccio.

Latin only:

Plautus's *Menaechmi.*

Ovid's *Metamorphoses* (details for *A Midsummer Night's Dream* are not found in Golding's English translation).

Wakefield Chronicle in manuscript.

Historia Major, by Matthew Paris.

Ciceronianus, by Gabriel Harvey.

Adagia, by Erasmus.

Henrici Quinti Angliae Regis Gest, by a chaplain in Henry 5's army.

Vita et Gesta Henrici Quinti, erroneously attributed to Thomas Elmham.

Rerum Scoticarum Historia, by George Buchanan.

De Origine, Moribus, et Rebus Gestis Scotorum, by John Leslie.

Timon: Comoedia Imitata, by Jakob Gretser, a German playwright.

Historia Regum Britanniae, by Geoffrey of Monmouth.

Greek: The Greek source for *Timon of Athens* (Lucian's *Timon, or the Misanthrope*) was also available in Latin, Italian, and French translations, but not in English. A ninth-century Greek source for *The Merchant of Venice,* called *Barlaam and Josaphat,* had been translated into Latin by the thirteenth century. But another source for *The Merchant of Venice,* the *Argonautica* by Apollonius of Rhodes, was not available in any language except Greek.

"Not of an age, but for all time"   *Ben Jonson*

Despite the author's prodigious scholarship, the Shakespearean plays have appealed to a wide range of audiences throughout history. In the author's own time, plays were attended by the lower-class "groundlings" who paid a penny to stand in the roofless courtyard of the theatre, as well as by the wealthy upper class who paid more to sit in the covered seats that rose around the courtyard. In the 1700s, Shakespeare's collected works were found in log cabins, saloons, and church halls across America, and by the late 1800s/early 1900s, Shakespeare had been propagated across America by the Woman's Club movement.[22] Today, the plays are still enjoyed by people of every age, race, color, religion, political preference, education level, income level, and social status—all over the world. They have been translated into almost every written language on Earth (including Klingon).

Shakespeare's contemporary, Ben Jonson, declared in 1623 that these works were "not of an age, but for all time." Little did Jonson know they would not only be for all ages, but also for all humankind.

The French writer Alexander Dumas (1802–1870) sums it up:

> Shakespeare contains the whole of humanity. Anybody who studies Shakespeare, studies at once Corneille and Molière, Racine and Regnard—plus Shakespeare. Shakespeare is as much a writer of comedy as Molière and Regnard: look at Falstaff and Mercutio.
>
> He is as tragic as Corneille and Racine: see *Othello* and *Richard 3*. Moreover, he's as much a dreamer as Goethe: see *Hamlet*; as dramatic as Schiller—think of *Macbeth*. As poetic . . . as ever poet has been: remember *Romeo and Juliet*.
>
> It results that, when an actor or actress has studied Shakespeare, they have studied everything . . . Shakespeare has divined everything.

---

22 Thane Whetstone, "Woman's Clubs: Dispersing Shakespeare Across America," in *Symbiosis: A Journal of Anglo-American Literary Relations*, 15.2 (2011), 193–203.

So Who Was This Person?

This author, who was so well-schooled in the craft of writing, so learned, knew so many languages and had access to so many books, so well-rounded in pursuits and passions, so brilliant at examining and communicating human emotion, so adept at turning a phrase more succinctly and elegantly than anyone before or since, and who has influenced writers, readers, and cultures all over the world for centuries—who *was* this person?

Part One
The Question

The center of this obsession
[of Shakespeare-worship], *then as
now, is the Shakespeare biography,
or rather lack thereof. It is by now
somewhat cliché to be reminded
that we know next to nothing
about Shakespeare's life, that our
knowledge is confined mainly to dry
legal records or unsatisfying contemporary references, and that so little
about him is "revealed" in his works.*

Michael Keevak, *Sexual Shakespeare:
Forgery, Authorship, Portraiture*

Documented Data

- There is no record, while Shakespeare was living, of anyone personally meeting him.

- There is no record that William Shakespeare was ever acknowledged by a patron.

- There is no record that he was ever paid for writing.

- There are no documents or even references to hearsay that Shakespeare acknowledged himself as a writer, nor did anyone in his family ever mention he was a writer.

- There is nothing from Shakespeare in his handwriting except six signatures on legal documents. One is illegible (on his will), and all are spelled differently. All were written within four years of his death.

- Not one piece of an original Shakespearean manuscript or draft has ever been found.

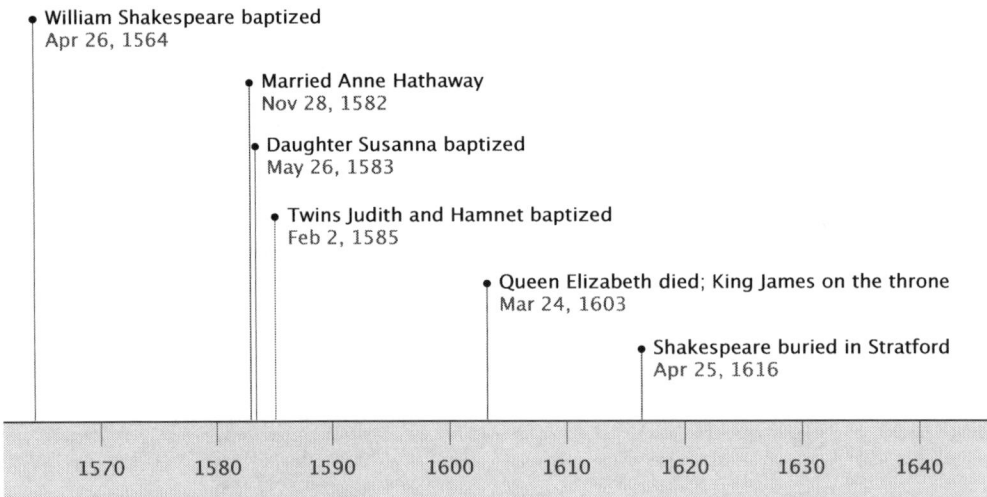

• William Shakespeare baptized
Apr 26, 1564

• Married Anne Hathaway
Nov 28, 1582

• Daughter Susanna baptized
May 26, 1583

• Twins Judith and Hamnet baptized
Feb 2, 1585

• Queen Elizabeth died; King James on the throne
Mar 24, 1603

• Shakespeare buried in Stratford
Apr 25, 1616

| 1570 | 1580 | 1590 | 1600 | 1610 | 1620 | 1630 | 1640 |

1 The Man Named William Shakespeare

HUNDREDS OF THOUSANDS OF BOOKS have been written about the man named William Shakespeare, the plays, the sonnets, and the Authorship Question—Shakespeare is literally the most researched subject on earth. Yet there is no other human being so famous about whom we know so little. It is often said that we have more documentation about the man named William Shakespeare than we do for any other dramatist of the time, with the exception of Ben Jonson—but what is missing from this documentation is any record that Shakespeare was a *writer*. We know he was an actor, but not a writer.

Let us be content with provoking second thoughts and not worry about convincing anyone.
Georges Braque, *Cahiers* 1882–1963

We do know these facts: William Shakespeare was born in April of 1564 in Stratford-upon-Avon, England. In 1582, at the age of 18, a marriage license was issued for Shakespeare to marry Anne Whateley of Temple Grafton, a village five miles from Stratford; the following day, two friends of Anne Hathaway's dead father signed a financial guarantee for Shakespeare to marry Anne Hathaway of Stratford-upon-Avon, who was eight years older than Shakespeare—and three months' pregnant. They had three children by the time he was twenty; their son died at age eleven.[1] His parents, wife, two daughters, and granddaughter were illiterate.[2]

---

1   These facts are in every biography about Shakespeare. S. Schoenbaum's *William Shakespeare, A Compact Documentary Life* (Oxford: Oxford University Press, 1987) sometimes sticks closer to facts than most biographers.
    An honest biography is by Diana Price, *Shakespeare's Unorthodox Biography: New Evidence of an Authorship Problem* (Westport, CT, London: Greenwood Press, 2013).
    Be particularly wary when reading anything by A. L. Rowse as he presents ridiculous fabrications as if they are facts. In general, read any biography of Shakespeare with a discerning mind and a highlighter; see pages 49–55.

2   There is a signature of Shakespeare's oldest daughter, Susanna Hall in 1647, but she was not able to read or even recognize her husband's handwriting. The signature is suspect because it is in what is called secretary hand; women generally wrote in italic hand (see page 216). The others in Shakespeare's family signed with marks. Schoenbaum, *William Shakespeare*, 291.

At some point between the ages of twenty and thirty, Shakespeare left his wife and children to go to London where he was sometimes an actor and a shareholder in various acting companies. He returned now and then to Stratford-upon-Avon where he bought the second-largest house and other properties, sued people for small sums and was sued, sold a load of stone to a Mr. Chamberlin, illegally held eighty bushels of grain during a shortage, owed a shepherd two pounds which was unpaid on the shepherd's death, and defaulted on his property taxes several times. He died in 1616 in Stratford at the age of 52 and was buried in an unmarked grave at the front of the village church.

What We Don't Know

*They say I'm a genius, but I still had to **study** physics.*

attributed to
Albert Einstein
1879–1955

We don't know if William Shakespeare went to school. There was a local grammar school he might have attended from about five to ten years of age. Yet Stratfordians insist that "Shakespeare received in the Stratford grammar school a formal education that would daunt many college graduates today."[3] With this supposedly remarkable public education in town, it's interesting to note that of the nineteen leaders of the town at the time (aldermen and burgesses), only six of them could write their names.[4] Shakespeare's own father was a high bailiff for a short time, and he signed documents with an X, even though this grammar school had been endowed since 1482.[5]

Other than legal signatures, not one piece of handwriting exists that was penned by the man named William Shakespeare. Not one letter from him, not one note, not a journal or a diary, not a poem, not one scrap of a manuscript for a play—nothing exists except six signatures on legal documents, and each is spelled differently. All signatures are within the last four years of his life, three of them are on his will, and even these are suspect, as David Thomas points out: signatures were often "supplied" by the scribe, not the dying person.[6]

3 Stephen Orgel and A.R. Braunmuller, "Shakespeare, the Stage, and the Book," in the digital edition of *William Shakespeare: Comedies, Histories, & Tragedies* (Oakland, California: Octavo, 2001), 27. www.RareBookRoom.org. I would think this comment would offend millions of students and professors—five years (average time of attendance) of schooling from ages five to ten in a village grammar school would daunt college graduates today?

4 Charles Knight, *William Shakespere, A Biography* (New York: Routledge, 1865), 15.

5 Levi Fox, *The Early History of King Edward VI School, Stratford-upon-Avon* (Oxford: Dugdale Society, 1984), 3.

6 David Thomas, *Shakespeare in the Public Records* (London: Public Records Office, 1985), 34.

There is only one letter written to William Shakespeare—a request for a loan—and that letter was never sent.

Because books were so valuable, it was standard practice at the time to put a bookplate or at least your name inside. Ardent Stratfordians have scoured the land for centuries and never found a book Shakespeare owned or even appears to have used.

Philip Henslowe was the most important theater owner, manager, and company banker of the time. He recorded letters to and from writers and actors, but not one letter to or from William Shakespeare. In his account books, called a "diary," Henslowe recorded personal and business contacts from 1592 through 1603, Shakespeare's most prominent years. "The importance of his diary and papers to dramatic history cannot be overemphasized."[7] Although Henslowe was most closely associated with the Rose theater, as opposed to the Globe theater where Shakespeare was a shareholder, he recorded a number of performances of five plays in the Shakespearean canon, but never mentions the man named Shakespeare.[8]

Who Met William Shakespeare?

The Elizabethan/Jacobean era was a time of prolific publishing, letter-writing, diary-keeping, gossip-mongering, satires, and recorded comments by everybody about everybody, thus it is remarkable that "No one who met [William Shakespeare] made a record during his lifetime of what he was like or what he said or did."[9]

Katherine Duncan-Jones notes that, "We do not have a single letter written by Shakespeare, nor even a single incontrovertibly genuine passage of his handwriting, and the Shakespeare biography-industry did not get going until nearly a century after his death. By the time of Nicholas Rowe's biographical essay in 1708 [92 years after Shakespeare's death] oral traditions had proliferated, but there was no one alive who remembered Shakespeare."[10]

Legends about Shakespeare began to spring up in Stratford as soon as there was a demand for them. Legends are a stupid man's excuse for his want of understanding. They are not evidence.

John Masefield, 1911
Shakespeare Home Library

---

7   Oscar James Campbell, ed., *The Reader's Encyclopedia of Shakespeare* (New York: MJF Books, 1998), 358.

8   E. K. Chambers, *William Shakespeare: A Study of Facts and Problems*, vol. 2 (Oxford: Clarendon Press, 1930), Appendix D. The plays that Henslowe mentions are *Titus Andronicus, Henry 6, King Lear, Hamlet,* and *The Taming of a Shrew.*

9   John Michell, *Who Wrote Shakespeare?* (London: Thames and Hudson, 1996), 53.

10 Katherine Duncan-Jones, *Sir Philip Sidney, Courtier Poet* (New Haven: Yale University Press, 1991), ix.

Diana Price points out, "Shakespeare is the only alleged writer of any consequence from the period who left no personal contemporaneous records revealing that he wrote for a living." [11]

There is no record that Shakespeare was personally acquainted with any of the other writers, philosophers, or intellectual thinkers of the time, with the exception of Ben Jonson. Jonson mentioned him years after Shakespeare died. [12] Shakespeare is listed as an actor in two of Jonson's plays, one of which was booed off the stage. [13]

If He were a Rich Man

There are a few more than twenty documentary records (as opposed to literary references) that mention the activity of William Shake-speare. What is stunning is that among the details we have about his life, there is not one word noting that he was a playwright. For instance, it is documented that William Shakespeare held varying portions of the leases of the Blackfriars gatehouse and the Globe theater, that he received 4.5 yards of red cloth as an *actor*, and once received £20 to share with the Lord Chamberlain's troupe for a performance of a play. [14] *But there is no documented evidence that William Shakespeare was a **writer**.*

Nonetheless, with no record of income, Shakespeare became quite wealthy and bought various homes and pieces of property: In 1597 he paid £60 cash for the summary record to transfer the second-largest house in Stratford, called New Place, into his name (we don't know how much he actually paid for the house). [15] In May of 1602 he paid £320 cash for 107 acres of land. In September that same year he acquired another quarter-acre of land with a cottage and garden. Also in September he paid a fee equal to one-fourth the yearly value of New Place; in July of 1605 he paid £440 cash for a half-interest in a lease of

---

11 Diana Price, *Shakespeare's Unorthodox Biography: New Evidence of an Authorship Problem* (Westport, CT, London: Greenwood Press, 2001), 150.

12 Three years after Shakespeare died, a poet named William Drummond wrote down a conversation he had with Ben Jonson in which Jonson mentioned that Shakespeare "wanted art" (lacked any trained skill). Jonson complained of *The Winter's Tale* shipwreck in Bohemia where there is no coast, and criticized a line in *Julius Caesar*. Drummond's original record has been "lost," which puts it in the same category as most of Shakespeare's paper trail—lost, forged, or suspicious.

13 Rosalind Miles, *Ben Jonson: His Life and Work* (London and New York: Routledge & Kegan Paul, 1986), 77.

14 Please see Appendix E for a comparison of money from then to now.

15 S. Schoenbaum, *William Shakespeare, A Compact Documentary Life* (Oxford: Oxford University Press, 1987), 234.

tithes; in 1613 he paid £140 for the Blackfriars' gatehouse, £80 of which was in cash (the gatehouse was a living establishment near the Blackfriars theater in London).[16] This totals to a rough equivalent today of around U.S. $1,000,000—cash—that Shakespeare spent in the village of Stratford in little more than a decade, with no record of where it came from.

It is remarkable that there are so many financial records for William Shakespeare—yet no record of income. It's a mystery acknowledged by many Shakespearean researchers. "If Shakspere* had sold all 37 known Shakespeare plays, he would have earned somewhere between £185 and £350 during his lifetime (the going rate for plays increased from roughly £5 to £10 after James I came to the throne). There is not one record to verify a penny of that alleged income."[17]

*Some writers use the spelling "Shakspere" to indicate the man from Stratford, as opposed to the spelling "Shakespeare" to indicate the author of the works.

Yet Gerald Bentley, in *The Profession of Dramatist in Shakespeare's Time*, reports of playwrights in general, "Fortunately there are a good many records of the financial rewards of the playwright."[18] Not even Bentley's research, however, could find one record referring to William Shakespeare as playwright or as getting paid. And in the records Bentley did find of other writers of the day, none made as much money as Shakespeare spent. Around 1615 one of the more successful playwrights, Philip Massinger, wrote a letter to William Herbert (Mary Sidney's son), the Lord Chamberlain at the time, complaining about the poverty of playwrights.[19]

In 1599, Shakespeare became part of the shareholders' syndicate for the Globe; in 1608 the King's Men, of which Shakespeare was a member in some capacity, assumed the lease of the Blackfriars theater. Shakespeare shared the income from the two theaters during these years, but he also had to help pay the expenses for the leases, upkeep, costumes, actors, and operations. This income was not a significant source of wealth for any of the shareholders.

---

16 Ibid., 271–72. The title-deed lists three co-purchasers, but "Shakespeare was evidently the sole buyer. He put up the purchase money; the others merely acted as trustees in his interest." Why? "The practical effect would be to deprive Shakespeare's widow of presumed dower right to a third share for life in this part of the estate." 274.

17 Price, *Shakespeare's Unorthodox Biography*, 103.

18 Gerald Eades Bentley, *The Profession of Dramatist in Shakespeare's Time, 1590–1642* (Princeton: Princeton University Press, 1971), 97.

19 Michael G. Brennan and Noel J. Kinnamon, *A Sidney Chronology 1554–1654* (Basingstoke: Palgrave Macmillan, 2003), 213.

As Diana Price explains in *Shakespeare's Unorthodox Biography*, "All of Shakspere's undisputed personal records are non-literary, and that is not only unusual—it is bizarre. Statistically, it is also a virtual impossibility. Over seventy historical records survive for Shakspere, but not one reveals his supposed primary professional occupation of writing. . . . All the Shakespearean literary allusions are either impersonal, confined to literary criticism, or ambiguous."[20]

Even Professor Stanley Wells, honorary president of the Shakespeare Birthplace Trust in Stratford-upon-Avon, admits there is no single document that can prove William Shakespeare of Stratford wrote the plays or was even a writer. When asked by a reporter what would settle the Authorship Question for good, Wells responded:

> I would love to find a contemporary document that said
> William Shakespeare was the dramatist of Stratford-
> upon-Avon written during his lifetime. There's lots and lots
> of unexamined legal records rotting away in the national
> archives; it is just possible something will one day turn up.
> That would shut the buggers up![21]

The "buggers," of course, are those who doubt that William Shakespeare of Stratford wrote the Shakespearean works.

Literary References to Shakespeare

Stratfordians (those who insist the man from Stratford wrote the plays) regularly cite items such as the following as "proof" that the person who wrote the reference was a friend of William Shakespeare's and personally knew that he wrote the plays—but no such assurance exists.

> *These may suffice for some Poetical descriptions of our ancient Poets,*
> *if I would come to our time, what a world could I present to you out*
> *of Sir Philip Sidney, Ed. Spencer, Samuel Daniel, Hugh Holland,*
> *Ben: Johnson, Th. Campion, Mich. Drayton, George Chapman,*
> *John Marston, William Shakespeare, & other most pregnant wits*
> *of these our times, whom succeeding ages may justly admire.*
> William Camden (1605)
> from *Remains of a greater Work concerning Britain, Poems* [22]

---

20 Price, *Shakespeare's Unorthodox Biography*, 149.

21 Robert Gore Langton, "The Campaign to Prove Shakespeare Didn't Exist" in *Newsweek* (December 29, 2014). https://www.newsweek.com/2014/12/26/ campaign-prove-shakespeare-didnt-exist-293243.html

22 Chambers, *Shakespeare: A Study of Facts and Problems*, vol. 2, 215.

There are twenty-one contemporaneous reviews *of the works attributed to William Shakespeare;* not one mentions the man himself as a person. Here are two more examples:

> *Will you read Virgil? Take the Earl of Surrey. Catullus? Shakespeare*
> *and Marlowe's fragment. Ovid? Daniel. Lucan? Spencer. Martial?*
> *Sir John Davies and others. Will you have all in all for Prose and*
> *verse? Take the miracle of our age, Sir Philip Sidney.*[23]
> Richard Carew, 1614

> *To Master W. Shakespeare.*
>
> *Shakespeare, that nimble Mercury thy brain,*
> *Lulls many hundred Argus-eyes asleep . . .*
> *Who loves chaste life, there's* Lucrece *for a Teacher:*
> *Who list read lust there's* Venus and Adonis,
> *True model of a most lascivious lecher.*[24]
> Thomas Freeman, 1614

Note that Carew considers Sir Philip Sidney to be a better writer than Shakespeare. Sidney had been dead for almost thirty years by this time.

*This is not an honorific mention—**Mercury** bored **Argus** to sleep by talking non-stop.*

These writers were clearly familiar with *the work attributed to* the name William Shakespeare, but there are no details in their statements that suggest they were *personally acquainted* with a dramatist by this name.

Many critics claim that the most significant proof of his authorship is Shakespeare's name on the title pages of printed editions of the plays. Yet the name "William Shakespeare" is also printed on other plays published during his lifetime, such as *A Yorkshire Tragedy, The London Prodigal, Locrine* (by W.S.), and *Thomas Lord Cromwell*—but experts insist Shakespeare did NOT write these other plays. So is the name on the printed title page proof or not proof? Either it is or it isn't: Either the name proves Shakespeare wrote *A Yorkshire Tragedy* and *The London Prodigal*, or it does NOT prove he wrote *The Merchant of Venice* and *Much Ado About Nothing*. It can't do both.

Only half of the Shakespearean plays were in print during Shakespeare's lifetime; see Chapter 15.

Millions of books are in print with the name "George Eliot" as author on the covers, and thousands of reviews of George Eliot's work refer to George Eliot as the author. But that does not prove there was a man named George Eliot who actually wrote the work. There was no man named George Eliot, of course—Mary Ann (or Marian) Evans wrote the work attributed to the male pseudonym.

23 Ibid., 219.
24 Ibid., 220.

Erasmus, in 1516, did a survey of false attributions among classical and biblical works. He wrote, "The man who is satisfied with the name of the author on the title-page regardless of how it got there will read fourteen Gospels, I think, instead of four. Nothing is easier than to place any name you want on the front of a book."[25] Gerald Bentley, in 1966, agrees even when specifically discussing title pages with Shakespeare's name on them: "We accept them because no other information is available. Yet we know from the history of the Shakespeare Apocrypha, if from nothing else, that printers dishonestly or mistakenly printed the names of the wrong authors on their title pages. . . . even in the time of Charles I, title pages cannot be accepted without question."[26] In the multivolume *Cambridge History of English Literature*, the editors write, "The appearance of [Shakespeare's] name on the Stationer's Register, or on the title-page of a play, is of interest as showing the extent of his popularity with the reading public of his time, but is no evidence whatever that the play is his."[27]

Missing: William Shakespeare

The complete lack of any personal reference to William Shakespeare as a writer is extraordinary. If even one written statement existed from anyone during Shakespeare's lifetime that clearly indicates that person personally knew William Shakespeare and connected him to the great author of plays, we wouldn't have an Authorship Question.

"The allusions to Shakespeare that perhaps speak the loudest are the ones that are not there."[28] So begins Diana Price in a description of some of the contemporaneous documents that do NOT mention the great William Shakespeare. This includes Thomas Lodge complimenting fellow writers Lyly, Spenser, Daniel, Drayton, and Nashe—but not Shakespeare. Or the historian William Camden, quoted earlier, in his work of 1607 in which he neglected to mention Shakespeare when discussing the important people in Stratford-upon-Avon, even though 1607 was the height of Shakespeare's supposed popularity. The author of *The New Metamorphosis* (1600–1615) did not name Shakespeare in a list of more than thirty poets and playwrights of the day. In a 1613

25 Cited by Harold Love, *Attributing Authorship: An Introduction* (Cambridge: Cambridge University Press, 2002), 19–20.

26 Gerald Eades Bentley, "Authenticity and Attribution in the Jacobean and Caroline Drama, in *Evidence for Authorship: Essays on Problems of Attribution*, eds. David V. Erdman and Ephim G. Fogel (Ithaca: Cornell University Press, 1966), 183.

27 A. W. Ward and A. R. Waller, eds., *Cambridge History of English Literature*, vol. 5, "The Drama to 1642" (Cambridge: University Press, 1910), 265.

28 Price, *Shakespeare's Unorthodox Biography*, 139.

defense of poetry called *Abuses Stript, and Whipt,* the author George Wyther praises Spenser, Daniel, Sidney, Drayton, Jonson, Chapman—but not Shakespeare. In 1598, Francis Meres published *Palladis Tamia: Wits Treasury,* in which he mentions eleven known plays of Shakespeare's by name (and one as yet unknown play); yet when Meres updated this book in 1634 and again in 1636, he did not add any more information regarding Shakespeare's plays.

Especially telling is Ben Jonson's *Timber, or Discoveries,* a collection of thoughts published twenty-four years after Shakespeare's death, in which Jonson recommends the best authors to read—Sidney, Donne, Gower, Chaucer, and Spenser—but not Shakespeare. This is most interesting considering Jonson had written the poem in the First Folio calling Shakespeare the "Soul of the Age" and the "Star of Poets."

Ms. Price muses, "Most people would rank Shakespeare with the major figures of his day, such as Francis Bacon, Spenser, Jonson, Sir Francis Drake, or Sir Walter Raleigh. Historical records prove that these men interacted with each other or were personally recognized for the activities with which their names are linked. If Shakespeare personally interacted with any of the opinion-setters, decision-makers, or influential personages of the time, the historical record is inexplicably and uncharacteristically silent."[29]

The following page charts this discrepancy: It is true that we have a greater number of extant records about the man named William Shakespeare than we do of any other dramatist of the time, with the exception of Ben Jonson. But within all the documentation, no one says Shakespeare was a playwright. We have *less* documentation for the other writers, but in their fewer papers, it is clear they wrote for a living.

29 Ibid., 139–41.

The Literary Paper Trail

	1. Evidence of education	2. Record of correspondence, esp. concerning literary matters	3. Evidence of having been paid to write	4. Evidence of a direct relationship with a patron	5. Extant original manuscript	6. Handwritten inscriptions, receipts, letters, etc. touching on literary matters	7. Commendatory verses, epistles, or epigrams contributed or received	8. Miscellaneous records (e.g., referred to personally as a writer)	9. Evidence of books owned, written in, borrowed, or given	10. Notice at death as a writer, written within a year of death
Ben Jonson	Yes	Yes	Yes	Yes	Yes	Yes	Yes	Yes	Yes	Yes
Thomas Nashe	Yes	Yes	Yes	Yes	Yes	Yes	Yes	Yes	Yes	•
Philip Massinger	Yes	Yes	Yes	Yes	Yes	Yes	Yes	Yes	•	•
Gabriel Harvey	Yes	Yes	•	Yes	Yes	Yes	Yes	Yes	Yes	•
Edmund Spenser	Yes	Yes	•	Yes	•	•	Yes	Yes	Yes	Yes
Samuel Daniel	Yes	Yes	Yes	Yes	Yes	Yes	Yes	Yes	•	Yes
George Peele	Yes	Yes	Yes	Yes	Yes	Yes	Yes	Yes	Yes	•
Michael Drayton	•	Yes	Yes	Yes	•	Yes	Yes	Yes	•	Yes
George Chapman	•	Yes	Yes	Yes	•	Yes	Yes	Yes	Yes	•
William Drummond	Yes	Yes	•	•	Yes	Yes	Yes	Yes	Yes	•
Anthony Mundy	•	•	Yes	Yes	Yes	Yes	Yes	Yes	•	Yes
John Marston	Yes	Yes	Yes	•	•	Yes	Yes	Yes	Yes	•
Thomas Middleton	Yes	•	Yes	•	Yes	Yes	•	Yes	•	•
John Lyly	Yes	Yes	•	Yes	•	Yes	Yes	Yes	•	•
Thomas Heywood	•	•	Yes	•	Yes	Yes	Yes	Yes	•	Yes
Thomas Lodge	Yes	Yes	•	Yes	•	•	Yes	Yes	Yes	•
Robert Greene	Yes	•	Yes	Yes	•	•	Yes	Yes	•	Yes
Thomas Dekker	•	Yes	Yes	•	•	Yes	Yes	Yes	•	•
Thomas Watson	Yes	•	•	Yes	•	•	Yes	•	•	Yes
Christopher Marlowe	Yes	•	•	Yes	•	•	•	Yes	•	Yes
Francis Beaumont	Yes	•	•	•	•	•	Yes	Yes	•	Yes
John Fletcher	•	•	Yes	•	•	•	Yes	Yes	Yes	•
Thomas Kyd	Yes	Yes	•	Yes	•	•	•	Yes	•	•
John Webster	•	•	Yes	•	•	•	Yes	Yes	•	•
William Shakespeare	•	•	•	•	•	•	•	•	•	•

Diana Price, *Shakespeare's Unorthodox Biography: New Evidence of an Authorship Problem* (Westport & London: Greenwood Press, 2011), 302–13; updated from her web site: www.Shakespeare-Authorship.com. Used with permission from Greenwood Publishing Group.

Proof by Patron

All biographies of Shakespeare insist that the Earl of Southampton was his patron, based on the dedication of Shakespeare's two lengthy poems (*Venus and Adonis* and *The Rape of Lucrece*) to the young Earl, who was nineteen years old at the time, ten years younger than William Shakespeare. Yet there is absolutely no evidence that the Earl ever acknowledged William Shakespeare as a patron—or in any other capacity.

Of this era, John Berryman affirms that for patronage, "Poets dedicated often at random, fishing."[30] In *Literary Patronage in the English Renaissance,* Michael G. Brennan elaborates: "Generally, aristocratic patronage involved a patron's personal assistance only for a minority of writers, and they were usually those who either lived within the patron's household or were privileged to mingle with members of the nobility on terms of friendly intimacy. For the rest, panegyric dedications brought no guarantee of either acceptance or reward, nor did patrons necessarily consider themselves responsible for the contents or quality of works which were prefaced by their names. Numerous literary tributes were addressed to members of the aristocracy on a purely speculative basis—many of them achieving nothing."[31]

Or as Arthur Marotti points out, "One is well advised to view with some skepticism writers' claims of having special relationships with the patrons whose favors they sought. This is especially so in the case of [Thomas] Churchyard who, in a touching moment of candor, revealed to [Sir Walter] Raleigh that of the sixteen books he had by then published, he was seldom even acknowledged by those to whom they were dedicated."[32]

Alistair Fox explains the situation clearly:

> The evidence of the dedications taken by itself, however, cannot be trusted. Without corroborating evidence of benefits actually received by clients, there is no proof that a dedication ever secured for an author the desired reward, or even the benevolence of the patron to whom the work was addressed. Even the wording of dedications cannot be trusted,

30 John Berryman and John Haffenden, eds., *Berryman's Shakespeare* (New York: Farrar, Straus and Giroux, 1999), 34.

31 Michael Brennan, *Literary Patronage in the English Renaissance: The Pembroke Family* (London, New York: Routledge, 1988), 78.

32 Arthur Marotti cited in David Linton, "Shakespeare as Media Critic: Communication Theory and Historiography," in *Mosaic* (June 1996), 9.

as they are constructed from topoi invariably couched in a language codified in courtesy theory, and as such need to be decoded. Decorum dictated that a suitor engage in a fulsome type of flattery that is itself part of the process of indirect negotiation between client and patron. . . . Dedications were thus a ritual means of constructing potential roles for both patron and suitor, according to desires that the aspiring client hoped would be fulfilled. No client, however, could be certain that these roles would actually be fulfilled, and often they were not.[33]

"Richard Robinson, who published from 1576 to 1600," says Bentley, "set down his receipts for a number of his publications . . . . Apparently he tried for a gift from a patron in connection with each publication, but he was only intermittently successful."[34] For instance, from the Earl of Warwick, Robinson received nothing. For a dedication to the president of the London Archery Society, he received 5 shillings; to the Dean of St. Paul's, 10 shillings; to Sir Philip Sidney, £2, plus 10 shillings more (half a pound) added by Sidney's father; the Earl of Rutland and Sir Christopher Hatton both gave him £3 for works dedicated to them. (For these values in today's money, see Appendix E).

Neither the Earl of Southampton, anyone who corresponded with the Earl, nor anyone who wrote about the Earl ever mentioned the name William Shakespeare in connection with Southampton in any way. Charlotte Stopes spent twenty-eight years in research for her book on the life of this Earl, but never found a single reference to Shakespeare.[35] Neither did G. P. V. Akrigg who more recently studied newly discovered archives of the Southampton family.[36] The two narrative poems, *Venus and Adonis* and *The Rape of Lucrece,* were published in 1593 and 1594, five years before the first printed play appeared with Shakespeare's name on it. Never again did Shakespeare dedicate any written work to the Earl of Southampton (nor to anyone)—a difficult proof of patronage, at best.

33 Alistair Fox, "The Complaint of Poetry for the Death of Liberality: The Decline of Literary Patronage in the 1590s" in *The Reign of Elizabeth I: Court and Culture in the Last Decade,* ed. John Guy (Cambridge: Cambridge University Press, 1995, reprt. 1999), 231–32.

34 Bentley, *The Profession of Dramatist in Shakespeare's Time,* 89.

35 Charlotte Stopes, *Life of Henry, Third Earl of Southampton, Shakespeare's Patron* (Cambridge University Press, 1922).

36 G. P. V. Akrigg, *Shakespeare and the Earl of Southampton* (Cambridge: Harvard University Press, 1968).

It is an undocumented assumption that Shakespeare had a patron. The idea suits the mythology of Shakespeare, particularly since he would have needed funding in his formative years, so the assumption is presented as a documented fact. Even Berryman admits, "He seems not to have known Southampton much."[37]

Traditions vs. Truth

Many legends, often called traditions, have been handed down about William Shakespeare, casting him as a schoolmaster or as a butcher in his father's trade killing calves while making speeches in high style. Some maintain he "must have been" a law clerk, or that he poached deer on Sir Lucy's land—all gossip dispensed almost a century after Shakespeare's death. We read about Shakespeare drinking with Michael Drayton and Ben Jonson—hearsay almost forty years after Shakespeare's death. Numerous posthumous anecdotes came into popular belief, but no contemporaneous documentation for any of these events exists.

But those who shape the popular imagination usually find fiction more memorable than fact.
Peter W. M. Blayney
1997

But there *is* contemporaneous documentation for several anecdotes that we don't hear so much about. For instance, there is a record that "Shakespeare the Player" got his coat-of-arms under a false pretense—having a coat-of-arms gave a man the official title of "gentleman," which in the English social system was a step up the ladder.[38] Stratfordians make much of the fact that he became a "gentleman" and little of the fact that he came by it dishonestly. Note that when the accusation was made in 1602, at the height of his supposed writing career, Shakespeare is pejoratively referred to as a "player," not as a dramatist, writer, or poet. (A subsequent hearing defended the eligibility of Shakespeare's *father*, in whose name William had applied.)

There is documentation that Shakespeare was sued along with two women and Francis Langley, owner of the Swan theater, for an incident in which another man was in "fear of death" from Shakespeare. Langley himself is a man whose "biography is a litany of

---

37 Berryman, *Berryman's Shakespeare*, 33.

38 Campbell, *The Reader's Encyclopedia of Shakespeare*, 741. "In 1900, a Mr. Pearson showed Sidney Lee a document he discovered in the Tixall Library that listed 23 persons who reportedly got their coats-of-arms under false pretenses. Under a drawing of a coat-of-arms were the words, 'Shakespeare Ye Player.'" The herald was accused of "elevating base persons" to the class of gentleman. Notice Shakespeare is identified as a player, not a writer or poet.

unscrupulous activities, greed, and extortion."[39] Shakespeare and several other "wicked people" were fined in Stratford for hoarding grain during a shortage; Shakespeare had the second-largest hoard. He is also listed as dodging his property taxes several times; one past-due amount is recorded of 13 shillings and 4 pence.

And there's the story that he often stopped at a place called The Tavern on his way to and from London and had an affair with the innkeeper's wife and even had a son by her, named William Davenant, a story perpetuated by the boy himself as he grew up.[40]

The only gossip written about Shakespeare as a man while he was alive, as opposed to a reference to the poems or plays, was written in a diary belonging to a law student, and even this notice is believed to be a forgery. It refers to Shakespeare as an actor, *not* as a playwright: A woman told the actor Richard Burbage, after seeing a performance in which Burbage played Richard the Third, to come to her house that night under the name of Richard the Third. Shakespeare supposedly overheard the invitation, went to the woman's house, and was "entertained, and at his game ere Burbage came." When the message was brought that Richard the Third had arrived to meet the woman, Shakespeare sent back a message that William the Conqueror came before Richard the Third. The diarist added a note, "Shakespeare's name William," indicating that Shakespeare was not so famous that everyone would know his first name.[41]

If we collect the contemporaneous, documented events in Shakespeare's life, which are more reliable than the posthumous and apocryphal "traditions" in the law clerk and poacher category, we must admit these facts: Shakespeare married an older woman whom he had already impregnated, then abandoned this wife and his three children to run off to London; he was a cheat and a tax evader; while carousing with an extortionist and two women (one of them married), created such trouble that a man feared for his life; and he never paid back the shepherd from whom his wife had to borrow two pounds.

39 Price, *Shakespeare's Unorthodox Biography*, 52.

40 Schoenbaum, *Shakespeare's Lives*, 61–65. William Davenant grew up to become England's poet laureate upon Ben Jonson's death. The cartilage in Davenant's nose was destroyed during third-stage syphilis, but he got married three times, even without his nose.

41 Chambers, *Shakespeare: A Study of Facts and Problems*, vol. 2, 212.

All is True, except when it isn't

Many legends that surround Shakespeare have been spun from thin threads in the desperation to find something that relates the Stratford man to the author of the plays and sonnets. For instance, in 1592 Henry Chettle published a 46-page pamphlet, *Greenes, Groats-worth of witte,* supposedly written by Robert Greene and published after his death by Henry Chettle. This possible reference and the resultant apology has been perverted into "proof" that Shakespeare was already established as a playwright in London by 1592. With the typical sleight-of-hand of Stratfordian biographers, the honorific references to the writer's civility, uprightness, honesty, and grace are given to William Shakespeare. This helps to counteract the only facts we have, which tend to be pejorative (tax defaulter, violent potential murderer, illegal hoarder, womanizer, deadbeat dad, etc.). So biographers grab onto Chettle's description and apply it to Shakespeare. But Chettle's apology is clearly *not* referring to Shakespeare. Jonathan Bate, rare among Stratfordian biographers, admits, "It is most likely that the first man [to whom Chettle writes] was Marlowe and the apology was to Peele: Chettle says that those who have taken offense are one or two of the play-makers *to whom Greene's remarks were addressed,* and Shakespeare was not one of those. The upstart crow does not rate a mention."[42] [emphasis is Bate's] No records have been found that mention Shakespeare from the birth of his twins in 1585 in Stratford until Greene's possible mention of him as "Shake-scene" the plagiarist in 1592 in London. Thus the reference in *Groats-worth* has become a foundation for the construction of the mythology of Shakespeare.

A similar example is the story that during "Shakespeare's" play about Henry the Eighth in June 1613, a cannon was set off on stage and caught the thatch roof on fire and burnt down the entire theater. It is indeed true and well documented that a cannon did this, but the play during which this happened was a play called *All is True.* There are several letters that detail this event, and every one mentions the play called *All is True;* a letter from Henry Wotton calls it "a new Play" and mentions that it is "representing some principall pieces of the raign of

A *groat* is a coin worth very little money; by Shakespeare's time it had devalued to about a penny.

42 Jonathan Bate, *Soul of the Age: A Biography of the Mind of William Shakespeare* (New York: Random House, 2009), 35.

Henry 8" and describes scenes not in Shakespeare's play.[43] A ballad printed two days after the event details the fire and the knights, lords, Richard Burbage, the Fool, Henry Condye (Condell), and Heminges at the scene, but no reference to Shakespeare. Shakespeare's play, which was not in print until 1623, had no Fool, although a contemporary play about Henry the Eighth, written by Samuel Rowley, does indeed have a Fool. The inexplicable thing is that we are now definitively told that Shakespeare's play of *Henry the Eighth* was originally called *All is True* and burnt down the Globe, as if it is a documented fact.

We are also told that in early 1601 the followers of the Earl of Essex went to the Globe playhouse and asked the Lord Chamberlain's Men to perform *Richard 2,* hoping to incite the citizens of London to revolt with Essex against the Queen because Shakespeare's play *Richard 2* shows the deposing of Richard by Bolingbroke, who went on to become Henry 4. Scholars make much of Essex's choice of a play, as if to prove Shakespeare himself was so incredibly popular. But not once in the records of the court trial of Essex is it mentioned that the play Essex requested was *written by William Shakespeare* or that they requested *a play by William Shakespeare*—they requested a play called *Henry the Fourth,* not a play called *Richard the Second.*[44] In Shakespeare's play of Richard 2, the phrase "Henry, fourth of that name" is the only reference to King Henry 4, and that's not until Act 4, thus no one would consider this to be a play about Henry 4. There were several other plays about Henry 4 at the time. Proving that the play requested is not the one by Shakespeare is the fact that one of the Lord Chamberlain's actors was called to the stand, but never the playwright, even though Shakespeare's name had been on various editions of the printed play of *Richard the Second* since 1598. Most importantly, the deposition scene, which was the point of Essex asking for the play, was not in the play until the 1608 quarto, five years after the death of Queen Elizabeth and seven years after Essex requested a play.

Most recently, it is now claimed even by the British Museum that a page and a half of an unpublished play written about 1591–1593, *Sir Thomas More,* is definitively in Shakespeare's handwriting, even though

---

43 Izaak Walton, ed., *Reliquiae Wottonianae,* third edition (London: T. Roycroft, 1672), 425–26. Logan Pearsall Smith's edition of the letters, *The Life and Letters of Sir Henry Wotton,* vol. 2 (Oxford: Clarendon Press, 1907), 33, includes a footnote re the burning of the Globe: "It is generally *supposed* that an *adaptation* of Shakespeare's Henry VIII was being acted." [emphasis added]

44 E. K. Chambers, *The Elizabethan Stage* (Oxford: The Clarendon Press, 1923), vol. 2, 419–22.

there is no agreement about this among traditional Stratfordian scholars—for numerous good reasons that are belabored elsewhere, not the least of which is that to compare handwriting from Shakespeare's few signatures on his deathbed with handwriting written almost 25 years earlier is unacceptable in professional handwriting analysis. Also, it must be held suspect that in the first book on the *Sir Thomas More* issue, published in 1923, A. W. Pollard states in the Preface that, "if Shakespeare wrote these three pages, the discrepant theories which unite in regarding the 'Stratford man' as a mere mask concealing the activity of some noble lord . . . comes crashing to the ground."[45] As Ron Rosenbaum states, this was part of "a very successful resistance movement against the anti-Strats that was led by A. W. Pollard from 1916–1923."[46] So this whole idea of Shakespeare's handwriting comprising three pages of the manuscript of *Sir Thomas More* began and still continues with the intent to try to demolish the Authorship Question.

Over the past four hundred years, Shakespeare's image has been selectively polished and deified with many similar assumptions. Yet most of what is passed off as truth about his life is fabricated. How did that happen?

The Shakespeare Biography Industry

When you next read a biography of William Shakespeare, take a highlighter and mark every phrase such as "surely," "must have," "doubtless," and "almost certainly." It will become obvious how much of what is written about Shakespeare is speculative fiction.

In the long run it is far more dangerous to adhere to illusion than to face the actual fact.

David Bohm, physicist 1948

Because there is so little to work from in creating a life of William Shakespeare, biographers embellish various elements deliberately, thus shaping our image of the man. For example, in 1693 (77 years after Shakespeare died) an antiquarian named Mr. John Dowdall wrote an account of his visit to Stratford. He was told by the clerk who showed him the church that Shakespeare himself wrote his own epitaph, which reads like a nursery rhyme:

> *Good friend, for Jesus' sake forbear*
> *To dig the dust enclosèd here.*
> *Bles't be the man that spares these stones*
> *And curs't be he that moves my bones!*

---

45 A. W. Pollard, "Preface," in *Shakespeare's Hand in the Play of* Sir Thomas More, ed. by W. W. Greg (Cambridge: Cmbridge University Press, 1923), v.

46 Ron Rosenbaum, *The Shakespeare Wars: Clashing Scholars, Public Fiascoes, Palace Coups* (New York: Random House, 2006), 125.

Says Oscar James Campbell in *The Reader's Encyclopedia of Shakespeare,* "The attribution does no credit to the poet and is generally rejected." [47] Yet the same account from Dowdall also states that Shakespeare ran away from his apprenticeship as a butcher, went to London, and was received in the playhouse as a servitor. Campbell says, "The most interesting piece of information in this report is that Shakespeare's first position in the theater was that of a servitor or hired man." [48] So Campbell claims one statement in the letter as fact and another in the same letter as fictitious, based on nothing except it "does no credit to the poet."

Unfortunately, this sort of "scholarship" is widely practiced, apparently to compensate for a scarcity of facts. It seems to be irresistible. Alden Brooks, an amateur Shakespearean sleuth, complained in 1937, "As an example of an almost universal procedure, take this statement of principle made by Beeching. 'If the evidence is good enough, if it fits in with the mental picture we have formed of the dramatist from his plays, and is not inconsistent with contemporary testimony, we shall incline to accept it, giving the great man the benefit of any doubt.'" Brooks is incredulous and continues, "In what other field of study would such a principle have authority? Imagine a scientist accepting as 'good enough' evidence, evidence that must first pass muster by agreeing with a preconceived idea, and that for this acceptance has none the less received the benefit of any doubt." [49]

Canon Beeching was a highly respected scholar.

Unfortunately, some writers don't differentiate between documented facts and speculative fiction. For instance, in his 2,500-page *Annotated Shakespeare,* 1943, editor A. L. Rowse claims, "When the actor-playwright met the fascinating half-Italian Emilia Lanier . . . he fell completely under her spell, partly out of pity for her unhappiness." Rowse goes on to explain that Shakespeare begged his dear friend, the nobleman Southampton, to write to the woman on his behalf because she was "driving the poet to distraction." [50] Shakespeare was "a strongly sexed heterosexual" who couldn't help himself. Every detail of this comes directly from Rowse's fevered imagination, but is presented in his ponderous tome as manifest

---

47 Campbell, *Reader's Encyclopedia of Shakespeare,* 213.

48 Ibid., 187.

49 Alden Brooks, *Will Shakspere, Factotum and Agent* (New York: Round Table Press, Inc., 1937), 14.

50 A. L. Rowse, ed., *The Annotated Shakespeare* (New York: Greenwich House, 1988), 1943.

facts. Recent books by Michael Wood (*In Search of Shakespeare*), Stephen Greenblatt (*Will in the World*), and James Shapiro (*Contested Will: Who Wrote Shakespeare?*) are almost as speculative, presenting many fanciful notions as if they are confirmed facts.

Don Foster, Professor of English at Vassar College, who recently proved that a poem called "A Funeral Elegy" was written by William Shakespeare —and was subsequently proven wrong—candidly admits in his book, *Author Unknown*, "Professors of literature are rarely required to be 'right' about anything. In my academic discipline, we don't usually produce facts—we produce incredibly clever interpretive commentary." [51]

It's no wonder that the entire Authorship Question has often been dismissed as "poppycock"—with professional scholars contributing unprofessional interpretation and embellishment and knowingly perpetuating myths disguised as facts. Students and the general public have been deluded into thinking that much more is known about Shakespeare than is truthfully known.

Shakespeare's Silence

Andrew Gurr notes in *The Shakespearean Stage 1574–1642*, "One can count as many as thirty-four complaints from almost all the dramatists of the time (except Shakespeare) about the kind of reception their plays were given." [52] Other authors complained of their works being pirated, but not Shakespeare. Shakespeare's own family is never recorded as having mentioned that he was a writer.

William Shakespeare himself wrote not one word outside the plays and poems—not a word about anyone's death or life or marriage or beauty, not even a word about himself nor a letter to anyone. John Berryman remarked about this lack, "Through an age brimming with eulogy and lament, his friends will publish and die, his son will die, Essex fall, Southampton languish in the Tower and emerge, the Queen lie speechless sweating and perish, James be crowned, without poems from Shakespeare." [53]

---

51 Don Foster, *Author Unknown: On the Trail of Anonymous* (New York: Henry Hold and Company, 2000), 70.

52 Andrew Gurr, *The Shakespearean Stage 1574–1642*, (Cambridge: Cambridge University Press, 1992, reprt. 2001), 227.

53 Berryman, *Berryman's Shakespeare*, 34.

Oops—He Died

Shakespeare wasn't the only one who was silent. When Shakespeare died in 1616 there was no mention of his death, no eulogies, and no record of his funeral. Numerous public, documented tributes were made upon the deaths of other literary figures of the time: Philip Sidney, Ben Jonson, Francis Beaumont, Michael Drayton, Edmund Spenser, John Fletcher, George Chapman, Philip Massinger.

"The Renaissance elegy was a form 'accessible to writers of all ages and abilities'. . . . This may have been even more true for women, since the need to commemorate the dead could override gender restrictions, making the elegy one of the few forms of original writing open to women."[54] So even though commemorating the dead was so important that even *women* were *allowed* to write elegies, not one person wrote a poem for William Shakespeare on his death.

In his will, Shakespeare gave away clothes, money, silver, a sword, alms for the poor, money for friends to buy rings, money for three actors to buy rings (inserted between the lines), and the famous (and only) bequest to his wife, one that was also inserted between the lines as an apparent afterthought, of his "second-best bed."

But there is not a single mention of any of the expensive books and manuscripts that we know the author of the plays read and studied. Nor does Shakespeare's will mention one word about anything he ever wrote—no reference to a poem, play, or written work of any kind. Shakespeare is buried in an unmarked grave inside the Stratford village church, while other, whom today we consider "lesser," poets and dramatists of his day—such as Jonson, Spenser, Beaumont, and Drayton, as well as Chaucer—are buried in Poets' Corner of Westminster Abbey in London. A statue of Shakespeare was not installed in Poets' Corner until 1740, more than a century after he died.

---

54 Margaret Hannay, et al., eds., *The Collected Works of Mary Sidney Herbert, Countess of Pembroke*, vol. 1 (Oxford: Clarendon Press, 1998), 120.

The Sum of the Whole is Greater than the Parts

In a list of the apparent deficiencies of William Shakespeare as the author of the Shakespearean canon, it is easy to dismiss each item one at a time. For each of the facts shown on the left, the Stratfordians' stock responses are on the right, every one one of which I have either heard or read.

No appeal to evidence can ever convince true believers, because nothing can disprove their fixed idea.
Scott McCrea, *The Case for Shakespeare*, 2005

Facts	Excuses
There is no indication that William Shakespeare had an extensive or even an adequate education. If he went to school, it was to the local small-town grammar school from about the ages of five to ten years old.	"**Of course** he attended the local school and had a remarkable education there. We see evidence of his education in the plays." "He was a genius who didn't need formal schooling." "There is no evidence of extensive book learning in the plays."
He owned no books.	"He didn't put his name in his books." "He **surely** studied in the library of a local aristocrat." "He got books from his fellow Stratfordian, Richard Field, who was a printer in London." "He browsed the book stalls and learned everything he needed to know."
His entire family was illiterate.	"So what." "Just because his daughter Susanna couldn't recognize her husband's handwriting doesn't mean she was illiterate." "Just because his father, mother, wife, daughter Judith, and granddaughter Elizabeth each signed with an X doesn't mean they were illiterate."
There is no record that he had the education or training in any of the specialty areas of which he writes.	"He **surely** read about the speciality areas." "He **surely** had training; it's just not recorded." "He was a genius and didn't need training." "He was a really good listener." Peter Holland "He picked up information in whorehouses and barber shops." Louis Marder

Facts	Excuses
He had no friends among the literati.	*"Just because no other writer mentioned him in writing doesn't mean he didn't have any literary friends."* *"Everyone just forgot to write it down."*
No one who knew him personally, such as his family and Stratford friends, referred to him as a writer.	*"Merely an oversight on the part of his family and friends."*
There is no record, while he was alive, that anyone mentioned meeting the playwright William Shakespeare.	*"All the records that mention Shakespeare from the gossipy English and Europeans have been lost."*
There is no indication that he was ever recognized by a patron or spent time in a noble household.	*"Those records did exist and have simply been lost."*
He never referred to himself as a writer.	*"Surely he mentioned it and the documents simply haven't been found yet."*
There is no documentation he was ever paid as a writer.	*"It's lost."* *"So what."*
The greatest writer in the English language never wrote a single thing outside the printed works.	*"It's lost. All lost."* *"He was just a working man writing plays to put bread on the table."*
There are no scraps of Shakespeare's handwriting outside of the six signatures on legal documents.	*"They're lost."* *"So what."*
There is no shred of an original manuscript.	*"Manuscripts were regarded as superfluous after printing and the paper they were written on was recycled."* (See Chapter 16.) *"We have no manuscripts of plays written by well-known writers of the time that were performed on the public stage and that were put into printed form."* (See Chapter 16.) *"The manuscripts were all burned in the great London fire of 1666."* (Although this makes one question why so many *printed* versions of the plays are still extant.)

Facts	Excuses
Nobody noticed when he died.	*"This is not unusual."*
He is buried in an unmarked grave in a village church instead of in Poet's Corner in Westminster Abbey, where lesser writers were laid to rest with honor. (Since it is unmarked, how do we know it is Shakespeare's?)	*"His unmarked grave is at the front of that village church, which proves he was very important."*
He is not known to have associated with any other great writers or thinkers of his time, nor to have participated in the two most important literary circles of his time.	*"So what."* *"He **surely** associated with writers, thinkers, philosophers, statesmen, and participated in the literary circles. It just wasn't documented."*

Each of these facts, taken individually, can be dismissed. But when these facts are viewed as a collection, the situation starts to look a little suspect. What if you come home from work and notice the following:

A window is broken.

Inside the house there are muddy footprints.

A light is on that wasn't on when you left the house.

A dresser drawer is open.

Clothes have been thrown onto the floor.

Your diamond brooch is not in the drawer where you keep it.

The back door is unlocked and open.

Each of these individual circumstances has a possible explanation: The kids playing ball broke the window; your teenager walked in with muddy feet; your husband came home to get something and left a light on; the housekeeper left a dresser drawer open, etc. *But when you view the facts as a collection,* you might entertain a different possibility, one that needs to be explored.

To be able to credit the most influential literary canon in human history to the man named William Shakespeare, one has to accept a mass of assumptions which range from implausible to outlandish— one might wonder if it's a conspiracy. Taken all together, the Authorship Question becomes urgent—not only to consider new possibilities, but to insist on rigorous documentation from original sources.

But Wait . . .

THERE ARE LITERALLY MILLIONS of extant documents from the sixteenth and seventeenth centuries that are still in readable condition.[55] I mentioned earlier that not one document records anyone meeting, dining, listening to, or speaking with the supposedly great William Shakespeare.

That might not be quite true. There was a letter, written in 1603, that was described in 1865 by William Cory, a reputable historian and tutor living at Wilton House in England. The letter was from the aristocrat Mary Sidney Herbert, the Countess of Pembroke, to her younger son Philip asking him to bring King James from Salisbury back to Wilton House. She wanted to plead with the king on behalf of Sir Walter Raleigh, who was shortly to be executed. Cory claimed that Mary Sidney mentioned that the play *As You Like It* was to be presented. And Mary supposedly wrote, "We have the man Shakespeare with us."[56] Unfortunately, the letter is now lost; some scholars question whether it ever existed.

But it is documented that King James held court at Wilton House for most of the autumn in 1603 to escape the plague that was making its periodic sweep through London. The King's Men were paid £30 to perform before the King at Wilton House on December 2, 1603.[57] And Mary did prevent the execution of Raleigh at that time, although he was eventually beheaded in 1618 at the age of 66.

Who was this woman, Mary Sidney Herbert, the Countess of Pembroke—possibly the only person to have mentioned meeting the man named William Shakespeare?

---

55 One of the reasons we have so many documents from this era is that paper made from wood pulp hadn't been invented yet—and wouldn't be until the mid-1800s in North America. People wrote either on parchment (sheep skin), vellum (calf, goat, or lamb skin), or 100 percent "rag" paper, which was literally made of rags of linen or cotton cloth, all of which is much more durable than wood-pulp paper. Dard Hunter, *Papermaking: The History and Technique of an Ancient Craft*, 2nd ed. (New York: Dover Publications, Inc., 1978), 13–14.

In 1666, "To save linen and cotton for the papermakers, a decree was issued in England prohibiting the use of these materials for the burial of the dead; only wool could be used for this purpose. In England at this time 200,000 pounds of linen and cotton were saved annually in this manner." Hunter, 482.

56 Twenty-three years after William Cory wrote about the letter, the "Lady Herbert, then not in very good memory, believed that a copy was at the B.M. [British Museum], or possibly the R.O. [Record Office]. Nothing has since been heard of it." In Chambers, *Shakespeare: A Study of Facts and Problems*, vol. 2, 329.

57 Chambers, *The Elizabethan Stage*, vol. 4, 168.

Part Two

The Woman

Make the doors upon a woman's wit,
and it will out at the casement;
shut that, and 'twill out at the key-hold;
stop that, 'twill fly with the smoke
out at the chimney.

Rosalind in *As You Like It*, 4.1.154–157

Documented Data

- Mary Sidney was the most educated woman in England of her time, comparable only to Queen Elizabeth.

- She owned an extensive private library and developed a personal alchemy laboratory.

- She hunted, hawked, bowled, sang, played musical instruments, composed music, stitched needlework, and studied medicine.

- She managed several large estates requiring expertise in logistics, accounting, medicine.

- She read, wrote, and spoke multiple languages fluently.

- She developed the most important literary circle in English history.

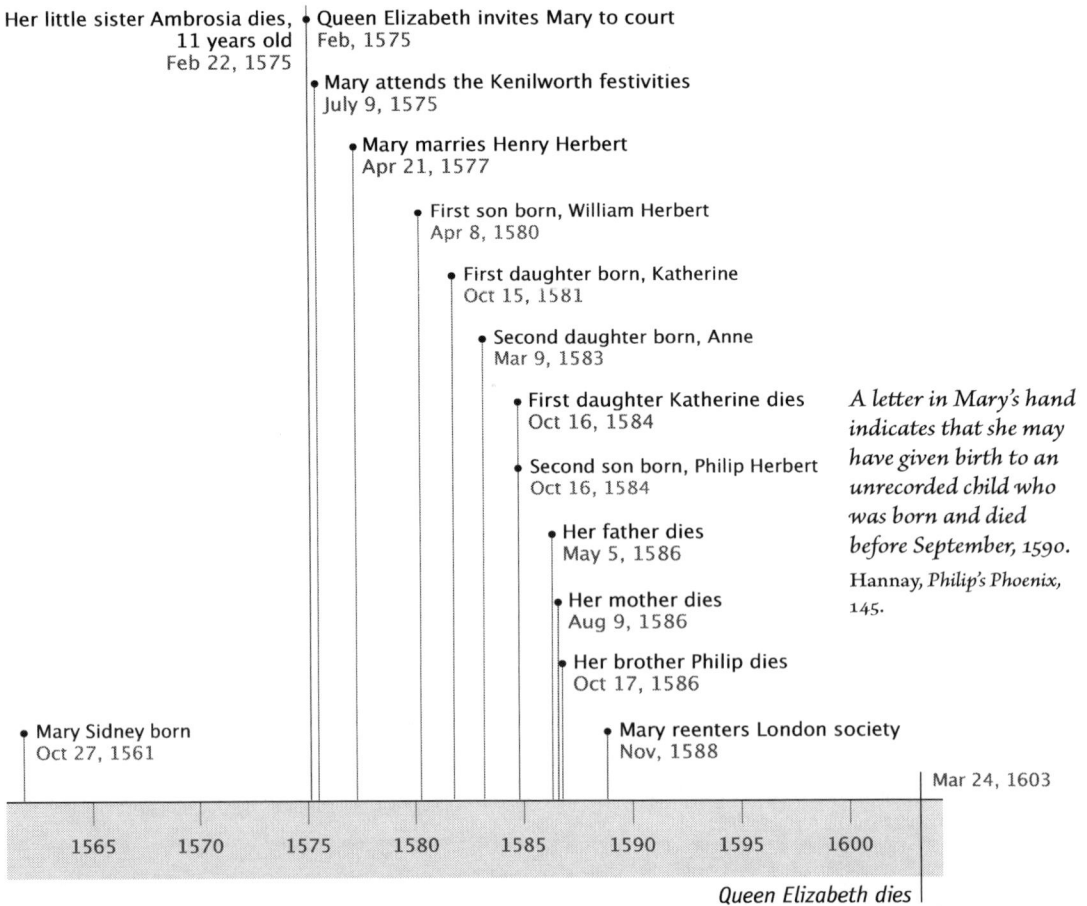

Her little sister Ambrosia dies, 11 years old Feb 22, 1575

Queen Elizabeth invites Mary to court Feb, 1575

Mary attends the Kenilworth festivities July 9, 1575

Mary marries Henry Herbert Apr 21, 1577

First son born, William Herbert Apr 8, 1580

First daughter born, Katherine Oct 15, 1581

Second daughter born, Anne Mar 9, 1583

First daughter Katherine dies Oct 16, 1584

Second son born, Philip Herbert Oct 16, 1584

Her father dies May 5, 1586

Her mother dies Aug 9, 1586

Her brother Philip dies Oct 17, 1586

Mary reenters London society Nov, 1588

Mary Sidney born Oct 27, 1561

A letter in Mary's hand indicates that she may have given birth to an unrecorded child who was born and died before September, 1590.

Hannay, *Philip's Phoenix*, 145.

Mar 24, 1603

1565   1570   1575   1580   1585   1590   1595   1600

Queen Elizabeth dies

2 Mary Sidney as a Young Woman

IN TICKENHILL MANOR, near the Severn River on what used to be the border of Wales in Bewdley, Worcestershire, England, Mary Sidney was born.[1] It was October 27, 1561, three years before William Shakespeare's birth.

Her mother, Mary Dudley Sidney, was sister to Robert Dudley, the Earl of Leicester (Queen Elizabeth's closest friend; some say, lover). The Dudley and Sidney families had been members of the English royal court for generations. Thus "before Mary was eleven, her family had consolidated so much power in this alliance of faith and blood that it controlled approximately two thirds of the land under Elizabeth's rule: Ireland, Wales, Warwickshire [home of William Shakespeare], and the north, as well as vast holdings scattered throughout England."[2]

Mary Dudley Sidney (the mother) is well-known historically as the woman who nursed Queen Elizabeth through smallpox, then caught the disease herself, almost died, and was so horribly disfigured that she never appeared in public again without a veil (Mary Sidney, the daughter, was one year old at the time).

Mary grew up mainly on the Sidney family estate in Kent, called Penshurst Place, with many summers spent in Ludlow Castle on the border of Wales. She was exceptionally well educated. While her older brother, Philip, attended Shrewsbury School for his primary education, Mary was tutored at home along with her younger brothers (Robert, who later enrolled in Oxford at age 12, and Thomas) and her two surviving sisters (Elizabeth and Ambrosia). She read, wrote, and spoke

Discovery consists of looking at the same thing as everyone else and thinking something different.

Albert Szent-Györgyi, biochemist, Nobelist 1893–1986

---

1   See page 341 for a list of biographies and other books about Mary Sidney and her family for further information.

2   Margaret Hannay, *Philip's Phoenix: Mary Sidney, Countess of Pembroke* (Oxford: Oxford University Press, 1990, 22.

Latin, French, and Italian, probably Greek (several dedications to her are in Greek) and Welsh, and possibly some Hebrew and Spanish (her mother interpreted Spanish for the Queen, and Mary had Spanish books in her library).[3]

She was trained in poetry, rhetoric, and the classics, as was expected of every well-bred person, and medicine, as was expected of every female head of household, especially women who were to run large manors. Several medical remedies created in her own laboratory have been preserved, as well as her formula for invisible ink.[4] She created exquisite needlework for which she was well known, she sang, read and composed music, and played the lute, virginals (an early spinet or small harpsichord), and possibly the violin. It seems there was always music in the house—her father paid almost £67 for violins "that perhaps represents the initial costs of establishing a violin consort in his household."[5] The family even had their own jester, or fool; her father paid for "3 yards of motley to make his coat."[6]

I am ambitious for a motley coat.
Jaques in
As You Like It, 2.7.43

Family records show she grew up riding horses, hawking, hunting, using a bow and arrow, and later had a lawn bowling green on her estate.

Mary's father, Henry Sidney, was Lord President of the Marches (border counties) of Wales and later the Lord Deputy Governor of Ireland. "Because Henry Sidney had a particular interest in geography and cartography, his children were probably better schooled in those fields than most."[7]

Mary was exposed to and involved in theater all her life. The account books of the Sidney family indicate that troupes of actors reenacted the adventures of Robin Hood and his merry men, singers celebrated May Day, and minstrels played at midsummer.[8] The account books at Ludlow Castle during her lifetime record performances of children's theater troupes, the Lord of Sussex players, and Lord Stanford players.[9]

3   Michael Brennan, *Literary Patronage in the English Renaissance: The Pembroke Family* (London, New York: Routledge, 1988), 99.

4   *The Rare SECRETS of the English Countess Mary of Pembroke* (Nuremberg: Gabriel Nicolaus Raspe, 1763), 116.

5   Peter Holman, *Four and Twenty Fiddlers: The Violin at the English Court, 1540–1690* (Oxford: Clarendon Press, 2002), 125.

6   J. Alan B. Somerset, *Records of Early English Drama, Shropshire*, vol. 2: Editorial Apparatus (Toronto: University of Toronto Press, 1994), 645.

7   Hannay, *Philip's Phoenix*, 27.

8   Ibid., 27.

9   Ibid., 124.

An elaborate Christmas season at the castle while Mary was in attendance included the nobility performing in a production of *King Arthur's
Knights of the Round Table.*

A regular stream of acting companies are recorded as having
performed throughout the years Mary was at Ludlow: Acting troupes
sponsored by the Lords Stafford, Bergavenny, Burghley, Berkeley,
Hunsdon, Chandos, Essex, Darcy, the Earls of Worcester, Oxford,
Pembroke, and Leicester, the Queen's Men from both Queen Elizabeth
and Queen Anne, the Master of the Revels players, as well as sundry
musicians, minstrels, and jesters all provided theater and music.[10]
"Some players [actors] were obviously known to the Sidneys, since Sir
Philip [Mary's older brother] later stood as godfather to the son of
Richard Tarlton, an actor in Leicester's company."[11] Leicester was
Mary's uncle, Robert Dudley.

This active family interest and household participation in theater was
a lifelong passion of hers. Even in her forties, the royal court records
show that Mary Sidney was one of three women who participated in
all four masques (plays intended for amateur performance by the
nobility in the royal court, not on the public stage) written by Ben
Jonson. The other two women were Queen Anne (James' wife) and
Mary's daughter-in-law, Susan de Vere (married to Philip).

Mary Sidney grew up surrounded by literary pursuits. Her mother
was well-educated and interested in writing—verses penned by her
and Mary's father in Latin and English, with French phrasing), are
extant. Her mother's female friends were also well educated, such as
the five remarkable Cooke sisters who were among the first generation
of female humanist scholars. Her mother's best friend was Mildred
Cooke, married to William Cecil, Lord Burghley, the Queen's chief
minister. Another good friend, Anne Cooke, was the mother of Sir
Francis Bacon. Mary's aunt Frances Sidney, the Countess of Sussex,
was the founder of Sidney Sussex College at Cambridge in 1589, when
Mary was 28 years old.

We often think of any era before our own as a bad time for women,
believing a woman was merely chattel to be used at her husband's
discretion and allowed no rights at all and hardly allowed education.
But this isn't quite so. The era in which Mary Sidney lived was filled
with women of financial power, real estate power, with writers, artists,

10 Somerset, *Records of Early English Drama, Shropshire,* vol. 2, 395.
11 Hannay, *Philip's Phoenix,* 124.

musicians, tavern owners, printshop owners, entrepreneurs and builders, philosophers, scholars, patrons, and important political figures.[12] For example, in the publishing arena, Katherine Parr (1512–48, d. 36 y.o.), sixth and last wife of Henry 8, is the first Queen to publish in England under her own name. Lady Ann Bacon (1528—1610, d. 82 y.o.) was a linguist and published her own religious translations. Anne Locke (1530–1607, d. 77 y.o.) published the first sonnet sequence in English, *A Meditation of a Penitent Sinner,* twenty-six sonnets based on Psalm 51. Lady Jane Lumley (1537–1578, d. 41 y.o.) is the first person to translate Euripides' *Iphigeneia at Aulis* into English from the original Greek and Latin; she gave the manuscript to her husband on their wedding day—when she was 13 years old. Her sister Mary's translations from Greek to Latin are still extant; Mary died after childbirth at 17 years old. Isabella Whitney (fl. 1567–1573) published the first printed collection of original secular poems in English. Amelia Lanyer (1569–1645, d. 76 y.o.) published the first volume of religious poetry (which includes strident anti-Semitism) by a woman in the seventeenth century, in 1611. Elizabeth Cary (1585–1639, d. 54 y.o.) is the first woman to publish an original play, as opposed to a translation, in English; it was a closet drama, not meant for the public stage, called *The Tragedy of Mariam,* published in 1613. There were other women too numerous to mention here.

As Alexander Witherspoon states, "There was probably never an age in which women held a greater sway physically and intellectually than during this period."[13]

Mary Sidney is not an anomaly in her time. Granted, there were still plenty of restrictions on women—especially in any area that put a woman in the public sphere, such as publishing—but Mary had strong sources for role models and encouragement, and she was not the only woman pushing against the boundaries.

12 Carole Levin, Anna Riehl Bertolet, and Jo Edlridge Carney, eds., *A Biographical Encyclopedia of Early Modern Englishwomen: Exemplary Lives and Memorable Acts, 1500–1650* (London and New York: Routledge, 2017).

13 Alexander Maclaren Witherspoon, *The Influence of Robert Garnier on Elizabethan Drama* (New York: Phaeto Press, 1968), 68–69.

"One daughter of very good hope"

When Mary was six years old, her seven-year-old sister Elizabeth died, and when Mary was thirteen, her beloved eleven-year-old sister Ambrosia died. Family documents tell us she and Mary often dressed in matching outfits. She was now the only surviving daughter. Queen Elizabeth wrote a condolence letter to the parents and suggested that since God had left them yet "one daughter of very good hope," she should come to live at court.[14] Thus Mary Sidney became one of the Queen's maids-of-honor at thirteen. (The term "maid-of-honor" is a phrase invented by Mary.[15])

Her first experience of court spectacle was the nineteen-day extravaganza at Kenilworth, the magnificent estate of her uncle Robert Dudley, the Queen's dear friend, or "favorite." It is documented that she attended with her parents and her older brother, Philip Sidney. The festivities at Kenilworth were an extravagant display of merry-making—allegorical figures, sibyls, and mythological creatures all spouting poetry at every turn, musical concerts, lavish hunting expeditions, dancing, fireworks, bearbaiting, theater, a movable island on the lake, barges carrying musicians, Italian tumblers. "Besides all this, they had upon the pool a Triton riding on a mermaid eighteen feet long; as also Arion on a dolphin's back, with rare music."[16]

After Kenilworth, the royal court progressed to other castles and country estates, then on to Woodstock. Here, "Mary's first notice from a poet appropriately stressed her lineage and intelligence":[17]

> Tho young in years yet old in wit, a gest due to your race,
> If you hold on as you begin, who is it you'll not deface?
>
> paraphrase according to the meanings of the words when they were written:
> Though you are young, you are intelligent and quick
> beyond your years, a bearing attributable to your family heritage;
> If you continue as you've begun, who is it you'll not
> confront fearlessly?

At 13 years old, she is already recognized as an extraordinary young woman.

The earth hath swallow'd all my hopes but she—She is the hopeful lady of my earth.
Thirteen-year-old Juliet's father in Romeo and Juliet, 1.2.14–15

Thou rememberest Since once I sat upon a promontory, And heard a mermaid on a dolphin's back...
Oberon in A Midsummer Night's Dream, 2.1.149–50

...for I never knew so young a body with so old a head.
The Duke in The Merchant of Venice, 4.1.162, referring to Portia who is disguised as a judge

14 As quoted in Hannay, Philip's Phoenix, 31.
15 Margaret Hannay, et al., eds., The Collected Works of Mary Sidney Herbert, Countess of Pembroke, vol. 1 (Oxford: Clarendon Press, 1998), 65.
16 William Dugdale, The Antiquities of Warwickshire, Illustrated (1656; reprint, Manchester: E. J. Morten, Ltd., 1730), 166.
17 Hannay, Philip's Phoenix, 35.

Back at the royal court, Mary's exposure to and involvement in theater continues. "In general, [Queen Elizabeth] was one of the theater's most devoted patrons. Numerous plays were put on at court throughout the Christmas holidays, sometimes as many as eleven in one season."[18]

Theater was provided not only by the public acting troupes sponsored by noblemen, but the production of plays was a common pastime among the lords and ladies at court. Noted poets such as Ben Jonson, Francis Beaumont, and John Fletcher wrote masques. Family and court records document that Mary Sidney actively participated throughout her life as an actress in these productions.

Henry Herbert, 2nd Earl of Pembroke

At court, Mary caught the eye of Henry Herbert, the second Earl of Pembroke. He was a widower and "the one great Protestant earl who was not a member of the Dudley family."[19] Her uncle Robert Dudley arranged a politically motivated marriage with Henry when Mary was 13 years old; they married when she was 15 and the Earl was 43.

Not long after their wedding they went to live at Wilton House, his estate on 14,000 acres in Wiltshire, just outside of Salisbury, given to the Earl's father by King Henry 8. The river Avon flowed through her land. The estate is very near to Stonehenge, about 80 miles south of Stratford-upon-Avon, and only a few miles from another town on the Avon called Stratford-sub-Castle.

The Earl indulged Mary in her passion for alchemy, chemistry, mineralogy, and medicine at Wilton House where she established a complete laboratory. Sir Walter Raleigh's half-brother Adrian Gilbert was an assistant in her lab.[20] Gilbert also acted as a landscape architect and developed the elaborate gardens at Wilton based on symbolic geometry "in such admirable art-like fashion, resembling both divine and moral remembrances."[21]

---

18 Anne Somerset, *Elizabeth I* (New York: St. Martin's Griffin, 1991), 368.

19 Hannay, *Philip's Phoenix*, 35. Henry Herbert had an earlier marriage at 19 years old to Katherine, age 14, the sister of Lady Jane Grey, reluctant queen for nine days in 1553. The marriage was unconsummated and annulled before Lady Jane's head was smit off.

20 Adrian Gilbert, Mary, her brother Philip, his dear friend Edward Dyer, as well as Mary's mother, were good friends with and students of Dr. John Dee, the astrologer and "magician." See Peter French, *John Dee, the World of an Elizabethan Magus* (London: Routledge, 1972).
    Giordano Bruno was also close to her brother Philip; Bruno dedicated his two most important works to Philip. See Katherine Duncan-Jones, *Sir Philip Sidney, Courtier Poet* (New Haven: Yale University Press, 1991), 271.

21 Roy Strong, *The Renaissance Garden in England* (London: Thames & Hudson, 1998), 122–23.

Mary collected an extensive private library, regarded as an exceptionally large one for its time. Around 1660 John Aubrey mentioned his visit to it in *The Natural History of Wiltshire*: "Here was a noble library of books, choicely collected in the time of Mary Countess of Pembroke. I remember there was a great many Italian books; all their poets; and books of politics and history."[22] Aubrey also noticed a Latin manuscript written in Julius Caesar's time, and *The Book of Hawking and Hunting*, by Juliana Berners, printed in 1486 (yes, an English woman wrote this book on hawking and hunting).[23]

"Wilton soon established itself as a base away from town not only for the Herberts, but also for the Dudleys and Sidneys. In such a group, so closely knit by familial and marital bonds, it was difficult to spot where a family gathering ended and a political summit began."[24]

Mary and Philip Sidney

To begin to understand Mary Sidney's influence in the literary world developing around her, it is first important to understand her brother Philip's part, as well as Mary's attachment to this brilliant older brother. The entire Sidney family is known for their devotion to each other. Mary was very close to all three of her brothers—Philip, Robert, and Thomas—but especially to Philip. He was the quintessential Elizabethan courtier: learned, traveled, cultured, courteous, athletic, intelligent, handsome, and single. "He was the rising sun in the Court of an ageing and childless Queen."[25] He has been compared with the late John Kennedy, Jr., in his charm, charisma, "great expectation," and tragic early death.[26]

When Philip was a young boy, he was sent to a private school in Shrewsbury for his education. At the age of 13, he entered Christ Church College at Oxford. At 17, Philip left for his European tour, considered to be the finishing school for young aristocrats in preparation for their lives in the service of the Crown.

---

22 John Aubrey, *Aubrey's Natural History of Wiltshire*, originally written between 1656 and 1691 (Wiltshire: David & Charles Reprints, 1969), 86.
23 Juliana Berners' book was the first printed book in England in which colored inks were used in the illustrations. Hunter, *Papermaking*, 477.
24 Alan Stewart, *Philip Sidney: A Double Life* (New York: St. Martin's Press, 2000), 202.
25 Katherine Duncan-Jones, *Sir Philip Sidney: Courtier Poet* (New Haven: Yale University Press, 1991), x.
26 The phrase "that friendly foe, great expectation" is in Philip Sidney's *Astrophel and Stella*, sonnet 21, line 8.

Philip was welcomed into all the royal courts of Europe and so impressed the heads of states that while still seventeen years old he was created a Baron by the King of France. (This title did him no good in England, however; Queen Elizabeth disdained foreign titles for her courtiers and had remarked, "My dogs wear my collars.")

Unfortunately, on his return to England Philip still did not receive from the Queen the favors she routinely bestowed upon other courtiers. Whether the Queen was angered by his foreign honors, his meetings in Prague with the English Catholic priest Edmund Campion, his familial relation to Robert Dudley, Earl of Leicester, or any of several other perceived transgressions, she constantly passed him over for honors and even refused to knight him.

"The grandson of a duke, godson of a king, nephew to four earls, brother-in-law of an earl, brother of an earl, and uncle to three earls, he was himself, through nearly all his life, an untitled commoner . . . the only title which he in fact received, that of knight, was granted for the sorriest of reasons and brought him neither commendation nor reward." [27]

Philip was eventually knighted in January, 1583, at age 28, but not by the Queen. He became a knight through an old friend, the German Prince Casimir. Casimir nominated Philip as his proxy when he was unable to attend his own installation as a Knight of the Garter at Windsor Castle, but a proxy had to be someone of sufficient rank so Philip was hastily knighted.

Philip exercised his literary skills in various forms at court. "Sidney played an increasingly public role in Elizabethan high society as a deviser of and participant in . . . 'royal pastimes.'" These included tiltyard appearances, playlets, and allegorical displays ranging from the "pastoral show" at Wilton, the mini-drama "The Lady of May," to the elaborate and mysterious *Triumph of the Four Foster Children of Desire,* "which made use of elaborate machinery, lavish costumes and armor, caparisoned horses, and 'special effects' on a grand scale." [28]

27 Tucker Brooke and Matthias A. Shaaber, *A Literary History of England,* vol. 2, *The Renaissance (1500–1660),* 2nd ed. (New York: Appleton-Century-Crofts, 1967), 472.

28 Katherine Duncan-Jones, ed., *Sir Philip Sidney, A Critical Edition of the Major Works* (Oxford: Oxford University Press, 1989), ix.

But then Philip wrote his famous letter to the Queen against her proposed marriage with the French Duke of Alençon.[29] Plus Philip made an enemy of the nettlesome Earl of Oxford, and "withdrew from the Queen's presence, attaching himself instead to the society of his sister and the increasingly absorbing literary pursuits that he shared with her. . . . Though he was not explicitly banished from Court, he was tied up, if not muzzled, and had for the time being to abandon hopes for advancement in rank or a posting abroad."[30]

In his self-imposed "retirement" from court, Philip turned to writing full time, along with his worthy and admired sister. "The numerous dedications to [Mary Sidney] portray a chaste, pious, gracious and intelligent woman, the exact female counterpart of her famous brother: if Philip Sidney was depicted as the ideal Renaissance man, then Mary came to personify the ideal Renaissance woman."[31]

A Life of Literary Pursuits

At Mary's request, Philip composed *The Countess of Pembroke's Arcadia*, which has been declared "the most important work of prose fiction in English of the sixteenth century."[32] "None of the writers of his age approached his influence in the field of prose romance."[33] Philip also wrote an essay called *The Defense of Poesie*. "Considered the finest work of Elizabethan literary criticism, Sidney's elegant essay suggests that literature is a better teacher than history or philosophy."[34]

29 James M. Osborn, *Young Philip Sidney, 1572–1577* (New Haven and London: Yale University Press, 1972), 503.

   When Queen Elizabeth was negotiating marriage with the French Catholic Duc d'Anjou (Alençon), the great Protestant Earls (including Leicester and Pembroke), Sir Frances Walsingham, Sir Christopher Hatton, and others met at the Pembroke's Baynard's Castle in London. They chose Philip Sidney to represent them; he wrote a formal letter to the Queen frankly condemning the proposed marriage. There is no record of the Queen's response, but Philip shortly thereafter retired to his sister's estate, Wilton House.

   When John Stubbs, a man of lower class, wrote a protest against the marriage, the Queen had both the printer's and Stubbs' right hands cut off. A man who distributed the pamphlets was scheduled to have his hand cut off, but it was saved due to his age, above eighty years old.

30 Duncan-Jones, *Sir Philip Sidney: Courtier Poet*, 167.

31 S. Cerasano and Marion Wynne-Davies, eds., *Renaissance Drama by Women: Texts and Documents* (London and New York: Routledge, 1996), 13.

32 Merriam-Webster and Encyclopedia Britannica, eds., *Merriam-Webster's Encyclopedia of Literature* (Springfield: Merriam-Webster, 1995), 1030.

33 Brooke and Shaaber, *A Literary History of England*, vol. 2, *The Renaissance (1500–1660)*, 472.

34 Merriam-Webster, *Merriam-Webster's Encyclopedia of Literature*, 1030.

His lengthy sonnet sequence, *Astrophel and Stella*, popularized the sonnet form in England.[35] *Astrophel and Stella* "was to be followed by dozens of sonnet sequences in the 1590s, but it must be remembered that when Sidney wrote it there were no other sonnet sequences in English.... Sidney's is not only the earliest English sonnet sequence properly so described: it is also arguably the best, in terms of assured poetic technique, richness of tone, and subtlety of organization."[36]

It is important to keep in mind that at this time in history, the only place English was spoken was in England—it was rare to hear it used even in Wales, Ireland, or Scotland. According to Roma Gill, "At the start of the sixteenth century the English had a very poor opinion of their own language: there was little serious writing in English, and hardly any literature. Latin was the language of international scholarship, and Englishmen admired the eloquence of the Romans."[37]

Yet "When Sidney came to devote himself more fully to his 'unelected vocation' as a poet, he wrote entirely in English ... *he hoped to lay the foundations of a body of literature in his own language which might ultimately stand comparison with the Greek and Latin classics.*"[38] [emphasis added]

I want to emphasize the point that there were great works of literature in Greek, Latin, Italian, and French, but few in English. It became Philip Sidney's—and then Mary Sidney's—mission in life to create great works in the English language.

The Wilton Circle

Through their own writing, as well as the patronage and encouragement of other writers, Mary and Philip developed the most important and influential literary circle in England, referred to today as the Wilton Circle.

"The developments at Wilton in the 1580s, then, were an attempt on the part of the Sidneys to instigate a revival of English aristocratic culture. For her own part, in providing Wilton's hospitality and its unique atmosphere of these crucial years of Elizabethan literature, the Countess was also re-creating in her own, perhaps typically English,

---

35 Hardin Craig and David Bevington, eds., *The Complete Works of Shakespeare*, rev. ed. (Glenview, IL: Scott, Foresman and Company, 1973), 468.

36 Duncan-Jones, ed., *Sir Philip Sidney, A Critical Edition of the Major Works*, xvii.

37 Roma Gill, ed., *The Taming of the Shrew* (Oxford: Oxford University Press, 1996), 120.

38 Duncan-Jones, *Sir Philip Sidney: Courtier Poet*, 143

way a pattern of patronage by noble women that had flourished in Italy and France for a century or more."[39]

Scholars agree on the importance of the poetic and dramatic work of Mary and Philip Sidney. As John Buxton said in 1966, "We remember how much the Florentine Renaissance owed to the Medici, but we forget that a similar debt was owed by the English Renaissance to the Sidneys."[40] It is significant to note that in his writing, "[Philip] Sidney's development of women who are active and strong without being evil or dominant over men was something new in literary history."[41]

It is even more significant, in light of the Authorship Question, that "In his portrayal of women as intelligent, capable, and morally responsible human beings, *Sidney very likely paved the way for writers like Shakespeare* who came after him to develop strong, active heroines and to alter, however slightly and gradually, cultural perceptions of women."[42] [emphasis added]

Albert Baugh, in *A Literary History of England*, 1948, sums it up:

> In three directions, to be sure, Sidney's actual achievement
> ranks him among the very highest of the Elizabethan writers.
> None but Shakespeare and Spenser produced a finer sonnet
> sequence. None but Ben Jonson surpassed him as a literary
> critic. None of the writers of his age approached his influence
> in the field of prose romance. Yet if *Astrophel and Stella,* the
> *Defense of Poesy,* and the *Arcadia* had never been published,
> we should still have to regard Sidney as a cultural landmark.
> Seconded by his sister, he created through his personal efforts
> and his personal charm a new artistic atmosphere more
> stimulating than any other that then existed. Together—
> or more strictly in succession, for the Countess of Pembroke
> (1561–1621) was but twenty-five when her brother died—

---

39 John Buxton, *Sir Philip Sidney and the English Renaissance* (New York and London: St. Martin's Press, 1966), 31.

40 Katherine J. Roberts, *Fair Ladies: Sir Philip Sidney's Female* Characters (New York: Peter Lang Publishing, Inc., 1993), 121.

41 Ibid., 122.

42 Gary F. Waller, *Mary Sidney, Countess of Pembroke: A Critical Study of Her Writings and Literary Milieu* (Salzburg: Universität Salzburg, 1979), 39. Waller compares Mary and Wilton House with Marguerite de Navarre's palace academy, which was a source for *Love's Labor's Lost.*

they first produced what in the highest sense may be called the academic spirit in English letters.[43]

Mary and her brother Philip laid a remarkable groundwork for the future of the English language and literature. Devoted to each other and to the literary arts, they stimulated excellence and perfected their craft, while inspiring the writers of the Wilton Circle.

Give Sorrow Words

The early stage of the Wilton literary circle was also the beginning of a devastating period for Mary. Her first son, William Herbert, was born when she was eighteen years old, and she had two daughters in the next three years. Tragically, on the very day Mary gave birth to her second son, Philip Herbert, her little girl Katherine died, the day after her third birthday. In the Sidney family Psalter it is written of this little girl that she was "a child of promised much excellency if she might have lived."[44]

Little more than a year after Katherine's death, Mary's father died. Mary's brother Philip, recently married, was away in the Netherlands fighting for the Queen, who did not allow him to return home to comfort their mother nor to attend their father's funeral.

Three months after her father's death, Mary's mother died.

> "[Philip] Sidney could have borne the news of his parents' death, [Dr. Thomas] Moffett thought, if he had received no other bad news: but it was reported to him also that his sister was mortally ill—'such a sister . . . as no Englishman, for aught I know, had ever possessed before.'"[45]

As Moffett mentions, Mary was near death herself when, two months after her mother's burial, she received news that her beloved brother Philip had been killed in the war, fighting for the Protestant cause in Zutphen, Netherlands—a musket ball shattered his thigh bone during a battle and he died twenty-five days later.

---

43 Albert C. Baugh, ed., *A Literary History of England* (New York: Appleton-Century-Crofts, Inc., 1948), 472.

44 Hannay, *Philip's Phoenix*, 55.

45 Pearl Hogrefe, *Women of Action in Tudor England: Nine Biographical Sketches* (Ames, Iowa: Iowa State University Press, 1977), 120.

Philip Sidney was the first "commoner" (meaning his father had no title) in English history to be given a state funeral at St. Paul's Cathedral. This would not happen again until Lord Nelson (1805) and Sir Winston Churchill (1965) were also so honored.

Forward—in All Directions

In November of 1588, two years after Philip's death, Mary returned strong and energetic once again to the London court for the season. And she returned in style:

> On Thursday the wife of the Earl of Pembroke made a superb entrance into this city. She has been for more than a year on her estates in the country. Before her went forty gentlemen on horseback, two by two, all very finely dressed with gold chains. Then came a coach in which was the Countess and a lady, then another coach with more ladies, and after that a litter containing the children, and four ladies on horseback. After them came forty or fifty servants in her livery with blue cassocks.[46]

She was barely twenty-seven years old. Thus fourteen years after her introduction to the royal court as a thirteen-year-old maid-of-honor, Mary returns to the royal court—older, sadder, wiser, stronger, and with a mission. The literary mantle had been passed to her by her beloved mentor, Philip.

This is the profile of the author of the Shakespearean canon: Extremely intelligent; superbly educated; literate in a number of modern and classical languages; holder of a celebrated library of books; politically involved; active in the sports, artistic, and intellectual pursuits that appear in the plays; living in the society about which the plays are written—and all of this well documented.

But that's far from the end of the story.

---

46 Hannay, *Philip's Phoenix*, 59–60.

Documented Data

- Mary Sidney's single-minded mission in life was to create great works in the English language. She studied the art and craft of writing.

- She translated work from Italian and French.

- She *published* her own "appropriate"—and pioneering—work.

- She is the first woman to *publish* a play in the English language; it is in blank verse (unrhymed iambic pentameter), the form of the Shakespearean plays.

- She is the first woman to *publish* original pastoral poetry.

- She circulated other work in manuscript form: a translation of Petrarch, the Psalms of David, and other lyrics and poems.

- She is the first English woman who did not apologize for publishing her work.

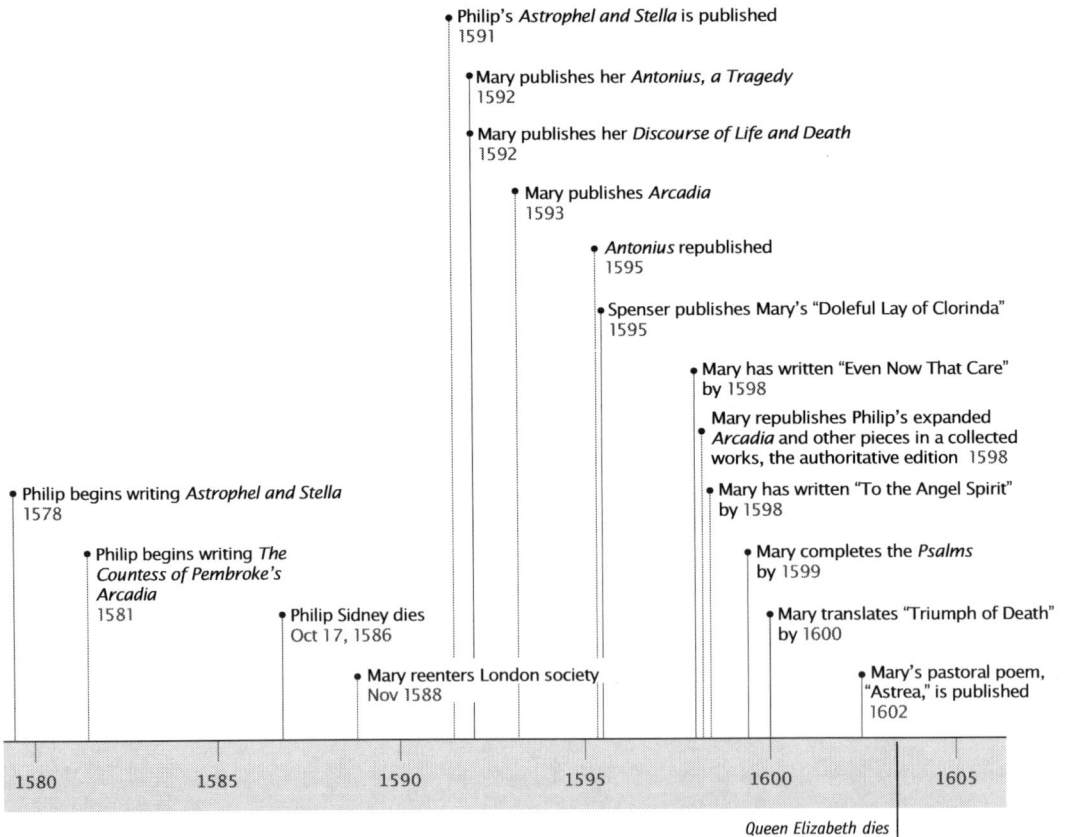

Philip's *Astrophel and Stella* is published
1591

Mary publishes her *Antonius, a Tragedy*
1592

Mary publishes her *Discourse of Life and Death*
1592

Mary publishes *Arcadia*
1593

Antonius republished
1595

Spenser publishes Mary's "Doleful Lay of Clorinda"
1595

Mary has written "Even Now That Care"
by 1598

Mary republishes Philip's expanded *Arcadia* and other pieces in a collected works, the authoritative edition 1598

Philip begins writing *Astrophel and Stella*
1578

Mary has written "To the Angel Spirit"
by 1598

Philip begins writing *The Countess of Pembroke's Arcadia*
1581

Mary completes the *Psalms*
by 1599

Philip Sidney dies
Oct 17, 1586

Mary translates "Triumph of Death"
by 1600

Mary reenters London society
Nov 1588

Mary's pastoral poem, "Astrea," is published
1602

| 1580 | 1585 | 1590 | 1595 | 1600 | 1605 |

Queen Elizabeth dies

Some dates are approximate.

3 Mary Sidney's Life of Literature

MARY SIDNEY's primary biographer, Margaret P. Hannay, describes the countess:

> Mary Sidney, like her brother Philip, was brilliant, learned, witty, articulate, and adept at self-presentation. . . . In an age when women were required to be chaste, silent, and obedient, she may have been chaste—but she was certainly eloquent and assertive. She was able to challenge the norms for women while appearing to follow them, empowered by her own clever self-promotion, her brother's legendary death, and her husband's money.[1]

Mary Sidney—brilliantly educated, passionate about literature, her life informed with marriage, birth, joy, loss, and grief—was determined to take up her brother's literary mantle. Her Wilton estate "became a workshop for poetical experimentation, the seedbed of a literary revolution. Centered upon Wilton's congenial and hospitable lifestyle, on Sidney's example, and on his sister's enlightened enthusiasm, it became the still center of the rapidly turning world of late Elizabethan literature."[2]

Until recently, Mary Sidney has been, it seems fair to state, the most unjustly underestimated poet of her age.
Gary F. Waller, 1979

---

1 Margaret Hannay, *Philip's Phoenix: Mary Sidney, Countess of Pembroke* (Oxford: Oxford University Press, 1990), vix.
2 Gary F. Waller, *Mary Sidney, Countess of Pembroke: A Critical Study of Her Writings and Literary Milieu* (Salzburg: Universität Salzburg, 1979), 45.

Gary F. Waller remarks:

> After [Philip's] death, it was at Wilton that the Countess
> gathered the poets and men of letters to continue her brother's
> work to improve English literature.[3]

> Indeed, it would seem . . . that after Sidney's death in 1586, the
> Countess took a more active part in the literary experiments of
> the Circle, and developed a much more highly organized salon,
> closer to its continental models.[4]

> She presumably felt her duty was to further the revolution
> begun by her brother—and probably in the process discovered
> that her own talents lay not merely in enlightened encour-
> agement [of other writers] but in actively writing herself.[5]

Navarre shall be
the wonder of the world;
Our court shall be
a little academe,
Still and contemplative
in living art.

King Ferdinand in
Love's Labor's Lost, 1.1.12–14

In awe and admiration, contemporaries called Wilton House a "little
university," an "academie," and Mary Sidney's own "court." She
gathered the greatest writers around her, acted as an active patron to
many, requested specific works from various poets, and encouraged
others to develop their writing talents and expand their skills.

> Wilton did indeed become "like a College"; writers like Spenser,
> Greville, Daniel, Drayton, Breton, Watson, and Fraunce
> gathered formally or informally around "the Lady of the plain,"
> dedicating their common efforts to what they saw as the
> betterment of English letters.[6]

> This circle of Lady Pembroke became one of the most
> interesting coteries in the history of English literature.[7]

> For almost two decades Mary Sidney and her household
> at Wilton became one of the most dynamic cultural influences
> in late Elizabethan England, and at the center of Wilton's life
> were her writings.[8]

Mary Sidney dedicated herself to the discipline and craft of writing.
She also acted as mentor to other writers in her circle. Numerous
documents refer to her indirectly or directly educating others. The

---

3   Ibid., 17.
4   Ibid., 71.
5   Ibid., 66.
6   Ibid., 18.
7   Alexander Maclaren Witherspoon, *The Influence of Robert Garnier on Elizabethan Drama* (New York: Phaeton Press, 1968), 68.
8   Waller, *Mary Sidney, Countess of Pembroke,* 29.

poet Thomas Churchyard wrote "A Pleasant Conceit" in 1593 in which he celebrates twelve of the young ladies in Queen Elizabeth's court, and says of Mary Sidney:

> *A gem more worth than all the gold of Ind,*
> *For she enjoys the wise Minerva's wit,*
> *And sets to school our poets everywhere,*
> *That doth presume the laurel crown to wear.*[9]

The **laurel** wreath, or **crown,** is an ancient symbol of an accomplished or celebrated writer.

The renowned and gentle poet Samuel Daniel was a lifelong friend of Mary's. In 1607 he wrote a dedication to her son William Herbert and gave credit to Mary for having taught him to write:

> *Having been first encouraged and framed thereunto by your*
> *most worthy and honorable mother, and received the first*
> *notion for the formal ordering of those compositions at Wilton,*
> *which I must ever acknowledge to have been my best school and*
> *thereof always am to hold a feeling and grateful memory.*[10]

The doctor in her employ, Doctor Thomas Moffett, gently chastised Mary for working too hard. Referring to her translations of Petrarch and her work versifying the Psalms of David, he wrote:

> *Vouchsafe a while to lay thy task aside,*
> *Let Petrarch sleep, give rest to Sacred Writ,*
> *Or bow or string will break, if ever tied.*
> *Some little pause aideth the quickest wit.*[11]

Mary was celebrated as a writer of the highest distinction in her own time. An indication of her reputation can be seen in the book of miscellaneous verse titled *Bel-vedére*, published in 1600, in which she is ranked as a writer alongside Edmund Spenser, Philip Sidney, and William Shakespeare with no notice of her gender. Three quotations from one of Mary's works are also cited. Queen Elizabeth is the only other female writer mentioned in the book (but she is, of course, compared only to King James; one would not dare compare the Queen with a mere citizen). "Such presentation of a non-royal woman author was unprecedented in England, for women were admonished to be silent, not to write and publish."[12]

---

9   Frances Berkeley Young, *Mary Sidney, Countess of Pembroke* (London: David Nutt, 1912), 174.
10   Ibid., 164.
11   Ibid., 181.
12   Margaret Hannay, et al., eds., *The Collected Works of Mary Sidney Herbert, Countess of Pembroke,* vol. 1 (Oxford: Clarendon Press, 1998), 22.

Mary is also the only woman (again, besides Queen Elizabeth) mentioned as a writer in Francis Meres' *Palladis Tamia: Wits Treasury,* the publication so important to literary history because it lists the known Shakespearean plays up to 1598. Meres, comparing Mary to Octavia as a patroness, exclaims that "she is a most delicate Poet," and finds her comparable to Sappho as the Tenth Muse.[13]

> *Octavia . . . was exceedingly bountiful unto Virgil . . . so learned Mary, the honorable Countess of Pembroke, the noble sister of immortal Sir Philip Sidney, is very liberal unto Poets; besides she is a most delicate Poet, of whom I may say, as Antipater Sidonius writeth of Sappho: Dulcia Mnemosyne demirans carmina Sapphus, Quaesivit decima Pieris unde foret.**

*Sweet Mnemosyne (goddess of memory), amazed at the poems of Sappho, asked from whence she became the tenth Muse.

13 Francis Meres, *Palladis Tamia* (1598; reprint, New York: Scholars' Facsimiles & Reprints, 1978), 285.

The Doleful Lay of Clorinda

The Renaissance elegy was one of the rare literary forms open to women. This is one of several elegies Mary wrote for her brother, although she wasn't allowed to publish them in the university collections upon his death in 1586. Why was she not allowed? Because she was a woman.

"The Doleful Lay of Clorinda" (a lay is a ballad) was published in Edmund Spenser's "Astrophel" in *Colin Clouts Come Home Again* in 1595 and attributed by Spenser to Mary Sidney. It is probably written about 1586, when Mary was 24 years old. Below are the first four stanzas of the sixteen-stanza lay.

AY ME, to whom shall I my case complain
That may compassion my impatient grief?
Or where shall I unfold my inward pain,
That my enriven heart may find relief?
    Shall I unto the heavenly powers it show?
    Or unto earthly men that dwell below?

To heavens? Ah, they alas the authors were,
And workers of my unremedied woe:
For they foresee what to us happens here,
And they foresaw, yet suffred this be so.
    From them comes good, from them comes also ill,
    That which they made, who can them warn to spill.

To men? Ah, they alas like wretched be,
And subject to the heaven's ordinance:
Bound to abide what ever they decree,
Their best redress, is their best sufferance.
    How then can they like wretched comfort me,
    The which no less, need comforted to be?

Then to my self will I my sorrow mourn,
Sith none alive like sorrowful remains:
And to my self my plaints shall back return,
To pay their usury with doubled pains.
    The woods, the hills, the rivers shall resound
    The mournful accent of my sorrow's ground.

To whom should I complain? Did I tell this, who would believe me?

Isabella in
Measure for Measure,
2.4.172

Translations

Most of Mary's known major works are translations. The literary form of translation was an acceptable genre for an Elizabethan noblewoman, especially if she translated what was considered to be "appropriate" works. "Translations were 'defective' and therefore appropriate to women; this low opinion of translating perhaps accounts for why women were allowed to translate at all. . . . By engaging in this supposedly defective form of literary activity, women did not threaten perceptions of male superiority; any competence they displayed could be dismissed by denigrating the task of translation itself."[14] If translations (of the work of men) are barely allowable, you can imagine how much more despicable it was considered to write plays for the public stage.

The Tragedy of Antonie

Mary's published writings include *Antonius* or *The Tragedy of Antonie*, a translation from French of Robert Garnier's *Marc Antoine*. Mary first published it in 1592 with *A Discourse of Life and Death*, then separately in 1595.

> *Antonie* was the first public expression of the Countess' dedication to her brother's literary ideals; it was a deliberate step to further the literary revolution he had started. . . . *She was deliberately taking up the matter of raising literary standards in a form which was becoming increasingly popular—the drama.*[15] [emphasis added]

With this translation, Mary "initiated a courtly Senecan movement . . . . This movement produced plays strikingly unlike other English drama of these years and had far-reaching consequences for English drama more generally.[16] It is truly striking that we have no evidence in the literary movement of the man named William Shakespeare.

---

14 Mary Ellen Lamb, "The Cooke Sisters: Attitudes toward Learned Women in the Renaissance," in *Silent but for the Word: Tudor Women as Patrons, Translators, and Writers of Religious Works*, ed. Margaret Hannay (Ohio: Kent State University Press, 1985), 116.

15 Waller, *Mary Sidney, Countess of Pembroke*, 108.

16 Stuart Gillespie, *Shakespeare's Books: A Dictionary of Shakespeare Sources*, 2nd ed. (London: Bloomsbury Arden Shakespeare, 2016), 146.

Below are several examples from Mary's translation of *Antonie*, which is written in blank verse (unrhymed iambic pentameter), the same form as the Shakespearean plays.

ANTONIUS:
Well; be her love to me or false, or true,
Once in my soul a cureless wound I feel.
I love, nay burn, in fire of her love:
Each day, each night, her image haunts my mind,
Her self my dreams: and still I tired am,
And still I am with burning pincers nipp'd.
Antonius, lines 919–924

CLEOPATRA:
Ah, weeping Niobe, although thy heart
Beholds it self enwrapp'd in causeful woe
For thy dead children, that a senseless rock
With grief become, on Sipylus thou stand'st
In endless tears: yet didst thou never feel
The weights of grief that on my heart do lie.
Antonius, lines 1909–1914

LUCILIUS:
                    All war's affairs,
But battles most, daily have their success
Now good, now ill: and though that Fortune have
Great force and power in every worldly thing,
Rule all, do all, have all things fast enchain'd
Unto the circle of her turning wheel:
Yet seems it more than any practice else
She doth frequent Bellona's bloody trade;
And that her favor, wavering as the wind,
Her greatest power therein doth oftenest show.
Whence grows, we daily see, who in their youth
Get honor there, do lose it in their age,
Vanquish'd by some less warlike than themselves,
Whom yet a meaner man shall overthrow.
Her use is not to lend us still her hand,
But sometimes headlong back again to throw,
When by her favor she hath us extoll'd
Unto the top of highest happiness.
Antonius, lines 1119–1136

Regarding Mary's *Antonie,* Cerasano and Wynne-Davies point out:

> Recent criticism suggests that we should interpret the play as
> an innovative and important contribution to a radical form of
> historical drama which employed the past as a veiling device
> for acute comment upon the contemporary political situation.
> Instead of closeting herself within a classical and Sidneian past,
> the Countess of Pembroke explored new forms of theater
> which allowed her to offer covert criticism of the government
> of her own day.[17]

This is particularly interesting in regard to the Authorship Question
in that critics continually note the political agenda of many of the
Shakespearean plays, especially the histories with *their* "covert
criticism of the government of the day."

But Mary went beyond the step of merely writing—for an Elizabethan
noblewoman, she took an unusually aggressive path and actually
published her own work. She took *Antonie* to press in 1592 and thus
became the first woman in England to publish a play; it was reprinted
in 1595, 1600, 1606, and 1607. *Antonie,* a closet drama, was meant to be
read aloud by aristocrats at social gatherings in great houses rather
than performed on a public stage—thus it was on the edge of what
was acceptable for a woman to publish. Nevertheless, it was widely
influential.

Mary Sidney is also one of the first dramatists in English to use blank
verse, the form taken up by the author of the Shakespearean plays.

Just as important as the act of publishing are the dedications with
which Mary Sidney prefaced her books. Every woman who had
published works wrote dedications that were apologies for being so
brazen as to publish and included assurances that the woman was still
a good wife and a good mother. Often they laid the "blame" on God.
However, "[Mary Sidney] Pembroke never apologizes for or even
mentions her own role as a woman writer, thereby making her most
powerful statement on gender."[18]

---

17 S. Cerasano and Marion Wynne-Davies, eds., *Readings in Renaissance Women's
    Drama: Criticism, History, and Performance, 1594–1998* (London and New York:
    Routledge, 1998), 16.

18 Margaret Hannay, "'Bearing the livery of your name': The Countess of Pem-
    broke's Agency in Print and Scribal Publications," *Sidney Journal* 18:1 (2000), 41.

Triumph of Death

In the late 1590s, Mary Sidney translated from Italian a "magnificent version of Petrarch's *Trionfo della Morte*" called *Triumph of Death*.[19]

Gary Waller's analysis of *Triumph of Death* is particularly pertinent as he notes Mary's expertise in the art of writing. After describing the clumsy and wordy earlier translations of Lord Morley and William Fowler, Waller states:

> Her translation is, however, undoubtedly the finest rendition into English of any part of the work before Ernest Hatch Wilkin's modern version, and *the only one* to reproduce Petrarch's terza rima in English. . . . The most outstanding technical feature of the Countess's translation is her reproducing Petrarch's original stanzaic pattern. Petrarch's poem is written in terza rima, where the middle line of one stanza rhymes with the outer lines of the next tercet: *aba, bcb, cdc,* etc. In the Countess's version, each of Petrarch's terzine is, almost without exception, rendered by an equivalent in English, yet as D. G. Rees remarks, "in spite of this close adherence to her originals she succeeds in maintaining that fluency and naturalness which version translations often lack." It is a remarkable performance. She shows constant ingenuity in changing the original eleven-syllable line into English iambic decasyllables and her determined practice to adhere closely to the original is remarkably successful demonstrating, as with so many of her psalms, that she had both an acute ear for the movement and tone of both the English poetical line and that of her original, and a consistent grasp of the high emotional level required.[20]

Several critics notice in Mary Sidney's translation that the speech of Petrarch's Laura is enhanced, more regal, and she speaks with more authority and eloquence than in the work of other translators, such as Lord Morley's. Mary Sidney presents Laura as a "vibrant figure of joy and power."[21]

---

19 Waller, *Mary Sidney, Countess of Pembroke,* 89.

20 Ibid., 146–149.

21 Hannay, *The Collected Works of Mary Sidney Herbert,* 265.

Below are the opening lines to Mary's translation of Petrarch's *Triumph of Death*.[22] Two other pieces follow from the lengthy work.

> *That gallant lady, gloriously bright,*
> > *The stately pillar once of worthiness,*
> > *And now a little dust, a naked sprite,*
> *Turn'd from her wars a joyful conqueress,*
> > *Her wars, where she had foil'd the mighty foe*
> > *Whose wily stratagems the world distress,*
> *And foil'd him not with sword, with spear, or bow,*
> > *But with chaste heart, fair visage, upright thought,*
> > *Wise speech, which did with honor linkèd go.*
> > > *lines 1–9, first chapter*

> *Alive am I, and thou as yet art dead,*
> > *And as thou art shalt so continue still,*
> > *Till, by thy ending hour, thou hence be led.*
> *Short is our time to live, and long our will:*
> > *Then let with heed thy deeds and speeches go,*
> > *Ere that approaching term his course fulfill.*
> > > *lines 23–28, second chapter*

> *That life's best joy was almost bitter cheer*
> > *Compared to that death, most mildly sweet,*
> > *Which comes to men, but comes not everywhere.*
> *For I that journey pass'd with gladder feet*
> > *Than he, from hard exile, that homeward goes;*
> > *(But only ruth of thee) without regret.*
> > > *lines 71–76, second chapter*

Mary Sidney never published this particular work. It exists only in a corrupt scribal manuscript copy held at London's Inner Temple.

---

22 Gavin Alexander, a modernized edition on the Sidneiana web site: www.english. cam.ac.uk/ceres/sidneiana/triumph.htm

A Discourse of Life and Death

In 1590, Mary translated Philippe de Mornay's *A Discourse of Life and Death* from French. She first published it in 1592. About this work, Diane Bornstein notes that:

> [Mary] Sidney's most notable additions are her continuations or expansions of metaphors that appeared in the original. . . . At a time when English syntax was still in an unsettled state, the countess translated Mornay's sophisticated French prose into a smooth, idiomatic English that fully reflected its rhetorical ornaments. A comparison with Edward Aggas' translation [the first English translation], with its awkward phrases and excess words, shows how skillful the Countess' work was. Her changes even improved the original by making it more concise, more specific, and more metaphorical. One can only regret that the Countess limited herself to the silent art of translation and did not write her own meditations.[23]

The following pages present the opening paragraphs of *A Discourse of Life and Death*. On the left-hand page is the translation by Edward Aggas, a contemporary of Mary's, as a comparison to Mary's version from the French original, on the right-hand page.

---

23 Diane Bornstein, "The Style of the Countess of Pembroke's Translation of Philippe de Mornay's 'Discours de la vie et de la mort,'" in *Silent but for the Word*, 134.

published in 1577 ## Edward Aggas, opening of *A Discourse of Life and Death*

It is a strange matter wherat I cannot sufficiently marvel, to behold how the laborer to the end to cease from his labors doth even in manner hasten the course of the Sun. The Mariner for the attaining unto the desired Haven, saileth forward amain, and from as far as he can espy the coast, to shout out for joy. And the Pilgrim or traveler, to take no rest before his journey be ended. And yet that man in the meantime being bound to perpetual labor, tossed with continual tempests, and tired with many rough and miry paths, is nevertheless unwilling to look upon or come near to the end of his journey, sorrowful to see the Haven of his assured rest, and with horror and fear to draw toward his lodging and peaceable dwelling place.

Our life resembleth a right Penelope's web, which still must be woven and woven again, a Sea abandoned to all winds, which sometime inwardly sometime outwardly tormenteth it, and a troublesome path, through frost and extreme heat, over steep mountains and hollow valleys, among deserts and thievish places.

This is the communication that we do use, being at our work, pulling at our oar, and passing through this miserable path and rough way. And yet when death cometh to finish our labors, when she stretcheth forth her arm to help us in to the Haven, and when after so many passages and troublesome hostelries, she seeketh to bring us into our true habitation; into a place of comfort and joy, where we should take heart at the view of our land, and drawing toward our happy dwelling place, should sing and rejoice; we would if we might have our own wills, begin our work again, return our Sails into the wind, and voluntarily retire back into our journey.

Mary Sidney, opening of *A Discourse of Life and Death*   published in 1592

It seems to me strange, and a thing much to be marvelled, that
the laborer to repose himself hasteneth as it were the course of
the Sun; that the Mariner rows with all force to attain the port,
and with a joyful cry salutes the descryed land; that the traveller
is never quiet nor content till he be at the end of his voyage;
and that we in the meanwhile tied in this world to a perpetual
task, tossed with continual tempest, tired with a rough and
cumbersome way, cannot yet see the end of our labor but
with grief, nor behold our port but with tears, nor approach
our home and quiet abode but with horror and trembling.

This life is but a Penelope's web, where we are always doing
and undoing; a sea open to all winds, which sometime within,
sometime without never cease to torment us; a weary journey
through extreme heats and colds, over high mountains, steep
rocks, and thievish deserts. And so we term it in weaving at
this web, in rowing at this oar, in passing this miserable way.

Who would these
fardels bear,
To grunt and sweat
under a weary life,
But that the dread
of something
after death—
Hamlet in *Hamlet,*
3.1.77–79

Yet lo when death comes to end our work, when she stretcheth
out her arms to pull us into the port, when after so many
dangerous passages and loathsome lodgings she would conduct
us to our true home and resting place; instead of rejoicing at
the end of our labor, of taking comfort at the sight of our land,
of singing at the approach of our happy mansion, we would fain
(who would believe it?) retake our work in hand, we would
again hoist sail to the wind, and willingly undertake our
journey anew.

Ending Mary's translation:

Neither ought we to fly death, for it is childish to fear it; and
in fleeing from it, we meet it. . . . It is enough that we constantly
and continually wait for her coming, that she may never find
us unprovided. For as there is nothing more certain than death,
so is there nothing more uncertain than the hour of death,
known only to God, the only Author of life and death, to
whom we all ought endeavor both to live and die.

> Die to live,
> Live to die.

It seems to me most
strange that men
should fear,
Seeing that death,
a necessary end,
Will come
when it will come.
Caesar in *Julius Caesar,*
2.2.34–37

To sue to live,
I find I seek to die,
And, seeking death,
find life.
Claudio in *Measure*
for Measure, 3.1.42–43

85

These short examples of Mary's *Psalms* alongside the Geneva Bible versions show the inventiveness and skill she used in making the *Psalms* her own verse. The spellings here are modernized.

Psalm 69, first verse, **Geneva Bible:**

> Save me, O God, for the waters are
> entered even to my soul.
>
> I stick fast in the deep mire, where no
> stay is: I am come into deep waters,
> and the streams run over me.
>
> I am weary of crying: my throat is dry,
> mine eyes fail, whiles I wait for my God.

Psalm 69, first verse, **Mary Sidney:**

> Troublous seas my soul surround:
>   Save, O God, my sinking soul,
> Sinking, where it feels no ground,
>   in this gulf, this whirling hole,
>   waiting aide, with earnest crying:
>   calling God with bootless crying—
> Dim and dry in me are found
> Eye to see, and throat to sound.

Psalm 57, line 4, **Geneva Bible:**

> My soul is among lions:
> I lie among the children of men,
> that are set on fire:
>   whose teeth are spears and arrows,
>   and their tongue a sharp sword.

Psalm 57, line 4, **Mary Sidney:**

> My soul encagèd lies with lion's brood,
>   villains whose hands
>   are fiery brands,
> Teeth more sharp than shaft or spear,
> Tongues far better edge do bear
>   Than swords to shed my blood.

Psalm 140, first verse, **Geneva Bible:**

> Deliver me, O Lord, from the evil man:
> preserve me from the cruel man:
>
> Which imagine evil things in their heart,
> and make war continually.
>
> They have sharpened their tongues like a
> serpent: adder's poison is under their lips.

Psalm 140, first verse, **Mary Sidney:**

> Protect me, Lord, preserve me, set me free
>   From men that be
>   So vile, so violent:
>   In whose intent
>   Both force and fraud doth lurk
>   My bane to work:
>   Whose tongues are sharper things
>   Than Adder's stings,
> Whose rusty lips enclose
> A poison's sword, such as in the Aspic grows.

aspic = asp

Portion of Psalm 58, **Geneva Bible:**

> Break their teeth, O God, in their mouths:
> Break the jaws of the young lions, O Lord.
>
> Let them melt like the waters, let them
> pass away: when he shooteth his arrows,
> let them be as broken.
>
> Let him consume like a snail that melteth,
> and like the untimely fruit of a woman,
> that hath not seen the sun.
>
> And men shall say, Verily there is fruit
> for the righteous: doubtless there is a
> God that judgeth in the earth.

Portion of Psalm 58, **King James Bible**

> Break their teeth, O God, in their mouth:
> break out the great teeth of the young lions,
> O Lord.
>
> Let them melt away as waters which run
> continually: when he bendeth his bow to shoot
> his arrows, let them be as cut in pieces.
>
> As a snail which melteth, let every one of them
> pass away: like the untimely birth of a woman,
> that they may not see the sun.
>
> So that a man shall say, verily there is a reward
> for the righteous: verily he is a God that
> judgeth in the earth.

Portion of Psalm 58, **Mary Sidney:**

> Lord crack their teeth,
>   Lord crush these lions' jaws,
>
> So let them sink as water in the sand:
>   When deadly bow their aiming fury draws,
>   Shiver the shaft ere past the shooter's hand.
>
> So make them melt as the dishoused snail,
>   Or as the embryo, whose vital band
>   Breaks ere it holds,
>   And formless eyes do fail to see the sun,
>   Though brought to lightful land.
>
> While all shall say, the just rewarded be,
> There is a God that carves to each his own.

Even without the advantage of training in rhetorical devices and poetic analysis, one can see that these comparisons provide a sense of the mastery, art, and experimentation of Mary Sidney's superb translations.

Religious Works

Women were allowed to read and write religious works because their "undisciplined" minds needed the influence of the Bible to prevent them from improper thinking—or so the Elizabethan men believed. But in Mary's project there is a quandary involved in a woman having the audacity to actually *rewrite* the Psalms; that is, instead of a woman being under the authority of the text, here she asserts her own authority over the Biblical word. This is just one example of the force that Mary Sidney exerted in pushing against the boundaries of what was allowed her as a woman.

As noted below, she used 163 different stanzaic patterns in a collection of 164 poems, leading Debra K. Rienstra to call Mary's *Psalms* "a fascinatingly unique work: a brother-sister collaboration, a translation, a paraphrase, a scholarly meditation, an artist's sketchbook of poetic forms."[24] This is a product of the lifelong study that one expects of a writer of the caliber of the Shakespearean works.

The Psalms of David

In her project to metaphrase and versify the *Psalms of David*, Mary consulted a French psalter and the 1560 Geneva Bible, among other psalm versions, as well as commentaries in English, French, and Latin. Margaret Hannay also believes she consulted Hebrew texts.[25] This project was begun by her brother Philip but unfinished at his death in 1586; he had rewritten just 43 of the 150 psalms.

Professor Gary Waller explains that Mary "revised [Philip's] versions and then finished the remainder herself. She [did so], however, not merely with a mere literal versification; her psalms involve an unprecedented degree of literary experimentation, and are the basis of her claim to literary, as opposed to mere historical, significance."[26]

"At their best the Countess' psalms, even more than [Philip] Sidney's, display a remarkable intensity of poetic evocation, formal inventiveness, and intellectual subtlety."[27]

24 Debra K. Rienstra, "Mary Sidney, Countess of Pembroke, Psalmes," in *A Companion to Early Modern Women's Writing*, ed. Anita Pacheco (Oxford: Blackwell Publishing, 2008), 113.
25 Hannay, et al., *The Collected Works of Mary Sidney Herbert*, vol. 2, 13–19.
26 Gary F. Waller, *Mary Sidney, Countess of Pembroke*, 101.
27 Ibid., 181.

Other experts agree on Mary's achievements in the *Psalms:*

> The Countess' virtuosity in experimenting with stanzaic
> and metrical forms is most striking. Overall . . . her Psalms
> contain 164 distinct stanzaic patterns, with only one repeated.
> There are, as well, 94 quite distinct metrical patterns.[28]

> Indeed, there is no collection of lyrics in English which uses
> such a wide range of meter.[29]

> This was an unprecedented achievement in English verse,
> leading Hallett Smith to call the Sidneian *Psalms* a "School
> of English Versification."[30]

> Pembroke's "technical virtuosity in inventing verse forms can
> scarcely be exaggerated" and suggests that had she chosen a
> different "poetic matter" than the *Psalms,* "her accomplishment
> might be better appreciated today."[31]

> In this work, [Mary] Sidney perhaps found a legitimate means
> of imitating the language, patterns, and images often used to
> construct a masculine paradigm of authorship.[32]

> In these *Psalms,* Lady Pembroke's ability as a translator is
> admirably shown. The consensus of critical opinion seems to
> be that her part shows more literary merit than her brother's,
> especially in the skill and ingenuity of the versification.[33]

And what an ironic statement R. E. Pritchard has made:

> If the Countess, as Elizabethan lady, could not easily speak out
> publicly, she could at least, as mouthpiece for the Psalmist's
> (male) voices, and like some of Shakespeare's heroines, speak
> most for herself when speaking as another. [34]

---

28 Ibid., 190.

29 Cerasano and Wynne-Davies, *Readings in Renaissance Women's Drama,* 15.

30 Hannay, et al., *The Collected Works of Mary Sidney Herbert,* vol. 1, 57.

31 Ibid., 57n5.

32 Wendy Wall, *The Imprint of Gender: Authorship and Publication in the English Renaissance* (Ithaca and London: Cornell University Press, 1993), 313.

33 Frances Berkeley Young, *Mary Sidney, Countess of Pembroke* (London: David Nutt, 1912), 139.

34 R. E. Pritchard, ed., *Mary Sidney (and Sir Philip Sidney): The Sidney Psalms* (Manchester: Carcanet Fyfield Books, 1992), 18.

Other Written Work

Mary also produced other original poems, among them a dedication to Queen Elizabeth in her manuscript book of *Psalms,* and another elegy for her brother, "To the Angel Spirit of the most excellent Sir Philip Sidney."

Around 1599, Mary wrote a poem entitled "Thenot and Piers in Praise of Astrea." It is a singing match between two shepherds and was created for presentation to the Queen on her proposed summer progress, or tour, of the Wiltshire area. Typically the aristocrat who was entertaining the visiting monarch commissioned and paid a professional poet to write glorious accolades, but Mary Sidney boldly broke convention once again to write her own pastoral dialogue for the Queen.

"Thenot and Piers" was published in 1602 in a collection called *A Poetical Rhapsody,* edited by Francis Davison. Thus Mary Sidney is the first woman to publish original dramatic verse in English. "Far from the light froth expected from a lady, 'Astrea' (as it was also known) is a tightly constructed dialogue between the Neoplatonic Thenot and the Protestant Piers, one that questions the very nature of language."[35]

Even her personal letters were praised. There are fourteen extant letters from Mary Sidney, three of which were included in a volume printed in 1660 to provide models of elegance in epistolary prose.[36]

Gary Waller remarks on her overall body of work:

> The Countess' technical virtuosity is, then, important and remarkable for her time; with few models available in English, she extends the technical range of English versification, and thus contributed to the revolution in both form and sensibility observable in poetry over the next forty years or so. . . . What is more important is the impressive range of appropriate tones and the variations in stylistic level that her virtuosity affords.[37]

---

35 Hannay, *Philip's Phoenix,* 165.

36 Josephine A. Roberts, *The Poems of Lady Mary Wroth* (Baton Rouge and London: Louisiana State University Press, 1983), 15. Three letters are included in *A Collection of Letters by Sir Tobie Matthew,* ed. John Donne, 1660.

37 Waller, *Mary Sidney, Countess of Pembroke,* 198.

Recently Found

A book printed in Germany in 1755 claims to be translated from an English manuscript. The writer of the English manuscript professes to have known Mary Sidney and her brother, Philip. He describes what was apparently a popular parlor game in Germany that was invented by Mary—an elaborate game in which spirits (named Auriel, Barthiel, Curiel, Daphniel, Ephtiel, Frugiel, Gaziel, and Honiel) tell your Future Fate in rhyme. But don't worry, the translator assures the reader, the spirits will not actually appear.

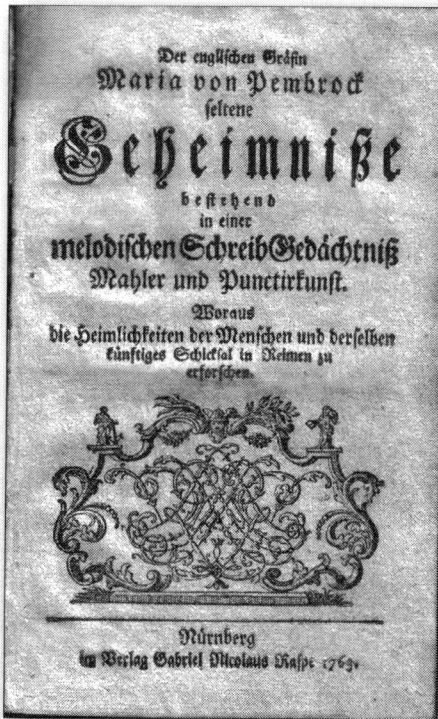

The English Countess
Mary of Pembroke
rare
Secrets
preserved
in a
Melodic Written Script
of the art of painting and stippling.
Thus
exploring in rhymes
the unfathomable future fate
of human beings.

Nürnberg
Publisher Gabriel Nicolaus Raspe 1763

An expanded edition of this book (due to popular demand, it claims), was printed in 1763, shown above, and includes not only the parlor game, but three other "secret procedures." One describes how Mary could remember long strings of numbers and repeat the same string days or weeks later, and could even repeat the list backwards. She wouldn't tell the author the secret, but he relates that her brother Philip disclosed to him the mnemonic device:

Translated from my copies of the book by Ute, Steven, and Malte Forstat in Germany.

> Imagine, gracious lady, how could I play the role of teacher
> of *Mnemonica arithmetica* since Mary of Pembroke never
> revealed this secret to me. To tell the truth, if I hadn't had

the good fortune to have been on a journey to Germany, Hungary, and Italy with Philip Sidney, a brother of this learned Countess, it would have remained forever a hidden secret. He had learned this art from his sister, and having a gregarious and pleasant personality, finally revealed it to me, after I had continuously questioned him.

The secret is this: Each number represents a letter of the alphabet, so Mary would actually rattle off the numbers that represent the characters in a line of poetry. Still an impressive feat.

The book also provides a musical code supposedly developed by Mary. Each letter of the alphabet is represented by a particular measure, so on the written sheet of music one can send an encoded message:

I once paid a visit to this English Sappho, when she actually had a violin in her hands, and was performing a piece of music. As you probably know, this Countess has gained as great a fame among her fellow countrymen through her music as through poetry. I almost went into raptures while listening to it. I could not think of enough praise to compliment the Countess on this piece of music, which in fact was enchanting. She laughed, however, and told me that by no means was this a perfect work of musical art, but nothing other than the transcription of a melodic missive, which she had sent off to Count M. one hour earlier.

The third procedure is a recipe for invisible ink, "the secret and disappearing art of drawing." You can paint or write with it, and when the ink dries, it is invisible. But hold the page near a candle or fire (or a light bulb), and the heat makes the ink reappear:

It is my intention to reveal this Countess' art of secret and disappearing drawing, which to this hour has been known to only some of her best friends. I am in possession of two such works of art which she created with her own hand. The first depicts a perspective view of the Tower or the citadel of London. The second is a floor plan of a fortress. Each is in the center of a sheet of fine Dutch writing paper. These artistic representations are invisible unless the paper is held near the heat of a fire for a short time. Soon thereafter they become visible, all green, in fact to such an

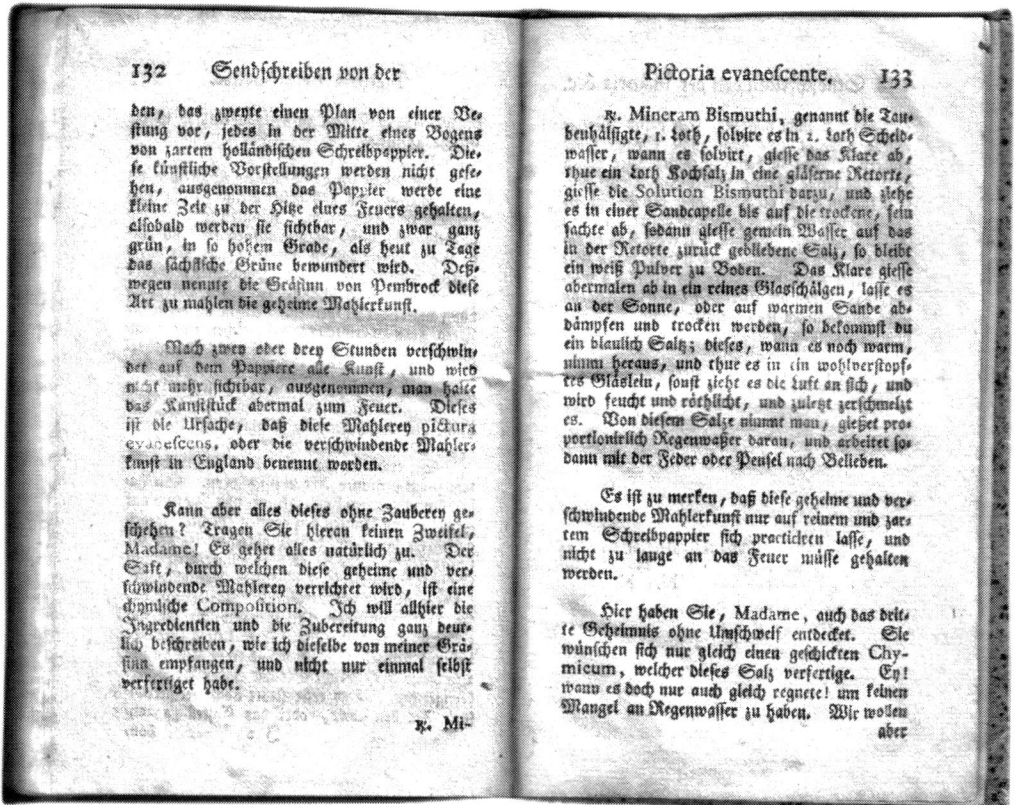

On the right-hand page is the recipe for invisible ink made with bismuth and salt.

extent as the "Green of Saxony" is marvelled at. For this reason, the Countess of Pembroke called this method the secret art of drawing.

After two or three hours, the drawing disappears from the paper and is no longer visible, unless it is held to the fire again. This is the reason why in England this technique is called *pictura evanescens* or the art of disappearing drawing.

It's not clear yet what we can consider as factual in this author's account, but it is intriguing to think of an impressive young woman with these diverse and creative pursuits. At the very least, it shows how far-reaching, both geographically and in time, the reputation of Mary Sidney had reached.

Conventional Yet Covert

Samuel Daniel, the tutor for Mary's children and a writing member of the Wilton Circle, provides a fascinating insight into Mary Sidney in the introduction to his play *Cleopatra* in 1611, a play that Mary requested him to write. Daniel sees Mary as someone determined to set an example and to provide role models for strong and intelligent women. What a powerful medium the public stage could be for this sort of message.

> *Behold the work which once thou didst impose,*
> *Great sister of the Muses' glorious star,*
> *Of female worth, who didst at first disclose*
> *Unto our times, what noble powers there are*
> *In women's hearts, and sent example far*
> *To call up others to like studious thoughts.*

Scholars regard Mary as being seditious, covert, revolutionary, and unprecedented, as in this typical remark from S. P. Cerasano and Marion Wynne-Davies:

> Throughout her life and work Mary Sidney appears to have been able to sustain a balance between what was customarily expected of a Renaissance noblewoman and what could have been considered shocking and subversive. . . . In this way, the Countess of Pembroke's own work should be viewed, not as a simple continuation of Philip's greater genius, but as a point of transition, *signaling a shift from male to female creativity and heralding a new age for women playwrights in her own family and beyond.*[38] [emphasis added]

In Margaret Hannay's words:

> Mary Sidney herself, by remaining within the established limits, became the most important woman writer and patron of the Elizabethan period, *one who demonstrated what could and what could not be accomplished in the margins.*[39] [emphasis added]

How did Mary Sidney balance this combination of apparent conventionality and subtle subversion? From the studies of Cerasano and Wynne-Davies:

38 Cerasano and Wynne-Davies, *Readings in Renaissance Women's Drama*, 17.
39 Hannay, *Philip's Phoenix*, x.

First, after her marriage she chose to retain the Sidney coat of arms as a form of identification, thereby asserting her familial inheritance and suggesting that the link with them was more important to her sense of self than the alliance with her husband. In other words, *Mary Sidney presented herself to the court as a woman of culture,* and not as a wife and mother. [emphasis added]

Second, the year 1586, in which her parents and her brother all died, proved a watershed for the Countess, and it is from this point that she seems to have taken on the Sidney mantle, transforming her home, Wilton House, into an academy for artists of all kinds, and reconstructing herself as a Sidneian scholar, fully capable of continuing the textual endeavors initiated by her brother.

However, rather than interpreting, as many commentators have done, Mary's post-1586 literary activity as a refuge from grief, it is more perceptive to discern a brilliant woman who, having been nurtured within the safety of a cultured familial group and then suddenly finding herself that family's most potent representative, rose to the challenge with exemplary skill and an extraordinary sense of purpose.[40]

Louise Schleiner concurs: "To sum up the observations here of how the Countess of Pembroke, uniquely among Elizabethan women, developed the sustained authorial identity that allowed her to speak with this voice, she did so through interacting with a fairly consistent circle of committedly Protestant writers and other contemporaries. And she had essential advantages that no other woman of her time and place possessed in such measure . . ." including wealth and position, a literary group, support from other poets, and her passion for continuing and developing the ideology she had first established with her brother.[41]

A spirited, courageous woman is revealed. An extraordinarily gifted writer, she used her skill to push against boundaries without apologies. As Schleiner notes, Mary Sidney had advantages that no other woman of the time possessed. But she was still a woman of that time, inexorably held to "honorable" behavior and responsible for upholding the reputation of her entire family.

---

40 Cerasano and Wynne-Davies, *Readings in Renaissance Women's Drama*, 17.

41 Louise Schleiner, *Tudor & Stuart Women Writers* (Bloomington and Indianapolis: Indiana University Press, 1994), 81.

John Tollett

Wilton House   "Under heaven it was my greatest happiness that of this world I ever found, to light into the courtlike house of a right worthy honorable Lady. . . . For in her eye was the seat of pity, in her heart the honor of virtue, and in her hand the bounty of discretion. . . . Her house being in a manner of kind of little Court, her Lord in place of no mean command, her person no less than worthily and honorably attended, as well with Gentlewomen of excellent spirits, as diverse Gentlemen of fine carriage. . . . where first, God daily served, religion truly preached, all quarrels avoided, peace carefully preserved, swearing not heard of, where truth was easily believed, a table fully furnished, a house richly garnished, honor kindly entertained, virtue highly esteemed, service well rewarded, and the poor blessedly relieved, might make much for the truth of my discourse."

Nicholas Breton, *Wits Trenchmour,* 1597,
writing of Mary Sidney and Wilton House

And Where Was William Shakespeare?

Gary Waller has noted:

> Wilton and the spirit it embodied and furthered were
> central to late Elizabethan high culture, and there were few
> major poets who were not in some way connected with it.[42]

William Shakespeare, the man purported to be the greatest writer in England, was never mentioned in connection with the greatest literary circle or by any of the people in it.

Besides the Wilton Circle, the Mermaid Tavern in London "was Elizabethan London's literary and dramatic venue.... The membership of the Mermaid Club reads like a roll-call of famous Elizabethans."[43] The writers, philosophers, and thinkers who belonged called themselves the First Friday Club because they met on the First Friday of each month, and the tavern was located where Bread and Friday Streets come to a point, nor far from St. Paul's in London. In all the contemporaneous stories and documentation about the Mermaid Tavern, William Shakespeare's name is never mentioned, although Stratfordians always claim he was *surely* there.

Many of the most celebrated contemporary literary works were dedicated to Mary Sidney. Scholar and critic John Buxton exclaims:

> There are indeed few poets of the time who, whether or not
> they received any favors from her, failed to insert some praise of
> her in their poems. Myra, Amaryllis, Urania, Clorinda, Miriam,
> Pandora, Pembrokiana, Poemenarcha—she is addressed by
> countless names, and addressed always as the living inspiration
> of the English Renaissance.[44]

One writer who never dedicated a work to Mary Sidney is William Shakespeare.

---

42 Waller, *Mary Sidney, Countess of Pembroke*, 31.

43 Sir Peter Hall, *Cities in Civilization* (New York: Pantheon Books, 1998), 125. The Mermaid Tavern burned down in the Great Fire of 1666, but today there is a pub on the same corner called The Seahorse, even though the owners had no idea this was the previous site of The Mermaid.

44 John Buxton, *Sir Philip Sidney and the English Renaissance* (New York and London: St. Martin's Press, 1966), 233.

Documented Data

- Shortly after the turn of the century, Mary Sidney's life became much more difficult.

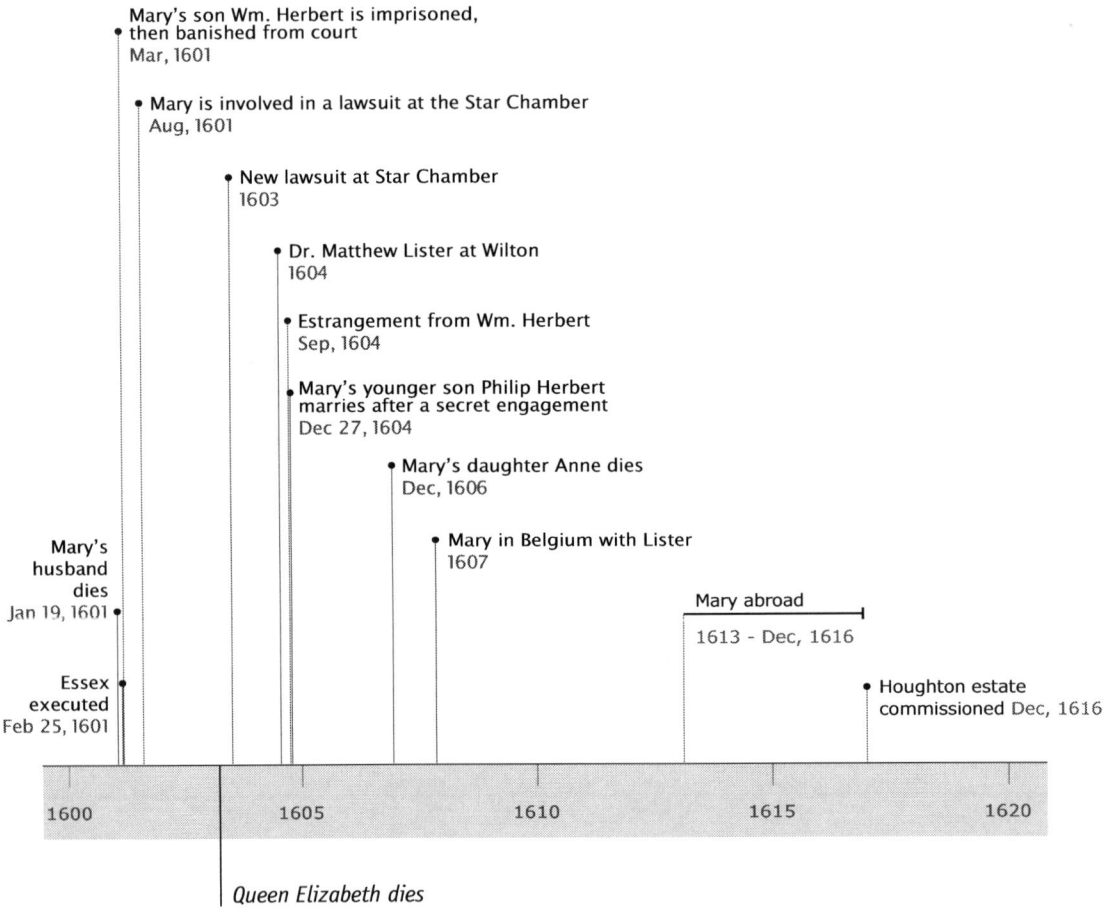

Mary's son Wm. Herbert is imprisoned,
then banished from court
Mar, 1601

Mary is involved in a lawsuit at the Star Chamber
Aug, 1601

New lawsuit at Star Chamber
1603

Dr. Matthew Lister at Wilton
1604

Estrangement from Wm. Herbert
Sep, 1604

Mary's younger son Philip Herbert
marries after a secret engagement
Dec 27, 1604

Mary's daughter Anne dies
Dec, 1606

Mary in Belgium with Lister
1607

Mary abroad
1613 - Dec, 1616

Mary's
husband
dies
Jan 19, 1601

Essex
executed
Feb 25, 1601

Houghton estate
commissioned Dec, 1616

| 1600 | 1605 | 1610 | 1615 | 1620 |

Queen Elizabeth dies

98

4 Mary Sidney as an Older Woman

THE EARLY YEARS OF MARY SIDNEY'S LIFE were rich in education, languages, court life, politics, childbirth, raising children, grief, travel, literary experimentation, alchemical studies, a literary salon, day to day administration of several large estates, acting in court masques and aristocratic closet dramas, singing, publishing, playing instruments, composing music, hunting and hawking, and more. Even as she grew older, Mary never settled into a mundane existence. Her last twenty years were as lively and abundant as the first forty—if not always as comfortable.

Well then, must I work otherwise what I may.

Mary Sidney in a letter to Sir Julius Caesar, July 14, 1603

The contentment in her married life with Henry Herbert, the Earl of Pembroke is difficult to ascertain. It is well documented, though, that Herbert was quick to make enemies, engaged in bitter feuds, was "disastrously lacking in tact," and in the last five years of his life was "a sick and melancholy man. On Christmas Eve, 1595, he sent a poignant note to his friend, Sir Francis Hastings, in which his seasonal greetings were tempered with the sad lament: 'I dream of nothing but death, I hear of little but death, and (were it not for others' further good) I desire nothing but death.' His condition steadily worsened until he was by late 1599 little more than a semi-invalid."[1]

---

1   Michael Brennan, *Literary Patronage in the English Renaissance: The Pembroke Family* (London, New York: Routledge, 1988), 101.

A Change for the Worse

When Mary's husband died in January of 1601, her life changed drastically. "Pembroke's death was a severe blow to Mary Sidney. As soon as he took his last breath, she lost not only her husband, but also her position, much of her wealth, the writers who sought her patronage, and most of her influence at court."[2]

This is intriguing, as for many years scholars have noted the shift that takes place in the Shakespearean plays around the turn of the century, a shift from history and light, joyous comedy to more melancholic and tragic perceptions of life. What might have caused this shift in William Shakespeare's life is impossible to determine, but in Mary Sidney's we see a string of upsetting events over the next several years. By 1601, not only is her husband gone, but by this time all of her influential relatives at court are gone: her parents, two of her brothers (Thomas had died in 1595 at the age of 26), her powerful uncles (the earls of Leicester, Warwick, and Huntingdon), and Sir Francis Walsingham (her brother Philip's father-in-law). Her younger son Philip is only seventeen and her older son William is banished from court and imprisoned.

Mary is 39 years old. At Henry Herbert's death she inherited, among other holdings, the town of Cardiff.

> Left with the responsibility for administering the extensive properties she retained under her jointure and [the Earl of] Pembroke's will, she contended with jewel thieves, pirates, and murderers, finally bringing them to trial after two and a half years of complex political and legal maneuvers. She continued to administer her castle and town of Cardiff, despite violent local attempts to shake off the seigneurial rule of the Pembrokes. Each time she was crossed, this indomitable woman found a way to "work otherwise."[3]

Trouble with Essex

Shortly after her husband dies, Mary's younger brother Robert storms the house of the Earl of Essex and negotiates with Essex and his small band of rebels during their ill-fated uprising against the Queen. This must have been especially difficult for Mary as Essex was a close friend

2   Margaret Hannay, *Philip's Phoenix: Mary Sidney, Countess of Pembroke* (Oxford: Oxford University Press, 1990), 169.
3   Ibid., xi.

of the family. He had been one of her brother Philip's dearest friends—on his deathbed, Philip had willed Essex his best sword, and Essex married Philip's widow (thus he was step-father to Mary's niece, Elizabeth). Essex was executed on February 25, 1601.

Trouble with William

At the same time, Mary's older son causes her grief. William, not yet twenty-one, had impregnated Mary Fitton. This young Mary was 23 years old and a maid-of-honor to Queen Elizabeth. A contemporary reference tells us that "during the time that the Earl of Pembroke favored her she would put off her head tire [headdress] and tuck up her clothes and take a large white cloak and march out as though she had been a man, to meet the said Earl out of the Court."[4]

William admitted paternity but obstinately refused to marry her. The Queen threw William in the Fleet prison for a month, then banished him to Wilton House where he was thoroughly miserable. It wasn't until Queen Elizabeth died two years later that William was able to go back to the royal court. Mary Fitton's baby, a boy, died at birth.

LUCIO: I was once before him for getting a wench with child.

DUKE: Did you such a thing?

LUCIO: Yes, marry, did I. But I was fain to forswear it; they would else have married me to the rotten medlar.

Measure for Measure, 4.3.169–72

Trouble in civil court

By August of 1601, Mary was writing to William Cecil, Lord Burghley, regarding administrative problems at Cardiff Castle, an estate she owned in Wales. She entered a complaint with the Star Chamber against a number of citizens of Cardiff who had pulled down parts of her castle, arrested several of her men, and beaten her servants. She went through lengthy legal battles over this.

In 1603 she went once again to the Star Chamber when one of her employees, Hugh David, was brutally attacked while transporting the Countess's money and jewels to London. David's skull was broken in six places with a cudgel, and the assailant escaped with the goods on a horse belonging to the Justice of the Peace of Cardiff. This same Justice of the Peace then represented Edmund Matthew, one of the accused, who happened to be a former employee of Mary's whom she had fired and replaced with Hugh David.

The Star Chamber was the highest court in England, controlled by the monarch. The court met in a room in Westminster Hall in London; the ceiling of this room was decorated with stars.

Sir Hugh, persuade me not; I will make a Star Chamber matter of it.

Shallow in *The Merry Wives of Windsor*, 1.1.1

4   Lady Newdigate, ed. and transcriber, *Gossip from a Muniment Room, being Passages in the Lives of Anne and Mary Fytton, 1574–1618* (London: David Nutt in the Strand, 1897), 36.

Edmund Matthew had been prosecuted years earlier by the Star Chamber for cruelly and unlawfully embezzling, taking bribes, and levying illegal fines. According to the documentation studied by Margaret Hannay, Matthew was able to convince the civil court that Mary was merely a hysterical woman.[5]

Hugh David languished for three months in ghastly pain before dying. The other accused man, Philip Llen, an accomplice of Matthew's, was asked if he did this dreadful deed, the accused man said no, and the court told Mary Sidney to go home—illustrating the particular vulnerability of a single woman under English law at the time.

Trouble with the boys

How sharper than a serpent's tooth it is, To have a thankless child.
King Lear in *King Lear*, 1.4.287–288

Inferences in several extant letters imply that Mary's oldest son William Herbert was not speaking to her at this time, even though many of the legal battles she was fighting were for the advantage of his inherited estate.

Mary's second son, Philip Herbert, was an irresponsible playboy who also caused her much distress. He was enrolled at Oxford University at eight years old, but stayed only a few months; he entered the royal court when fifteen years old. "As one of [King] James's favorite young men, he achieved wealth and position not by service to the state—as had his uncle, father, and grandfathers—but by hunting, tilting, gambling, and performing in masques."[6]

By his twentieth birthday in 1604, Philip had secretly engaged himself to Susan de Vere, daughter of the Earl of Oxford. Although Oxford was dead by the time the lovers negotiated their own marriage, it's hard to say how Mary felt about this since her brother Philip Sidney had shared "the uncomfortable distinction of being one of those the Earl of Oxford said he wanted to kill."[7] This might be a reason why the marriage negotiations were secret. The girl's great-uncle, Robert Cecil, was disturbed about the match and it was only the King's intervention that allowed Philip Herbert and Susan to marry at the

---

5   Hannay, *Philip's Phoenix*, 173–84.

6   Ibid., 212.

7   Katherine Duncan-Jones, *Sir Philip Sidney: Courtier Poet* (New Haven: Yale University Press, 1991), 174. Contrary to the insistence of many Oxfordians, Philip never did reconcile with Oxford. Oxfordians claim that Philip was Oxford's second in the "Callophisus" tournament as the White Knight, but Duncan-Jones proves Philip was the Blue Knight. The White Knight was Oxford's nephew, Edward, Lord Windsor. *Courtier Poet*, 202–03.

end of the year. Philip later went on to openly keep a mistress, as did his older brother William.

After one particular scene where Philip did not behave as befitted a nobleman, Francis Osborne recorded in his *Historical Memoirs* that "I have been told the mother of [Philip] Herbert tore her hair at the report of her son's dishonor." [8]

Death leads to love

In 1604, the estate physician at Wilton House, Dr. Moffett, died and was buried at Wilton. He had been an integral part of her family and even her literary circle for many years. His place was taken by Dr. Matthew Lister. This must have been a bright spot during these difficult years, because Mary and Lister developed an ardent and romantic relationship that lasted for the rest of her life, although marriage was out of the question because of the difference in social status. In 1604, Mary was 43 years old; Lister was 33, only nine years older than Mary's son, William Herbert. Was this the cause of her estrangement from William—an affair with a younger man who was in a considerably lower social class?

Death of Anne, her adult daughter

Then in late 1606, Mary's 23-year-old unmarried daughter Anne supposedly died in Cambridge, apparently of a recurring illness.[9] Records exist of Mary and her daughter participating in masques and dances at court together. Anne is described as taking part in story-telling evenings that Mary sponsored at Wilton House, and Mary Ellen Lamb believes that Anne was also a writer.[10] Of Mary's four (or possibly five) children, she now had only two sons; of her six siblings, she and her younger brother Robert were the only survivors.

---

8   Francis Osborne, *Historical Memoirs of the Reigns of Queen Elizabeth and King James* (London: T. Robinson, 1658). Quoted in Hannay, *Philip's Phoenix*, 212.

9   Robert Hayes, "Lady Anne Herbert: Another Wilton Secret?" in *The Cygnet* (Santa Fe, NM: Wilton Circle Press, 2013), 2:8–17, argues that Anne did not die in Cambridge. There is no official record of her death, nor a record of a burial place in Cambridge. There is, however, a marriage certificate between an Anne Herbert and a Francis Higginson who studied in Cambridge and became a priest, then a Puritan. This Anne and Francis emigrated to the New World. A copy of a letter written by Anne in Salem, Massachusetts, is extant.

10 Michael G. Brennan and Noel J. Kinnamon, *A Sidney Chronology, 1554–1654* (Basingstoke and New York: Palgrave Macmillan, 2003), 187.

Traveling and Hosting Again

In 1607 she was in Spa (the original Forest of Ardennes in *As You Like It*) with Dr. Lister. From 1613 to 1616, Mary sailed, traveled abroad, and lived in Nérac, Amiens, and Calais in France; Flushing in the Netherlands; Flanders, Antwerp in Belgium, as well as Spa, where she held a noted literary salon. She spent part of one winter in Mechlen, the lace-making capital of Europe. Is this where she commission the swan lace collar and wrist ruffs shown in her final portrait?

In Spa, aged 52, Mary Sidney shot pistols with her great friend the Countess of Barlemont. Their lodgings became the central "court" for the visiting English for entertaining, dancing, and playing. In a town where people gathered from all over Europe to take the waters for their health, Mary Sidney "complains chiefly of a common disease and much troublesome to fair women, *senectus* [old age], otherwise we see nothing amiss in her."[11]

She smoked tobacco, shot pistols, danced, sang, played cards, and consorted with her younger lover. She had such a grand time in Europe that she wrote to her friend, Sir Toby Matthew, "For if you saw me now, you would say, [Spa] had created a new creature. Therefore, let all Pictures now hide themselves; for, believe me, I am not now, as I was then."[12]

In 1616, once again back in England, Mary built an estate with her lover, Matthew Lister, called Houghton House—now in elegant ruins near the town of Ampthill, Bedfordshire.[13]

The stately ruins of Houghton House.

11 Ibid., 214–15.

12 Hannay, *Philip's Phoenix*, 198.

13 It is thought that Houghton House is the "House Beautiful" that John Bunyan refers to in *The Pilgrim's Progress*. Outside the town of Ampthill is a hill that is thought to be his "Hill Difficulty."

Writing Again

And she continued to write. Letters from Mary to her friends Sir Edward Wotton and Sir Toby Matthew intriguingly mention manuscripts that are now presumed lost.

Gabriel Harvey's question in his 1593 work, *Pierce's Supererogation,* also implies there were other works of hers:

> Yet I dare undertake with warrant, whatsoever she writeth must needs remain an immortal work . . . She is neither the noblest, nor the fairest, nor the finest, nor the richest lady: but the gentlest, and wittiest, and bravest, and invinciblest gentlewoman that I know.

> And what if she can also publish more works in a month, than [Thomas] Nashe hath published in his whole life, or the pregnantest of our inspired Heliconists can equal?

Heliconists are poets who call on the Grecian Muses who live on Mount Helicon in central Greece.

What were all these pieces, published or not?

It is encouraging to see that missing or unknown works are regularly discovered. In 1973, a bound manuscript containing the largest collection of lyric poetry of the early modern age was sold at auction; it had been in the library at Warwick Castle for the previous hundred years, mistakenly ascribed—the manuscript was actually written by Mary's younger brother Robert. Similarly, in 2009 a 41-page journal written in 1618 was discovered among the Aldersey family papers in Cheshire, England; the journal is an account of the legendary journey of Ben Jonson when he walked to Scotland. It has always been assumed that Ben walked alone, but this journal was written by his companion.

Mary Sidney has only recently been rediscovered—who knows what works of hers are quietly sitting on a library shelf, waiting to be found?

Still Within the Margins

In Mary Sidney we find an exceptionally intelligent, strong, assertive, and dedicated woman who developed the most important literary circle in English history and whose single-minded mission in life was to create great works in the English language. As forward-thinking as she was, however, the barriers for women were still formidable, and what was considered acceptable behavior was strictly defined. Inappropriate conduct could affect entire families, and in Mary Sidney's case, could directly impact the fortunes and futures of both her sons.

Before we look at Mary's connections with the Shakespearean plays and what might have prevented her from publishing them in her name, let's first look at the documented evidence that ties her so closely to the Shakespearean sonnets.

Part Three

The Sonnets

Never durst poet touch a pen to write
Until his ink were tempered with Love's sighs.
Berowne in *Love's Labor's Lost*, 4.3.320–21

Documented Data

- The first seventeen sonnets implore a handsome, unmarried man to have a baby to carry on his beauty.

- Most of the other sonnets are passionate love poems written to a younger man.

- The poet thinks the younger man is having an affair with a dark-haired, dark-eyed, newly married woman.

- Scholars believe the sonnets were taken to the printing press without the poet's permission.

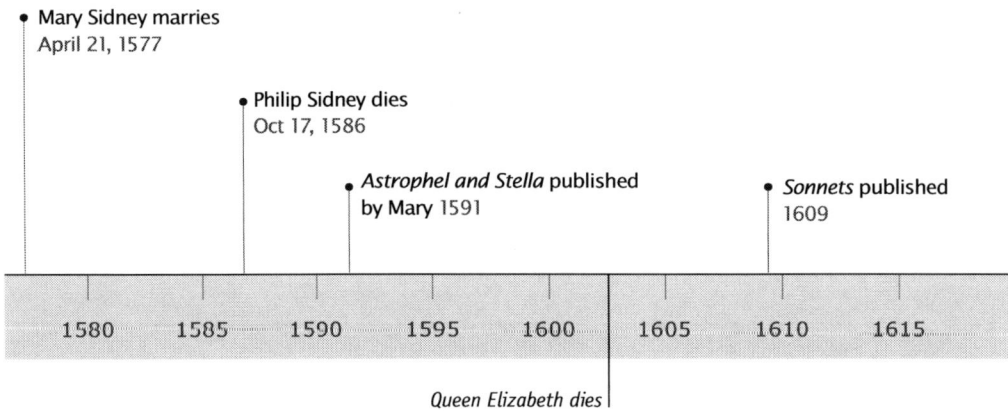

• Mary Sidney marries
April 21, 1577

• Philip Sidney dies
Oct 17, 1586

• *Astrophel and Stella* published
by Mary 1591

• *Sonnets* published
1609

| 1580 | 1585 | 1590 | 1595 | 1600 | 1605 | 1610 | 1615 |

Queen Elizabeth dies

5 Introduction to the Sonnets

AHH, THE SONNETS. This collection of 154 poems presents the most perplexing mystery about the man named William Shakespeare. Many of the sonnets are difficult to understand, and there has never been consensus on what an individual poem actually means: "Editors and commentators have violently disagreed about the meaning of various words, phrases, and passages."[1]

Most experts do agree that the sonnets appear to be intensely auto-biographical. Harold Bloom remarks on their sense of the intimate, "Perhaps the extraordinary voice we hear in the Sonnets is as much a fiction as any other voice in Shakespeare, though I find that very difficult to believe."[2]

But no one can explain how the sonnets fit into Shakespeare's life. "After nearly two hundred years of speculation and scholarship, we have made remarkably little progress toward uncovering the 'true story' behind Shakespeare's Sonnets, if indeed there is a story to be uncovered."[3] Experts also agree the sonnets were not meant for publication and were taken to press without the poet's cooperation. The publisher (not the poet) dedicated the collection, "To the onlie begetter of these ensuing sonnets, Mr. W. H."

And this is the biggest issue with these passionate and often desperate love poems: most of them are written to a man.

> *The relationship between an artist's biography and his writing is always a difficult subject, but there can be no other important writer since the invention of printing for whom we are unable to demonstrate any relationship at all.*
> Dr. Blair Warden, Oxford University, speaking of Shakespeare

1   Hyder Edward Rollins, ed. *A New Variorum Edition of Shakespeare: The Sonnets*, vol. 1 (Philadelphia & London: J. B. Lippincott Company, 1944), vi.
2   Harold Bloom, *Shakespeare: The Invention of the Human* (New York: Riverhead Books, 1998), 731.
3   Donald Foster, "Master W.H., R.I.P.," in *Shakespeare's Sonnets, Critical Essays*, ed. James Schiffer (New York: Garland Publishing, Inc., 1999), 15.

Stratfordians generally believe Henry Wriothesley, Earl of South-ampton, ten years younger than Shakespeare, is the younger man to whom the sonnets were written. Why Southampton? Because the narrative poems published in 1593 and 1594, *Venus and Adonis* and *The Rape of Lucrece* (which in my opinion are *not* written by Mary Sidney), each had a dedication to Southampton from "William Shakespeare." Sixteen years later, in 1609, the *publisher* dedicates the printed book of sonnets "to Mr. W. H." Weirdly, Stratfordians believe that the initials "W. H." are really *supposed to be* "H. W." and therefore the dedicatee *must be* Henry Wriothesley, and thus Henry Wriothesley, Earl of Southampton, has come down through history labeled as Shakespeare's "patron." There is not one jot of documented evidence to support this speculation, and even as speculation, it's quite silly.

In *A Literary History of England*, Brooke and Shaaber discuss the sonnets:

> Of all the Elizabethan sonnet sequences, Shakespeare's
> is the least typical. It celebrates not the idealized love of
> an idealized mistress but the affection of an older man
> for a gilded and wayward youth. Even the twenty-five
> sonnets addressed to a dark lady express repulsion as
> well as fascination. On the showing of the sonnets,
> Shakespeare's experience of love and friendship was
> turbid and disheartening. They abound in meditations
> on estrangement, failure, and death. They bewail the
> poet's outcast state, death's dateless night, the anxieties
> of separation, time's giving and taking away, even world-
> weariness. The conclusion, however, is triumphant—
> an uncompromising affirmation of the transcendence of
> love. The later sonnets (100–126) assert and reassert that
> love, and love alone, withstands the onslaught of time,
> eternal amidst the world's ruin and decay.[4]

---

4   Tucker Brooke and Matthias A. Shaaber, *A Literary History of England*, vol. 2, *The Renaissance (1500–1660)*, 2nd ed. (New York: Appleton-Century-Crofts, 1967), 482.

Depending on how homophobic an individual scholar is, they might give you one of the four excuses written by James Boswell, Jr., printed in 1821 in the late Edmond Malone's version of the collected works of Shakespeare.[5] About these excuses, Peter Stallybrass says in a recent essay, "The final page of Boswell's introductory remarks on the Sonnets are dedicated to proving that Shakespeare was not a pederast. In the process he produces, as hysterical symptom, the lines of defense that have governed nearly all subsequent readings of the Sonnets." [6]

In the table on the following pages is the essence of Boswell's excuses for the sonnets, followed by responses from more recent scholarship.

5   James Boswell, *The Plays and Poems of William Shakespeare, with the Corrections and Illustrations of Various Commentators*, vol. xx (London: C. Baldwin, 1821).
6   Peter Stallybrass, "Editing as Cultural Formation," in *Shakespeare's Sonnets, Critical Essays*, ed. James Schiffer (New York: Garland Publishing, Inc., 1999), 77.

Excuse	Response
1] During the English Renaissance, men talked to each other like this, "in a fondness of classical imitation."[7]	James Schiffer: "No serious reader can any longer make the facile assumption that the relationship between poet and friend is nonsexual or assume as Malone did (and as many have argued since) that the amorous tone of so many of the Sonnets is typical of the way Neoplatonic male friends spoke to one another in Elizabethan times."[8]
	David Bevington: "His emphasis on friendship seems new, for no other [sonnet] sequence addressed a majority of its sonnets to a friend rather than to a mistress . . . ."[9]
	David Bevington: "Still, the bond between poet and friend is extraordinarily strong, and certainly there is a danger that traditional scholarship has minimized the erotic bond between the poet and his friend out of a distaste for the idea."[10]
	Michael Keevak: "The main issue, then as now, is the (apparently undeniable) fact that most of the 154 poems are addressed to a man. This has always been the Sphinx's riddle of Shakespeare sonnet criticism. Was Shakespeare engaged in a sodomitical relationship with another man?"[11]
	Michael Keevak: "It is remarkable how many of the controversies that surround the sonnets are inextricably bound up with the issue of sexuality, and with sodomy between men in particular. . . . Whether or not Shakespeare 'himself' was (or should have been) 'gay,' the sonnets are nonetheless queer, and perhaps a lot queerer than most modern critics have been willing to allow."[12]

7   Boswell, *The Plays and Poems of William Shakespeare*, vol. XX, 221.

8   James Schiffer, "Reading New Life into Shakespeare's Sonnets," in *Shakespeare's Sonnets, Critical Essays*, ed. James Schiffer (New York: Garland Publishing, Inc., 1999), 46.

9   David Bevington, ed., *The Complete Works of Shakespeare*, 6th ed. (New York: Pearson Longman, 2009), 1710.

10 Ibid., 1711.

11 Michael Keevak, *Sexual Shakespeare: Forgery, Authorship, Portraiture* (Detroit: Wayne State University Press, 2001), 30–31.

12 Ibid., 39.

Excuse	Response
2] Shakespeare wrote to get patronage (money and political support) from a nobleman ten years younger, Henry Wriothesley, the Earl of Southampton, "written with a view of remonstrating against a premature vow of celibacy," as proposed by Dr. Drake.[13]	Joseph Pequigney: "There is no evidence to support the idea that the young friend is an aristocratic patron, or a patron of any kind."[14]
	E. K. Chambers: "The case for [the Earl of Southampton] as the friend of the sonnets is now very generally accepted. . . . I do not think it a convincing one. If it were sound, one would expect to find some hints in the sonnets of the major interests of Southampton's early life, his military ambitions, his comradeship with Essex, the romance of his marriage. There are none."[15]
	A. C. Bradley: "The sonnets to the friend are, so far as we know, unique in Renaissance sonnet literature in being a prolonged and varied record of the intense affection of an older friend for a younger, and of other feelings arising from their relations. They have no real parallel in any . . . occasional sonnets to patrons or patron-friends couched in the high-flown language of the time."[16]
	John Dover Wilson: "A poet who rebukes, however gently, a young man for loose living (Sonnets 95, 96), for making himself cheap (69), for his love of flattery (84, line 14), for self-satisfaction (67, line 2), for keeping the said poet up for hours waiting for an appointment he fails to observe (57, 58), is going a queer way about to curry his favor."[17]
	Colin Burrow: "For a printed poem by a commoner to address an Earl as the 'master mistress of my passion' would be audacious beyond belief."[18]

13 Boswell, *The Plays and Poems of William Shakespeare*, vol. XX, 218.

14 Joseph Pequigney, "Such Is My Love: A Study of Shake-speare's Sonnets," in *Shakespeare's Sonnets*, 13.

15 E. K. Chambers, *William Shakespeare: A Study of Facts and Problems*, vol. 1 (Oxford: Clarendon Press, 1930), 595.

16 A. C. Bradley, "Shakespeare the Man," *Oxford Lectures on Poetry* (New York: Macmillan & Co. Ltd., 1909), 330.

17 J. Dover Wilson, *The Sonnets* (Cambridge: Cambridge University Press, 1969), l–li.

18 Colin Burrow, ed., *The Complete Sonnets and Poems* (Oxford: Oxford University Press, 2002), 100.

Excuse	Response
3] The poems are merely conventional—they're not really about "being in love," but about the transcendent state of love itself, sonnets being "the favorite mode of . . . embellishing a work of fiction."[19]	James Schiffer: "The fact that the Sonnets exploit conventional images and themes does not in itself prove that the poems are 'literary exercises' rather than the key to Shakespeare's heart."[20]
Richard Barnfield wrote homoerotic poems in the late 1590s.	Stanley Wells: "Although the sonnet sequence was a fashionable and conventional form, I have been struck by ways in which Shakespeare's poems differ from other sequences. A very obvious one is that, like some of Barnfield's but none, so far as I know, by any other sonneteer of the period, many of Shakespeare's sonnets are explicitly addressed to, or concern, a man. And all of them idealize him. On the other hand the woman, in another reversal of convention stretching back to Petrarch and beyond, is reviled."[21]

Excuse	Response
4] The poems are simply experiments in writing, "merely the effusions of his fancy, written upon various topics for the amusement of a private circle."[22]	Stanley Wells: "These surely are poems in which the poet is talking to himself, trying to work through and to gain control over an emotional crisis by imposing poetic form upon an expression of feelings that no words can ultimately assuage."[23]
	A. C. Bradley: "No capable poet, much less a Shakespeare, intending to produce a merely 'dramatic' series of poems, would dream of inventing a story like that of the sonnets, or, even if he did, of treating it as he treats it. The story is very odd and unattractive. . . . It is all unnatural, well-nigh incredibly unnatural, if, with the most skeptical critics, we regard the sonnets as a free product of mere imagination."[24]

19 Boswell, *The Plays and Poems of William Shakespeare*, vol. XX, 220.

20 Schiffer, *Shakespeare's Sonnets, Critical Essays*, 30.

21 Stanley Wells, "Objects of Desire," *Around the Globe, The Magazine of Shakespeare's Globe* 22 (Autumn 2002), 16.

22 Boswell, *The Plays and Poems of William Shakespeare*, vol. XX, 220.

23 Wells, "Objects of Desire," *Around the Globe*, 16.

24 Bradley, "Shakespeare the Man," 331.

The literary scholar L. P. Smith sums it up: "The story Shakespeare recounts of his moral—or rather his immoral—predicament . . . must certainly, in the interests of the British Empire, be smothered up; the business of proving and re-proving, and proving over again . . . that our Shakespeare cannot possibly mean what he so frankly tells us, has become almost a national industry."[25]

Was Shakespeare Gay?

Homosexuality is certainly not out of the question if the man named Shakespeare actually did write the sonnets. It's just not a very plausible theory because there are no other indications that the man named William Shakespeare from Stratford was gay. Besides being married with three children, we have more documented gossip about his escapades with women than about his acting: In 1596, when Shakespeare was charged with deadly assault, he was out with two women and another man. In 1602, the third-hand diary story (described on page 46) is about Shakespeare in a tryst with a female fan from the theater. William Davenant, the poet laureate of England from 1638–68, claimed he was an illegitimate child of Shakespeare's.

Homosexuality is not a modern creation—it has been a fact of life throughout all recorded history. The "good King Richard" of Robin Hood tales, Richard the Lionheart, was gay. King Edward 2, who ruled England from 1307–1327, was also famously gay.[26] We know that other men of Shakespeare's time were gay, such as Christopher Marlowe and Sir Francis Bacon (his mother complained about it in letters). King James I, of the *King James Bible*, who succeeded Queen Elizabeth, is well documented as having been gay. He openly nuzzled his favorite young men in public, including his greatest love, the Duke of Buckingham.[27]

If Ben Jonson had noticed Shakespeare was gay, scholars assume he would have added that comment to the other disparaging remarks he made about Shakespeare after his death.

---

25 L. P. Smith, "On Reading Shakespeare," quoted in Schiffer, *Shakespeare's Sonnets*, 30.
26 Antonia Fraser, ed., *The Lives of the Kings & Queens of England* (Berkeley: University of California Press, 1998), 87–93.
27 Ibid., 216–23.

Babies and Lovers

The first seventeen of the Shakespearean sonnets—often called the "procreation" sonnets—implore a handsome man to marry and have a baby, an heir, a son to carry on his beauty and his name.

Most of the other sonnets are intensely passionate (not just warm) letters to a younger man, younger than the poet, the "friend." In the plays, the word "friend" refers to a lover of either sex.

Eventually, the famous "Dark Lady" appears, so called because the poet mentions her dark eyes and hair. The sonnets assumed to be written about the woman, this Dark Lady, are not love poems, but are negative and sometimes hateful—the poet believes the Dark Lady and the Young Friend are having an affair. Eventually the poet and the young man get back together and continue their intensely emotional and apparently sexually consummated relationship. There is also mention of a rival poet, a male, in several of the sonnets—whom Jonathan Bate believes is John Davies of Hereford, Mary's secretary.[28]

Intriguingly, in an essay titled "The Silent Speech of Shakespeare's Sonnets," George T. Wright observes the following:

> [Philip] Sidney and Shakespeare are "the only two love poets to make central to their sonnet sequences the issue of showing in verse what is truly in the heart."[29]

> It is so much the more curious, then, that, as the only playwright among those Elizabethans who participated in the sonnet-writing vogue of the 1590s, [Shakespeare] alone should have written sonnets in a style that stresses the solitude of the poet-speaker and the silence of his speech . . . .[30]

> But Shakespeare, following Sidney, moves toward the charging of an inner verbal current, with what sounds like authentic "autobiographical material."[31]

28 Jonathan Bate, *Soul of the Age: A Biography of the Mind of William Shakespeare* (New York: Random House, 2009), 217–19.

29 George T. Wright, "The Silent Speech of Shakespeare's Sonnets," in *Shakespeare's Sonnets*, 157–58.

30 Ibid., 140.

31 Ibid., 148.

Hundreds of books that focus on the sonnets as authored by William Shakespeare raise more questions than they answer. My questions are:

> What if the sonnets were not written by a gay or bisexual man to his younger, male lover, but by a woman, Mary Sidney, to her younger, male lover?

> Could the love sonnets be written to and about her younger lover who, for a time, she suspected of having an affair with her dark-haired, dark-eyed, newly married niece?

> Could some of the sonnets be written to her adored and single brother encouraging him to procreate, to have an heir to carry on his name and beauty?

In the following chapter we'll first look at the documented evidence that demonstrates how Mary's romantic life was fully mirrored in the sonnets that are about or addressed to a younger, male lover, in which she at times laments the younger lover's supposed affair with the dark lady.

Documented Data

- After Sonnet 18, most of the sonnets are passionate love poems to a younger, male lover.
- The poet thinks the younger man is having an affair with a dark-haired, dark-eyed, newly married woman.
- After her husband died, Mary Sidney had a younger lover for the rest of her life.
- There is documented evidence that for a time she believed her younger lover was having an affair with a dark-haired, dark-eyed, newly married woman.

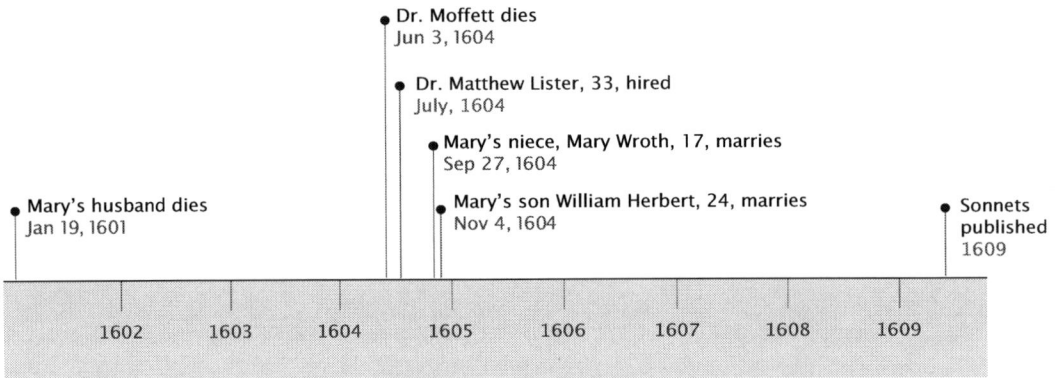

Dr. Moffett dies
Jun 3, 1604

Dr. Matthew Lister, 33, hired
July, 1604

Mary's niece, Mary Wroth, 17, marries
Sep 27, 1604

Mary's husband dies
Jan 19, 1601

Mary's son William Herbert, 24, marries
Nov 4, 1604

Sonnets published
1609

| 1602 | 1603 | 1604 | 1605 | 1606 | 1607 | 1608 | 1609 |

Katherine Duncan-Jones states, "Recent stylometric studies point to 1603–04 as a plausible time for the composition or completion of most of the 'fair youth' sonnets after [sonnets] 1–17." [1]

6 The Love Sonnets

SCHOLARS AGREE that the poet who wrote the Shakespearean sonnets was in love with a younger man.

In the later sonnets, the poet apparently thinks this younger man is having an affair with a dark-haired woman, even though the dark-haired woman is married to someone else, someone who seems to be named "Will." The sonnets that address this "Dark Lady" are not love poems, but verses berating the woman for lust and betrayal. Because so much has been written in trying to connect Shakespeare's life to these poems, it is only natural so see if these details mirror any documented details of Mary Sidney's life.

In 1601, when Mary was 40 years old, her husband died at 67 years of age. In 1604, Dr. Moffett, the estate physician, died and was buried at Wilton. A month or so later Dr. Matthew Lister, who was to become a prominent doctor to the nobility and royalty, began to live at Mary's estate as the resident physician. Dr. Moffett had introduced Lister to Mary Sidney a year or two earlier.

Matthew Lister was ten years younger than Mary—she was 43 and he was 33—yet they fell deeply in love and stayed together for the rest of her life (Lister lived on to the age of 86). Understanding that most single men his age married nubile 15-year-old girls, we can appreciate that Mary, as a mistress, was considerably older than her lover by the standards of the time.

Mary and Matthew would never have been allowed to marry because of the difference in their social classes, "for all responsible persons accepted that it was inappropriate for individuals of unequal wealth and status to marry one another." [1] Also, the land and properties Mary inherited from her husband in his will stipulated that they were only hers until she remarried.

The sonnets are too rich and ambiguous to count as history, but they are something as good or better— a portrait of the artist as lover, painted by his own hand.
Robert Crosman, 1990

---

1   Anne Somerset, *Elizabeth I* (New York: St. Martin's Griffin, 1991), 347.

With this in mind, consider these excerpts from the love sonnets below as though a beautiful, widowed noblewoman is writing to her younger lover. Then read them again with the standard assumptions in mind—as if the baseborn tradesman named William Shakespeare is writing to a highborn, aristocratic, younger, male patron, assumed (on remarkably slim evidence, as explained on page 112) to be Henry Wriothesley, Earl of Southampton.

O, let me, true in love, but truly write,
And then believe me, my love is as fair
As any mother's child.
Sonnet 21

Now see what good turns eyes for eyes have done:
Mine eyes have drawn thy shape, and thine for me
Are windows to my breast, where-through the Sun
Delights to peep, to gaze therein on thee.
Sonnet 24

An *argument*
is the subject matter.

O know, sweet love, I always write of you,
And you and love are still my argument.
Sonnet 76

Those lines that I before have writ do lie,
Even those that said I could not love you dearer;
Yet then my judgment knew no reason why
My most full flame should afterwards burn clearer.
Sonnet 115

[paraphrase]
The poems I wrote earlier are lies,
Especially when I said I couldn't love you more
*   than I already do.*
But at the time I couldn't imagine
That my love for you would grow even stronger.

The following is Sonnet 108 in full with a paraphrase following.

What's in the brain that ink may character,
Which hath not figured to thee my true spirit?
What's new to speak, what now to register,
That may express my love, or thy dear merit?

Nothing, sweet boy, but yet like prayers divine,
I must each day say o'er the very same,
Counting no old thing old, thou mine, I thine,
Even as when first I hallowed thy fair name.

The term "boy" was used as a familiar term in addressing or speaking of a grown person. The Fool calls King Lear "boy."

So that eternal love in love's fresh case,
Weighs not the dust and injury of age,
Nor gives to necessary wrinkles place,
But makes antiquity for aye his page,

> *Finding the first conceit of love there bred,*
> *Where time and outward form would show it dead.*

[paraphrase]

What is in the mind that I can write in ink
Which has not already portrayed to you how faithful I am?
What else can I say, what else can I record
> *That can express how much I love you,*
> *or how I value your precious worth?*

Nothing more can be said, sweet boy; but yet, like divine prayers
Every day I must say it over and over again,
Appreciating all old and repeated thoughts as new,
> *you are mine and I am yours,*
Just like the first time I enshrined your beautiful name.

Eternal love, expressed as new once again
Ignores the way our bodies change for the worse as we grow older
And pays no attention to the inevitable wrinkles,
But love makes old age the paper upon which it writes, for eternity,

> *Having discovered the first passions of love in the body*
> *Even though time and our aged bodies might be expected*
> > *to give love and affection the appearance of being dead.*

Lysander in *A Midsummer Night's Dream*

"The course of true love"

Mary Sidney is the only authorship candidate with *documented evidence* of a younger, male lover, but what about the Dark Lady?

The poet, Stratfordians claim, was writing sonnets to Henry Wriothesley, but then Wriothesley began having an affair with the Dark Lady. This dark-haired, dark-eyed woman is newly married and her husband seems to be named "Will," based on the text of the sonnets. This is a visual representation of the traditional and accepted theory:

The poet . . .	is in love with a younger man, but believes the younger man is having an affair with . . .	a dark-haired, dark-eyed, newly married woman who seems to be married . . .	to someone named Will.
William Shakespeare	Henry Wriothesley, the Earl of Southampton	Mary Fitton, one of the candidates for the Dark Lady	The mysterious "Will"

No Dark Lady in Shakespeare's life (or in the life of any other authorship candidate) has ever been found, although many fantastic theories abound. However, Mary Sidney, a strawberry-blonde, had a dark-haired goddaughter and niece, her brother Robert's daughter, named Mary Wroth (née Sidney). This young Mary, whose nickname as a child was "Little Mall," spent a great deal of her childhood in Mary Sidney's home. In a letter to her sister-in-law, Mary Sidney sends "my blessing to my pretty daughter," referring to her young niece Mary.[2] Margaret Hannay describes them: "The lives of these two writers, Mary Sidney Wroth and Mary Sidney Herbert, Countess of Pembroke, were intertwined from the moment of young Mall's birth."[3] Portraits of Mary Wroth show her dark hair and dark eyes.

---

2 Michael G. Brennan and Noel J. Kinnamon, *A Sidney Chronology, 1554–1654* (Basingstoke and New York: Palgrave Macmillan, 2003), 125. Wroth is her married name. This Mary's maiden name was also Sidney.

3 Margaret Hannay, *Mary Sidney, Lady Wroth* (Farnham: Ashgate Publishing Limited, 2010), 23.

Mary Wroth is well known in academic circles as a writer.[4] One of the pieces she wrote is an unpublished play called "Love's Victory" that provides a clue to the story that seems to play out in the Shakespearean sonnets.[5] Scholars who have studied the work of Wroth say, "Indeed, an awareness of Mary Wroth's biography is essential to the understanding of her work, for the characters in her romances, poems, and play represent the people she knew, those she loved and those she despised."[6]

In her play, "Love's Victory," Mary Wroth uses a popular technique of the time in which she uses quasi-anagrams for the character names that represent Mary Sidney and her younger lover, Matthew Lister, as well as for herself and Mary Sidney's oldest son, William Herbert.

Mary Wroth included William Herbert, her first cousin, in this play because she was in love with him, even though they were both married to other partners within a month of each other. Mary Wroth eventually had two illegitimate children with William Herbert after her husband died.

In her play, the character who (according to Waller and others) represents William Herbert is in love with the character of Mary Wroth.[7] The character representing Matthew Lister, Mary Sidney's lover, swears he will never fall in love, but the goddess Venus brings him together with Mary Sidney. They fall fiercely in love with each other, but soon their relationship is deeply troubled by an unfounded rumor that breaks them apart—the rumor is that Matthew Lister (the younger lover) is in love with the dark-haired, dark-eyed Mary Wroth (Mary Sidney's niece), and she with him.[8]

4   Mary Wroth was the first English woman to write an original (as opposed to translated) dramatic comedy, a prose romance, a sonnet sequence, and an original pastoral drama.
5   The manuscript copy of "Love's Victory" is in the Huntington Library in San Marino, California. It was probably written in the early 1620s for private performance. The entire play is reproduced in S. Cerasano and Marion Wynne-Davies, eds., *Renaissance Drama by Women: Texts and Documents* (London and New York: Routledge, 1996), 91–125.
6   Cerasano and Wynne-Davies, *Renaissance Drama by Women*, 91. If the character named Rustic in the play represents Mary Wroth's husband, Robert Wroth, as the scholars say, Mary Wroth certainly does despise him, and so does everyone else.
7   Gary Waller, *Sidney Family Romance* (Detroit: Wayne State University Press, 1993), 242.
8   Also in the play, Mary Sidney berates Lister for being fickle, for professing vows of love to another woman, and for reviling a particular woman to Mary's face but wooing her behind Mary's back.

In the play, Mary Wroth herself discovers the trouble and helps to reunite Mary Sidney and Lister with vows of eternal love. "The other half of Act 4 presents [Mary Wroth] as a loyal and effective friend, intervening in a quarrel between [Mary Sidney] and [Matthew Lister]."[9] And they become, as a character named Musella says, "the couple Cupid best doth love."

The historical events that Mary Wroth incorporates into her play are the same events that surface in the Shakespearean sonnet sequence after Sonnet 18: Mary Sidney as the author/poet of the sonnets, Matthew Lister the younger lover, and Mary Wroth the Dark Lady.

Are these the poems that Mary Sidney, in love with Matthew Lister, wrote when she thought her adored 19-year-old niece, Mary Wroth, whom she helped raise and who was recently married, was having an affair with Matthew Lister?

Excerpts from the "Dark Lady" sonnets:

> *That thou hast her it is not all my grief,*
> *And yet it may be said I loved her dearly,*
> *That she hath thee is of my wailing chief,*
> *A loss in love that touches me more nearly.*
>
> *Loving offenders, thus I will excuse ye:*
> *Thou dost love her, because thou knowst I love her,*
> *And for my sake even so doth she abuse me,*
> *Suff'ring my friend for my sake to approve her.*

Sonnet 42; is this directed at Matthew Lister?

> *Thou art as tyrannous, so as thou art,*
> *As those whose beauties proudly make them cruel;*
> *For well thou knowst to my dear doting heart*
> *Thou art the fairest and most precious Jewel. . . .*
> > *In nothing art thou black save in thy deeds*
> > *And thence this slander as I think proceeds.*

Sonnet 131; directed at her beloved niece, Mary Wroth?

---

9 Louise Schleiner, *Tudor & Stuart Women Writers* (Bloomington and Indianapolis: Indiana University Press, 1994), 143.

Beshrew [curse] *that heart that makes my heart to groan*
For that deep wound it gives my friend and me.

Sonnet 133; directed at Mary Wroth? The word "friend"
is used in the plays to refer to a lover of either sex.

O call not me to justify the wrong
That thy unkindness lays upon my heart,
Wound me not with thine eye but with thy tongue,
Use power with power, and slay me not by Art,
Tell me thou lov'st else-where; but in my sight,
Dear heart, forbear to glance thine eye aside.

Sonnet 139; written to Lister, thinking he is "changing eyes"
with Mary Wroth?

O me! What eyes hath love put in my head,
Which have no correspondence with true sight,
Or if they have, where is my judgment fled,
That censures falsely what they see aright? . . .

                O how can love's eye be true,
That is so vexed with watching and with tears?

Sonnet 148; has she discovered she is wrong to have accused them?

It turns out Wroth wasn't having an affair with Lister after all, just as
Mary Wroth wrote in her play. But Mary Sidney does discover that
her niece (Mary Wroth) is actually in love with her son (Will
Herbert), who is also newly married. This, of course, presents an
emotional quandary of another kind for Mary Sidney.

Who ever hath her wish, thou hast thy Will,
And Will *to boot, and* Will *in over-plus . . .*
So thou, being rich in Will *add to thy* Will,
One Will *of mine to make thy large* Will *more.*

Sonnet 135; written to Mary Wroth?

The word **will** also means
desire or *lust.*

In loving thee thou knowst I am forsworn
    [I have sworn falsely on your love, thinking it true]
But thou art twice forsworn to me love swearing;
In act thy bed-vow [marriage vow] *broke and new faith torn . . .*

Sonnet 152; written to Mary Wroth?

Thus it is clear that there is a *documented* love story, the only one during this time period, that matches the story of the sonnets:

The poet . . .	is in love with a younger man, but believes the younger man is having an affair with . . .	a dark-haired, dark-eyed, newly married woman who seems to be married . . .	to someone named Will.

Mary Sidney	Dr. Matthew Lister	Mary Wroth	Will Herbert

It wasn't discovered until 1935 that Mary Sidney's son William had two illegitimate children with his first cousin Mary Wroth.[10] Gary Waller, author of *The Sidney Family Romance*, affirms, "The modern discovery of the affair is a fascinating one of an almost total cover-up by the Sidneys for nearly three hundred years."[11] The cover-up, which

10 M.A. Beese, "A Critical Edition of the Poems Printed by John Donne the Younger in 1660, As Written by William Herbert, Earl of Pembroke, and Sir Benjamin Ruddier," unpublished dissertation, Oxford University, 1935. Discussed in *The Sidney Family Romance*, 122.

Sharon Valiant argues that Mary Wroth, through her illegitimate daughter Catherine Lovell, may be the great-grandmother of the writer Aphra Behn. "Sidney's Sister, Pembroke's Mother . . . and Aphra Behn's Great-Grandmother?", a paper presented at the American Society of Eighteenth Century Studies Conferences, New Orleans, 1989. Ms. Behn is the first woman to make a living by writing in English. She had seventeen plays produced on the London stage in seventeen years, among many other amazing accomplishments in and out of the literary world. Yet Aphra Behn also "constitutes an example of almost every technique men have used to abuse, devalue, and erase women." Dale Spender, *Women of Ideas & What Men Have Done To Them* (London: Routledge, 1982), 34. Aphra Behn claimed Shakespeare as an ally, as an honorary woman writer, in her 1673 preface to her comedy stage play, *The Dutch Lover*. Was she speaking from a knowledge of her family history?

11 Gary Waller, *Sidney Family Romance* (Detroit: Wayne State University Press, 1993), 122. William Herbert had no living children with his own wife—after twelve years of marriage, their first baby died at birth, and five years later another baby died as an infant. Mary Wroth's only child with her husband was born ten years into her marriage, one month before her husband died. The baby died when two years old.

included destroying documentation, was perpetrated by the same man to whom the First Folio (the hard-bound collection of Shakespearean plays) is dedicated, and possibly the sonnets, "Mr. W. H."—William Herbert. Was this a precedent for handling subsequent family secrets?

Documented Data

- The sonnet mania in England was started by the publication of the sonnet sequence written by Mary's brother, Philip Sidney, called *Astrophel and Stella*.
- This sonnet sequence was published after Philip's death by Mary Sidney.
- With no home of his own, Philip often lived at Mary's Wilton House estate, writing and developing the literary circle with her.

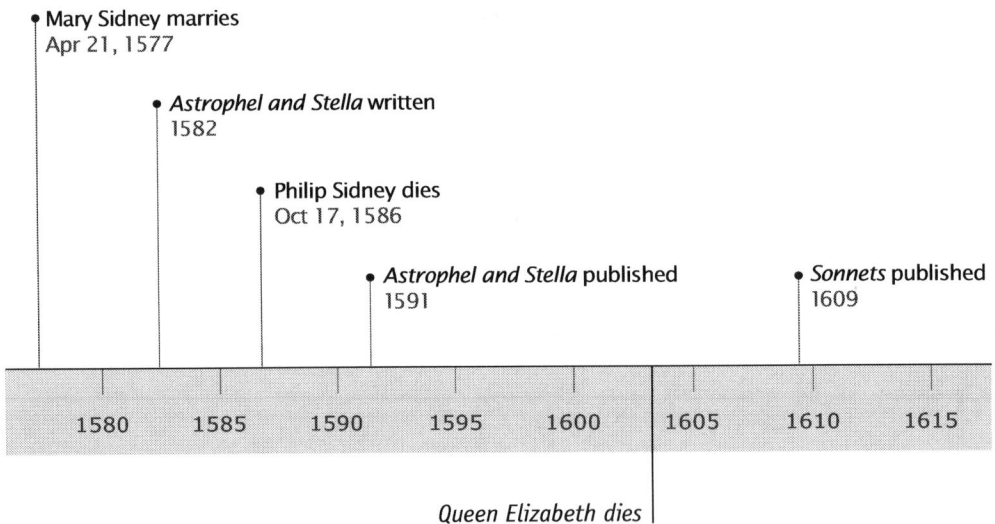

• Mary Sidney marries
Apr 21, 1577

• *Astrophel and Stella* written
1582

• Philip Sidney dies
Oct 17, 1586

• *Astrophel and Stella* published
1591

• *Sonnets* published
1609

| 1580 | 1585 | 1590 | 1595 | 1600 | 1605 | 1610 | 1615 |

Queen Elizabeth dies

7 The Procreation Sonnets

THE SHAKESPEAREAN SONNETS WENT TO PRESS in 1609. Critics say the height of the public passion for sonnet writing and reading was about fifteen years earlier, which is one reason it is often assumed this particular collection was not meant for publication—besides the fact that the "man" who wrote them was apparently gay and surely wouldn't want his supposed relationship exposed through the sonnets' publication.

More folly has been written about the sonnets than about any other Shakespearean topic.

Sir Edmund Chambers
1866–1954

As David Bevington writes, "Sonneteering was the rage in England in the early and mid 1590s . . . gaining new momentum in 1591 with the publication of Sir Philip Sidney's *Astrophel and Stella*."[1] Philip wrote this sonnet sequence around 1582; he died in 1586. An unauthorized and corrupt version was printed in 1591, then recalled by Mary Sidney, who corrected and edited the collection, and immediately reprinted it.[2] So the passion for English sonnets started with the poems of Mary's brother Philip, work that was published by Mary Sidney herself.

"The first [sonnet series] to follow was Samuel Daniel with his *Delia* (1592). Daniel was the protégé and neighbor of Lady Pembroke, to whom his sequence was dedicated. . . . He uses almost exclusively the easy Shakespearean form."[3] It is very interesting that Samuel Daniel, employed in Mary's home, most likely as a tutor for her daughter, credits Mary Sidney as having taught him to write, as evidenced in a dedication he wrote to her oldest son:[4]

---

1 David Bevington, ed., *The Complete Works of Shakespeare*, 6th ed. (New York: Pearson Longman, 2009), 1708.

2 Michael G. Brennan and Noel J. Kinnamon, *A Sidney Chronology, 1554–1654* (Basingstoke and New York: Palgrave Macmillan, 2003), 130.

3 Tucker Brooke and Matthias A. Shaaber, *A Literary History of England*, vol. 2, *The Renaissance (1500–1660)*, 2nd ed. (New York: Appleton-Century-Crofts, 1967), 480.

4 Margaret Hannay, *Philip's Phoenix: Mary Sidney, Countess of Pembroke* (Oxford: Oxford University Press, 1990), 162–63.

Having been first encouraged and framed thereunto by your most worthy and honorable mother, and received the first notion for the formal ordering of those compositions at Wilton, which I must ever acknowledge to have been my best school, and thereof always am to hold a feeling and grateful memory.[5]

In the Shakespearean sonnets, the first seventeen poems implore a man to have a baby, which is why they are today called the "procreation sonnets." Over and over and over, the poet gives impassioned reasons for some man to marry and have a child.

Philip had a series of ineffectual marriage alliances with Anne Cecil, daughter of Lord Burghley; Penelope Devereux, Lady Rich (sister of Essex); various European princesses; Penelope's sister Dorothy; a daughter of Henry, Lord Berkeley; and finally, nearly thirty years old, Philip married sixteen-year-old Frances Walshingham.[6]

John Dover Wilson notes a remarkable coincidence between Philip Sidney's work and the Shakespearean procreation sonnets: "But this marriage section had a source peculiar to itself . . . namely a famous passage in the *Countess of Pembroke's Arcadia,* which Sir Philip Sidney wrote for his sister . . . which consisted of a series of arguments virtually identical with those Shakespeare advances to the youth."[7]

We must consider, then, this possibility: What if the first seventeen sonnets (some are excerpted below) were written by a young woman who is studying the art of writing along with her beloved brother who is educated, worldly, handsome, charming, almost thirty years old, unmarried, childless, and the sole heir to the entire fortunes of the two most powerful noblemen in England, his uncles Robert Dudley, the Earl of Leicester, and Ambrose Dudley, the Earl of Warwick? If a nobleman dies without heirs, his fortune and lands revert to the crown, so there is an extremely practical side to the desire for an heir, as well as the natural desire of a woman, who is herself a mother, to see the brother she cherishes fulfilled in this way.

---

5   Ibid., 117. Samuel Daniel wrote this to Mary's son, William Herbert, in the dedication to his "A Defense of Rhyme."

6   Margaret P. Hannay, Michael G. Brennan, and Mary Ellen Lamb, *The Ashgate Research Companion to The Sidneys, 1500–1700, Volume 1: Lives* (Surrey: Ashgate Publishing Limited, 2015), 47.

7   J. D. Wilson, *The Sonnets* (Cambridge: Cambridge University Press, 1969), 89.

Read the following sonnet snippets with Mary Sidney in mind, writing
with and about her beloved older brother, then re-read them with the
image of a low-born player writing to a nobleman.[8]

> *Is it for fear to wet a widow's eye*
> *That thou consum'st thyself in single life?*
> Sonnet 9

> *Make thee another self for love of me,*
> *That beauty still may live in thine or thee.*
> Sonnet 10

> *Oh, that you were your self! But, love, you are*
> *No longer yours than you yourself here live.*
> *Against this coming end you should prepare,*
> *And your sweet semblance to some other give.*
> Sonnet 13

> *If I could write the beauty of your eyes*
> *And in fresh numbers number all your graces,*
> *The age to come would say, "This poet lies;*
> *Such heavenly touches ne'er touched earthly faces."*
>   *But were some child of yours alive that time,*
>   *You should live twice, in it and in my rhyme.*
> Sonnet 17

> *Dear my love, you know*
> *You had a father; let your son say so.*
> Sonnet 13

> *Thou art thy mother's glass [mirror], and she in thee*
> *Calls back the lovely April of her prime.*
>
> Sonnet 3. Perhaps a reference to their mother
> who, as an adult, was horribly scarred by smallpox?

It's interesting to
note in these last two
examples that the poet
refers to both the man's
father and **mother.**

---

8   If you saw the television series *Downton Abbey,* consider how realistic a homosexual relationship might be between the Earl of Grantham and a lower class
actor on the public stage, who would be lower in status than a footman in a noble
house. Consider it, and then take it three hundred years backwards in society.

The author C. S. Lewis wrote of the sonnets:

> His language is too lover-like for that of ordinary male
> friendship; and though the claims of friendship are
> sometimes put very high in, say, the *Arcadia*, I have found no
> real parallel to such language between friends in sixteenth-
> century literature. Yet, on the other hand, this does not seem
> to be the poetry of full-blown pederasty. . . . The incessant
> demand that the Man should marry and found a family
> would seem to be inconsistent . . . with a real homosexual
> passion. It is not even very obviously consistent with normal
> friendship. It is indeed hard to think of any real situation in
> which it would be natural. What man in the whole world,
> except a father or a potential father-in-law, cares whether
> any other man gets married? Thus the emotion expressed in
> the Sonnets refuses to fit into our pigeonholes.[9]

The sonnets do not fit into pigeonholes. They do not fulfill any of the
pat explanations of Renaissance male friendship. They do not
resemble the sonnets written by any other man of the time. Perhaps
a man did not write these sonnets.

At almost thirty years of age, Mary's brother Philip did finally marry
sixteen-year-old Frances Walsingham, the daughter of Sir Francis
Walsingham, the Queen's Secretary of State. It's ironic that so many
of these first sonnets implore the man to have a child before he dies,
and Philip did indeed die very early in his life, not long after his
daughter Elizabeth was born. (His wife Frances was pregnant with a
second child when Philip died, but she miscarried at about five
months.)

Is it possible that Mary Sidney wrote these early sonnets, the procreation sonnets, to express her feelings to and about her brother Philip,
who at the time had yet to get married and have a child? Might they
also be studies in her craft, experimenting in the sonnet form
alongside her brother as he wrote the sequence of *Astrophel and Stella*,
Certain Sonnets, and the book *The Countess of Pembroke's Arcadia*?

---

9   C. S. Lewis, *English Literature in the Sixteenth Century* (Oxford: Oxford University
     Press, 1954), 503–05.

"Death shall not brag . . ."

If the first seventeen sonnets are Mary writing to Philip, encouraging him to have a child and heir before he dies, then Sonnet 18, one you might be familiar with, may be read as a shattered goodbye to a youthful Philip upon his death in war.

John Dover Wilson muses on the procreation sonnets: "One recalls the weeping crowds in February 1587 when Sir Philip Sidney was carried to his grave leaving no son to perpetuate his name."[10]

Regarding the third line, Katherine Duncan-Jones notes, "The image of often-spoiled spring blossoms hints at early death."[11] In regard specifically to this sonnet, Wilson writes, "And then comes sonnet 18; and there is no talk of marriage in it, or for ever afterwards."[12]

> Shall I compare thee to a summer's day?
> Thou art more lovely and more temperate:
> Rough winds do shake the darling buds of May,
> And summer's lease hath all too short a date.
>
> Sometime too hot the eye of heaven shines,
> And often is his gold complexion dimmed;
> And every fair from fair sometime declines,
> By chance, or Nature's changing course untrimmed:
>
> But thy eternal summer shall not fade,
> Nor lose possession of that fair thou owest,
> Nor shall Death brag thou wand'rest in his shade,
> When in eternal lines to Time thou growest.
>
> > So long as men can breathe or eyes can see,
> > So long lives this, and this gives life to thee.

A paraphrase of this sonnet is on the following page.

10 Wilson, *The Sonnets*, 90.
11 Katherine Duncan-Jones, ed., *The Arden Shakespeare, Shakespeare's Sonnets* (Walton-on-Thames: Thomas Nelson and Sons, Ltd., 1997), 146.
12 Ibid., 92.

Below is a paraphrase of Sonnet 18; keep in mind the multiple layers of meanings in every line.

Shall I compare you to a summer's day?
You are lovelier than a summer's day and less extreme.
In summer, rough winds shake the sweet new buds that sprouted in May;
And the summertime itself is much too short.

Sometimes on a summer's day the sun shines too hot,
And often it doesn't shine much at all;
And everything that is beautiful eventually becomes less so,
Either by chance, or simply from the progression of Time and Nature.

But the eternal summer of your soul shall not fade, even though you are dead,
Nor will you lose the beauty that you own,
Nor will Death brag that he has overtaken you.
I have written about you in these lines of my poem, and so
the memory of you will be as eternal as Time.

As long as men can breathe or eyes can see,
This poem about you lives just as long, and this poem
gives life to you, long after you are gone.

Philip's Influence

In Anne Ferry's exploration of *The "Inward" Language: Sonnets of Wyatt, Sidney, Shakespeare, Donne,* she discovers the remarkable influence that Philip Sidney had on the author of the Shakespearean sonnets:

> "O let me true in love but truly write" is the plea of the speaker in Shakespeare's Sonnet 21. The deliberate echo of the opening of *Astrophel and Stella* is verified by the poem as a whole, which assimilates many characteristic means invented by Sidney for representing Astrophel's struggle to show the truth of his love in verse. The issues involved in that effort about the relation of poetic language to inward experience are first raised in Shakespeare's sequence in this sonnet, which is so closely, complexly, and successfully patterned after a characteristic Sidneian model as to prove that Shakespeare there understood the issues in Sidney's terms, and learned his means for exploring them.[13]

Anne Ferry continues, "Shakespeare, *alone among English writers of love sonnets after Sidney,* followed him in making these questions a central concern, assimilating their most far-reaching implications for what amounts to a new conception of human nature. Other poets, by contrast, borrowed only details of phrasing from Sidney, or imitated his motifs and manner."[14] [emphasis added]

Ferry explores Philip Sidney's influence in shared themes and motifs, his vocabulary about art, imitations of specific personifications "like a quarrelsome personal Muse, or a neglectful Cupid," and even echoes of individual lines.[15] She shows that the poet of the Shakespearean sonnets "repeatedly turned to *Astrophel and Stella* for models," adapted individual poems, borrowed simultaneously from multiple poems, and combined "specific echoes with adaptations of devices more generally characteristic of Sidney's style."[16]

---

13 Anne Ferry, *The "Inward" Language: Sonnets of Wyatt, Sidney, Shakespeare, Donne* (Chicago, London: The University of Chicago Press, 1983), 170.

14 Ibid., 172.

15 Ibid., 192.

16 Ibid., 77–78.

Beyond influences of writing style and subject, Anne Ferry demonstrates that the Shakespearean poet absorbed "fundamental assumptions about human nature which are new to English poetry in *Astrophel and Stella*."[17] She also notes that, "The fullness and power of Shakespeare's adaptations show how profoundly he understood what were Sidney's different assumptions."[18]

It is curious, inconsistent, and unlikely that William Shakespeare, who never met Philip Sidney, could have "understood" him and his work so intimately and completely. Only Mary Sidney among all the authorship candidates was in such close collaboration with Philip Sidney as to be able to explore and develop so deeply these new ideas in literature.

17 Ibid., 198.
18 Ibid., 205.

8 Sonnet Miscellany

IN ADDITION TO THE PROCREATION AND LOVE SONNETS, there are a number of other intriguing features in the Shakespearean sonnets. For instance, not all of the sonnets in the collection are love poems. It's puzzling to note how often the poet laments of obscurity, frustration, and disgrace. But why would William Shakespeare complain of obscurity and disgrace when the sonnets were written and published during the supposed height of his achievements and popularity? David Honneyman remarks that "there is a persistent sense of failure, of disappointment, and of complaints against Fortune which are out of phase with Shakespeare's accelerating prosperity."[1]

O! let my books be then the eloquence And dumb presagers of my speaking breast.
Sonnet 23

The sonnets were published in 1609. By this time it is theorized that all but three or four of the plays had been written (Shakespeare died in 1616).

Could these be the laments of a brilliant woman?

> *When, in disgrace with Fortune and men's eyes,*
> *I all alone beweep my out-cast state,*
> *And trouble deaf heaven with my bootless [useless] cries,*
> *And look upon my self and curse my fate,*
> *Wishing me like to one more rich in hope,*
> *Featured like him, like him with friends possess'd,*
> *Desiring this man's art, and that man's scope,*
> *With what I most enjoy contented least . . .*
> Sonnet 29

"What I am most gifted with gives me the least satisfaction," because she cannot claim her art to the world?

---

1   David Honneyman, *Shakespeare's Sonnets and the Court of Navarre* (Lewiston: The Edwin Mellen Press, 1997), 3.

Stars can refer to fortune or fate, and they can also refer to the members of the royal court.

Let those who are in favor with their stars
[those who are born male?]
Of public honor and proud titles boast
[men who can publish openly?]
Whilst I, whom fortune of such triumph bars . . .
[because she is a woman?]
Sonnet 25

So I, made lame by Fortune's dearest spite . . .
Sonnet 37   "I am handicapped by a grievous spite of fortune," by being born a woman?

My name be buried where my body is,
And live no more to shame nor me, nor you . . .
Sonnet 72

Sonnet 81 is another melancholy complaint. If Mary Sidney is creating work for which William Shakespeare takes credit, could she have written this with him in mind?

Or means whether.

Or I shall live your Epitaph to make,
Or you survive when I in earth am rotten,
From hence your memory death cannot take,
Although in me each part will be forgotten.

Your name from hence immortal life shall have,
Though I (once gone) to all the world must die,
The earth can yield me but a common grave,

Note the pun on **lie.**

When you entombèd in men's eyes shall lie.

Your monument shall be my gentle verse,
Which eyes not yet created shall o'er-read;
And tongues to be, your being shall rehearse,
When all the breathers of this world are dead:

> *You still shall live (such virtue hath my Pen)*
> *Where breath most breathes, even in the mouths of men.*

[paraphrase of Sonnet 81]

Whether I live long enough to write your epitaph,
Or if you're still living when I'm long dead,
From here on out, death cannot take the memory of you
*   from this world,*
But me, all of my accomplishments will be forgotten.

From now on your name will have immortal life,
But me, once I'm dead, the entire world will forget me.
I will have an ordinary grave of no particular distinction,
But you shall be seen forever, even after you're dead, in men's eyes.

Because my ennobling compositions will be your memorial,
And people who aren't even born yet will read them over and over,
And people who aren't even born yet will speak of you.
When everyone now alive in the world is dead:

*   You shall live on forever, for my writing has that much power/*
*   operative influence,*
*   You shall live on where spoken words are most spoken,*
*   especially/that is to say in the mouths of men.*

The Publication Issues

Another of the mysterious elements about these sonnets is that there is no dedication from the author. Rather, the dedication is from the publisher, "to Mr. W. H." as "the only begetter of these ensuing sonnets."

Experts believe the poet did not authorize the printing because typically an author would check the finished pages as they came off the press and make corrections. When multiple copies of a finished book are compared, one can see the corrections, but in the book of Shakespearean sonnets, the mistakes went uncorrected.

The book was a flop. Katherine Duncan-Jones compares the success of the Shakespearean narrative poems printed in 1593 and 1594, *Venus and Adonis* and *The Rape of Lucrece,* with the book of sonnets: "Whereas the early narrative poems were received with immediate enthusiasm, prompting dozens of early allusions, citations, and imitations, the 1609 Q seems to have been greeted largely in silence—a silence the more surprising given Shakespeare's literary celebrity in 1609, in contrast to his relative obscurity in 1593–94."[2]

Q is a quarto, a small paperback edition.

2   Katherine Duncan-Jones, ed., *The Arden Shakespeare, Shakespeare's Sonnets* (Walton-on-Thames: Thomas Nelson and Sons Ltd., 1997), 69.

In a book of essays, James Schiffer concurs that "these poems were virtually ignored for their first 170 years of existence."[3]

John Dover Wilson noticed this: "That Thorpe engaged two book-sellers to unload his treasure trove on to the public suggests that he anticipated a brisk sale. Yet no second edition was called for."[4]

Wilson wonders about the failure of the book. "The usual explanation given is that by 1609 the poetry-reading public had grown tired of sonnets: the sonnet craze, dating from the appearance in 1591 of Sidney's *Astrophel and Stella,* being supposedly exhausted eighteen years later. It was declining, no doubt, but Drayton's *Idea's Mirror* had been reprinted six times since its appearance in 1590 and was reprinted three times after 1609."[5]

Once again we have conflicting information—traditional Shakespearean scholarship assures us that the "sonnet craze" had passed and no one wanted to read sonnets anymore, an excuse created to explain the failure of Shakespeare's book. But even Wilson has to question this, since records show that the sonnets of other authors continued to be popular and reprinted for many years.

Why was this book of poems so demonstrably unsuccessful? Why was the book not circulated? Scholars generally agree that apparently someone other than the poet sent the sonnets to press under Shakespeare's name. When William Shakespeare saw the homosexual implications of the poems with his name on them, did he demand their suppression?

Schiffer says, "Various explanations have been offered as to why the 1609 Quarto did not achieve more initial success. The most dramatic theory, offered by John Dover Wilson and others, is that the 'unauthorized' volume was suppressed by Shakespeare, with the help of a powerful friend (in Dover Wilson's theory, that friend is William Herbert, the Earl of Pembroke), presumably because of the embarrassing true-life story the Sonnets presumably reveal."[6]

Responding to the theory that someone beseeched William Herbert, Mary's oldest son, to suppress the sale of the sonnets, the *Reader's*

---

3   James Schiffer, "Introduction," in *Shakespeare's Sonnets, Critical Essays,* ed. James Schiffer (New York: Garland Publishing, Inc., 1999), 16.

4   J. Dover Wilson, *The Sonnets* (Cambridge: Cambridge University Press, 1969), xli.

5   J. Dover Wilson, *An Introduction to Shakespeare's Sonnets for Historians and Others* (New York: Cambridge University Press, 1964), 30.

6   Oscar James Campbell, ed., *The Reader's Encyclopedia of Shakespeare* (New York: MJF Books, 1966), 872. The book referred to is *St. Augustine of the Citie of God,* 1610.

Encyclopedia of Shakespeare notes that the publisher, Thomas Thorpe, did something unusual: "In this connection, it is interesting to note that in the next year Thorpe published a volume which he dedicated, in extremely obsequious terms, to William Herbert, Earl of Pembroke and one of the candidates for the title of Mr. W. H."[7]

Is Mary's son, William Herbert, the "Mr. W. H." whom the publisher, Thorpe, acknowledged as "the only begetter" of these poems? We do know that it was during this time that Mary and her son William were estranged. Was it because of her affair with the doctor? Was it due to William's affair with his cousin Mary Wroth? Had William Herbert discovered by this time that his mother was writing plays for the public theater? Did he take this collection of sonnets to press and have them published under William Shakespeare's name? Did Mary Sidney's secretary, John Davies of Hereford, take them to press under a pseudonym?

A Puzzling Epigram

Shortly after the publication of the sonnets, an English poet named John Davies of Hereford wrote a short and cryptic epigram titled:

"To our English Terence, Mr. Will. Shake-speare."

Terence was an impoverished writer, a freed slave, in ancient Rome who made a living by publishing the works of noblemen under his own name. "It is commonly said that Scipio [a Roman aristocrat] and Laelius [tribune, legate, governor] assisted the author in his plays; and indeed, Terence himself increased that suspicion by the little pains he took to refute it." To remove the aspersion of plagiarism, Terence took a boat to Greece and was never heard from again. John Davies seems to allude in "our English Terence" that Shakespeare is a front for an aristocrat.

An engaging connection between Mary Sidney and this allusion is that its author, John Davies of Hereford, was Mary's secretary.[8] A secretary, as explained by Alan Stewart and Heather Wolfe, "as the etymology of his name suggests, was often privy to his master's most intimate

---

7   Alfred Bates, *The Drama, Its History, Literature and Influence on Civilization*, vol. 2 (London: Historical Publishing Company, 1906), 205–207. The Elizabethans knew Terence's reputation, as evidenced by the writings of Robert Ascham and John Florio. Terence was about 25 or 30 years old when he disappeared.

8   Gary Waller, *Sidney Family Romance* (Detroit: Wayne State University Press, 1993), 9.

secrets. The secretary was therefore a man in which infinite trust had to be placed and who had the power to use or abuse that trust."[9]

Did John Davies quietly suspect—or know—that Mary was writing the plays for which William Shakespeare was getting credit, as Terence received credit for the plays of the noblemen?

Below is the first half of Davies' epigram, which has been interpreted in a wide variety of ways by a diverse group of scholars, which indicates that no one really knows what it means. "In fact, biographers find Davies' poem almost incomprehensible."[10]

> **To our English Terence Mr. Will: Shake-speare.**
> SOME say, good *Will* (which I, in sport, do sing)
>   Had'st thou not played some Kingly parts in sport,
> Thou hadst been a companion for a *King*;
>   And, been a King among the meaner sort.[11]

Since there are so many speculations about this poem, here is another one: "If you had not played some Kingly parts on stage (which means you are in the lower caste of Jacobean society), you would have been a great companion for King James, who is also gay, as your sonnets show you to be. And you then would have been a King among your own "meaner" or lower class peers."

---

9   Alan Stewart and Heather Wolfe, *Letterwriting in Renaissance England* (Washington D.C.: Folger Shakespeare Library, 2005), 55.

10   Diana Price, *Shakespeare's Unorthodox Biography: New Evidence of an Authorship Problem* (Westport: Greenwood Press, 2001), 64.

11   Davies' epigram continues:

> Some others rail; but rail as they think fit,
> Thou hast no railing, but, a reigning Wit:
> And honesty thou sow'st, which they do reap;
> So, to increase their Stock which they do keep.

In Davies' book, the Terence/Shakespeare epigram is preceded by standard sorts of epigrams to Samuel Daniel, Ben Jonson, Inigo Jones, and Isaac Simonds.

The Terence poem is followed by two other mysterious epigrams:

> **To his most constant, though most unknown friend: No-body.**
> You shall be served; but not with numbers now;
> You shall be served with nought; that's good for you.

> **To my near-dear well-known friend; Some-body**
> You look that as myself I you should use;
> I will, or else myself I should abuse;
> And yet with rhymes I but myself undo,
> Yet am I some-body with much ado.

A Sonnet Collection?

Mary was surrounded by writers in her family—her parents wrote eloquently in several languages, her brother Philip is one of the most famous poets of the time, her brother Robert wrote the lengthiest manuscript collection of lyric poetry in English history, her son William published a book of sonnets, her daughter is believed to have been a writer, her niece was a prolific writer. Might Mary have encouraged her lover, Matthew Lister, to write sonnets? Did the published book of sonnets that went to press against her will inadvertently include poems from others in her close circle?

Many scholars believe that not all of the sonnets published in the collection are by the same author, including the lengthy poem that was printed at the end of the book, "A Lover's Complaint." Brian Vickers completed a lengthy and comprehensive study on this poem and argues that it was actually written by John Davies of Hereford.[12] Such a remarkable coincidence? Clinton Heylin, in *So Long as Men Can Breathe: The Untold Story of Shakespeare's Sonnets,* not only believes that Davies wrote "A Lover's Complaint," but details the reasonable likelihood that Davies is also the person who took the sonnets to press, slipping his own poem into the collection, and also procured the Shakespearean plays for the printers over the years.[13]

And what does Davies mean in this epigram that he wrote about Mary Sidney?

> *And didst thou thirst for Fame (as all Men do)*
> *Thou wouldst, by all means, let it come to light.*

Is Davies, as her secretary, her keeper of secrets? He married three times, and it is noted that each time the woman was surprisingly above his station, surprising after his "long years of struggles and straits."[14] Was this somehow an advantage due to his work for Mary Sidney? Davies' will gives away jewels, plate, brass implements, chains and bracelets of gold; one house in Fleet Street, London, and all his books to his son; and to his living wife he gives the lease to his house and garden on St. Martin's Lane, London.[15] Considering both Davies and

12 Brian Vickers, Shakespeare, *A Lover's Complaint, and John Davies of Hereford* (Cambridge: Cambridge University Press, 2007).

13 Clinton Heylin, *So Long as Men Can Breathe: The Untold Story of Shakespeare's Sonnets* (New York: Da Capo Press, 2009), 188–266.

14 A.B. Grosart, ed., *The Complete works of John Davies, with introduction and notes,* two volumes (Blackburn, Lancashire: Chertsey Worthies Library, 1878), vol. 1, 17.

15 Ibid., 17–18.

Shakespeare rose above their stations to achieve success, Davies' will is an interesting comparison to Shakespeare's will in which there was no mention of books and an interlinear delegation of only a bed to his wife, no mention of the house they lived in nor the accouterments. But *surely* there is a reason for that.

If Mary Sidney is the author of most of the sonnets, there are still unanswered questions, but she is the only person of this entire era who even begins to have personal, documented evidence that can help unravel the story line shown in the Shakespearean sonnets.

Part Four

The Sources

My library was dukedom large enough.
Prospero in *The Tempest*, 1.2.109

Documented Data

- More than 200 books have been acknowledged by experts as sources for the Shakespearean plays. Often several editions of the same book were used.

- About two dozen of the French, Italian, and Latin sources had not been translated into English during Shakespeare's lifetime.

- No book owned or used by William Shakespeare has ever been found.

- The Sidney and Herbert libraries contained more than 5,000 books and manuscripts in a number of languages.

9 Sources of and Connections to the Plays

FOR MORE THAN A HUNDRED YEARS scholars and critics have acknowledged not only contemporary references to current events incorporated into the Shakespearean plays, but entire stories, specific plot lines, literary motifs, characterizations, philosophies, and verbatim lines taken from existing books. The lengthy list of books that scholars know the author read or consulted is shown in the Prologue on pages 24–28.

But suppose we question the general assumption, and look for the evidence.
Gerald Eades Bentley
1971

But not one book has ever been found that was owned by William Shakespeare or anyone in his family, and there were no public libraries at the time.[1] Nor have documented connections been made between Shakespeare and any of the source books or authors.

Mary Sidney, on the other hand, is intimately associated with many of the sources for the plays: Either she wrote the source material herself, her brother wrote it, someone in her literary circle wrote it, it was dedicated to her or to her brother, the book includes information about or connected with her family, or the book is known to have been owned by her family. There are also a number of remarkable "coincidences" in her life that connect her to the works; although coincidences cannot prove authorship, they are certainly lacking in the biography of William Shakespeare.

Source research to date is presented on the following pages with Sidney and Shakespeare connections paralleled.[2]

---

1   There were no public libraries in England until September, 1852, when one was opened in Manchester. The first public library in America had opened a few years earlier, 1848, in Boston.

2   Unless otherwise noted, the list of sources are from David Bevington, ed., *The Complete Works of Shakespeare*, 6th ed. (New York: Pearson Longman, 2009), A23–A60; *The Riverside Shakespeare, The Complete Works*, 2nd ed. (Boston, New York: Houghton Mifflin Company, 1997), 78–87; Stuart Gillespie, *Shakespeare's Books: A Dictionary of Shakespeare Sources* (London: Bloomsbury Arden Shakespeare, 2016); and various Arden editions of the plays.

Source	Mary Sidney	Shakespeare
About two dozen of the reference books used in the plays were available only in French, Italian, or Latin, with no English translations during Shakespeare's lifetime. See page 28 for a list.	Mary translated works from French and Italian, is known to have been proficient in Latin, and owned books in those as well as other languages, such as Spanish, Greek, and Hebrew.	There is no evidence that Shakespeare was fluent in any foreign language.
Raphael Holinshed's book, *The Chronicles of England, Scotland, and Ireland,* was used in twelve plays.[3] Specifically, the second edition was used, printed in 1587.	The 1587 edition includes a memorial account of Mary's brother Philip, as well as an account of the "excellent" death of Mary's mother, Mary Dudley Sidney. Book 2 is dedicated to her uncle Robert Dudley and Book 3 is dedicated to her father, Henry Sidney.	No recorded connection.
The Countess of Pembroke's Arcadia, which Bevington calls the "greatest of all Elizabethan prose romances," was used as a source for five plays, including the story of an "unkind king" and a father being blinded by his bastard son.[4] Regarding the several debts to *Arcadia* in *King Lear,* Bevington also says, "Albany's speeches about anarchy . . . recall one of [Philip] Sidney's deepest concerns."[5]	*Arcadia* was written by Mary's brother Philip, for Mary, at Mary's request. It was written mostly in Mary's home and Mary published it. In 1685, John Aubrey says about *Arcadia,* "but many or most of the verses in the *Arcadia* were made by her Honor [Mary], and they seem to have been writt by a woman."[6]	No recorded connection.

3   *King John; Richard 2; Richard 3; Henry 4 parts 1 and 2; Henry 5; Henry 6 parts 1, 2, and 3; Henry 8; Macbeth; Cymbeline.*

4   *King Lear; Two Gentlemen of Verona; Midsummer Night's Dream; Twelfth Night; Pericles.*

5   Bevington, *Complete Works of Shakespeare,* A-50.

6   John Aubrey, *Aubrey's Natural History of Wiltshire* (originally written between 1656 and 1691) (Wiltshire: David & Charles Reprints, 1969), 89.

Source	Mary Sidney	Shakespeare
The works of Samuel Daniel, including *The First Four Books of the Civil Wars* (1595), were used as sources for five plays.[7]	Samuel Daniel was Mary's protégé. As mentioned previously, Daniel credits Mary with having been his best teacher of writing.[8] This particular work about the Civil Wars was begun at Wilton. The expanded edition of 1609 is dedicated to Mary. A set was in the Sidney library.	No recorded connection.
Thomas Kyd's *Cornelia*, translated from the French Senecan tragedy *Cornélie*, by Garnier, is a source for *Julius Caesar*.	"[Mary Sidney] diverted Thomas Kyd from his true vocation as a writer for the popular stage by persuading him, about 1594, to translate another play of Garnier's, *Cornélie*."[9]	No recorded connection.
The Reader's Encyclopedia states, "Romeo's last speech in the tomb contains echoes of *Astrophel and Stella* and Daniel's *Complaint of Rosamond*."[10]	*Astrophel and Stella* was written by Mary's brother, Philip Sidney. As mentioned above, Daniel was a protégé of Mary's. In his *Complaint of Rosamond* he refers to Mary Sidney and Delia on the Avon.	No recorded connection.
The original Latin version of Ovid's *Metamorphoses* and the 1567 translation by Arthur Golding were used in four plays.[11]	Arthur Golding was personally known to Mary; he completed one of Philip's unfinished translations after Philip died. This particular 1567 translation was dedicated to Mary's uncle, Robert Dudley, the Earl of Leicester. Numerous volumes of various works of Ovid were in the Sidney Library.	If he went to grammar school (there are no records), he may have read Ovid.

7   *Romeo and Juliet; Antony and Cleopatra; Richard 2; Henry 4 parts 1 and 2.*

8   Gary F. Waller, *Mary Sidney, Countess of Pembroke: A Critical Study of Her Writings and Literary Milieu* (Salzburg: Universität Salzburg, 1979), 72.

9   John Buxton, *Sir Philip Sidney and the English Renaissance* (New York and London: St. Martin's Press, 1966), 200. Navarre was a small kingdom that straddled the Pyrenees mountains on the border between France and Spain. Its capital was Pamplona. Henri 3 of Navarre (later Henry 4 of France) was Marguerite de Navarre's grandson. His wife was also named Marguerite, but of Valois.

10 Oscar James Campbell, ed., *The Reader's Encyclopedia of Shakespeare* (New York: MJF Books, 1966), 813.

11 *Titus Andronicus; Midsummer Night's Dream; Merry Wives of Windsor; The Tempest.*

Source	Mary Sidney	Shakespeare
In *Twelfth Night*, 5.1.113–116, Orsino makes a reference to "the Greek romance *Ethiopica* by Heliodorus."[12]	An Italian edition of this book was in the Sidney Library.[13]	No recorded connection.
There are references in two plays to a book called *Tottel's Miscellany*, also called *Songs and Sonnets*, with epigrams by Surrey, Wyatt, and other anonymous contemporaries.[14]	A 1574 edition of *Songs and Sonnets* was in the Sidney library.[15] *"I had rather than forty shillings I had my book of Songs and Sonnets here."* Slender in *The Merry Wives of Windsor*, 1.1.182–183	No recorded connection.
In an article in the *Sidney Journal*, Katherine Duncan-Jones writes, "By the mid-1590s, then, it seems that Shakespeare was beginning to be importantly influenced by [Philip] Sidney's writings, both in terms of their verbal and metaphoric detail, and in terms of their literary ideals. It seems likely that [Shakespeare] had some access to Sidney's writings in manuscript, in advance of their print publication."[16]	In *Literary Patronage in the English Renaissance: The Pembroke Family*, Michael Brennan states, ". . . during the decade following Sidney's death [in 1586], the Countess's households at Wilton and Baynard's Castle, along with those of Robert Sidney, Fulke Greville [Philip's best friend] and the Countess of Rutland [Philip's daughter], remained the most likely locations where writers might gain access to Sidney's literary works before they became generally available in print."[17]	No recorded connection.

12 Keir Elam, ed., *Twelfth Night* (London: Arden Shakespeare, 2008), 330n114.
13 Warkentin, *The Library of the Sidneys*, 188, 71v25.
14 Stuart Gillespie, *Shakespeare's Books: A Dictionary of Shakespeare Sources* (London: Bloomsbury Arden Shakespeare, 2016), 391. References are in *The Merry Wives of Windsor* and in *Hamlet*.
15 Warkentin, *The Library of the Sidneys*, 154, 51v05.
16 Katherine Duncan-Jones, "Liquid Prisoners: Shakespeare's Re-writings of Sidney," *Sidney Journal* 15:2 (Fall 1997), 10.
17 Michael Brennan, *Literary Patronage in the English Renaissance: The Pembroke Family* (London, New York: Routledge, 1988), 77–78.

Source	Mary Sidney	Shakespeare
As a source for *Antony and Cleopatra*, "Most important for Shakespeare were *The Tragedy of Antony*, translated from Robert Garnier's *Marc Antoine* by Mary [Sidney] Herbert, Countess of Pembroke . . . and *The Tragedy of Cleopatra* [1594] by Samuel Daniel."[18] Bevington also states, regarding these sources, "Shakespeare certainly gained from such works as these a sense of tragic greatness in his protagonists."[19] "*Cleopatra* had been a closet drama, designed only for reading to the highly cultured ears of the Wilton art circle."[20] "Both [Mary] Pembroke and Shakespeare emphasize Antony's cross-dressing, a detail absent in Garnier."[21]	Mary wrote *The Tragedy of Antony*, also called *Antonius* or *Antonie*. "The influence of her translation may be seen in Shakespeare's *Antony and Cleopatra*, which echoes structural and thematic elements of *Antonius* as well as occasional phrasing. "Verbal parallels establish that Shakespeare knew Garnier in [Mary] Pembroke's translation. . . . the parallels are too numerous to be coincidental."[22] Samuel Daniel writes in the dedication that his play *Cleopatra* was written at Mary's request and under her tutelage, "'the work the which she did impose,' for she bade him 'To sing of State, and tragic notes to frame.'"[23] It was "designed as a companion piece to *Antony* and dedicated to the Countess of Pembroke."[24]	No recorded connection.
Mary Renault shows that Shakespeare knew the work of Xenophon, a Greek historian, particularly his *Anabasis*, in *Henry 5*.[25]	Mary's library included a volume of the various works of Xenophon.[26] Robert Sidney's library included numerous volumes; a copy exists that is signed by Philip Sidney.[27]	No recorded connection.

18   Bevington, *Complete Works*, A-51.

19   Ibid., A-51.

20   Alvin Kernan, *Shakespeare, the King's Playwright* (New Haven: Yale University Press, 1995), 174.

21   Margaret Hannay, et al., eds., *The Collected Works of Mary Sidney Herbert, Countess of Pembroke*, vol. 1 (Oxford: Clarendon Press, 1998), 39.

22   Ibid., 40.

23   Geoffrey Bullough, *Narrative and Dramatic Sources of Shakespeare*, vol. 5 (London: Routledge and Kegan Paul; New York: Columbia University Press, 1960), 229.

24   John Wilders, ed., *The Arden Shakespeare, Antony and Cleopatra* (New York: Routledge, 1995), 63.

25   Mary Renault, "Shakespeare and Xenophon" in the *Times Literary Supplement*, 12 July: 749.

26   *Catalogue of a Selected Portion of the Renowned Library at Wilton House, Salisbury*, collected in the sixteenth and seventeenth centuries, sold at auction by Sotheby, Wilkinson & Hodge (London, 1914), 70.

27   Warkentin, *The Library of the Sidneys of Penshurst*, 367.

Source	Mary Sidney	Shakespeare
Scholars recognize not only the number of references in the plays to Seneca, an early Roman tragedian, but also the elements throughout the plays that are inspired by his style.	"In 1590 Mary Sidney, Countess of Pembroke, initiated the courtly Senecan movement which led several members of her circle to write Roman tragedies within the next ten or fifteen years."[28] "The [Senecan] genre was also particularly suited for women who desired to write plays but would not be permitted to write for the public arena."[29] Several volumes of Seneca were in the Sidney library.	No recorded connection.
"Shakespeare . . . seems to be indebted to [Mary's translation of] *Discourse* for some of the Senecan elements in *Measure for Measure*."[30]	As noted above, Mary initiated the Senecan literary movement, and she is the author of this source, *A Discourse of Life and Death*.	No recorded connection.
Both the 1570 and the 1583 editions of John Foxe's *Acts and Monuments of Martyrs* were sources for five of the history plays.[31]	In 1573, "The Sidneys purchased a copy of 'two books of Martirs' (the two volumes familiarly known as Foxe's *Book of Martyrs*) when Mary Sidney was a child. The book records tales of heroic death, including that of her aunt Lady Jane Grey."[32]	No recorded connection.
Edmund Spenser's book *The Faerie Queene* was a source for three of the plays.[33]	Spenser was a protégé of Philip's and a member of the Wilton Circle. Spenser praised Mary in a dedicatory sonnet in *The Faerie Queene* and again in *Colin Clout's Come Home Again*. He dedicated *The Ruins of Time* to her and dedicated *Shepherd's Calendar* to Philip.[34]	No recorded connection.

28   Bullough, *Narrative and Dramatic Sources*, 232.
29   Hannay, *The Collected Works of Mary Sidney Herbert*, 41.
30   Ibid., 34.
31   *Henry 6 parts 1, 2, and 3; King John; Henry 8.*
32   Hannay, *The Collected Works of Mary Sidney Herbert*, 211.
33   *The Tempest; Midsummer Night's Dream; Henry 6 plays.*
34   Hannay, *The Collected Works of Mary Sidney Herbert*, 122.

Source	Mary Sidney	Shakespeare
A book by Matteo Bandello called *Novelle* (1554) was the source for three plays.[35] "Shakespeare seems to have relied more on the Italian version by Matteo Bandello and its French translation by Belleforest, *Histoires Tragiques*."[36]	This book belonged to Mary's brother Philip. "It is a copy of the French version of Bandello's romances, *Histoires Tragiques*."[37] Philip's copy of this book still survives, complete with its inscription. Also, a writer named Geoffrey Fenton dedicated a collection of translations of *Novelle* to Mary's mother.	No recorded connection.
John Stow's books, *Holinshed's Chronicles of England* (1580) and particularly *The Annals of England* (1592 edition) were used in three of the English history plays.[38]	The 1592 edition of *The Annals of England* includes an account of a spectacular entertainment for the Queen that Mary's brother Philip wrote, designed, and participated in. This book also includes an account of the battle in which Philip died; in fact, "The description in Stow's *Annals* tells of [Philip] Sidney gathering his men before the attack and addressing them in terms similar to King Henry's before the walls of Harfleur."[39] "John Stow tells of how Philip, a mile away from their destination, made a speech to the soldiers—which, to the modern ear, might eerily prefigure Shakespeare's Henry 5 before Agincourt.... This oration 'did so link the minds of the people that they desired rather to die in that service than to live in the contrary.'"[40]	No recorded connection.

35 *Much Ado About Nothing; Twelfth Night; Hamlet.*
36 Bevington, *Complete Works*, 220.
37 Katherine Duncan-Jones, *Sir Philip Sidney: Courtier Poet* (New Haven: Yale University Press, 1991), 29–30.
38 *Henry 4 parts 1 and 2; Richard 3.*
39 James M. Osborn, *Young Philip Sidney, 1572–1577* (New Haven and London: Yale University Press, 1972), 515.
40 Alan Stewart, *Philip Sidney: A Double Life* (New York: St. Martin's Press, 2000), 303.

Source	Mary Sidney	Shakespeare
Ariosto's *Orlando Furioso*, originally written in Italian in 1516, translated into English by Sir John Harington in 1591, was consulted for *Much Ado About Nothing*.	In Harington's translation of *Orlando Furioso*, he praises Mary in an allegory.[41] Harington was a good friend of both Mary and her brother Robert, was several times at Wilton, and praised Mary's *Psalms* as "precious leaves [that] shall outlast Wilton walls."[42]	No recorded connection.
Sir Thomas North's 1579 English translation of *Plutarch's Lives of the Noble Grecians and Romans* was the most-often used source for Shakespeare plays after 1600.	In discussing Mary's translation of *The Tragedy of Antonie*, Hannay says, "In her 'Argument,' she mentions only Plutarch, which she used primarily in Sir Thomas North's 1579 English translation of *Plutarch's Lives of the Noble Grecians and Romans*, the work that was also the basis for Shakespeare's Roman History plays."[43]	No recorded connection.
Thomas Moffett's book, *Of the Silkworms and their Flies*, was not in print until 1599, about five years after it was used as a source in *A Midsummer Night's Dream*. The playwright read the unpublished manuscript.[44]	This book was dedicated to Mary Sidney and refers to Mary (as "Mira") in the book. She had access to the unpublished manuscript because the author, Dr. Moffett, was her estate physician and lived at Wilton until his death.	No recorded connection.
A Journal of the Siege of Rouen, written by Sir Thomas Coningsby, was used as a source for *1 Henry 6*, according to *The Riverside Shakespeare*. This manuscript was not printed until 1847.	Sir Thomas Coningsby was a good friend of Mary's brother Philip. Coningsby accompanied Philip on his European tour. Later he married Mary's cousin Philippa..	No recorded connection.

41 Hannay, *The Collected Works of Mary Sidney Herbert*, 33n48.

42 H. R. Woudhuysen, *Sir Philip Sidney and the Circulation of Manuscripts, 1558–1640* (Oxford: Oxford University Press, 1996), 344.

43 Hannay, *The Collected Works of Mary Sidney Herbert*, 140.

44 Kenneth Muir, *The Sources of Shakespeare's Plays* (London: Routledge Library Editions, 1977), 73.

Source	Mary Sidney	Shakespeare
"It was natural that England's greatest living playwright, William Shakespeare, in penning his dramas, should make use of the *Geneva Bible*, rather than the official translations urged on the English people by the church authorities." [45]	Mary used the *Geneva Bible* as one of her main sources while versifying the *Psalms*.	No recorded connection.
Four Paradoxes, or Politique Discourses by Thomas and Dudley Digges was used as a source for *Coriolanus*.	This book honors Mary's brother Philip. Thomas Digges was with Philip in Zutphen during the battle in which Philip was fatally wounded. [46]	No recorded connection.
In 1599, Lewis Lewkenor translated Gasparo Contarini's Italian book into *The Commonwealth and Government of Venice*. "The first book in English to deal exclusively with Venice, it may have been read in manuscript by Shakespeare and used for the legal background of Shakespeare's *Merchant of Venice*. The book was definitely used by the poet for *Othello*, not only for information about Venice, but for Othello's defense against the charge of witchcraft." [47] *The Merchant of Venice* was registered as a play in July, 1598, a year before the publication of Lewkenor's translation.	Philip Sidney owned a copy of Contarini's original, probably purchased in Venice in 1574. [48] Lewkenor wrote two books that included Philip Sidney's actions during the war in Flanders in 1586. *A Discourse of the Usage of the English Fugitives, by the Spaniards* includes Philip's involvement in taking Axel, and it details the cruel and tyrannous butchering of the men whom Philip had sent into the town of Gravelines. [49] When Lewkenor returned to England from the European continent in 1590, he was one of the first to appeal to Mary's younger brother Robert Sidney for patronage. [50]	Sir Lewkenor had a "remote kinship with the Combe family of Stratford with whom Shakespeare was friendly." [51]

45   Alister E. McGrath, *In the Beginning: The Story of the King James Bible and How It Changed a Nation, a Language, and a Culture* (New York: Doubleday, 2001), 129.

46   Michael G. Brennan and Noel J. Kinnamon, *A Sidney Chronology, 1554–1654* (Basingstoke and New York: Palgrave Macmillan, 2003), 181.

47   Campbell, *Reader's Encyclopedia of Shakespeare*, 598.

48   Brennan and Kinnamon, *A Sidney Chronology*, 38.

49   Stewart, *Philip Sidney: A Double Life*, 305.

50   Millicent V. Hay, *The Life of Robert Sidney, Earl of Leicester (1563–1626)* (Washington: The Folger Shakespeare Library, 1984), 127.

51   Campbell, *Reader's Encyclopedia of Shakespeare*, 460.

Source	Mary Sidney	Shakespeare
Scholars attribute Richard Tarlton's *News Out of Purgatory* as a source for *The Merry Wives of Windsor*. *The Riverside Shakespeare* also attributes the unpublished manuscript of *The Famous Victories of Henry 5*, generally ascribed to Tarlton, as a source for *Henry 5*.[52] *The Reader's Encyclopedia of Shakespeare* states that "Hamlet's advice to the players may have been prompted by Tarlton's practice."[53] Also, "Scholars have conjectured that Tarlton was the model for Yorick whose skull Hamlet recovers from the graveyard."[54]	Richard Tarlton, the famous comic genius with the Queen's Men, was a servant of Mary's uncle Robert Dudley, the Earl of Leicester. Tarlton was an actor and playwright, and a member of Leicester's Men, the acting troupe sponsored by Dudley. For years Tarlton worked and traveled with Mary's uncle. Mary grew up with these acting companies providing entertainment in their great houses. Mary's brother Philip was godfather to Tarlton's son in 1582.[55]	No recorded connection. Richard Tarlton died in 1588, several years before William Shakespeare is believed to have gone to London.
Julius Caesar and *The Tempest* use John Florio's translation of Montaigne's *Essays*. "Shakespeare could have read Montaigne in the French original or, if he had access to a manuscript, in John Florio's English translation published in 1603."[56] Gary Taylor argues that Shakespeare read Florio's translation of Montaigne two to three years before it was published.[57]	Mary could have read the French version, of course, but she also had access to the unpublished manuscript of this translation of Montaigne because Florio was closely connected with the Wilton Circle; the published book is in the Sidney library.[58] His second volume of *Essays* is dedicated to Mary's niece, Philip's daughter Elizabeth.	No recorded connection.

52 *Riverside Shakespeare*, 2nd edition, 82 and 83.

53 Campbell, *Reader's Encyclopedia of Shakespeare*, 851.

54 Duncan-Jones, *Sir Philip Sidney: Courtier Poet*, 148.

55 Hannay, *Philip's Phoenix*, 124.

56 Bevington, *Complete Works of Shakespeare*, A-45.

57 Gary Taylor, *Reinventing Shakespeare: A Cultural History, from the Restoration to the Present* (New York: Grove Press, 1989), 252.

58 Germain Warkentin, Joseph L. Black, and William R. Bowen, *The Library of the Sidneys of Penshurst Place, circa 1665* (Toronto: University of Toronto Press, 2013), 254.

Source	Mary Sidney	Shakespeare
The most important source for *The Tempest* was a letter written by William Strachey, the secretary to the Virginia Company, describing the shipwreck in the Bermudas. The letter was not made public until 1625 (nine years after Shakespeare died) to prevent unpleasant publicity about the Virginia Company's explorations.	Mary, her brother Robert, and both sons were founders and stockholders of the Virginia Company, to which the Strachey letter was written.[59] Her son, William Herbert, was its second-largest contributor. Her brother Robert Sidney had an active part in the management of the organization. Intriguingly, Strachey's letter was specifically addressed to an unidentified "Excellent Lady." Of the 1001 men who signed the charters, there were also eight women. Mary had a lifelong interest in New World exploration—the Sidneys helped finance Sir Martin Frobisher's voyages in the 1570s and Edward Fenton's voyage in the 1580s as well.[60]	Shakespeare had a friend who had a stepson who was involved with New World exploration who "could have been the playwright's source for the 1610 letter by William Strachey," although this stepson was not connected with the Virginia Company, nor did he have a speaking relationship with his stepfather. During the time of the Strachey letter, the stepson had been harassing his stepfather "for years with a long, acrimonious lawsuit."[61]
Why look you pale? Sea-sick, I think, coming from Muscovy. Rosaline in *Love's Labor's Lost*, 5.2.393–394	Her father, as well as Adrian Gilbert, Mary's assistant in her alchemy lab, were both involved with the Muscovy Company.	
Also regarding *The Tempest*, scholars agree that the author kept up with the New World travel accounts of Sir Walter Raleigh.	Sir Walter Raleigh was a close friend of Mary's. At one point she successfully appealed to the King to prevent Raleigh from being executed.[62]	No recorded connection.

59   www.let.rug.nl/usa/documents/1600-1650/the-third-virginia-charter-1612.php
60   Hannay, *Philip's Phoenix*, 42.
61   Charles Boyce, ed., *Shakespeare A to Z* (New York: Roundtable Press, 1990), 156 and 568.
62   Ibid., 123.

Source	Mary Sidney	Shakespeare
For *Richard 2*, the author used a French eyewitness account available only in manuscript, Jean Créton's *Histoire du Roy d'Angleterre Richard*. John Dee is known to have had a copy.[63]	John Dee was a tutor to the Dudley children in their home.[64] In the next generation, Mary's brother Philip was considered one of Dee's best pupils.	No recorded connection.
Several of George Whetstone's literary works were used in *Much Ado About Nothing* and as a chief source in *Measure for Measure*.	Whetstone was a member of the Wilton Circle. He published a contemporary account of the battle in which Philip died, based on information from his own brother Bernard who had fought at Zutphen with Philip. And "it has been suggested that the main characters of [Whetstone's] work may reflect something of Philip and Mary Sidney themselves."[65]	No recorded connection.
One of the probable sources for *Two Gentlemen of Verona* is a children's play presented at Elizabeth's court in 1577, a play about two friends, Titus and Gisippus.[66]	Mary was living at court in 1577.	No recorded connection.
Two of the few songs that have definite sources (in *As You Like It* and *Twelfth Night*) are in music books by Thomas Morley, one of the greatest Elizabethan composers of madrigals and lute songs.[67]	Morley dedicated his manuscript score *Canzonets* to Mary, not requesting patronage for the dedication, but merely for the honor of her acceptance of his songs.[68]	For several years Shakespeare lived in the same area of London as Thomas Morley.[69]

63 Peter Ure, ed., *The Arden Shakespeare, King Richard 2* (Surrey: Thomas Nelson & Sons Ltd., 1998), xlv.
64 Margaret P. Hannay, Michael G. Brennan, and Mary Ellen Lamb, *The Ashgate Research Companion to The Sidneys, 1500–1700, Volume 1: Lives* (Surrey: Ashgate Publishing Limited, 2015), 31.
65 Waller, *Mary Sidney, Countess of Pembroke*, 57.
66 Bevington, *Complete Works of Shakespeare*, A-25.
67 Campbell, *Reader's Encyclopedia of Shakespear*, 558.
68 Hannay, *Philip's Phoenix*, 115–16.
69 Campbell, *Reader's Encyclopedia of Shakespeare*, 558.

Source	Mary Sidney	Shakespeare
The 19-day royal extravaganza in July, 1575, at Kenilworth Castle has long been thought by many scholars to have supplied several images for *A Midsummer Night's Dream*.[70]	Mary attended the 1575 extravaganza at Kenilworth, home of her uncle Robert Dudley, Earl of Leicester, along with her parents and her brother Philip.[71]	No recorded connection. "Surely he climbed up and looked over the wall."
E. K. Chambers identifies the source of several images in *A Midsummer Night's Dream* as a water fête presented by Edward Seymour, the Earl of Hertford, to the Queen in 1591 at his Elvetham estate.[72]	The Earl of Hertford had long been associated with Mary and her family. A few years after the water fête, which the Sidney family attended, the Earl, 62 years old, made an unsuccessful attempt to marry Anne Herbert, 16 years old.[73]	No recorded connection.
"The only instruments not used in the theatre were the organ and the virginals . . . . That Shakespeare knew this instrument [the virginals] is indicated by the jealous Leontes' 'Still virginalling upon his palm' as he observes Polixenes caressing his wife's hand."[74] In *The Winter's Tale*, 1.2.125–126.	Mary played the virginals, which is like a small harpsichord, as evidenced by the family household records that detail the maintenance of her virginals.[75]	No recorded connection. The virginals is most typically played by young women.
"The wording of Berowne's famous monologue in praise of love from *Love's Labor's Lost* mirrors a similar speech from Bruno's *The Expulsion of the Triumphant Beast*."[76]	Bruno dedicated *The Expulsion of the Triumphant Beast* to Mary's brother Philip.[77]	No recorded connection.

70 S. Schoenbaum, *William Shakespeare, A Compact Documentary Life* (Oxford: Oxford University Press, 1987), 115–16.

71 Hannay, *Philip's Phoenix*, 33–35.

72 E. K. Chambers, *William Shakespeare: A Study of Facts and Problems*, vol. 1 (Oxford: Clarendon Press, 1930), 358.

73 Brennan, *A Sidney Chronology*, 129.

74 Campbell, *Reader's Encyclopedia of Shakespeare*, 575.

75 Hannay, *Philip's Phoenix*, 27, referencing the L' Isle family papers.

76 Michael White, *The Pope and the Heretic* (London: Little, Brown and Company, 2002), 180.

77 Ibid., 92.

Source	Mary Sidney	Shakespeare
"Many scholars have argued that [William Cecil, Lord Burghley] is being satirized as Polonius in *Hamlet*. Evidence of this view is believed to be found in Burghley's 'Certain Precepts, or Directions' (1616) which he wrote for his son, Robert Cecil, and which Shakespeare may have seen in manuscript."[78]	Robert Cecil, Burghley's son, was a close friend of Mary's. They had grown up together because their mothers, Mildred Cooke and Mary Dudley Sidney, were best friends. There are extant letters from Mary to both Burghley and his son Robert. Another close friend of Robert Cecil was Mary's oldest son, William Herbert. Mary's brother Philip was almost engaged at age 14 to Burghley's daughter, Anne, but Anne ran off instead with Edward de Vere, the Earl of Oxford, "who made her and her family thoroughly miserable."[79] Years later Mary went through extensive marriage arrangements for her older son, William, with Burghley's granddaughter Bridget. Since the girl's father (Oxford) had abandoned her long ago, grandpa Burghley was the one making arrangements. That deal fell through, but Mary's younger son Philip, after Oxford died, secretly arranged to marry Burghley's other grand-daughter, Susan.	No recorded connection. The letter wasn't published until the year Shakespeare died, which was fifteen years after *Hamlet* was written. The idea that William Shakespeare would have seen the original letter from the Queen's Secretary of State can be considered not only silly but desperate.
The Arden edition of *Antony and Cleopatra* states that several lines in the play are a terse translation of the Latin in Juvenal's *Satire*, which is "not attributable to mere coincidence."[80]	Numerous editions of Juvenal's *Satires* were in the Sidney library, one with a signature of Robert Sidney's.[81]	No recorded connection.

78 Campbell, *Reader's Encyclopedia of Shakespeare*, 471.
79 Hannay, *Philip's Phoenix*, 22.
80 M. R. Ridley, ed., *The Arden Shakespeare, Antony and Cleopatra* (London: Routledge, 1993 reprint), 43n5–8.
81 Warkentin, *The Library of the Sidneys of Penshurst*, 218.

Source	Mary Sidney	Shakespeare
Regarding the sonnets, Claes Schaar says, "The thesis that Shakespeare as a writer of sonnets was indebted to Daniel's *Delia* has become widely accepted in English literary history."[82]	Samuel Daniel dedicated his sonnet sequence *Delia* to Mary in 1592. The woman named "Delia" in the poems refers to Mary herself. It was at Wilton, where Daniel lived for years, that he learned to compose poetry under Mary's tutelage.[83]	No recorded connection.
William Camden's *Remains of a Greater Work Concerning Britain* is a minor source for *King Lear* and *Coriolanus*.[84]	This book was in the Sidney library.[85]	No recorded connection.
There is only one place in the world where the words to Desdemona's "Willow Song" in *Othello* are written—a music journal compiled "over quite a brief period of time and reflecting a single interest: an interest in the music used in and associated with the popular theatre."[86]	This manuscript includes handwritten music of two of Mary Sidney's psalms, several of Philip Sidney's sonnets, a song from Philip's *Old Arcadia* (available only in manuscript and only in the Sidney circle), which includes a line of Falstaff's, "Have I caught my heavenly jewel?" in *The Merry Wives of Windsor*. It is not known who originally compiled the journal, but most of the musicians included have a direct connection to Mary Sidney.	No recorded connection.
The translation of Richard Robinson's *Gesta Romanorum* was a source for *The Merchant of Venice* and probably for *Pericles* and *The Comedy of Errors.*	Mary's father, Henry Sidney, and her brother Philip were generous patrons of Richard Robinson. Robinson was also the scribe of one of the *Arcadia* manuscripts.[87]	No recorded connection.

82   Claes Schaar, *An Elizabethan Sonnet Problem* (Lund: Håkan Ohlssons Boktryckeri, 1960), 7.

83   Hannay, *Philip's Phoenix*, 72.

84   Gillespie, *Shakespeare's Book: A Dictionary of Shakespeare Sources*, 62.

85   Warkentin, *The Library of the Sidneys at Penshurst*, 304.

86   Mary Joiner, "British Museum Add Ms. 15117: A Commentary, Index and Bibliography," *RMA Research Chronicle*, 1969, 7, 51–109 (51).

87   Brennan and Kinnamon, *A Sidney Chronology, 1554–1654*, 177–78.

Source	Mary Sidney	Shakespeare
Richard Grafton's 1569 edition of *A Chronicle at Large* is a source for the *Henry 6* plays and *King John*.	Mary's parents owned the 1548 edition of this work, and then bought another one in 1573/74, which would be the 1569 edition, for which they paid 21 shillings. Both Mary's father and mother wrote Latin and English verses in the margins of the 1548 edition.[88]	No recorded connection.
For *Macbeth*, "It is much more likely that Shakespeare had read Buchanan's *History of Scotland* in its original Latin."[89]	George Buchanan's *History of Scotland* in the original Latin was in the Sidney library.[90] Philip Sidney praises this book in his *Defense of Poesie*.	No recorded connection.
Regarding the fictional Captain Fluellen in *Henry 5*, "Shakespeare may have found his inspiration for Fluellen in a member of Elizabeth's court," one of Essex's companions named Roger Williams.[91]	This same Roger Williams was a very close friend of Mary's brother Philip, who spent most of his adult years at Mary's home.	No recorded connection.
"It has been suggested that David Gam is the original of Shakespeare's Fluellen. This is not at all an improbable conjecture, as Fluellen is plainly a corruption of Llewelyn, and David was generally called David Llewelyn, or ab Llewelyn."[92] David, known as Davy Gam, is listed as dying on the battlefield at the end of *Henry 5*.	Davy Gam was the great-great-great grandfather of Mary Sidney's husband. Gam's daughter became the mother of William Herbert, 1st Earl of Pembroke in the Herbert house. "Gam" is a nickname meaning "squinty-eyed."	No recorded connection.

88 Brennan and Kinnamon, *A Sidney Chronology*, xxii, 39.
89 Kenneth Muir, ed., *Arden Shakespeare Second Series, Macbeth* (London: Arden Shakespeare, 1984), xl.
90 Warkentin, *The Library of the Sidneys of Penshurst Place*, 95.
91 J. Madison Davis and A. Daniel Frankforter, *The Shakespeare Name Dictionary* (New York, London: Garland Publishing, Inc., 1995), 170.
92 Ibid.

Source	Mary Sidney	Shakespeare
The playwright wrote ten English history plays. "'Shakespeare worked like a historical scholar, and made his histories by collating authorities, cross-checking, and (in a word) Research.' There is no way of escaping from this conclusion. . . . Wilson found it necessary to suppose the existence of an intermediary, a dramatist 'soaked in the history of England,' who wrote Shakespeare's original, and so may be said to have done his research for him. This view is partly to be attributed to the difficulty we have in believing that Shakespeare worked on his material like a scholar-chronicler."[93] (See Chapter 11 for details.)	The Dudley genealogy of Mary's mother includes the families of Neville, Beauchamp, Percy, Mortimer, and Hastings; the Herbert genealogy goes back to a bastard son of King Henry 1.[94] The Kings Edward 4, Henry 7, Henry 8, the Earls of Pembroke, Warwick, Northumberland, Westmorland, Salisbury, Kent, and others are in Mary's direct lineage. Every one of these families appears in the history plays, as well as Mary's family homesteads and homelands such as Baynard's Castle, Ludlow, Shrewsbury, Kenilworth, Kent, Ampthill, and Wales, including Pembrokeshire and Milford Haven.[95]	No recorded connection.
Lord Berners' translation of Jean Froissart's *The Chronicles of England* was used as a source for *Richard 2*.	The Sidney family paid 27 shillings for a copy of this book in 1573/74.[96]	No recorded connection.

93   Peter Ure, ed., *The Arden Shakespeare, King Richard II* (Surrey: Thomas Nelson & Sons Ltd., 1998), l.

94   Hannay, *Philip's Phoenix*, 49.

95   Davis, *The Shakespeare Name Dictionary*, throughout.

96   Ibid., 39.

Source	Mary Sidney	Shakespeare
Rosencrantz and Guildenstern are the names of two schoolmates of Hamlet's in the play. Two Danish students named Rosencrantz and Guildenstern studied at the Padua University, along with Roger Manners, Fifth Earl of Rutland. Manners also spent time in Elsinore, the scene of *Hamlet*.[97]	Roger Manners, the Earl of Rutland, married Mary's niece, Elizabeth (Philip's daughter). Mary's estate physician, Dr. Moffett, went to Elsinore in 1582 to present the Order of the Garter to King Frederick at the newly renovated Kronberg Castle, by order of Walsingham.[98]	No recorded connection.
Dr. John Caius appears in *The Merry Wives of Windsor* as a foul-mouthed, irascible, excitable Frenchman. Some scholars see this Dr. John Caius as the same man who was founder of Caius College at Cambridge whose temperament was similar to the character in the play. He died in 1573, twenty-four years before *Merry Wives* was written.	Henry 8's son, the young King Edward 6, was the dearest friend of and died in the arms of Mary's father, Henry Sidney. One of King Edward's doctors was Dr. John Caius of Cambridge, indicating that Mary's father knew Caius well.	No recorded connection.
The constable Dogberry in *Much Ado About Nothing* is one of the few illiterate characters in the plays.	The constable in Wiltshire, where Mary lived, was illiterate. In 1616 he pleaded to be released from his office, "forasmuch as I am unlearned, and by reason thereof am constrained to go two miles from my house to have the help of a scrivener to read such warrants as are sent unto me."[99]	Of course, Shakespeare *surely* knew illiterate constables, even though it is not documented.

97 John Michell, *Who Wrote Shakespeare?* (London: Thames and Hudson, 1996), 215.

98 Sidney Lee, *Dictionary of National Biography.*

99 Woudhuysen, *Sir Philip Sidney*, 61.

Source	Mary Sidney	Shakespeare
Most scholars agree with this statement: "That Shakespeare was an ardent admirer of Essex seems almost certain."[100]	Robert Devereux, the Earl of Essex, was an intimate family friend and Mary's step-cousin. When Mary's brother Philip died, Essex inherited Philip's "best sword" and married his widow. A letter that Mary wrote to Essex still exists. Essex was the stepson, protégé, and chief heir of Mary's uncle, Robert Dudley.	No recorded connection.
In *The Merry Wives of Windsor*, it is believed that the incident involving the three German horse thieves and their Duke is an insider joke for Elizabeth's courtiers regarding Count Mompelgard, a German nobleman who was obsessively intent on being inducted as a Knight of the Order of the Garter. There are clear and obvious references to the Knights of the Garter and its investiture ceremonies in the play.	This was Mary's world, her peers and friends—the royal court and all its gossip. Mary's father, husband, two sons, and younger brother Robert were all invested as Knights of the Garter. Her brother Philip was knighted (not as K. G.) specifically so he could stand in as proxy for his close friend John Casimir, Duke of Bavaria, when Casimir was invested as a Knight of the Garter. Women were allowed to watch the ceremony from the upper level of the Great Hall of Windsor Castle.	No recorded connection.
In *Twelfth Night*, "Scholars have suggested that the Malvolio plot may reflect an incident at Queen Elizabeth's court in which the Comptroller of the Household, Sir William Knollys, interrupted a noisy late-night party dressed in only his nightshirt and a pair of spectacles, with a copy of the Italian pornographic writer Aretino's work in his hand."[101]	As mentioned above, this was Mary's world, her peers and friends—the royal court and all its gossip.	No recorded connection.

100 Campbell, *Reader's Encyclopedia of Shakespeare*, 215.
101 Bevington, *Complete Works of Shakespeare*, A-32.

Source	Mary Sidney	Shakespeare
Harold Bloom wonders, "Shakespeare seems to have gone home again, to Stratford, in late 1610 or early 1611 [based on Stratford records], but then to have returned intermittently to London until sometime in 1613. After that, in the nearly three years before his death [1613 to 1616], he was in Stratford, writing nothing. The rest was silence, but why?"[102]	"In 1613, [Mary Sidney] went abroad for almost three years. She was recorded at Flushing and Antwerp in 1614, and visited Stuttgart before returning to England in October 1616."[103]	No documented evidence regarding any literary involvement during this time.
It has been proposed that the work of Robert Barret, soldier and author of *The Theory and Practice of Modern Wars* (1598), is ridiculed in the character of Parolles in *All's Well that Ends Well*.[104]	Barret dedicated his book, *The Theory and Practice of Modern Wars,* to Henry Herbert and William Herbert, Mary's husband and son, and the book includes a reference to Mary's brother, Philip Sidney.	No recorded connection.

102 Harold Bloom, *Shakespeare: The Invention of the Human* (New York: Riverhead Books, 1998), 695.

103 Brennan, *Literary Patronage in the English Renaissance,* 157–58.

104 Nick de Somogyi, 'Barret, Robert (fl. 1586?–1607)', *Oxford Dictionary of National Biography,* Oxford University Press, 2004. http://www.oxforddnb.com/view/article/1519, accessed 17 Nov 2011.

Source	Mary Sidney	Shakespeare
The central assertion of *The Chemical Theatre* by Charles Nicholl is that "the symbols and themes of Renaissance alchemy are woven into the language and structure of Shakespeare's great tragedy, *King Lear*."[105] Nicholl also points out the many images and references to alchemy that appear in the plays and sonnets.	Mary had her own chemical/alchemy laboratory, as mentioned earlier. Aubrey said of Mary Sidney, "Her Honor's genius lay as much towards chemistry as poetry."[106] Mary's family, as well as her lab assistant Adrian Gilbert, was well acquainted with the famous alchemist and astrologer John Dee. "Dee had long been associated with Sidney's family, and probably began tutoring Sidney in alchemy and related magical pursuits in the early 1570s."[107] Giordano Bruno was the other most prominent alchemist and "magician" in Europe. Bruno and Philip Sidney were friends and kindred spirits; Bruno dedicated his two most important works to Philip Sidney.[108]	No recorded connection.

105 Charles Nicholl, *The Chemical Theatre* (The Akadine Press: New York, 1997), xii. Alchemy includes a "quintessence," the fifth spiritual element after earth, water, fire, and air. It is involved with vessels, distillation, volatile vapors, smoke, spirits being liberated from solid matter [as Ariel in *The Tempest*], probing, purifying, transforming, transmuting, "the capacity of chemical experiments to mirror both physic and cosmic meanings" (page 6), crystals, "good angels" (page 20), fire, death and rebirth, loss and restoration of form, purity, and the search for the "Universal Medicine," or Elixir, which fully perfects metals or imperfect bodies—the Philosopher's Stone. Out of pairs of the four qualities (cold, hot, moist, dry) arise the four elements: earth (cold and dry), water (cold and wet), fire (hot and dry) and air (hot and wet) (page 25). Also see the sonnets 44 and 45.

106 John Aubrey, *Brief Lives* (1680; reprint, Rochester, New York: The Boydell Press, 1997), 140.

107 Nicholl, *The Chemical Theatre*, 15.

108 Duncan-Jones, *Sir Philip Sidney, Courtier Poet*, 271.

Source	Mary Sidney	Shakespeare
A number of plays are set in Italy, specifically mentioning Verona, Padua, Milan, Mantua, Florence, Rome, and Venice.	Mary's older brother Philip spent more than three years in Europe and specifically stayed in Verona, Padua, Venice (which entailed going through Milan and Mantua), and Vienna, among other cities, including Prague, Hungary, and Cracow.[109] Philip "was certainly the most widely traveled of the major Elizabethan writers."[110]	No record of having left England. No recorded connection with travelers.
Some details about these places are surprisingly accurate, but the number of erroneous details indicate the author didn't actually go to these various places, such as Italy, but clearly used second-hand descriptions from someone who had traveled there. There are no Italian accents written into the plays, as there are Welsh, Irish, and Scots.	Mary's younger brother Robert Sidney traveled extensively in Europe, visiting the Netherlands, Spa, Strasbourg, Frankfurt, Prague, Paris, and parts between, and he also accompanied Princess Elizabeth to Heidelberg following her marriage to Frederick.[111] In her later years, Mary traveled extensively in northern Europe.	

Other plays take place in:		
Elsinore, Denmark	Spa/Ardennes, Belgium	Tyre in Lebanon
Milford Haven, Wales	Illyria (Balkan Peninsula)	Pentapolis/Libya
Rousillion, Paris, Marseille, Agincourt, Crecy, and many other towns in France	Bohemia (Czech Republic)	Navarre, northern Spain
Vienna, Austria	Actium, Athens, Mytilene on Lesbos, Thebes in Greece	Cyprus
	Philippi in Macedonia/Greece	Sicily
	Alexandria, Egypt	Ephesus, Troy, Antioch, Tarsus, and Sardis in Turkey

109 Philip also traveled to Paris, Strasbourg, Basle, Dresden, Leipzig, Frankfurt, Heidelberg, Cologne, Bruges, Antwerp, Zutphen (the Netherlands), among other places. Robert was fluent in English, Latin, French, German, Italian, and Spanish; see Warkentin, *The Library of the Sidneys*, 20.

110 Katherine Duncan-Jones, *Sir Philip Sidney: Courtier Poet* (New Haven: Yale University Press, 1991), xi.

111 Millicent V. Hay, *The Life of Robert Sidney, Earl of Leicester* (1563–1626) (Washington: The Folger Shakespeare Library, 1984), 34–35 and throughout.

Source	Mary Sidney	Shakespeare
The use of falconry images in the Shakespearean plays has long been noted, although there is only one scene that is actually about falconry. The author was so familiar with this sport that falconry images appear in such disparate ideas as political discussions, love banter, jealousy, philosophical musings.	In Mary's Psalm 83, she develops an extended metaphor from falconry to stress the hunting of God's people by their enemies. She uses technical falconry terms in Psalm 91.[112] In Psalm 73, she uses the falconry term "pitch" in the same sense as in Richard 2: *How high a pitch his resolution soars.* *Richard 2, 1.1* *So high a pitch their proud presumption flies.* *Psalm 73* Mary owned an important book about hunting with hawks and falcons, written by a woman. Falconry was a popular pastime among noblewomen.[113]	No recorded connection.

---

112 Hannay, *Philip's Phoenix*, 101.

113 Mary owned *The Book of Hawking and Hunting*, by Dame Juliana Berners, printed by Caxton in England in 1486; John Aubrey mentions seeing it in her library. Mary Queen of Scots often hunted with her merlins. Katherine Duncan-Jones reports in *Philip Sidney: Courtier, Poet*, 74, that Catherine Howard, sister of the executed Duke of Norfolk, was "so addicted to falconry that her dresses were covered with bird-droppings."

Source	Mary Sidney	Shakespeare
Many references, images, and dialects in the plays come directly from the areas of Kent, in southeast England, and Wales. Gilbert Slater noted, "Next to Kent, with London and Windsor, it is Wales that supplies the most local color to the Shakespeare plays."[114] Frederick J. Harries felt the influence of Wales was so strong that he produced an entire book, *Shakespeare and the Welsh*, and came to his own surprising conclusion that "it seems reasonably proved that [Shakespeare] had Welsh blood in his veins, and it may have been from the lips of a Welsh grandmother that he obtained his first knowledge of Welsh tradition and folklore, which . . . exerted no small influence upon his dramatic and lyrical genius."[115] More recent scholarship agrees that "Shakespeare knew more about the Welsh than about any other people except the English."[116] The characters Fluellen in *Henry 5* and Evans in *Merry Wives of Windsor* both speak with Welsh accents that are written directly into the dialogue in the plays.	Regarding Kent: Mary grew up in Kent at the Sidney family estate called Penshurst, now open to the public. Regarding London and Windsor: Mary had several homes in London and is documented as having spent time in Windsor by her extant letters from Windsor. Regarding Wales: Mary was born on the border of Wales and spent summers in Ludlow Castle on the Welsh border. Her father, and later her husband, was Lord President of the Council of the Marches (border counties) of Wales. Her husband, whose father preferred to speak Welsh rather than English, was the Earl of the Welsh county of Pembrokeshire and where they owned Pembroke Castle and the town of Cardiff in southern Wales, an estate that Mary administered. Her sister-in-law, Barbara Gamage, was also Welsh and spent months at a time in Mary's home.	There is no evidence that Shakespeare had Welsh ancestry, nor that he ever spent time in Wales.

114 Gilbert Slater, *Seven Shakespeares* (Oxford: Kemp Hall Press, Ltd., 1931), 106.

115 Frederick J. Harries, *Shakespeare and the Welsh* (London: T. Fisher Unwin, Ltd., 1919), 5.

116 Willy Maley, "Shakespeare, Wales and the Critics" in *Shakespeare and Wales: From the Marches to the Assembly* (Farnham: Ashgate Publishing LTd., 2010), eds. Willy Maley and Philip Schwyzer, 179.

Source	Mary Sidney	Shakespeare
There are sixty song lyrics in the plays, and more than one hundred other song lyrics are alluded to.[117] There are more than 500 references to music, many of which portray a high level of musical knowledge and ability. Louis Marder states that Shakespeare shows evidence of "more than superficial acquaintance with music" with "knowledge of the theory of resonance and the use of burden, close, crotchet, descant, diapason, division, ground, minim, rest, relish, and triplex." Marder then goes on to state that Shakespeare "would have" picked up this information in the barber shop while waiting to be shaved, in the brothel while chatting with the musicians, or from some mysterious education in a nobleman's household.[118]	"The Sidneys have long been celebrated by critics as important musical patrons. The extant tributes to Philip, Mary, and Robert Sidney, William Herbert, and Mary Wroth, which situate them within a veritable "Who's Who" of Musical Figures of the period, testify to the family's ongoing status within artistic and literary circles." [119] As mentioned in Chapter 2, Mary played the lute, virginals (an early spinet or small harpsichord), and probably the violin, and she composed music. Her father established a violin consort in the household. Gavin Alexander details the family account books that show regular expenditures for the hiring of musicians, music books, musical instruments, the upkeep of instruments, and musical patronage.[120]	No recorded connection or mention of Shakespeare in relation to music.

117 Ross W. Duffin, *Shakespeare's Songbook* (New York: W. W. Norton & Company, 2004).

118 Louis Marder, "Shakespeare's Musical Background" in *Modern Language Notes*, 65:7 (1950): 501–03.

119 Hannay, et al., *Ashgate Research Companion, vol 1: Lives*, 324.

120 Gavin Alexander, "Musical Sidneys" in the *John Donne Journal* 25 (2006): 65–105.

And more books

Books by Aesop, Catullus, Callimachus, Titus Livy, Apollonius of Rhodes, Quintillian, Homer, Ovid in Latin, Plautus, Julius Caesar, Boethius, Distichs of Cato, Dante, at least eighteen books by Cicero, plus Pliny, Seneca, Suetonius, Tacitus, Terence, Virgil, ancient Roman manuscripts, Greek grammar books, numerous books published in Greek, including the *Argonautica*, and more, many of them incunabula (printed before 1501), were still in Mary's library when a portion of it was sold in 1914.[121] Recently the catalog of the Sidney library in the family home of Penshurst was transcribed: "The 5,798 entries document one of the larger libraries possessed by a magnate of the period."[122] *This is the sort of library that one would expect from the writer of the Shakespearean works,* and indeed, the list of books used by this playwright insist on a library of this breadth and caliber.

Milford Haven and the Cave in Cymbeline

The following is a very interesting coincidence. In the play of *Cymbeline*, two young men were kidnapped as babies and raised in a cave with the courtier who kidnapped them; this cave, also called a rock, is mentioned thirteen times. The coastal town of Milford Haven in Wales is mentioned by name seventeen times. The heroine, Imogen, wakes up outside the cave from a dream and still half asleep, says:

> "Yes Sir, to Milford-Haven, which is the way?
> I thank you: by yond bush? pray how far thither?"
> 'Ods pittikins: can it be six mile yet?

Guiderius, who lives in the cave, smites off Cloten's head and says:

> I have taken
> His head from him: I'll throw 't into the creek
> Behind our rock, and let it to the sea,
> And tell the fishes, he's the Queen's son, Cloten.

So the playwright tells us the cave is six miles from the town of Milford Haven, and right outside the cave, or *rock* (a rock cavern), is a *creek* that runs to the sea. In 1600, a *creek*, as defined by the OED, was specifically a tidal estuary or an armlet of the sea that runs inland.

---

121 *Catalogue of a Selected Portion of the Renowned Library at Wilton House, Salisbury,* collected in the sixteenth and seventeenth centuries, sold at auction by Sotheby, Wilkinson & Hodge, London, 1914).

122 Warkentin, *The Library of the Sidneys of Penshurst Place,* vii.

There actually is a cave, a huge cave called the Wogan, exactly six miles by water from Milford Haven. It is situated directly under Pembroke Castle, and just outside the cave entrance is a creek that flows to the sea. The castle wall, built in the late 1100s, covers the entrance to the cave with an iron gate. *To access the cave, one must climb down fifty-three steps from inside the family apartments of Pembroke Castle, owned by Mary Sidney.*[123]

A Mutable Language

The Shakespearean plays and sonnets contain approximately 1,500 words that were new to the English language.[124] These words were either freshly created, or were existing words combined into new words or used with new meanings. Mary Sidney "is inventive in coining new words and recycling old ones."[125]

Mary Sidney is credited in the Oxford English Dictionary (OED) with the first recorded use of more than forty words as used in the plays, including *sea-monster* and *unpeopled* (among other uses, Cleopatra says to her servant, "I'll unpeople Egypt"), plus more than 140 words that Mary used for the first time in English in a particular sense, such as *eternize, measure, shallow, embowel, disaster, disposer, chamberer, imprison, infant, lease, self, waitress, unstate,* and *winged* (as a ship with sails), and which are used in the same sense in the plays.[126] In addition, there are words that Mary used earlier than the citations in the OED, such as *thunderstrike,* and other words that she used in the same senses as in the plays before their recorded use, such as *candy, oblivion, unsounded,* and *void.* For instance, the OED lists Shakespeare first using *lonely* in *Coriolanus* in 1607, but it was used in the same sense by Mary Sidney in her play, *Antonie,* published in 1592. She invented words such as *feathery, heart-broken, head-long, re-become, empearl, powerfulness, surrounded, mix* as a noun, *wondered* as used in *The Tempest, soundless deep* as used in Sonnet 80.[127]

---

123 www.CastleWales.com/pembroke.html; this site displays photos of the cave and creek. Also en.wikipedia.org/wiki/Pembroke_Castle.

124 Jeffrey McQuain and Stanley Malless, *Coined by Shakespeare* (Springfield: Merriam-Webster, 1998), viii.

125 Hannay, *The Collected Works of Mary Sidney Herbert,* 64.

126 Oxford English Dictionary, www.oed.com, Advanced Search: Countess of Pembroke as Quotation Author, First Quotation in Entry or Sense.

127 Hannay, *The Collected Works of Mary Sidney Herbert,* 64.

Compound adjectives, an oft-used device in the Shakespearean plays, were introduced into English poetry by Mary's brother, Philip Sidney. "Joseph Hall singled Sidney out for praise because of his introduction into English poetic practice of the French fondness for compound adjectives." [128] Mary, as well, often uses compound adjectives in her own work, such as *hunger-starvèd land, never-dying rhymes, brain-sick men, shadow-clothèd night, ghost-haunted tomb, angel-like delight*. The OED shows numerous compound adjectives she invented used in their sense for the first time in various of her works, such as *maid of honor, out-eat, over-grieve, proverb-like, mother-murdering, sail-winged, thunder-hid, world-dweller, wood-bred*, and others.

Mary Sidney's written works have so many similarities with the Shakespearean works in the use and inventiveness of language, rhyme, multilevel mastery of rhetorical devices, structure, imagery, character development, vocabulary, neologisms, and other aspects of the craft of writing. It is a very small leap to imagine her as the author of the plays and sonnets. Conversely, we have nothing in writing by the man named William Shakespeare (except a few signatures) with which to compare the vocabulary or usage in the plays and sonnets. How convenient.

As mentioned earlier, it is claimed that the doggerel on the tombstone was written by William Shakespeare. It is certainly interesting that the tombstone of Shakespeare's includes the odd curse—but not Shakespeare's name.

Just the Beginning

These are just the documented instances that I have found of Mary Sidney's direct connections to so many of the source books, as well as a couple of intriguing coincidences in her life. This work is just the beginning. I am confident that with continued rigor in documentation, many more connections linking Mary Sidney to the Shakespearean canon will be found.

---

128 H. R. Woudhuysen, "Sidney, Sir Philip (1554–1586)," *Oxford Dictionary of National Biography*, Oxford University Press, 2004; online edition, May 2005, www.oxforddnb.com/view/article/25522.

10 The Sources and How They Were Changed

ONLY FOUR PLAYS in the canon are original stories (*Love's Labors Lost, The Tempest, The Merry Wives of Windsor,* and *A Midsummer Night's Dream*), and even those four lean heavily on plot points, concepts, philosophies, even direct lines taken from other sources. The rest of the plays are based on a variety of sources established by and generally agreed upon by generations of scholars.

This chapter looks at how the author changed the original stories. As you read through this, do you see any patterns develop?

"Fool," said my Muse to me, "Look in thy heart, and write."
Philip Sidney, Sonnet 1, *Astrophil and Stella*

As You Like It

In the primary original source, three men are killed in the wrestling match; Celia/Aliena is kidnapped by outlaws whose purpose is to hand her over to her lecherous father as an incestuous gift; blood is shed when she is rescued; and her father is killed in a battle at the story's end. In contrast, there's not a hint of incest in *As You Like It,* and no one dies. Anne Barton in *The Riverside Shakespeare* describes it:

The incest, bloodshed, and father's death are removed.

> There are no outlaws either, only banished courtiers suffi-
> ciently tender-hearted to worry about preying upon the
> deer in the forest, let alone upon other human beings; and
> the usurping duke, Celia's father, never reaches the fatal
> battlefield [as in the original] because an old religious man
> meets and peaceably converts him on the way.[1]

David Bevington states:

> The conversion of Duke Frederick by a hermit instead
> of his being overthrown and killed is a characteristically

---

1   Anne Barton in *The Riverside Shakespeare* (Boston, New York: Houghton Mifflin Company, 1997), 399.

Shakespearean softening touch. Shakespeare's added characters are virtually all foils to the conventional pastoral vision he found in his source.[2]

Titus Andronicus

The love of a mother and two fathers for their children is added, as well as insurmountable heartache.

The chapbook on which *Titus* is thought to have been based does not include Titus's sacrifice of Tamora's son.[3] In the Shakespearean version, the sacrifice of her son gives Tamora a stronger motive to persecute Titus, making her less monstrous because she is a broken-hearted mother. Thus the play becomes a tale of two single parents, Tamora and Titus, who have seen their children cruelly mutilated, which motivates their revenge. The playwright also creates a strong theme about grief; revenge is a manifestation of the overwhelming grief.

The chapbook shows nothing of Aaron's love for his child; in the play, his love and care is a poignant hint of a redeeming quality in the otherwise hard-hearted Aaron.

The Taming of the Shrew

The misogyny is removed and Katherina's spirit is not only unbroken but appreciated.

The wife-taming plot in the Shakespearean version of *The Taming of the Shrew* differs markedly from the ballad considered to be its primary source, "A Merry Jest of a Shrewd and Curst Wife Lapped in Morel's Skin for Her Good Behavior." In the ballad, the husband confines his wife inside the skin of a dead horse named Morel. As Anne Barton explains in *The Riverside Shakespeare*:

> Verbal similarities indicate that Shakespeare knew this particular ballad; certainly he knew others like it, in which the approved remedy for a domineering wife was physical violence, the more ingenious and excruciating the better. By comparison with the husband who binds his erring spouse, beats her, bleeds her into a state of

---

2   David Bevington, ed., *The Complete Works of Shakespeare*, 6th ed. (New York: Pearson Longman, 2009), A-31.

3   This is from *The Riverside Shakespeare*. In Bevington's *Complete Works*, he states the chapbook has now been shown to be an expansion of the story based on a ballad of 1594, which was in turn modeled on the play. It's very interesting, whether the play was based on the chapbook or the chapbook on the play, that the author of the play as we know it softened various elements, and the author of the chapbook removed the softening elements.

debility, or (in the case of the ballad mentioned above) incarcerates her inside the salted skin of a dead horse Morel, Petruchio—although no Romeo—is almost a model of intelligence and humanity. His aim, moreover, is not the crude one of the traditional wife-tamer, out to pulverize the woman's will as well as, in most cases, her body. What Petruchio wants, and ends up with, is a Katherina of unbroken spirit and gaiety who has suffered only minor physical discomfort and who has learned the value of self control and of caring about someone other than herself.[4]

David Bevington also notes that "Shakespeare avoids the misogynistic extremes of this story despite the similarity of the narrative."[5] Keep in mind, regarding what Petruchio puts Katherina through in the play, that Petruchio does not inflict anything on Katherina that he does not inflict on himself as well: He gets wet and cold and muddy; he is the one who stays awake all night to keep *her* awake all night; he doesn't eat the choleric-inducing food either; he makes himself look like a fool just as he does Katherina, etc. Remember, which daughter in this play disobeys both her father and her husband?

Much Ado About Nothing

Although there are a number of sources for the plot of Hero and Claudio (some of which include slaying and poison), the addition of Beatrice—one of the brightest and wittiest characters in the canon—is original. Thus the scenes of the indissoluble bond between the women are also added. Beatrice finds herself in Act 4 three times wishing "that I were a man."

The story of Beatrice and Benedick is added, and thus the close bond of women is also added.

No source has been found for Dogberry, the illiterate constable, one of four illiterate characters in the canon (all male). It is documented, however, that the constable in Wilton, the village where Mary Sidney lived, was illiterate.[6] This doesn't prove anything, of course; it's simply interesting that even such a detail as this can be connected to Mary.

---

4 Barton, *The Riverside Shakespeare*, 138.
5 Bevington, *Complete Works*, A-26.
6 H. R. Woudhuysen, *Sir Philip Sidney and the Circulation of Manuscripts, 1558–1640* (Oxford: Oxford University Press, 1996), 61.

Measure for Measure

The woman does *not* sacrifice herself sexually for a man who committed an immoral act. She apparently chooses to stay true to her monastic ideals rather than marry.

There are several source stories, each built on the previous. In the first, the husband is a murderer; in the second, a young man has sex with a number of women; in the third, the brother rapes a young virgin. In all three, the Isabella character has sex with Angelo to expiate the sins of the violent, immoral men, and in all the sources (written by men), all characters believe she did the right thing to sacrifice herself sexually for the crimes committed by a degenerate criminal.

But in the Shakespearean play, the stakes are raised—Isabella's brother has done nothing worse than consensually sleep with his beloved Juliet just before they are to be married, and she's pregnant. Isabella is a novice just entering a convent. The Shakespearean version is the only one in which Isabella does *not* have sex with Angelo in exchange for her brother's life—she is willing to let her brother die rather than compromise her values. Nor does she respond to either of the Duke's offers of marriage in the final scene.

The Comedy of Errors

The women are more virtuous, even the courtesan. A sister is added and thus the scenes of the bond between women.

In the Shakespearean version, the author "plays down the role of the courtesan, dignifies the part of the wife, invents the sympathetic role of Luciana her sister."[7] Plautus, in his original story, uses a detached ironic tone and a casual depiction of courtesans and parasites, but these are replaced in the Shakespearean play "by a thematic emphasis on patience and loyalty in marriage."[8]

The Two Gentlemen of Verona

The woman remains faithful to her man and does not die for love of a different man.

In the Shakespearean version, Sylvia does *not* fall in love with the disguised Julia ("Sebastian") and die of unrequited love—Sylvia is a much pluckier spirit, remains loyal to Valentine, and follows him into banishment, after escaping from the tower in which her father kept her locked.

---

7   Bevington, *Complete Works*, A-23.

8   Ibid., A-23.

Twelfth Night

In the source story, Olivia takes Sebastian as her lover and after a one-night stand—in which she gets pregnant—he abandons her. Orsino throws Viola in jail. In the Shakespearean *Twelfth Night*, the playwright "eschews the pregnancy, the desertion, the imprisonment, and all of [Barnabe] Riche's stern moralizing [in the original] about the bestiality of lust."[9] Riche wrote his book for women and claims in the introduction that the story is for "the only delight of the courteous gentlewoman."

The woman does not take a lover or get pregnant before marriage.

Othello

In the original story, Othello has Iago bludgeon Desdemona to death with a sand-filled stocking, then together they make the ceiling collapse on her so it looks like she was brained with a rafter. But in the Shakespearean version, Othello suffocates Desdemona with a pillow, thus avoiding the appalling butchery of the original. "Most important," says Bevington, "Shakespeare transforms a sensational murder story into a moving tragedy of love."[10] "Speak of one that loved not wisely but too well," says Othello.

A murder becomes a love story. Private and close scenes between women are added.

Both Othello and Iago are held accountable for the crimes they have committed, unlike in the source story.

The playwright also adds the intimate scene between Emilia and Desdemona as she prepares for bed.

The Winter's Tale

In the original story, Pandosto/Leontes is incestuously in love with his daughter. His wife actually gave him cause for jealousy and has died. Pandosto/Leontes kills himself in a melancholic fit after his daughter marries a young man.

Incest is removed. Leontes' jealousy is increased. The Queen is more virtuous, and the brilliant Paulina is added. The fifteen-year secret between two women is added.

In the Shakespearean version, all signs of incest are removed. Leontes is more irrationally jealous and his wife more virtuous. The enterprising and dynamic character of Paulina is added, as well as the fifteen-year secret kept by the two women. "Leontes' purgative sorrow is more intense and also more restorative than in the source."[11]

9   Ibid., A-32.
10 Ibid., A-48.
11 Ibid., A-57.

Coriolanus

The women's roles are greater, stronger, and fiercer—and the men more cowardly.

In the Shakespearean version of this historical piece, Volumnia's role is magnified into a strong and capable matriarch in her son's life and in the lives of the Roman people. "Shakespeare therefore makes Volumnia more fierce than she is in Plutarch, and emphasizes the powerlessness of Virgilia's pacific spirit and her inability to affect the course of her husband's life, or even her son's." [12] However, Virgilia is the only person in the play willing and able to stand up to Volumnia—not even Coriolanus can do that.

The playwright makes the men in the mob more cowardly in war than they were in Plutarch's source.

Macbeth

The original strange women are recast into three goddesses of destiny, the Wyrd Sisters. Lady Macbeth is given a larger and more powerful role.

Historically, Duncan was an ineffectual king, and Banquo did conspire against him. In the play, Duncan becomes a well-beloved ruler, and Banquo (purported ancestor of King James) evolved into a more honorable man with a forceful ghost. The role of Lady Macbeth is considerably enhanced, and Shakespeare invents her sleepwalking scene.

In the source material, Macbeth hears the prophecies from "three women in strange and wild apparel, resembling creatures of elder world." [13] The playwright changes the strangely clad women to the more intriguing trinity of Wyrd Sisters, the three Anglo-Saxon Fates or goddesses of destiny. No one in the play refers to the women as "witches" except one of the Wyrd Sisters herself when relating a story in which a woman derogatorily uses the word.

Pericles

The woman's challenge is greater in the play, and the man she marries more dignified.

In other plays, this author consistently removed any incest that may have appeared in the source material. Act 1 of Pericles includes incest, but Act 1 is not believed to have been written by "Shakespeare" (for other reasons).

"Shakespeare has given a more sordid impression of the brothel in which Marina must dwell and has dignified the character of Lysimachus so as to render him worthy of marrying Marina." [14]

---

12 Frank Kermode in *The Riverside Shakespeare*, 1441.

13 Holinshed's *Chronicles, Volume V: Scotland*, 268.

14 Bevington, *Complete Works*, A-23.

The Merry Wives of Windsor

This play doesn't have a single direct source, but in similar stories, the wives do commit adultery. In the Shakespearean version, "Falstaff is tricked by a pair of wives who may be merry but are also fiercely chaste. It is the would-be lover [Falstaff] who is cleverly deceived, not the husband."[15]

The women are virtuous and clever. Rather than commit adultery, they make fools of the men.

Antony and Cleopatra

Regarding one of the sources, Mary Sidney's translation, *Antonie*, Tina Krontiris says, "[Mary Sidney's] play interrogates conventional definitions of masculine and feminine virtue, opposes the established association of overt female sexuality with loose morals, and reveals the psychological and sexual complexes of those holding political power. . . . *Antonie* offers a sympathetic view of the adulterous lovers, and especially of Cleopatra, the woman who up to that time had been presented to the English public as a seductress."[16]

Cleopatra is more sympathetic. Two woman have been added, creating scenes of the bond between women. Antony is less of a lush.

John Wilders, in the Arden edition of the play, states that the portrayal of Cleopatra in Mary Sidney's play, "unlike Plutarch, is consistently sympathetic," and that in the Shakespearean play, the playwright "may have been influenced by [*Antonie*] when he created the resolute, idealizing Cleopatra of the final scene."[17]

The characters of Iras and Charmian are developed from mere hints in the Plutarch source. And the playwright plays down Antony's bacchanalian nature.

15 Barton, *Riverside Shakespeare*, 322.
16 Tina Krontiris, *Oppositional Voices: Woman as Writers and Translators of Literature in the English Renaissance* (London and New York: Routledge, 1992), 69.
17 John Wilders, ed., *The Arden Shakespeare, Antony and Cleopatra* (New York: Routledge, 1995), 62.

The History Plays

The playwright consistently adds and enlarges scenes of powerful women who are barely noted in the historical record.

The women in the history plays—from Mistress Quickly who appears in both parts of *Henry 4* and also *Henry 5* (as well as in *The Merry Wives of Windsor*) to the daunting Queen Margaret, who appears in all three parts of *Henry 6* and also *Richard 3*—are active participants who vigorously comment on unfolding events, reveal the impact of these events on their families and themselves, and often oppose the historical progress.

King John: The incredible queens Eleanor (who is 78 years old when the play opens) and Constance, as forceful and unwavering mothers, are much more important in this play than alluded to in the sources. The scene of Constance's grief is invented by the playwright, as well as young Blanche's exasperation as her new husband leaves for bloody war.

Richard 2: The author adds three women to the Shakespearean play and invents three scenes that were not in any of the historical sources:

> Queen Isabel and the now-famous garden scene.
> Duchess of York as a protective mother who goes up against the king to save her son's life, while her husband is willing to have him executed as a traitor.
> Duchess of Gloucester mourning for her husband.

1 Henry 4: The author adds two women not included in the historical narrative, the witty wives of devoted husbands, Mortimer and Hotspur. And we are introduced to Mistress Quickly, who runs the tavern and appears in four plays.

1 Henry 6: Joan la Pucelle (Joan of Arc) not only leads the French army and wins battles, she physically fights with the dread Lord Talbot. She goes to her death taunting the Englishmen with salacious lies about herself.

2 Henry 6: The Duchess of Gloucester bids for power and loses as the young Queen Margaret (who appears in four plays) starts to feel her own strength.

3 Henry 6: The playwright invents the scene where the formidable Queen Margaret, remorseless defender of her son's right to the throne, takes down the most powerful man in the land, Richard, Duke of York.

Richard 3: The longest scene in this play, the first 135 lines in Act 4.4, invented by the author, is that of three commanding and passionate women on stage: Queen Margaret, Queen Elizabeth, and the Duchess of York. Not only has the playwright created them as daunting political figures throughout, but in this scene they are specifically angry and anguished as mothers and wives, bewailing the sons, husbands, and brothers who have been murdered.

The playwright includes Margaret in this play, the fourth she appears in, even though historically she was back in France.

A Pattern?

This playwright consistently ennobles and strengthens the female characters and makes them more virtuous than their original counterparts. All references to incest are eliminated. Women are often added where they didn't appear in the source material, and scenes of women's emotional, intimate bonds with each other are invented. There is an undeviating pattern of faithful, dedicated wives with an emphasis on loyalty in marriage, even though a surprising number of these wives have irrationally jealous husbands. In the history plays, women who are barely mentioned or ignored in the historical record are given strong voices and powerful statements.

This playwright, unlike any other dramatist of the time, displays a reverence for the wit, intelligence, maternity, capacity, and strength of women.

A fascinating parallel when considering Mary Sidney as the author of these Shakespearean plays is that she is well known for removing material one might consider improper or offensive from her brother Philip's works. The early manuscript version of Philip's *The Countess of Pembroke's Arcadia*, not discovered until 1907, is now called the *Old Arcadia*. Philip died in 1586; in 1590, a small paperback quarto was published of the unfinished revision of this novel, probably by Fulke Greville, who may have been Philip's lover. In 1593, a folio (large hard-bound) version was published by Mary Sidney. In this publication, which Mary is known to have edited, she transformed a scene of sexual consummation by the unmarried lovers, Pyrocles and Philoclea, to a scene of an attempted elopement. A scene when Musidorus, meeting with Pamela to elope, is overcome with lust and attempts to rape her before the outlaws interrupt, is deleted by Mary.

This bowdlerizing is entirely consistent with the work of the author of the Shakespearean plays.

11 The Plays and Mary's Life

WRITERS, RESEARCHERS, Stratfordians, Oxfordians, Marlovians—everyone attempts to find parallels in the plays to a particular author's life. I hesitate to do this because one can make a case for just about any play to reflect just about any author. But—as an exercise in possibilities—we'll take a look at some intriguing (and documented) events in Mary's life and how they might connect to a few of the Shakespearean plays. After all, if she *is* the author of the plays, one would *expect* to find some reflections.

As Betsy Lerner states in *The Forest for the Trees: An Editor's Advice to Writers,* "Writing what you know is a given. Writing what you know is unavoidable. All people write what they know, for God's sake. It's the air you breathe."

Every writer, by the way he uses the language, reveals something of his spirit, his habits, his capacities, his bias . . . . creative writing is communication through revelation—it is the self escaping into the open. No writer long remains incognito.
E. B. White 1899–1985

Titus Andronicus

In Chapter 2 I talked of Mary Sidney's heartbreaking and agonizing year when her little girl Katherine died, her father died, her mother died, and her beloved brother Philip died of a battle wound, after an agonizing month with a bullet in his thigh bone. These deaths in such a close-knit family were particularly devastating. Because she was a woman, Mary was not allowed to participate in her brother Philip's elaborate state funeral, nor to contribute to the publications of elegies that were collected. Even the joyful promise of the pregnancy of her young sister-in-law Frances, Philip's widow, was destroyed when the baby miscarried. The year was 1586. Mary was barely 25 years old.

"Her love for her brother passes even her own understanding.... there is no doubt that the deepest emotional commitment of her life was to her brother, both before and also after his death."[1] Mary went into deep mourning and seclusion for two years. Did Mary Sidney, as a writer, use writing as solace (what we would today call "writer's therapy") and create *Titus Andronicus,* a violent, heart-wrenching, horrifying play that contains more tragedy than anyone could imagine living through?

John Klaus makes the following point in his article, "Politics, Heresy, and Martyrdom in Shakespeare's Sonnet 124 and *Titus Andronicus*": "The suggestiveness of plot, character, and allusion rather than any set of allegorical correspondences indicates that Shakespeare's mind in composing *Titus Andronicus* was engaged by the bloody history of Europe's and especially England's religious conflicts."[2] It was in one of these religious conflicts that Mary's brother Philip was killed.

Too often critics see only the gruesome surface layer of this remarkable and poetic play and fail to recognize the underlying layer of overwhelming grief. The play contains an astonishing collection of anguished cries, as shown on the opposite page.

---

1   Gary F. Waller, *Mary Sidney, Countess of Pembroke: A Critical Study of Her Writings and Literary Milieu* (Salzburg: Universität Salzburg, 1979), 100.
2   Ibid.

There greet in silence, as the dead are wont,
And sleep in peace, slain in your country's wars.
1.1.93–94

He lives in fame, that died in virtue's cause.
1.1.390

Sorrow concealèd, like an oven stopp'd,
Doth burn the heart to cinders where it is.
2.3.36–37

If I do dream, would all my wealth
     would wake me.
If I do wake, some planet strike me down,
That I may slumber in eternal sleep.
2.3.13–15

For these, tribunes, in the dust I write
My heart's deep languor and my soul's sad tears.
3.1.11–12

Therefore I tell my sorrows to the stones . . .
When I do weep, they humbly at my feet
Receive my tears and seem to weep with me.
3.1.37, 41–42

When will this fearful slumber have an end?
3.1.53

Titus, prepare thy agèd eyes to weep,
Or, if not so, thy noble heart to break —
I bring consuming sorrow to thine age.
3.1.59–61

Will it consume me? Let me see it then.
3.1.62

My grief was at the height before thou cam'st,
And now, like the Nile, it disdaineth bounds.
3.1.71–72

It was my dear, and he that wounded her
Hath hurt me more
     than had he kill'd me dead.
3.1.92–93

O, what a sympathy of woe is this.
3.1.149

Is not my sorrow deep, having no bottom?
Then be my passions bottomless with them.
3.1.217–18

If there were reasons for these miseries,
Then into limits could I bind my woes.
3.1.220–21

These miseries are more than may be borne.
3.1.244

I have not another tear to shed.
3.1.267

. . . when my heart, all mad with misery,
Beats in this hollow prison of my flesh.
3.2.9–10

Wound it with sighing, girl, kill it with groans,
Or get some little knife between thy teeth
And just against thy heart make thou a hole,
That all the tears that thy poor eyes let fall
May run into that sink and, soaking in,
Drown the lamenting fool in sea-salt tears.
3.2.15–20

She says she drinks no other drink but tears,
Brewed with her sorrow, mashed upon her cheeks.
3.2.37–38

O heavens, can you hear a good man groan
And not relent or not compassion him?
4.1.123–24

Yet wrung with wrongs more than our backs can bear.
4.3.49

                    . . . let him tell the tale,
While I stand by and weep to hear him speak.
5.3.93–94

O, take this warm kiss on thy pale cold lips,
These sorrowful drops upon thy bloodstained face.
5.3.152–53

I cannot speak to him for weeping;
My tears will choke me, if I ope my mouth.
5.3.173–74

Many a time he danc'd thee on his knee,
Sung thee asleep, his loving breast thy pillow;
Many a story hath he told to thee
And bid thee bear his pretty tales in mind,
And talk of them when he was dead and gone.
5.3.161–65

Bid him farewell; commit him to the grave;
Do him that kindness, and take leave of him.
5.3.169–70

Titus Andronicus is one of the first Shakespearean plays known to have existed. Because of what scholars refer to as its relatively amateur style, it is often considered to be the first play written by its author. Ben Jonson made a reference to the play that would date it to about 1588.[3] The first theater troupe to stage *Titus* in 1589 or 1590 was the Earl of Pembroke's Men, the acting company sponsored by Mary and her husband.[4]

Titus Andronicus was published anonymously in 1594. In 1658, Edward Ravenscroft, an English dramatist, wrote in the preface to his version of the play, "I have been told by some anciently conversant with the Stage that it was not Originally [William Shakespeare's], but brought by a private Author to be Acted, and he only gave some Master-touches to one or two of the Principal Parts or Characters."[5]

In 1588, just before the play was staged by Pembroke's Men, Mary Sidney was twenty-seven years old, had been married for twelve years, buried two sisters, birthed four children, buried her daughter, father, mother, and brother, and was the Lady of the House of four large estates. Imagination is an essential writer's tool, of course, but how much deeper a writer's work can become when informed with a vivid and abundant life.

The man named William Shakespeare was twenty-four years old and had very recently been named, along with his parents, in a legal action against a neighbor in Stratford, which suggests he was still living in the village.

3   Oscar James Campbell, ed., *The Reader's Encyclopedia of Shakespeare* (New York: MJF Books, 1966), 881.
4   "That the countess herself had some responsibility for the players is indicated by the will of the actor Simon Jewell, which bequeathed 'my share of such money as shalbe givenn by my ladie Pembrooke or by her means.'" Margaret Hannay, et al., eds., *The Collected Works of Mary Sidney Herbert, Countess of Pembroke*, vol. 1 (Oxford: Clarendon Press, 1998), 38.
5   Campbell, ed., *Reader's Encyclopedia of Shakespeare*, 677.

All's Well That Ends Well

All's Well That Ends Well is particularly interesting in regard to documented people and events in Mary's life.

a) This play is considered by most scholars to have been written around 1604. In it a Countess has a womanizing, profligate, arrogant, unmarried son, Bertram.

> In early 1604, Mary Sidney was a Countess with a womanizing, profligate, arrogant, unmarried son, William Herbert.
>
> In the original source story, there is no Countess; the author added a Countess to the story.

Is **Bertram** a loose anagram of William Herbert?

b) In the play, the husband of the Countess has died, and the son is heir to his father's estate.

> The husband of Mary, Countess of Pembroke, had recently died (1601), and her son is heir to his father's estate.

c) In the play, the doctor who lived in her house has more recently died.

> The doctor who lived in Mary's house, Dr. Moffett, had more recently died (early 1604). A new physician, Dr. Matthew Lister, has come to reside at her estate.

d) In the play, the deceased doctor left a daughter, Helena, who wants to marry the Countess's son, Bertram. The Countess thinks this is a splendid idea.

> Mary herself fell passionately in love with the handsome young doctor in her house. She was with him for the rest of her life, although they never married "for marriage out of one's degree was a debasing of the blood which blemished successive generations."[6]

e) The King promises Helena, the doctor's daughter, she can marry whomever she likes if she can cure the King's fatal illness. Helena cures the King and chooses to marry Bertram. Bertram is horrified at the idea of a high-born aristocrat such as himself marrying the daughter of a person of such an exceedingly inferior class as a doctor. (At the time, a doctor was of a

---

6   M. C. Bradbrook, "Shakespeare and Elizabethan Poetry," reprinted in the Signet Classic edition of *All's Well That Ends Well* (New York: New American Library, 1965), 182.

lower class than lawyers and soldiers and was not even considered as respectable as the "gentleman" class.) When the King insists he marry Helena, Bertram cries out to him:

> *But follows it, my lord, to bring me down*
> *Must answer for your raising? I know her well:*
> *She had her breeding at my father's charge:*
> *A poor Physician's daughter my wife? Disdain*
> *Rather corrupt me ever.*
> 2.3.113–117

Rather than marry her, let my **disdain** for her ruin me for**ever** in your eyes.

As M. C. Bradbrook says of Helena, "She is only the daughter of a poor gentleman belonging to the least dignified of the professions."[7]

f) The King lectures Bertram on the source of true nobility— the assessment of human worth by merit *earned* versus merit *inherited,* that which is outside of class distinctions—and wholeheartedly approves the union, much to Bertram's dismay.

> *She is young, wise, fair;*
> *In these to nature she's immediate heir,*
> *And these breed honor. That is honor's scorn*
> *Which challenges itself as honor's born*
> *And is not like the sire. Honors thrive*
> *When rather from our acts we them derive*
> *Than our foregoers. . . .*
> *If thou can like this creature as a maid,*
> *I canst [can] create the rest. Virtue and she*
> *Is her own dower; honor and wealth from me.*
> 2.3.131–144

The Countess in the play berates her son's behavior when she discovers how ill he has treated Helena.

> *There's nothing here that is too good for him*
> *But only she, and she deserves a lord*
> *That twenty such rude boys might tend upon*
> *And call her, hourly, mistress.*
> 3.2.79–82

---

7   Ibid., 181.

g) Bertram swears eternal love and service to a young virgin, Diana, if she will sleep with him. But after he sleeps with her (he *thinks* it's her), he immediately abandons her.

> William Herbert had recently created a scandal at court by sleeping with one of Queen Elizabeth's maids-of-honor, getting her pregnant, and abandoning her without remorse. The Queen threw him in prison.

All's Well That Ends Well was written at the beginning of Mary's love affair with the young doctor; he was ten years younger than Mary. About this same time, she had a disagreement with her oldest son, William (who was only nine years younger than the doctor), that separated them for the next decade.[8] Was the disagreement about Mary's romantic relationship with Dr. Lister, a relationship that embarrassed William as being shameful or degrading?

In this play, is Mary as the Countess trying to justify her liaison with the young doctor? In the original source, there is no Countess at all, just a dead Count.[9] Also in the source, the King does *not* approve of the marriage between Bertram and Helena, although he reluctantly agrees to it because of his bargain. In the Shakespearean play, Bertram is a more reprehensible scoundrel than he was in the source.

Dr. Matthew Lister. He was eventually knighted, years after Mary's death.

So why would William Shakespeare have chosen this story about which to write a play? (Or Oxford, Marlowe, Bacon—other possible candidates for authorship—for that matter?) Why would he add a Countess to the story? Especially a Countess who encourages her son to marry such a virtuous young woman regardless of propriety? Why would he change the original story to show a Countess who believes it to be perfectly appropriate, even commendatory, that her high-born son should marry the daughter of a doctor, and whose advice is supported by the King? The courtiers in the royal court well knew that noblemen and women ended up in jail or banishment from court for marrying outside of their social class. Yet Mary Sidney was, at the time of this play's conception, a widowed Countess desperately in love with a handsome young doctor, a situation that could only have upset her spoiled, arrogant, womanizing son.

8   Margaret Hannay, *Philip's Phoenix: Mary Sidney, Countess of Pembroke* (Oxford: Oxford University Press, 1990), 171 and 184.

9   The source is one of the stories in a section of Boccaccio's *Decameron* (Day 3), "Gigletta di Nerbona" (1313–1375).

There is no record that this play was ever performed or printed in either Shakespeare's or Mary Sidney's lifetime, and many scholars consider it to be an unfinished draft. Could it be a reflection of another difficult time in Mary's life?

Love's Labor's Lost

Navarre shall be the wonder of the world; Our court shall be a little Academe, Still and contemplative in living art.

King Ferdinand in Love's Labor's Lost, 1.1.12–14

Love's Labor's Lost, probably written around 1594, is one of the few plays that has an original plot. It explores the concept of an "academy" of aristocratic scholars. David Bevington says, "Certain historical facts about Henri of Navarre may well have provided Shakespeare a model for the play's action, especially the visit of Catherine de' Medici with her daughter [Marguerite de Valois] . . . to Henri's court in 1578 and a similar visit in 1586. *Published accounts of these visits were not available when Shakespeare wrote his play,* but he may well have heard the gossip."[10] [emphasis added]

Richard David, editor of the Arden edition of Love's Labor's Lost, is more definite about Shakespeare's lack of connection: "It is, however, extremely unlikely that Shakespeare had any direct knowledge of Navarre's academy."[11]

However, Henri of Navarre became one of Philip Sidney's closest friends after his visit to Navarre (in southern France) in 1572. They stayed in touch for the rest of Philip's life. As Gary Waller explains, "When Sidney visited France in the 1570s he met a number of the members of the palace academy centered on Marguerite de Navarre. . . . The developments at Wilton in the 1580s, then, were an attempt on the part of the Sidneys to instigate a revival of English aristocratic culture. For her own part, in providing Wilton's hospitality and its unique atmosphere of these crucial years of Elizabethan literature, the Countess [Mary Sidney] was also re-creating in her own, perhaps typically English, way a pattern of patronage by noble women that had flourished in Italy and France for a century or more."[12]

10 David Bevington, ed., *The Complete Works of Shakespeare,* sixth ed. (New York: Pearson Longman, 2009), A-24.
11 Richard David, ed., *The Arden Shakespeare, Love's Labor's Lost* (London: Routledge, 1994), xxx.
12 Gary F. Waller, *Mary Sidney, Countess of Pembroke: A Critical Study of Her Writings and Literary Milieu* (Salzburg: Universität Salzburg, 1979), 39.

Philip and Henri of Navarre's secretary, Ségur, visited Mary at her Wilton and Ramsbury estates in 1583.[13] Even after Philip's death, the Sidney family stayed close to the French court. Mary's younger brother Robert was chosen to go to Europe in 1593 as ambassador to Henri of Navarre.

A. H. Upham states that "the versatile career of the Countess of Pembroke was modeled considerably on that of Margaret of Navarre, the 'amiable mother of the Renaissance' in France."[14] Margaret Hannay agrees, "Before [Mary Sidney] Pembroke, no woman had achieved such a prominent public literary identity in England, although she may well have looked to France and Marguerite de Navarre as a role model."[15]

"There is every reason that Sidney's sister should have been familiar with the character of Margaret and the significance of her patronage of French letters; every reason too that she should have admired and imitated such a personality."[16] John Aubrey, not long after Mary's death, wrote, "We are now to consider it [Wilton House] within, where it will appear to have been an academy as well as palace."[17]

But the Navarre academy was not the only topical allusion in this play. "Many literary quarrels in England of the 1590s have been adduced as possible sources for Shakespeare's play [Love's Labor's Lost], especially the controversy between Thomas Nashe and Gabriel Harvey . . . ."[18] Intriguingly, both Mary's and Philip's names were involved in the decade-long Nashe-Harvey battle in print. "Whether the countess herself took any part in this quarrel, Harvey apparently wanted his readers—particularly Nashe—to think that she did," says Hannay. "If Mary Sidney was angry with Nashe, she would have had cause, quite apart from his quarrel with Harvey."[19]

---

13 Margaret Hannay, et al., eds., *The Collected Works of Mary Sidney Herbert, Countess of Pembroke*, vol. 1 (Oxford: Clarendon Press, 1998), 208.
    Also see Michael G. Brennan and Noel J. Kinnamon, *A Sidney Chronology*, (Basingstoke and New York: Palgrave Macmillan, 2003), 91.

14 A. H. Upham, *The French Influence in English Literature: From the Accession of Elizabeth to the Restoration* (New York: Columbia University Press, 1911), 58.

15 Hannay, *The Collected Works of Mary Sidney Herbert*, 24.

16 A. H. Upham, *The French Influence*, 60.

17 John Aubrey, *Aubrey's Natural History of Wiltshire*, originally written between 1656 and 1691 (Wiltshire: David & Charles Reprints, 1969), 89.

18 Bevington, *Complete Works of Shakespeare*, A-24.

19 Hannay, *Philip's Phoenix*, 141.

A number of references to people and events in the play have compelling connections to Mary. "It is possible that Shakespeare drew Holofernes [a 'pompous, conceited, ignorant village schoolmaster'] on the model of some well-known learned men of his day, like John Florio or Gabriel Harvey."[20] Mary knew both Florio and Harvey very well and had reason to mock them. She was not pleased with Florio because "the countess's literary judgment was attacked by John Florio in his dedication of Book II of Montaigne's *Essays* . . . ."[21] And Harvey, as mentioned above, had dragged her into a public literary quarrel.

In *The Poems of Robert Sidney*, the editor P.J. Croft includes an essay describing the influence of the work of Robert Sidney (Mary's younger brother) on the play *Love's Labor's Lost*. But Croft can't explain how Shakespeare would have read Robert's poetry—it was never published and the handwritten poems were circulated only within his family or, at most, to a select few who visited the family. "If a formal manuscript were presented, it seems that the Countess followed Robert's wishes in keeping it closely to herself."[22] This notebook of poems, only recently properly attributed, was inscribed "For the Countess of Pembroke."

The Tragic Plays

The earlier Shakespearean plays include *The Comedy of Errors, The Two Gentlemen of Verona, The Taming of the Shrew, Romeo and Juliet, As You Like It, Twelfth Night, A Midsummer Night's Dream*, and nine of the ten English history plays. Just after the turn of the century, the plays took a turn from light comedy and romance into the darker tragedies. Between 1601 and 1608 we get *Hamlet, Antony and Cleopatra, Othello, Macbeth, King Lear, Measure for Measure*. Dr. Charles G. Bell of St. John's College in Santa Fe calls it "The Tragic Divide." Most scholars believe the author must have gone through personally difficult and trying times during this period.

What is Mary Sidney doing in the early years of the seventeenth century? As mentioned earlier, this is a most difficult time: Her husband dies in 1601 and with him she loses much of her power, wealth, and influence. Many of those who had flocked around her

---

20 Campbell, *Reader's Encyclopedia of Shakespeare*, 471.

21 Hannay, *Philip's Phoenix*, 73.

22 P.J. Croft, *The Poems of Robert Sidney, Edited from the Poet's Autograph Notebook with Introduction and Commentary* (Oxford: Clarendon Press, 1984), 4. This book was discovered in the Warwick Castle Library in the late 1960s and properly attributed to Robert Sidney in the early 1970s.

disappear. The Earl of Essex, step-father of her niece, is captured by her brother and has his head smit off for trying to overthrow the Queen. Mary's son William is thrown in the Fleet prison for impregnating a young woman and is, as usual, embarrassingly unrepentant. Dr. Moffett, the estate physician and a member of her literary circle, dies in 1604 and is buried at Wilton. His replacement arrives, Dr. Matthew Lister, with whom she falls boldly in love (bold because it was socially disgraceful), but then she believes he is in love with her own niece, who is really having an affair with Mary's oldest son. The citizens of Cardiff rise against her, trying to pull down parts of her castle and beating her servants. She spends years in two hostile lawsuits, with no help from her oldest son in whose hereditary interests she is working.

It was around this time that her older son William stops speaking to her and her younger son Philip ingratiates himself with King James through "intimacies" with him. Philip also secretly arranges a marriage for himself. And in 1606 her 23-year-old daughter Anne dies. This was indeed a difficult and disappointing time of Mary's life, more than enough to inspire the writing of tragedies.

The English History Plays

There are ten English history plays that cover periods of time from 1199 (the opening of *King John*) to 1533 (the end of *Henry 8*). One might think history plays were a popular genre and that's why this author wrote so many. But they weren't. Shakespeare wrote more English history plays than any other dramatist. There is only one known history play written before the Shakespearean set, an anonymous one attributed to Richard Tarlton called *Famous Victories of Henry V*. David Bevington says Shakespeare "was an important innovator in the new genre of the history play" and that "the English history play as a recognizable form came into being with [the Shakespearean play] *Henry VI*." [23]

Why would an unknown upstart writer begin a body of work in an unproven form of drama? Especially a genre that not only entails such

---

23 Bevington, *Complete Works of Shakespeare*, 510. There is argument among scholars over whether the anonymous play published in 1591, *The Troublesome Raigne of John, King of England*, was earlier and used as a source or perhaps it was a "bad quarto." E. A. J. Honigmann believes *Troublesome Raigne* was based on the Shakespearean play, *King John. Troublesome Raigne* was reprinted in 1611 with "by W. Sh." on the title page, and the 1622 reprint attributed the play to "W. Shakespeare."

zealous historical research, but one that John Hayward counseled King James' son against:

> Men might safely write of others in manner of a tale, but in manner of a History, safely they could not: because, albeit they should write of men long since dead, and whose posterity is clean worn out, yet some alive, finding themselves foul in those vices, which they see observed, reproved, and condemned in others, their guiltiness maketh them apt to conceive that whatsoever the words are, the finger pointeth only at them.[24]

It is thus remarkable that Mary Sidney audaciously published her political drama, *Antonie* (a translation from Garnier). Margaret Hannay notes, "By importing Garnier's topical use of Roman history, [the Countess of] Pembroke paved the way for explicitly political history plays in English, including those of Shakespeare and Daniel."[25]

The history plays in particular indicate an intimate knowledge of life in the royal court and among noblemen. It is true that if William Shakespeare were the author, he might have picked up insider knowledge while hanging around court—once he became a famous writer and bought appropriate clothing and was even allowed to appear at court. But these history plays were some of the earliest written of the entire genre, as early as 1589; most of them were complete before Shakespeare had time to become well known and allowed at court.

Curious about Mary Sidney's connections with the history plays, I procured copies of her genealogy (the one her father commissioned when she married Henry Herbert) from the Bodleian Library in Oxford, England. I entered Mary's lineage into a genealogy program and I researched every family member. I also researched every historical person in the ten English history plays. Then I condensed a huge amount of data into a list.

Opposite is a list of Mary Sidney's relatives who appear in two of the history plays (the rest of the plays are in Appendix D). The code for the relationship is simple: "1C 2R" means that person is her first cousin (1C), 2 times removed (2R), or two generations ago, as shown on the previous page. "3G Grandmother" means that person is the great-great-great grandmother of Mary Sidney. The farther back in time the history play took place, the more removed the relatives are, of course.

---

24 Rebecca Lemon, "The Faulty Verdict in 'The Crown v. John Hayward,'" in *Studies in English Literature 1500–1900*, 41:1 (2001), 109–32.

25 Hannay, *Collected Works of Mary Sidney Herbert*, 39.

King John

Character	Relation to Mary Sidney
King John	11G Grandfather
Queen Eleanor	12G Grandmother
Prince Henry, afterward Henry 3	10G Grandfather
Arthur Plantagenet	1C 12R
Constance of Brittany	12G Aunt
William Marshall, 1st Earl of Pembroke	12G Uncle
Geoffrey FitzPeirs, 4th Earl of Essex	10G Grandfather
William Longsword, 3rd Earl of Salisbury	12G Uncle
Roger Lord Bigot, 2nd Earl of Norfolk	11G Grandfather
Hubert de Burgh	--
Philip, King of France	--
Lewis, the Dauphin	*married to Mary's 1C 12R*
Blanche of Castile	1C 12R
Cardinal Pandulph	--

mentioned in the play:

Richard the Lionheart	12G Uncle
Geoffrey Plantagenet, 3rd son of Henry 2	12G Uncle

Richard 2

Character	Relation to Mary Sidney
King Richard 2	1C 7R
Queen Isabel	*(by marriage)*
John of Gaunt, Duke of Lancaster	6G Grandfather
Eleanor de Bohun, Duchess of Gloucester	7G Aunt
Edmund of Langley, 1st Duke of York	7G Uncle
Duchess of York, mother of Aumerle	7G Aunt
Edward of Norwich, Duke of Aumerle	1C 7R
Henry Bolingbroke, Duke of Hereford, afterward King Henry 4	6G Uncle (half)
Thomas Mowbray, 1st Duke of Norfolk	5G Grandfather
Thomas Holland, Duke of Surrey	2C 5R
John Montacute, 3rd Earl of Salisbury	*his son married Mary's 2C 5R*
Thomas Lord Berkeley	6G Grandfather
Sir Henry Green	4G Uncle
Sir John Bushy	--
Sir William (or John) Bagot	--
Henry Percy, 1st Earl of Northumberland	7G Uncle
Henry Percy, called Hotspur	1C 7R
William Lord Ross	*married to 1C 7R*
William, 5th Baron Willoughby de Ersby	6G Uncle
Walter Lord Fitzwater	*very distantly related*
Thomas Marke, Bishop of Carlisle	--
William de Colchester, Abbot of Westminster	--
Thomas Holland, Lord Marshall	2C 5R
Sir Stephen Scroop (Scrope)	*unclear*
Sir Piers of Exton	--

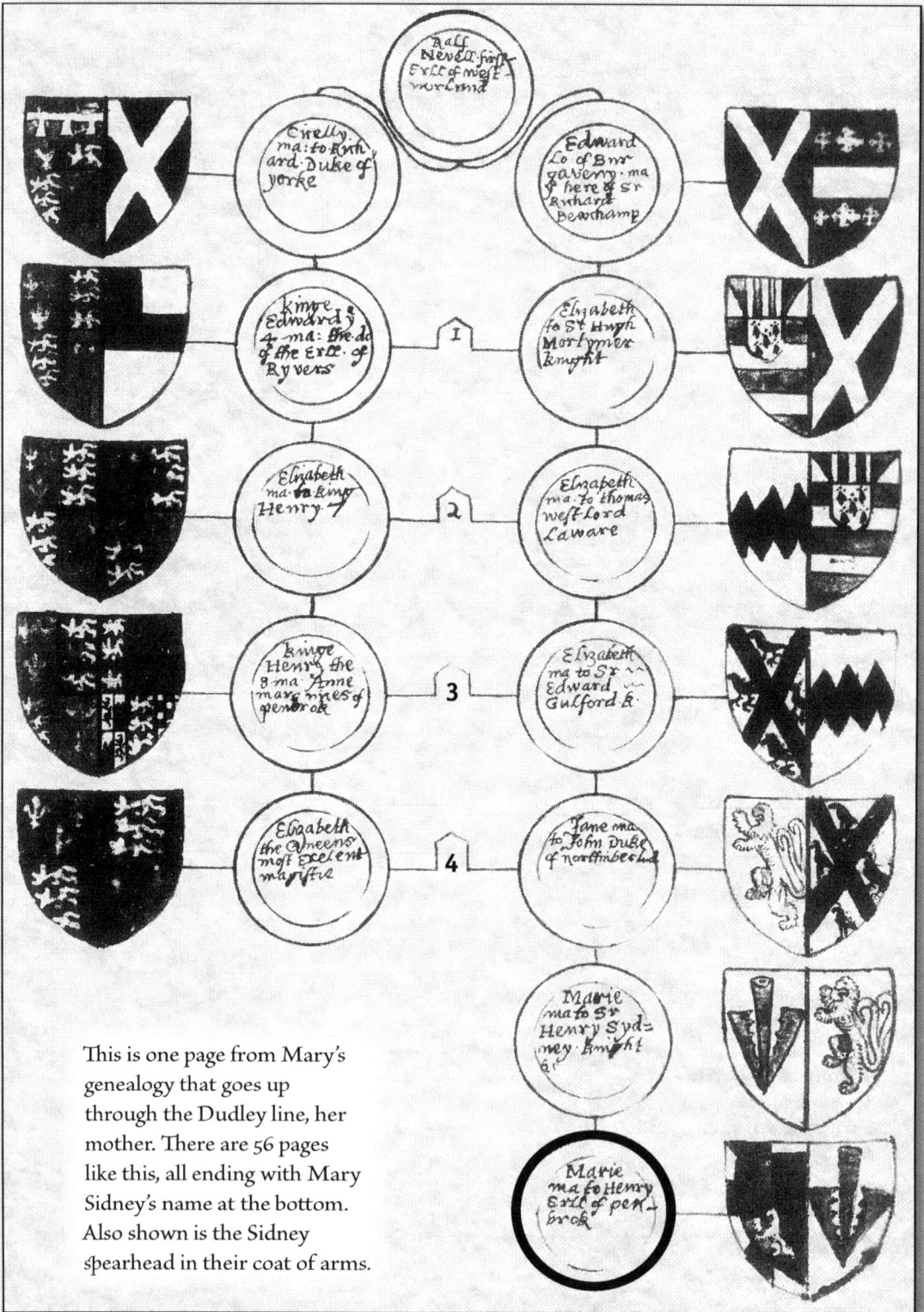

This is one page from Mary's genealogy that goes up through the Dudley line, her mother. There are 56 pages like this, all ending with Mary Sidney's name at the bottom. Also shown is the Sidney spearhead in their coat of arms.

Ralph Neville,
first Earl of Westmorland
father

Cecily [Neville],   ←siblings→   Edward [Neville],
married to Richard [Plantagenet],   Lord of Bergavenny, married the heir
Duke of York   of Sir Richard Beauchamp

King Edward the 4   ←first cousins→   Elizabeth [Neville]
married [Elizabeth Woodville]   married to Sir
the daughter of the Earl of Rivers   Hugh Mortimer, Knight

Elizabeth [of York]   ←second cousins→   Elizabeth [Mortimer]
married to   married to Thomas West,
King Henry 7   Lord Lawarre

King Henry the 8   ←third cousins→   Elizabeth [West]
married Anne [Boleyn],   married to
Marchioness of Pembroke   Sir Edward Guildford, knight

Elizabeth the Queen's   ←fourth cousins→   Jane [Guildford]
most excellent majesty   married to John [Dudley],
Duke of Northumberland

Mary [Dudley]
married to Sir Henry Sidney, knight

Mary [Sidney]
married to Henry [Herbert],
Earl of Pembroke

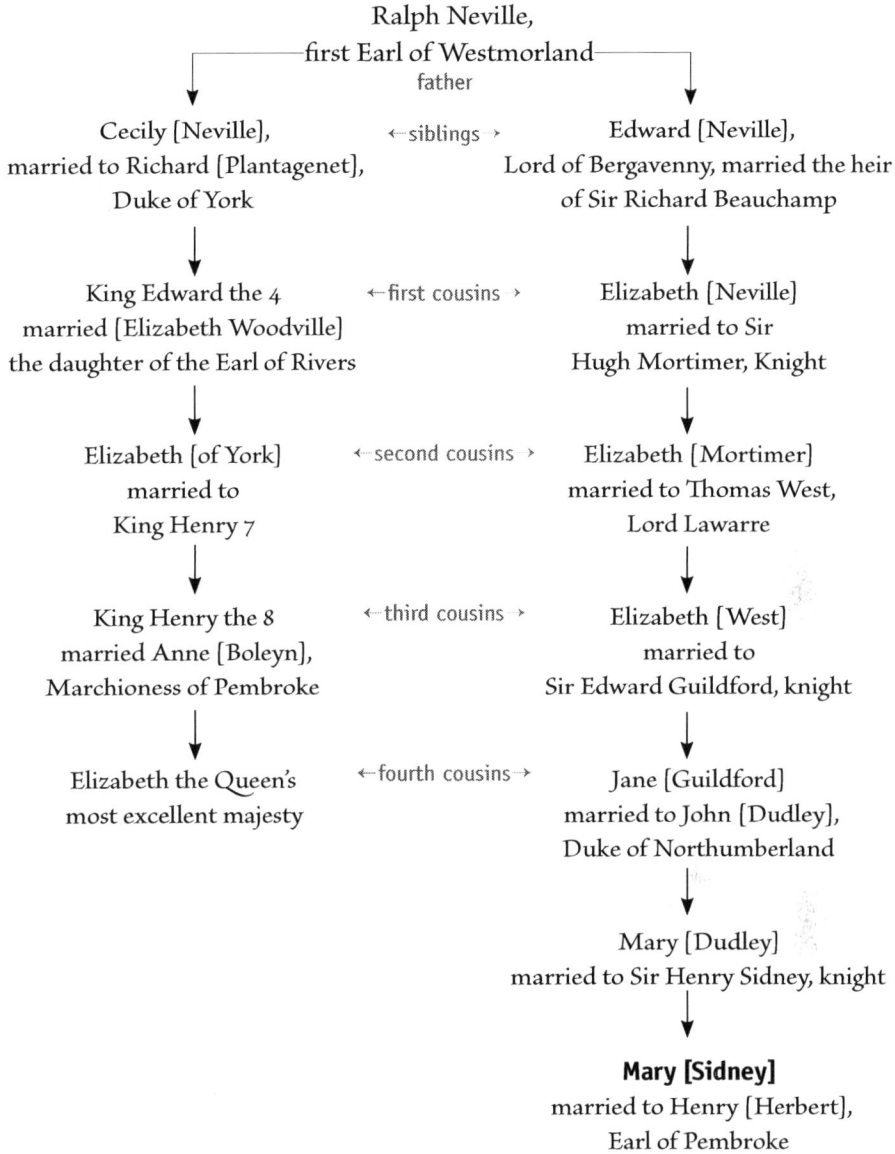

Above is a clarification of the page, shown opposite, of Mary Sidney's genealogy. Every person in the left-hand column, straight above, appears in one or more of the history plays.

This chart makes it easy to see how Mary is related to anyone else. For instance, you see above that Queen Elizabeth is Mary's fourth cousin (horizontal), twice removed (vertical).

As you can see, a large number of the noblemen and women in these plays are directly related to Mary Sidney. The aristocracy was a fairly large group: In Queen Elizabeth's time, there was one duke, two marquises, twenty-three earls, three viscounts, and fifty barons, and this group did not include the many untitled aristocrats such as Mary's father, Henry Sidney, and her brother Philip. Each day 133 court officials and their servants were entitled to dine in the Great Hall.

Holinshed wrote in 1587 about the court of King Richard 2, who reigned from 1377 to 1399: "He kept the greatest port and maintained the most plentiful house that ever any king in England did either before his time or since. For there resorted daily to his court above ten thousand persons that had meat and drink there allowed them."[26] Ten thousand is probably an exaggeration, but it indicates that the royal courts about which these plays are written include many more people than are mentioned in the plays.

But not everyone was related to everyone, as is so commonly believed. In all this research, I found almost no one from Mary's father's side, the Sidney family, showing up in the plays, nor many of their direct relations in the court system.

The Historical Records and How They Changed

It is interesting to note which historical persons this playwright chose to include in the plays and how they have been changed between the source material and the plays. For instance, in *Richard 2*, Henry Percy, the 1st Earl of Northumberland, is much more prominent in the play than in the historical record. Yet the playwright "omits the blackest of all Northumberland's acts, his perjury at Conway."[27] This Northumberland was not only Mary's 7G Uncle, but the title was in her family; her grandfather was the Duke of Northumberland (as shown on the previous two pages).

Also in *Richard 2*, "The character and behavior of Richard's uncle, John of Gaunt, Duke of Lancaster, constitute one of the most marked departures from Holinshed, and one of the greatest things in the play.

---

26 W. G. Boswell-Stone, *Shakespeare's Holinshed: The Chronicles and the Historical Plays Compared* (1896; reprint, New York, London: Benjamin Blom, Inc., 2003), 119.

27 Peter Ure, ed., The Arden Shakespeare, *King Richard II* (Surrey: Thomas Nelson & Sons Ltd., 1998), xxxiii.

... The Gaunt of Shakespeare is a father and patriot of grandiose stature, a prophet whose dying speech on England attracted the attention of the anthologist (for *England's Parnassus*) as early as 1600. Where did Shakespeare get this utterly unhistorical Duke of Lancaster?"[28] John of Gaunt, Duke of Lancaster, is Mary's 6G grandfather.

In *1 Henry 4*, Sir Walter Blunt dresses in armor to look like King Henry 4, as did several other men on the battlefield. Mistaking him for the king, Douglas kills Blunt, as well as the other similarly dressed men. The playwright emphasizes Blunt's role; he is "a good deal more important in the play than is the simple standard-bearer we know from Holinshed."[29] Sir Walter Blunt was Mary's 7G grandfather.

In *2 Henry 4*, the playwright attributes a particularly cold-blooded and treacherous deed to Bedford, brother of the king. Historically, this treachery was implemented by the Earl of Westmorland, Mary's 5G grandfather—but the author diverts it to someone else.

Although Orleans and Rouen were *not* recovered by the English as portrayed in *1 Henry 6*, "Shakespeare's intention is to suggest that France is lost through England's political divisions at home, not through any failure on the part of Lord Talbot. Shakespeare exalts Talbot's might and chivalry (hence the [invented] scene with the Countess of Auvergne) . . . ."[30] Lord Talbot and his son are Mary's 4G grandfather and 3G grandfather. As you can see by the contemporaneous comment shown to the right, the Shakespearean play is what positions Talbot in history as one of greatest heroes.

The Welsh Captain Fluellen, invented by Shakespeare, is thought to be based on Davy Gam, grandfather of William Herbert, 1st Earl of Pembroke in the Herbert house.

The murder in *3 Henry 6* of Richard, 3rd Duke of York, is much more emotional, powerful, and unforgettable than stated in the original historical source. York was Mary's 5G uncle.

In *Henry 8* there is a clear and elaborate reference to the Field of the Cloth of Gold, the meeting place where Henry 8 met the King of France, an event at which Mary's grandfather was present.

How it would have joyed brave Talbot (the terror of the French) to think that after he had lain two hundred years in his tomb, he should triumph again on the stage, and have his bones new embalmed with the tears of ten thousand spectators (at least) who, in the Tragedian that represents his person, imagine they behold him fresh bleeding?
Thomas Nashe
Pierce Pennilesse, 1592

---

28 Ibid., xxxiv.

29 John Julius Norwich, *Shakespeare's Kings: The Great Plays and the History of England in the Middle Ages: 1337–1485* (New York: Touchstone, Simon & Schuster, 1999), 145.

30 Bevington, *Complete Works of Shakespeare*, A-36.

The significance of these associations (and more) is yet to be determined, but it is worth considering how much of the historical material was Mary Sidney's birthright. Her brother Philip argues, in his *Defense of Poesie*, that "a feigned example hath as much force to teach as a true example," in that a dramatic presentation of a character as he *could* be is preferable to the literal imperfections of a historical figure, and the poet can beautify the historical action "both for further teaching, and more delighting . . . under the authority of his pen." Essentially, Philip prescribes that literature or drama is a better teacher than historical records. If Mary Sidney is the author of these plays, she carried this advice in her heart and work.

Part Five

The Women

I grant I am a woman, but withal
A woman that Lord Brutus took to wife;
I grant I am a woman, but withal
A woman well-reputed, Cato's daughter.
Think you I am no stronger than my sex,
Being so father'd and so husbanded?
Tell me your counsels, I will not disclose 'em:
I have made strong proof of my constancy,
Giving myself a voluntary wound
Here, in the thigh: can I bear that with patience.
And not my husband's secrets?

Portia in *Julius Caesar*, 2.1.293–303

Methinks a woman of this valiant spirit
Should, if a coward heard her speak these words,
Infuse his breast with magnanimity
And make him, naked, foil a man at arms.

Prince Edward, speaking of Queen Margaret, his mother,
as she leads the battle in 3 Henry 6, 5.4.39–42

The catastrophe of every play is caused always
by the folly or fault of a man; the redemption,
if there be any, is by the wisdom and virtue of
a woman, and, failing that, there is none.

John Ruskin,
Sesame and Lilies, 1865

Shakespeare was the first who understood
woman. If anyone doubts this, let him read
the women's characters in other men's plays,
and then come back to Shakespeare to
understand the human being.

Charlotte Carmichael Stopes, 1889

Shakespeare wholeheartedly believed
in the superiority of women.

Harold Bloom, in *Romeo and Juliet* lecture, 1998

12 *Do you not know I am a woman?*

Rosalind in *As You Like It*

THE WOMEN OF THE SHAKESPEAREAN PLAYS defy their fathers to marry the men they choose, defy their husbands when they feel it necessary, disguise themselves as men to accomplish what needs to be done, and regularly make fools of foolish men. They show themselves to be women of strength, intelligence, resilience, and independence in an Elizabethan/Jacobean male-dominated society where women were still considered property.

God made him, and therefore let him pass for a man.
Portia in *The Merchant of Venice*, 1.2.54

What is particularly interesting in the plays is the underlying thread of strength, wit, education, and intelligence in the female characters, even the minor ones, that underpins both plot and narrative of the plays and gives the group of women a collective power not often recognized. The creative ways in which these women gain their power is not merely a series of coincidences, but a pattern created by the author.

Please, understand that I am certainly *not* implying that a man is not capable of writing about women in this way, but we must consider this thought: If the Shakespearean plays present women in a manner *different from all other contemporary writers*, it just might be a clue that the author is different—in a significant way—from all other contemporary writers.

Froward Females

In an issue of *Shakespeare* magazine sponsored by Cambridge University Press and Georgetown University, the foreword to a series of articles about "Shakespeare's Froward Females" includes these statements:

> It is interesting, amazing really, that within this context [of the Elizabethan and Jacobean cultures] we see in Shakespeare's plays a number of women who defy male domination. They choose to avoid the time-honored path to marriage, they choose to find their own path to marriage, or they choose to follow their own consciences rather than obey a husband or father or male authority figure . . . . They know what society expects of them, they know what particular men expect of them, but they choose another course and—for a time at least—they are successful.[1]

In a different article in the same magazine:

> Shakespeare's women have the reputation of being unruly, and indeed many of them have minds of their own. They may defy authority, get what they want, and sometimes dominate the action. But what they think, what they want, and what they do can only be successful if they operate within limits acceptable to the admittedly changing social expectations of their time.[2]

The author of the plays was singular among writers of the day, creating complex female characters who defied and defined the mores. Anne Barton states in *The Riverside Shakespeare:*

> Shakespeare's sympathy with and almost uncanny under-standing of women characters is one of the distinguishing features of his comedy, as opposed to that of most of his contemporaries. His heroines not only tend to overshadow their male counterparts, as Rosalind overshadows Orlando, Julia Proteus, or Viola Orsino: they adumbrate and urge throughout the play values which, with their help, will triumph in the new, more enlightened society of the end.[3]

1   Wendy Greenhill and Paul Wignall, introduction to "Shakespeare's Froward Females: Women Who Defy Male Domination," in *Shakespeare,* 2:2 (Spring 1998), 7.
2   Jeanne Addison Roberts, "Are Shakespeare's Women Unruly?" in *Shakespeare,* 2:2 (Spring 1998), 11.
3   Anne Barton, *The Riverside Shakespeare* (Boston: Houghton Mifflin, 1974), 107.

In the book *Seven Shakespeares,* Gilbert Slater shows a reflection of Mary Sidney's position as a lady governing several estates and as a woman by birth and marriage involved in a politically powerful family, as he sees it in *Coriolanus*:

> All the political wisdom displayed by the Patricians in the play was concentrated in the person of Volumnia. Shakespeare's attitude in this play was, I think, that of a lady accustomed, in the absence of her lord on State business, to manage his estates, thus mastering the principles of government in a relatively small field, and accustomed also to discuss State affairs confidentially with relatives in Elizabeth's service.[4]

Professor Juliet Dusinberre concludes her thought-provoking book, *Shakespeare and the Nature of Women,* with this:

> Shakespeare saw men and women as equal in a world which declared them unequal. He did not divide human nature into the masculine and the feminine, but observed in the individual woman or man an infinite variety of union between opposing impulses. To talk about Shakespeare's women is to talk about his men, because he refused to separate their worlds physically, intellectually, or spiritually. Where in every other field understanding of Shakespeare's art grows, reactions to his women continually recycle, *because critics are still immersed in preconceptions which Shakespeare discarded about the nature of women.*[5] [emphasis added]

At a time when contemporaries created few memorable parts for women, the author of these plays opened a window into the complexity of human experience—as often through the eyes of the quiet and unassuming women as through the vital, outspoken ones.

On the following pages are more than fifty of the female characters in the plays with brief descriptions of their courageous acts—some bold, some subtle. There are several engaging patterns in their actions that are worth further discussion.

4 Gilbert Slater, *Seven Shakespeares* (Oxford: Kemp Hall Press, Ltd., 1931), 218.
5 Juliet Dusinberre, *Shakespeare and the Nature of Women,* 2nd ed. (New York: St. Martin's Press, Inc., 1996), 308.

Woman	Play	Description
Juliet	*Romeo and Juliet*	She defies her mother and father to marry the man of her choice.
Lavinia	*Titus Andronicus*	She defies her father to marry the man of her choice.
Anne Page	*The Merry Wives of Windsor*	She defies her mother and father to marry the man of her choice.
Hermia	*A Midsummer Night's Dream*	She defies her father to marry the man of her choice. She runs away into the forest at midnight.
Silvia	*The Two Gentlemen of Verona*	She defies her father to marry the man of her choice. Her father locks her in a tower; she escapes and is captured by outlaws.
Bianca	*The Taming of the Shrew*	She defies her father to marry the man of her choice.
Perdita	*The Winter's Tale*	She defies her lover's father to marry the man of her choice.
Imogen	*Cymbeline*	She defies her father and wicked stepmother to marry the man of her choice. She dresses as a man, runs away, and later joins the Roman army.
Jessica	*The Merchant of Venice*	She defies her father to marry the man of her choice. She dresses as a man and runs away.
Portia	*The Merchant of Venice*	She dresses as a man—a judge—and wins an eminent court case. She is the head of a large estate. She manipulates and shames her new husband for his fickleness.
Nerissa	*The Merchant of Venice*	She dresses as a man—a law clerk—to appear in court. She manipulates and shames her new husband for his fickleness.
Rosalind	*As You Like It*	She dresses as a man, runs away into the forest, buys property, arranges the forest society, and marries the man of her choice.
Viola	*Twelfth Night*	She dresses as a man, takes a job, and marries the man of her choice.
Joan of Arc	*1 Henry 6*	She dresses as a man and leads armies into battle. In this play she possibly has lovers.

Woman	Play	Description
Julia	*The Two Gentlemen of Verona*	She dresses as a man and runs away. She is a steadfast woman scorned by an inconstant lover.
Helena	*A Midsummer Night's Dream*	She is a steadfast woman scorned by an inconstant lover. She runs away into the forest at midnight.
Celia	*As You Like It*	She runs away from her father to be true to herself and to her girlfriend. She marries the man of her choice.
Cordelia	*King Lear*	She defies her father to be true to herself.
Olivia	*Twelfth Night*	She runs an estate and marries the man of her choice.
Beatrice	*Much Ado About Nothing*	She is a brilliant woman who wittily chooses not to marry—but eventually does marry the man of her choice. Against several powerful men, she remains true to her female cousin.
Helena	*All's Well That Ends Well*	With her medical knowledge, she cures a king of a fatal disease that his male doctors have been unable to treat. She travels from Paris to Florence as a pilgrim. She manipulates events to marry the man of her choice.
Isabella	*Measure for Measure*	She is a noble, virtuous woman who manipulates a powerful leader. She dupes a man with the bed-trick. There is no indication that she chooses to accept the twice-offered marriage proposal from the Duke.
Diana	*All's Well That Ends Well*	She conspires to hoodwink a profligate womanizer and plays the bed-trick on him.
Maria	*Twelfth Night*	She devises a plot to make a fool of a man.
Mrs. Page	*The Merry Wives of Windsor*	She is a middle-aged woman, wise and witty, who humiliates a seedy knight. She defies her husband's preference of a marriage choice for her daughter.

Woman	Play	Description
Princess of France & her ladies Rosaline, Maria, and Katharine	*Love's Labor's Lost*	The Princess of France is the political emissary for her country. These self-possessed women baffle and torment the men. They consign the men to a year of meditation, celibacy, and good deeds before they will even consider marrying them.
Regan and Goneril	*King Lear*	These indomitable, power-hungry sisters defy their father and husbands. Each takes a lover.
Queen Margaret	*1, 2, 3 Henry 6* and *Richard 3*	She rules her husband, leads an army into battle for the sake of her son, murders the usurper, takes a lover, and prophesies truths.
Queen Elizabeth (Grey)	*3 Henry 6* and *Richard 3*	She refuses the sexual advances of the King until he marries her and then manipulates life at court for the betterment of her family. She scorns Richard 3 and refuses him her daughter.
Constance of Bretagne	*King John*	She goes into battle for the sake of her son. Her intense grief over the imminent death of her son is scorned by the men.
Eleanor of Aquitaine	*King John*	Almost eighty years old, she marches off to lead the battle front in France.
Volumnia	*Coriolanus*	She rules the country while her son is away. She saves Rome from destruction by controlling her son, a powerful warrior.
Cleopatra	*Antony and Cleopatra*	She is a powerful ruler of her country. She loves whom she pleases and takes her own life rather than become a Roman trophy.
Fulvia	*Julius Caesar*	She leads a Roman army into war and is first on the field.
Tamora, Queen of the Goths	*Titus Andronicus*	She leads an army, loves whom she pleases, fights for her sons, orders murders to avenge the slaughter of her first-born child.
Queen Katherine of Aragon	*Henry 8*	She is a virtuous, steadfast woman who perseveres with grace through her husband's perfidy.
Katharina	*The Taming of the Shrew*	A complex woman who defies men and their marriage plans for her until "wooed" by one of her own mettle.

Woman	Play	Description
Lady Macbeth	*Macbeth*	She has the strength and mettle "of a man" to do what needs to be done to have power. She begs to have her feminine nature removed so she would have the capacity to be cruel.
Portia and Calpurnia	*Julius Caesar*	Their quiet wisdom and family values are ignored by their husbands. Portia commits suicide by holding hot coals in her mouth to avoid the shame of her husband's defeat.
Adriana and her sister Luciana	*The Comedy of Errors*	They debate "obedience" to a husband vs. "servitude."
Mistress Quickly	*1 & 2 Henry 4, Henry 5*	She runs a successful business, a tavern.
Mistress Quickly	*The Merry Wives of Windsor*	She takes advantage of all the men and makes buffoons of them.
Paulina	*The Winter's Tale*	Strong and undaunted, she stands up to powerful men, including the King. She keeps a secret with another woman for fifteen years, until the oracle is proven true.
Charmian	*Antony and Cleopatra*	Her loyalty to her woman-friend is so strong that she commits suicide with Cleopatra.
Iris	*Antony and Cleopatra*	Her loyalty to her woman-friend is so strong that she falls down dead in anticipation of dying in solidarity with Cleopatra.
Hero	*Much Ado About Nothing*	She is a virtuous woman unjustly accused of gross infidelity by her fiancé and thus also spurned by her own father and Don Pedro.
Hermione	*The Winter's Tale*	She is a virtuous wife unjustly accused of infidelity by a jealous husband. With her waiting woman, she secludes herself for fifteen years, until exonerated.
Mrs. Ford	*The Merry Wives of Windsor*	She is a virtuous wife unjustly accused by a jealous husband, whom she brings around with humor and a good nature. She also humiliates a lecherous and sleazy knight.
Desdemona	*Othello*	She is a virtuous wife unjustly accused by her insanely jealous husband. She defies her father and society to marry the man of her choice.

Another way of looking at the women

Below is the same list of women, just organized differently.

Women who defy their fathers to marry the men they choose

Desdemona in *Othello*.

Juliet in *Romeo and Juliet*.

Anne Page in *The Merry Wives of Windsor*.

Hermia in *A Midsummer Night's Dream*.

Silvia in *The Two Gentlemen of Verona*.

Bianca in *The Taming of the Shrew*.

Perdita in *The Winter's Tale* (defies her lover's father).

Imogen in *Cymbeline*.

Lavinia in *Titus Andronicus*.

Jessica in *The Merchant of Venice*.

Women who dress as men

Imogen in *Cymbeline*, to run away from her father
and stepmother and later to join the Roman army.

Jessica in *The Merchant of Venice*, to run away from her father.

Portia in *The Merchant of Venice*, as a judge to win a court case.

Nerissa in *The Merchant of Venice*, to act as law clerk in court.

Rosalind in *As You Like It*, to run away from her uncle
into the forest where she buys property.

Viola in *Twelfth Night*, to get a job.

Joan of Arc in *1 Henry 6*, to lead battles.

Julia in *The Two Gentlemen of Verona*, to run away
from her father and follow her lover.

Steadfast women who are scorned by inconstant lovers

Helena in *A Midsummer Night's Dream*.

Queen Katherine of Aragon in *Henry 8*.

Julia in *The Two Gentlemen of Verona*.

Helena in *All's Well that Ends Well*.

**Virtuous women who are unjustly accused of infidelity
by jealous husbands (or fiancé)**

Desdemona in *Othello*.

Hero in *Much Ado About Nothing*.

Hermione in *The Winter's Tale*.

Mrs. Ford in *The Merry Wives of Windsor*.

Imogen in *Cymbeline*.

Leaders of armies

Tamora, Queen of the Goths in *Titus Andronicus*.

Queen Margaret in *3 Henry 6* and *Richard 3*.

Constance of Bretagne in *King John*.

Eleanor of Aquitaine, eighty years old, in *King John*.

Cleopatra in *Antony and Cleopatra*.

Fulvia in *Julius Caesar*.

Women who make fools of men or expose them

Maria in *Twelfth Night.*
Mrs. Page in *The Merry Wives of Windsor.*
Mrs. Ford in *The Merry Wives of Windsor.*
Mrs. Quickly in *The Merry Wives of Windsor.*
Princess of France and her ladies in *Love's Labor's Lost.*
Diana and Helena in *All's Well that Ends Well.*
Isabella and Marianna in *Measure for Measure.*
Paulina and Hermione in *The Winter's Tale.*
Portia and Nerissa in *The Merchant of Venice.*

Female Relationships

It is thought-provoking to take a look at the close female-female relationships this author has created. As Virginia Woolf points out in 1929 in *A Room of One's Own*, "I tried to remember any case in the course of my reading where two women are represented as friends." This list is especially interesting when compared to the male-male relationships as described at the end of this chapter.

Rosalind and Celia in *As You Like It.*
Volumnia, Virgilia, and Valeria in *Coriolanus.*
Queen Margaret, Queen Elizabeth, Queen Ann,
    and the Duchess of York in *Richard 3.*
Maria and Olivia in *Twelfth Night.*
Julia and Silvia in *The Two Gentlemen of Verona.*
Juliet and her Nurse in *Romeo and Juliet.*

The asterisks* below indicate a female who was not in the original source material; the playwright added these women so as to create close relationships.

Adriana and Luciana* (sisters) in *The Comedy of Errors.*
Portia and Nerissa* in *The Merchant of Venice.*
Desdemona and Emilia* in *Othello.*
Hero and Beatrice* in *Much Ado About Nothing.*
Cleopatra with Charmian* and Iras* in *Antony and Cleopatra.*
Hermione and Paulina* in *The Winter's Tale.* ·

Three of the four plays that use original plots all depend on women and their close relationships for the story.

Hermia and Helena in *A Midsummer Night's Dream.*
The Princess of France and her maids of honor, Rosaline, Maria,
    and Katherine, in *Love's Labor's Lost.*
Mistress Ford and Mistress Page in *The Merry Wives of Windsor.*

Women in War

During scenes of war and battles, it is striking how often Shakespeare mentions mothers, daughters, children, babes, wives, and women in general. This is in notable contrast to the work of Shakespeare's contemporaries, as in both parts of Christopher Marlowe's *Tamburlaine*, or *The Battle of Alcazar*, attributed to George Peele, or *A Larum for London* by George Gascoigne. The author of the Shakespearean plays is much more conscious of the effect of war on females than any of the contemporary (male) authors and is virulently anti-war. The rape and defilement of women is regularly shown as one of the most horrid consequences of war. These are just a few of more than fifty examples:

*For many a thousand **widows***
*Shall this his mock mock out of their **dear husbands,***
*Mock **mothers from their sons,***
*And some are yet **ungotten and unborn***
That shall have cause to curse the Dauphin's scorn.
Henry 5, *Henry 5*, 1.2

*And in my conduct **shall your ladies come;***
From whom you now must steal and take no leave,
*For there will be **a world of water shed***
Upon the parting of your wives and you.
Glendower, *1 Henry 4*, 3.1

But if the cause be not good, the King himself
hath a heavy reckoning to make,
when all those legs and arms and heads,
chopped off in battle, shall join together
at the latter day and cry all,
"We died at such a place," some swearing,
some crying for a surgeon, some upon
their wives left poor behind them,
some upon the debts they owe,
some upon their children rawly left.
I am afeard there are few die well
that die in a battle . . .
Williams, *Henry 5*, 4.1

*If you do fight **in safeguard of your wives,***
***Your wives shall welcome** home the conquerors;*
*If you do **free your children from the sword,***
***Your children's children** quit it in your age.*
Richmond, *Richard 3*, 5.3

Let them break your backs with burdens,
take your houses over your heads,
ravish your wives and daughters
before your faces . . .
Jack Cade, *2 Henry 6*, 4.8

*Making the **mother, wife and child** to see*
***The son, the husband and the father** tearing*
His country's bowels out.
Volumnia, *Coriolanus*, 5.3

Posterity, await for wretched years,
*When **at their mothers' moist eyes babes shall suck,***
Our isle be made a nourish of salt tears,
And none but women left to wail the dead.
Duke of Bedford, *1 Henry 6*, 1.1

He is come to open
The purple testament of bleeding war;
But ere the crown he looks for live in peace,
Ten thousand bloody crowns of mothers' sons
Shall ill become the flower of England's face,
*Change the complexion **of her maid-pale peace***
To scarlet indignation, and bedew
Her pastures' grass with faithful English blood.
Richard 2, *Richard 2*, 3.3

In one speech, Henry 5 paints three images of virgins and daughters being raped:

And the flesh'd soldier, rough and hard of heart,
In liberty of bloody hand shall range
*With conscience wide as hell, **mowing like grass***
Your fresh-fair virgins and your flowering infants.
. . . .
What is 't to me, when you your selves are cause,
If your pure maidens fall into the hand
Of hot and forcing violation?
. . . .
If not, why, in a moment look to see
The blind and bloody soldier with foul hand
Defile the locks of your shrill-shrieking daughters . . .
Henry 5, *Henry 5*, 3.3

Women who Travel

Traveling for women, especially single women, has been dangerous every day and every where throughout history and around the world. There were times in Elizabethan England when it was actually forbidden by law. Even when not legally forbidden, "The female traveler was a woman at risk, unceasingly liable of breaching decorum, if not also natural and divine law."[6] So it is a bit surprising to see how many women this playwright bravely sends out into the world. Most often they are accompanied by men, which is of course practical, but some of them venture out alone. This list does not yet include the women in the history plays who travel.

Julia in *Two Gentlemen of Verona* dresses as a man and travels from Verona to Milan.

Helena in *All's Well that Ends Well* travels from Roussillon, a Catalan province in what was then Spain, to Paris and back again. Then she dresses as a pilgrim and travels to Florence, Italy, and back again.

Diana and the Widow in *All's Well that Ends Well* travel from Florence, Italy, to Roussillon, France.

Rosalind and Celia in *As You Like It* travel from the luxurious royal court out into the Forest of Ardennes, where these "female travelers effect cultural change."[7]

Viola in *Twelfth Night* was traveling on a ship when it was wrecked.

Volumnia and Valeria, with her little boy, in *Coriolanus*, travel from Rome to Antium, capital of their enemy, the Volsces.

Imogen in *Cymbeline* dresses as a man and travels from the royal court, apparently in London, to Milford Haven on the Welsh coast.

Perdita in *The Winter's Tale* travels from Bohemia to Sicily.

Desdemona in *Othello* travels from her home in Venice to an army camp in Cyprus.

Portia and Nerissa in *The Merchant of Venice* travel from their coastal home to Venice and back again.

Helena and Hermia in *a Midsummer Night's Dream* run away from home out into the forest in the night.

Princess and her three maids in *Love's Labors Lost* travel from Paris, France, to Navarre, in what is now the Basque Country.

---

6   Patricia Akhimie and Bernadette Andrea, eds., *Travel and Travail: Early Modern Women, English Drama, and the Wider World* (Lincoln: University of Nebraska Press, 2018), 82.

7   Ibid., 292.

Literacy among Women

There are only four clearly illiterate characters in the entire canon—all male.[8] All the noblewomen are literate, as is to be expected—letters are exchanged, leaves of books turned down, references are made to literary figures and books, metaphors of literacy are created. What is surprising is that the playwright also portrays the lower class women reading and writing, those whom today we expect would have been illiterate.

> The Nurse in *Romeo and Juliet* makes jokes using letters of the alphabet.
> The townswomen Mrs. Ford and Mrs. Page in *The Merry Wives of Windsor* are not only literate, but they discuss the iteration of the printing process.
> Phoebe the shepherdess in *As You Like It* not only reads but can also write, and she writes poetry.
> Perdita, raised in a shepherd's cottage, reads and writes in *The Winter's Tale*.
> Mopsa and Dorcas in *The Winter's Tale* not only read text, but also read music.

This is supposedly the signature of Susanna Hall, Shakespeare's daughter, married to Dr. John Hall.

A remarkable note about this is that Shakespeare's wife, daughter Judith, and daughter Susannah's daughter each signed with an x, indicating they could not write even their own names. As mentioned earlier, there are signatures of Susanna's on two documents, but oddly, the signature uses what is called secretary hand, but women were taught the italic hand, and Susannah could not recognize her husband's handwriting. Yet the playwright assumes literacy in all classes of women.

"Dishonor not your Mothers"

Too often I hear someone spout an old canard, "There are no mothers in Shakespeare." True, there are a few plays in which fathers play a large role and mothers are absent, such as *King Lear* or *As You Like It*, but there are remarkably potent and powerful mothers throughout the canon. I find this very interesting—why are all these mothers ignored? The longest scene in *Richard 3* is three powerful women discussing the fates of their children. Tamora is certainly a mother, and what about the astounding Volumnia, or the dynamic duo of Hermione and Paulina, mothers both? Why are they ignored?

---

8 The clearly illiterate men are Jack Cade in *2 Henry 6*, Dogberry in *Much Ado About Nothing*, a servant in *Romeo and Juliet*, and a young page with six lines in *Timon of Athens*.

Mother	Play	Description
Queen Margaret	1, 2, and 3 *Henry 6*, plus *Richard 3*	She is the mother of Prince Edward, who is murdered in *3 Henry 6*. Shakespeare wrote her into four plays. She went to war to ensure her son's right to the throne. *Oh, Ned, sweet Ned, speak to thy Mother, boy.*
Duchess of York	*Richard 3*	She is the mother of the reigning monarch, King Edward 4, and his brothers, George Duke of Clarence, Richard Duke of Gloucester (the future Richard 3), and young Rutland, who is murdered in *3 Henry 6*. *Was never Mother had so dear a loss.*
Queen Elizabeth Grey	*Richard 3*	She is the mother of Princess Elizabeth (whom she marries to Richmond), the two Princes Edward and Richard (who were killed in the Tower), as well as her older sons from a previous marriage, the Marquess of Dorset and Lord Grey. *I am their Mother; who shall bar me from them?*
Queen Gertrude	*Hamlet*	What would this play be without Gertrude? Her relationship with Hamlet guides the action. *The Queen, his Mother, lives almost by his looks.*
Countess of Roussillon	*All's Well That Ends Well*	She is the mother of the scoundrel Bertram and eventually the mother-in-law of Helena. *I say I am your Mother.*
Widow Capilet	*All's Well That Ends Well*	She is the mother of Diana, in Florence, who is pursued by Bertram. *I am her Mother, sir.*
Tamora, Queen of the Goths	*Titus Andronicus*	She is the mother of Alarbus, Demetrius, Chiron, and the newborn babe, child of Aaron the Moor. The ritual sacrifice of her first-born child, Alarbus, right in front of her, is what sets in motion the vengeful deeds of an angry mother. *Rue the tears I shed, a Mother's tears in passion for her son.*
Duchess of York	*Richard 2*	She is the mother of the Duke of Aumerle. She disobeys her husband to go plead with the King to forgive her son. Her husband is willing to turn in his son for a traitor. *And wilt thou pluck my fair son from mine age, And rob me of a happy Mother's name?*

Mother	Play	Description
Lady Montague	*Romeo and Juliet*	She is the mother of Romeo. *Alas, my liege, my wife is dead to-night; Grief of my son's exile hath stopped her breath.*
Lady Capulet	*Romeo and Juliet*	She is the mother of Juliet. *O sweet my Mother, cast me not away.*
Nurse	*Romeo and Juliet*	She is the mother of Susan, who died young. *Well, Susan is with God; she was too good for me.*
Volumnia	*Coriolanus*	She is the powerful mother of Coriolanus and the only one able to save Rome from destruction. *There's no man in the world more bound to 's Mother.*
Virgilia	*Coriolanus*	She is the mother of young Martius, the son of Coriolanus. She has the quiet strength to stand up to Volumnia. *Ay, and [my womb] that brought forth this boy, To keep your name living to time.*
Lady Macduff	*Macbeth*	She is the mother of several children, including the young boy we see on stage. She is the sole protection of her children from the wrath of Macbeth. Three men abandon her. *Wisdom? To leave his wife, to leave his babes?*
Lady Macbeth	*Macbeth*	She tells us she has had at least one child. *I have given suck, and know How tender 'tis to love the babe that milks me.*
Queen Eleanor	*King John*	78 years old, she is the mother of King John. She goes to war to retain her son's throne. *With him along is come the Mother Queen, An Ate stirring him to blood and strife.*
Constance	*King John*	She is the mother of young Prince Arthur. She arranges a war to put her son on his rightful throne. Young Arthur is killed; the grief of Constance is one of the most moving scenes in all Shakespeare. *He talks to me that never had a son.*
Queen Katherine of Aragon	*Henry 8*	Queen Katherine, on her death bed, writes a letter to Henry and commends their daughter. *And a little to love her for her Mother's sake, that loved him.*

Mother	Play	Description
Lady Faulconbridge	*King John*	She is the mother of Philip the Bastard and Robert. She was "seduced" by Richard the Lionheart. Richard the Lionheart was historically gay and had no children—Shakespeare invents the scene of the mother and her two boys. *O me, 'tis my Mother: how now, good Lady?*
Mrs. Page	*The Merry Wives of Windsor*	She is the mother of William and Anne Page. She is intelligent and witty and merry and forgives her daughter, Anne, who runs off with the the man she chooses to marry. *Good Mother, do not marry me to yond fool.*
Queen Hermione	*The Winter's Tale*	She is the mother of young Mamillius, who dies as a result of his father's abuse of his mother, and the newborn Perdita, whom her father abandons to a hillside (he really wanted to burn her alive) because he unjustly believes Hermione was sleeping with his friend. For sixteen years she waits for the truth to be revealed. *. . . a great King's daughter,* *The Mother to a hopeful prince.*
Paulina	*The Winter's Tale*	One of the most remarkable among Shakespeare's remarkable characters, Paulina is the mother of three daughters. She secretly cares for Queen Hermione for sixteen years, while controlling the King's life. *[She has] three daughters: the eldest is eleven;* *The second, and the third, nine and some five.*
Thaisa	*Pericles*	She is the mother of Marina. She gives birth on a ship and is thought to have died and so is thrown overboard in a casket. But she lives and becomes a vestal in the temple of Diana until reunited with her daughter and husband. *My Mother was the daughter of a King.*
Dionyza	*Pericles*	She is the foster mother of Marina and has her own daughter Marina's age. For love of her own daughter, she attempts to have Marina murdered. *How now, Marina? Why do you keep alone?* *How chance my daughter is not with you?*

Mother	Play	Description
Emilia the Abbess	*The Comedy of Errors*	She is the mother of twins and foster mother of another set of twins. She resolves all the issues at the end of the play by the story of her shipwreck, rescue, the kidnapping of her children, and her resourcefulness. *She became a joyful Mother of two goodly sons.*
Queen	*Cymbeline*	She is the mother of Cloten. For love of her son, she attempts to marry him to her step-daughter; failing that, she plots to murder the step-daughter so her son will inherit the throne. *They dare not fight with me, because of the Queen my Mother.*

More references to mothers

There are so many *references* to mothers who might not appear in the plays, as if they are never very far from the playwright's consciousness:

- Cleopatra, as a **mother,** mentions her children in *Antony and Cleopatra.*
- Euriphile is the foster **mother** of Guiderius and Arviragus in *Cymbeline.*
- Caliban's **mother** Sycorax is talked of in *The Tempest.*
- The Duke of York mentions his **mother** Anne, married to Richard Earl of Cambridge, in *2 Henry 6.*
- Jack Cade claims his **mother** was a Plantagenet in *2 Henry 6.*
- Cassius mentions his testy **mother** in *Julius Caesar.*
- The son who has killed his father in battle thinks of his **mother** in *3 Henry 6.*
- Gloucester mentions the **mother** of his bastard son, Edmund, and Edmund mentions her as well in *King Lear.*
- Lear mentions the **mother** of Regan in *King Lear.*
- Macduff mentions the **mother** of his children and his own **mother** in *Macbeth.*
- Isabella mentions her **mother** in *Measure for Measure.*
- Launcelot Gobbo mentions his **mother,** Margery, in *The Merchant of Venice.*
- Shylock mentions Jacob's **mother** in *The Merchant of Venice.*
- Jessica mentions her **mother** in *The Merchant of Venice.*
- Slender mentions his **mother** in *The Merry Wives of Windsor.*
- Mistress Quickly mentions her **mother** in *The Merry Wives of Windsor.*

Quince mentions Thisbe's **mother** in *A Midsummer Night's Dream*.

Bottom mentions Peaseblossom's **mother** in *A Midsummer Night's Dream*.

Titania describes the **mother** of the changeling child in *A Midsummer Night's Dream*.

Charles, King of France, mentions Helen, the **mother** of Constantine in *1 Henry 6*.

Edmund Mortimer mentions both his **mother** and Richard Duke of York's **mother** in *1 Henry 6*.

Young Talbot mentions his **mother** several times, as does his father in *1 Henry 6*.

The Shepherd mentions his wife as the **mother** of Joan la Pucelle in *1 Henry 6*.

Leonato mentions his wife as **mother** to his daughter, Hero, in *Much Ado About Nothing*.

Beatrice mentions her **mother's** birth pains in *Much Ado About Nothing*.

Desdemona mentions her **mother** twice in *Othello*.

Othello mentions his **mother** several times in *Othello*.

Prospero mentions Miranda's **mother** in *The Tempest*.

Miranda mentions her own **grandmother** in *The Tempest*.

Stanley mentions the **mother** of his step-son Richmond in *Richard 3*.

Young Lucius mentions his **mother** in *Titus Andronicus*.

Aaron's babe is given to a **mother** to suckle in *Titus Andronicus*.

Priam mentions Hector's **mother** in *Troilus and Cressida*.

Launce mentions his **mother** a number of times in *Two Gentlemen of Verona*.

Leontes mentions Florizel's **mother** in *The Winter's Tale*.

Antigonus's final soliloquy before his death is all about a **mother** in *The Winter's Tale*.

Imogen speaks of her **mother** in *Cymbeline*.

Prince Hal and Falstaff both mention Hal's **mother** in *1 Henry 4*.

Sextus Pompeius of Pompey mentions Antony's **mother** in *Antony and Cleopatra*.

Anne Bullen becomes a **mother**; her baby girl, who will change the world, is brought on stage in *Henry 8*.

Posthumous Leonatus sees his dead **mother** in a dream in *Cymbeline*.

Lady Macbeth mentions being a **mother** in *Macbeth*.

Richard 2's Queen provides a striking political metaphor using **motherhood** in *Richard 2*:

> *So, Green, thou art the midwife to my woe,*
> *And Bolingbroke my sorrow's dismal heir:*
> *Now hath my soul brought forth her prodigy,*
> *And I, a gasping new-deliver'd Mother,*
> *Have woe to woe, sorrow to sorrow, join'd.*

Hecuba, wife of Priam and **mother** of many children, is mentioned as a mother in *Coriolanus, Cymbeline, Titus Andronicus*, and *Hamlet*. Although she has no lines in *Troilus and Cressida*, she is mentioned six times in the play, always in reference to being a **mother** of many.

Mothers are mentioned five times in four sonnets:
Sonnets 3, 8, 21, 143

Babes and Children

More than any other playwright of the time, "Shakespeare's interest in and observation of children and child nature from babyhood are remarkable."[9]

> *As looks the Mother on her lowly babe*
> *When death doth close his tender dying eyes,*
> *See, see the pining malady of France.*
> Joan la Pucelle in *1 Henry 6*, 3.3.47–49

> *Ah, my poor princes! Ah, my tender babes,*
> *My unblown flowers, new-appearing sweets;*
> *If yet your gentle souls fly in the air*
> *And be not fixed in doom perpetual,*
> *Hover about me with your airy wings*
> *And hear your Mother's lamentation.*
> Queen Elizabeth Grey in *Richard 3*, 4.4.9–14

> *We do not know*
> *How he may soften at the sight o' the child:*
> *The silence often of pure innocence*
> *Persuades when speaking fails.*
> Paulina in *The Winter's Tale*, 2.2.39–42

---

9 Caroline Spurgeon, *Shakespeare's Imagery and What It Tells Us* (1935; reprint, Cambridge: Cambridge University Press, 1996), 137.

Showing King Leontes his new-born daughter, Paulina describes how the baby girl looks so much like him:

> *Although the print be little, the whole matter*
> *And copy of the father—eye, nose, lip,*
> *The trick of 's frown, his fore-head, nay, the valley,*
> *The pretty dimples of his chin, and cheek, his smiles:*
> *The very mold and frame of hand, nail, finger.*
>
> Paulina in *The Winter's Tale*, 2.3.99–100

A remarkable image in *Julius Caesar* is when Pindarus mistakenly reports that Titinius has been captured, leading Cassius to insist that his slave Pindarus kill him (kill Cassius). Pindarus does so, and when Messala discovers his dead body, the metaphor is of a child and of a birth gone wrong, during which the mother dies:

> *Mistrust of good success hath done this deed.*
> *O hateful Error, Melancholy's child:*
> *Why dost thou show to the apt thoughts of men*
> *The things that are not? O Error, soon conceiv'd,*   *soon: easily*
> *Thou never com'st unto a happy birth,*
> *But kill'st the Mother that engender'd thee.*   *engender: conceive, bear, or give birth*
>
> Messala in *Julius Caesar*, 5.3.65–70

A female focus?

Just this limited display in this chapter of the women in the Shakespearean plays makes it clear that this playwright is different from all others of the time. Of course, this does not prove the author was a woman—the man named William Shakespeare certainly might have been the most forward-thinking feminist of the era, even if he did not teach his own daughters or granddaughter to write. Surely he might have been.

But then again, if there is no other playwright of the time who has such a focus on the female characters, why might that be? If "Shakespeare saw men and women as equal in a world which declared them unequal," maybe we should wonder more about why this is.[10]

---

10 Dusinberre, *Shakespeare and the Nature of Women*, 308.

Questionable Men

Shakespeare has no heroes—he has only heroines. There is not one entirely heroic figure in all his plays.

John Ruskin,
Sesame and Lilies, 1865

It's curious that so many books and articles have been written about what "William Shakespeare" thought of women, but few about what Shakespeare thought of men. When their qualities are compiled in a list, it's remarkable how many of these men are cads, scalawags, or outright villains.

Now don't get all huffy and claim I am ignoring the bad women— obviously, there are a few wicked women in the plays, otherwise the canon would not be human, and it would be bland. Shakespeare creates Regan and Goneril, Lady Macbeth, Queen Margaret, Tamora, —all remorseless (well, Lady Macbeth has some remorse). And there are some wonderful men in the plays—Albany, France, and Edgar in *King Lear;* Horatio in *Hamlet;* Adam, Orlando, and Duke Senior in *As You Like It;* Ferdinand and Gonzalo in *The Tempest;* the King's sons in *Cymbeline;* the good-natured Sir Hugh Evans in *The Merry Wives of Windsor.* The professional Fools tend to be witty and kind-hearted.

I would there were no age between ten and three-and-twenty, or that youth would sleep out the rest; for there is nothing in the between but getting wenches with child, wronging the ancientry, stealing, fighting— Hark you now!

Old Shepherd in
The Winter's Tale, 3.3.58–64

But consider the top names in the canon: Richard 3, Othello, Iago, Macbeth, Romeo, Hamlet, Claudius—murderers all, not to mention their cadres of hired killers. Consider the idea that if Shakespeare's women were—just about every one of them—as evil and despicable as the majority of men, what would critics have written over the years?

The list of characters below is not complete, nor does it include most of the history plays.

Murderers

Titus in *Titus Andronicus*
Demetrius in *Titus Andronicus*
Chiron in *Titus Andronicus*
Aaron the Moor in *Titus Andronicus*
Romeo in *Romeo and Juliet*
Tybalt in *Romeo and Juliet*
Hamlet in *Hamlet*
Claudius in *Hamlet*
Laertes in *Hamlet*
Brutus and Cassius in *Julius Caesar*
Othello in *Othello*
Iago in *Othello*
Edmund in *King Lear*
Macbeth in *Macbeth*
Richard 3 in *Richard 3*
Achilles in *Troilus and Cressida*

Overbearing and/or barbaric fathers

Capulet in *Romeo and Juliet*

Mr. Page in *The Merry Wives
of Windsor*

Egeus (encouraged by Theseus)
in *A Midsummer Night's Dream*

Shylock in *The Merchant of Venice*

Portia's dead father in *The Merchant
of Venice*

Baptista Minola in *The Taming
of the Shrew*

Duke of Milan in *Two Gentlemen*

King Lear in *King Lear*

King Cymbeline in *Cymbeline*

Prospero in *The Tempest*

Duke Frederick in *As You Like It*

Insanely jealous husbands

Othello in *Othello*

Posthumous in *Cymbeline*

Leontes in *The Winter's Tale*

Mr. Frank Ford in *The Merry Wives
of Windsor*

Pompous and pedantic men

Don Adriano de Armado in
Love's Labor's Lost

Holofernes in *Love's Labor's Lost*

Sir Nathaniel in *Love's Labor's Lost*

Robert Shallow in *The Merry Wives
of Windsor*

Malvolio in *Twelfth Night*

Lucio in *Measure for Measure*

Polonius in *Hamlet*

Drunkards

Sir John Falstaff in *1 and 2 Henry 4,
The Merry Wives of Windsor*

Sir Toby Belch in *Twelfth Night*

Sir Andrew Aguecheek in *Twelfth Night*

Christopher Sly in *Taming of the Shrew*

Cowards, liars, hypocrites, extortionists

Parolles in *All's Well that Ends Well*

Angelo in *Measure for Measure*

Bertram in *All's Well that Ends Well*

Cloten in *Cymbeline;* attempted rape

Proteus in *Two Gentlemen;* attempted rape

Sir Eglamour in *Two Gentlemen*

Iachimo in *Cymbeline*

Sir John Falstaff in *1 and 2 Henry 4* and
The Merry Wives of Windsor

Men who get women pregnant out of wedlock

Gloucester in *King Lear*

Richard the Lionheart in *King John*

Claudio in *Measure for Measure*

Launcelot Gobbo in *Merchant of Venice*

Aaron in *Titus Andronicus*

Lucio in *Measure for Measure*

Bertram, sort of, in *All's Well that Ends Well*

Fickle men

Demetrius in *A Midsummer Night's Dream*

Bassanio, a gold-digger, in *The Merchant
of Venice*

Claudio in *Much Ado About Nothing*

Don Pedro in *Much Ado About Nothing*

Leonato in *Much Ado About Nothing*

Cassio in *Othello*

Proteus in *Two Gentlemen*

Romeo in *Romeo and Juliet*

Cruel men (besides the murderers)

Antonio in *The Merchant of Venice*

Don John in *Much Ado About Nothing*

Duke of Cornwall in *King Lear*

Thersites in *Troilus and Cressida*

Chiron and Demetrius in *Titus Andronicus;*
rape and mutilation

Titus in *Titus Andronicus*

Launcelot Gobbo in *The Merchant of Venice*

Obnoxious, loudmouthed, or hot-headed

Gratiano in *The Merchant of Venice*

Dr. Caius in *The Merry Wives of Windsor*

Oswald in *King Lear*

Kent in *King Lear*

—continued

Men who usurp or kill their own brothers, or attempt to

Duke Frederick in *As You Like It*
Oliver in *As You Like It*
Sebastian in *The Tempest*
Antonio in *The Tempest*
Hamlet senior, as Ghost in *Hamlet*
Claudius in *Hamlet*
Richard 3 in *Richard 3*
Don John in *Much Ado About Nothing*

Dimwits

Abraham Slender in *Merry Wives*
Christopher Sly in *Taming of the Shrew*
Gremio and Hortensio in *Shrew*
Thurio and Launce in *Two Gentlemen*
Anthony Dull in *Love's Labor's Lost*
The six rude mechanicals in
  A Midsummer Night's Dream
Dogberry and Verges in *Much Ado*
Silvius in *As You Like It*
Sir Andrew Aguecheek in *Twelfth Night*
Ajax in *Troilus and Cressida*
Elbow and Froth in *Measure for Measure*
Borachio and Conrade in *Much Ado*
Prince Cloten in *Cymbeline*
Trinculo and Stephano in *The Tempest*

Male Relationships

It's a bit alarming to look carefully at the male-male relationships in the plays. There are some heartwarming master/servant relationships (Lear/Kent, Hamlet/Horatio, Orlando/Adam), the brothers Guiderius and Arviragus in *Cymbeline*, or the odd relationship between Antonio and Bassanio in *the Merchant of Venice* or Sebastian and Antonio in *Twelfth Night*, but many men betray or murder their best friends.

Henry 5 executes four of his friends and abandons another,
  breaking his heart.
Richard 3 has his friends murdered.
Macbeth has his best friend murdered.
Romeo inadvertently causes the murder of his best friend
  and slays his wife's kinsman and Juliet's groom.
Leontes accuses his best friend of adultery with his wife
  and plots his murder.
Hamlet has his two school friends murdered.
Othello is destroyed by his trusted friend Iago.
Tullus Aufidius betrays and murders Coriolanus.
Proteus tries to steal his best friend's girlfriend
  and attempts to rape her.
Iachimo lies to his friend Posthumous about sleeping with his wife.

And yet in the general literary criticism written about the Shakespearean canon, the normalcy of all these men acting badly tends to be unquestioned and the prevailing complexity of the women (until recently) unexamined. Why is that?

13 The Imagery in the Plays

IN HER ENLIGHTENING AND HIGHLY RESPECTED BOOK, *Shakespeare's Imagery and What It Tells Us*, Caroline Spurgeon gathers every image from every play and sonnet to categorize them in a variety of ways. She demonstrates that *mere references* to law, religion, war, etc., are quite different from *images*: "The imagery [the playwright] instinctively uses is thus a revelation, largely unconscious, given at a moment of heightened feeling, of the furniture of his mind, the channels of his thought, the qualities of things, the objects and incidents he observes and remembers, and perhaps most significant of all, those which he does not observe or remember."[1] Following are some of the results Spurgeon discovered after charting her voluminous data.

From women's eyes
this doctrine I derive:
They are the books,
the arts, the academes
That show, contain, and
nourish all the world.
Berowne, *Love's Labor's Lost*, 4.3.324–27

Kitchen and living room

"Shakespeare has an unusually large number [of images] drawn from the daily work and occupations of women in a kitchen and living room: washing glass and knives, breaking glass and cracking china, scouring, wiping, dusting, sweeping, removing spots and stains, preparing food, knitting, patching, lining, turning and remaking clothes . . . steeping, scouring, wringing, sponging, wiping, and hanging out in the sun to dry . . . ."[2]

> *The cloyèd will—*
> *That satiate yet unsatisfied desire, that tub*
> *Both fill'd and running—*
> Iachimo in *Cymbeline*, 1.6.47–49

---

1   Caroline Spurgeon, *Shakespeare's Imagery and What It Tells Us* (1935; reprint, Cambridge: Cambridge University Press, 1996).
2   Ibid., 114.

Cooking

"His interest in and acute observation of cooking operations are very marked all through his work. . . . we see how extraordinarily close is his knowledge of different kinds of cooking—the kneading, baking, boiling, mincing, broiling, stewing, frying, stuffing, larding, basting, and distilling . . . ."[3] For instance, Richard 2 discusses his imminent death, now that Bolingbroke has invaded, in a metaphor that compares a grave with a covered pie:

> *And nothing can we call our own, but Death,*
> *And that small model of the barren Earth,*
> *Which serves as paste and cover to our bones.*
> Richard in *Richard 2*, 3.2.152–154

paste and cover: a pastry shell and cover for a pie. A pie shell was called a coffin.

Hamlet creates a cooking metaphor while raging against his mother:

> *Nay, but to live*
> *In the rank sweat of an enseamèd bed,*
> *Stew'd in corruption, honeying and making love*
> *Over the nasty sty.*
> Hamlet in *Hamlet*, 3.4.93–95

enseamèd: greasy

stewed: steamed in a slow, moist heat

"That which, next to an orchard and garden, has registered itself most clearly and continuously upon his mind is the picture of a busy kitchen, and the women's work forever going on in it."[4] In *Troilus and Cressida*, no less than twelve different processes of cooking are alluded to or described.[5] Pandarus tells Troilus, "He that will have a cake out of the wheat must tarry the grinding" and the bolting [sifting] and the leavening:

> *Ay, to the leavening; but here's yet in the word "hereafter"*
> *the kneading, the making of the cake,*
> *the heating of the oven and the baking;*
> *nay, you must stay the cooling too,*
> *or you may chance burn your lips.*
> Pandarus in *Troilus and Cressida*, 1.1.14–28

---

3   Ibid., 119–120.

4   Ibid., 205

5   Ibid., Chart VII.

Sewing and mending

"Shakespeare also noticed the women's sewing and mending which he saw going on round him, and there is clear evidence of his observation of and interest in needlework in the many images he draws from it and things pertaining to it, such as a bodkin [a thick, blunt needle], a silken thread, a twist of rotten silk . . . mending, ripping up an old garment, facing, lining . . . basting . . . showing a knowledge of trimming a garment, and the way a needlewoman would set about preparing it, which is somewhat unusual."[6]

Sleep that knits up the raveled sleave of care . . .
Macbeth in *Macbeth*, 2.2.41

raveled: tangled
sleave: skein of soft floss silk

Deep clerks she dumbs; and with her needle composes
Nature's own shape, of bud, bird, branch, or berry,
That even her art sisters the natural roses;
Her inkle, silk, twin with the rubied cherry . . . .
Gower in *Pericles*, Act 5 Prologue

deep clerks: well-versed scholars
dumbs: renders speechless
inkle: linen thread

No, girl, I'll knit it up in silken strings
With twenty odd-conceited true-love knots.
Julia in *The Two Gentlemen of Verona*, 2.7.45–46

odd-conceited: strangely devised
true-love knots: an intertwined stitch that symbolizes eternal love

Nay, mock not, mock not. The body of your discourse
is sometime guarded with fragments,
and the guards are but slightly basted on neither . . . .
Benedick in *Much Ado About Nothing*, 1.1.273–76

guarded: decorated
fragments: poor rags
guards: decorations
basted: sewn on lightly and temporarily

. . . thou idle immaterial skein of sleave-silk,
thou green sarcenet flap for a sore eye, thou
tassel of a prodigal's purse, thou?
Thersites in *Troilus and Cressida*, 5.1.30–32

skein: a quantity of thread wrapped in a loose knot
sleave-silk: floss silk that is unwoven and thus worthless
sarcenet: a soft silk cloth
tassel: ornamental bunch of silk threads

6   Ibid., 124–125.

Lawn bowling

"Of all the games and exercises Shakespeare mentions—tennis, football, bowls, fencing, tilting, wrestling—there can be no doubt that bowls [lawn bowling] was the one he himself played and loved best. He has . . . more than thrice as many as from any other game . . . . Although we know the game of bowls was popular in Shakespeare's day . . . yet this image cannot be classed as a commonplace of Elizabethan writers. . . . So that Shakespeare's interest in it is unusual and is a personal characteristic."[7]

At the reference to bowling in *The Winter's Tale* (4.4.330), David Bevington points out that bowling was "a game played mainly by the aristocracy."[8] There is a topographical painting by Leonard Knyff, painted about 1700, of Mary's Wilton estate that shows an enlarged inset of the bowling green.[9] The painting can still be viewed at Wilton House.

rub: an obstacle or impediment that diverts the ball from its course

'Twill make me think the world is full of rubs,
And that my fortune runs against the bias.
Queen Isabel in *Richard 2*, 3.4.4–5

subtle ground: deceptively irregular
past the throw: overshot the mark

Nay, sometimes,
Like to a bowl upon a subtle ground,
I have tumbled past the throw . . . .
Menenius in *Coriolanus*, 5.2.22–24

bowl: small wooden ball
bias: an off-center weight inside the ball that makes it roll in an oblique or curving path

Well, forward, forward—thus the bowl should run,
And not unluckily against the bias.
Petruchio in *The Taming of the Shrew*, 4.5.24–25

7 Ibid., 110–111.

8 David Bevington, *The Complete Works of Shakespeare*, updated fourth edition (Chicago: Longman, 1997), 1237 n339. Intriguingly, the reference to this sport being one played mainly by aristocrats has been removed in subsequent editions.

9 John Bold with John Reeves, *Wilton House and English Palladianism, Some Wiltshire Houses* (London: Her Majesty's Stationery Office, 1988), 79.

War images

"Next come his war images, and in this selection of them I find nothing which indicates any direct knowledge of war or of fighting."[10] "Bacon, compared with Shakespeare, has very few 'war' images, but he definitely asserts that he strongly approves of war, and believes it to be as necessary to a State as healthy exercise to a man's body. Shakespeare hates war and condemns it . . . he constantly symbolizes it by and associates it with loud and hideous noises, with groans of dying men, with 'braying trumpets and loud churlish drums, clamors of hell.'"[11] Also see Chapter 12 regarding war images and women.

> Now for the bare-picked bone of majesty
> Doth doggèd War bristle his angry crest,
> And snarleth in the gentle eyes of Peace.
> The Bastard in *King John*, 4.3.148–150

> The King himself
> Of his wings destitute, the army broken,
> And but the backs of Britons seen, all flying
> Through a straight lane; the enemy full-hearted,
> Lolling the tongue with slaughtering, having work
> More plentiful than tools to do 't, struck down
> Some mortally, some slightly touch'd, some falling
> Merely through fear, that the straight pass was damm'd
> With dead men hurt behind, and cowards living
> To die with lengthen'd shame.
> Posthumous Leonatus in *Cymbeline*, 5.3.

> . . . all those legs and arms and heads, chopped off in a battle,
> shall join together at the Latter Day and cry all,
> "We died at such a place"—some swearing, some crying for a surgeon,
> some upon their wives left poor behind them,
> some upon the debts they owe, some upon their children rawly left.
> I am afeard there are few die well that die in a battle . . . .
> Michael Williams, soldier, in *King Henry 5*, 4.1.136–142

> What would you have me do? Go to the wars,
> would you, where a man may serve seven years
> for the loss of a leg and have not money enough
> in the end to buy him a wooden one?
> Bolt in *Pericles*, 4.6.171–74

---

10 Ibid., 36.
11 Ibid., 28–29.

The war imagery in the plays is particularly intriguing. The few mentions of tactical maneuvers are copied from the historical sources. Armed conflicts in the plays are merely described in the stage directions as "Alarums. They Fight." This playwright describes battle scenes in the form of human interactions, of connections and dissensions, of emotionally charged confrontations between individuals.

In *1 Henry 4*, Prince Hal saves his father, Henry 4, in a battle. The author's stage directions state only: "They fight. Douglas flieth." The point of the scene is not the fight, but the relationship between father and son.

In *Henry 5*, the King wanders among the soldiers at night to philosophize on life and death and the responsibilities of kingship.

In *3 Henry 6*, a young man drags a soldier he has killed onto the stage to steal his goods, only to discover it is his own father; an older man drags a soldier he has killed onto the stage to steal his goods, only to discover it is his only son. The father cries:

> *These arms of mine shall be thy winding-sheet;*
> *My heart, sweet boy, shall be thy sepulcher,*
> *For from my heart thine image ne'er shall go;*
> *My sighing breast shall be thy funeral bell . . .*
> *I'll bear thee hence and let them fight that will,*
> *For I have murder'd where I should not kill.*

Father in *3 Henry 6*, 2.5.114–22

winding sheet: a sheet in which a corpse is wrapped for burial; a shroud

sepulcher: tomb

Says Henry 6 upon seeing these events:

> *O piteous spectacle! O bloody times!*
> *Whiles lions war and battle for their dens,*
> *Poor harmless lambs abide their enmity.*
> *Weep, wretched man, I'll aid thee tear for tear;*
> *And let our hearts and eyes, like civil war,*
> *Be blind with tears, and break o'er-charg'd with grief.*

Henry 6 in *3 Henry 6*, 2.5.73–78

Also in *3 Henry 6*, Queen Margaret has Clifford murder young Rutland, son of Richard, Duke of York. When her men have captured York, she taunts him mercilessly with the murder of his son, then gives him a handkerchief steeped in Rutland's blood to wipe away his tears. It is a highly emotional exposé of the humanity and inhumanity of war, not a technical account of a particular battle. This playwright is concerned about the human relationships during wartime, not martial strategies. There is nothing in the plays that indicates the writer was ever in a battle or witnessed one, and this author clearly condemns and vilifies war. As the herald says in *King John*, "This day hath made much work for tears in many an English mother."

Animal sports

"Shakespeare's attitude as seen in his images [of animal sports] is unique among the dramatists of his time, for he shows a sympathy with and understanding of the animal's point of view and sufferings which no one else in his age approaches." [12]

> *To the which place a poor sequestered stag,*
> *That from the hunter's aim had ta'en a hurt,*
> *Did come to languish. And indeed, my lord,*
> *The wretched animal heavèd forth such groans*
> *That their discharge did stretch his leathern coat*
> *Almost to bursting, and the big round tears*
> *Cours'd one another down his innocent nose*
> *In piteous chase. And thus the hairy fool,*
> *Much markèd of the melancholy Jaques,*
> *Stood on th' extremest verge of the swift brook,*
> *Augmenting it with tears.*
> First Lord in *As You Like It*, 2.1.33–43

---

12 Spurgeon, *Shakespeare's Imagery*, 27.

Compared to contemporaries

Ms. Spurgeon makes a lengthy comparison of the images in Shakespeare's plays with those in the works of Francis Bacon, a contender for the authorship of the plays. She finds "this type of difference, betrayed unconsciously or accidentally through individual or accumulated images, is the most subtle, and to my thinking, the most irrefutable proof of individuality of authorship that can be found."[13] She sees two different world views, different experiences, an interest in and familiarity with different everyday objects, different tastes in games and sports, and even different aspects of their interest in the same subject, such as astronomy.

She also compares the work of five other playwrights: Ben Jonson, Christopher Marlowe, George Chapman, Thomas Dekker, and Philip Massinger. She is able to note some observable differences, such as that Chapman's favorite images are war and weapons; Dekker loves explosives; Jonson and Chapman are "chiefly interested in the fairly well-to-do town types, which interest Shakespeare comparatively little."[14] And Shakespeare uses imagery of children and babes seventy-five times more than does Marlowe.

Authorship cannot be proven by this kind of information, of course, but it is difficult to claim that the unconscious images a writer develops mean nothing at all.

13 Ibid., 28.
14 Ibid., 34.

Part Six

The Antagonist

*I hate ingratitude more in a man than
lying, vainness, babbling, drunkenness,
or any taint of vice . . . .*
Viola in *Twelfth Night*, 3.4.355–357

*Ingratitude, thou marble-hearted fiend,
More hideous when thou show'st thee in a child
Than the sea-monster.*
King Lear in *King Lear*, 1.4.257–259

Documented Data

- Mary Sidney's oldest son, William Herbert, became the wealthiest and most powerful man in England, second only to King James.

- William Herbert successfully changed the power structure at court by acting as bawd (pimp) for the King. As Lord Chamberlain from 1615 until his death in 1630, William controlled the printing of all plays, books, and other documents in England.

- Mary Sidney's younger son, Philip Herbert, gained his title and power in the royal court through "intimacies" with King James.

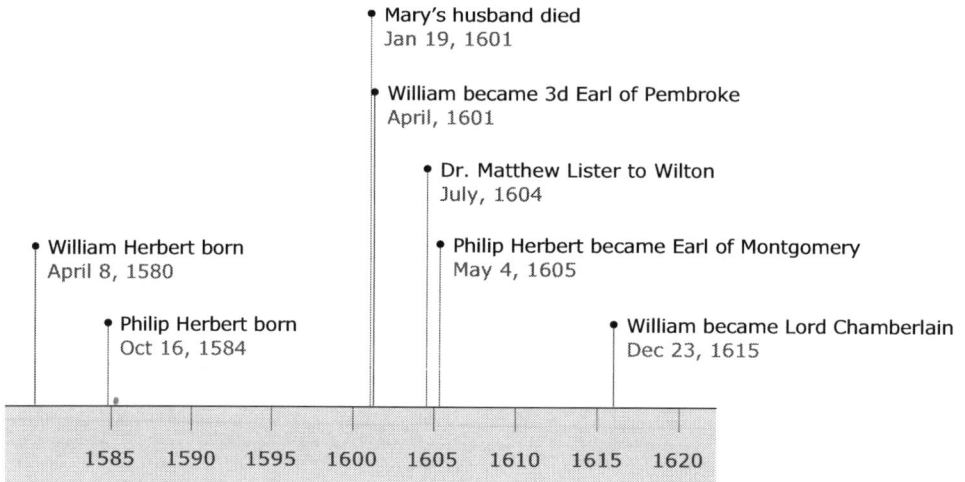

Mary's husband died
Jan 19, 1601

William became 3d Earl of Pembroke
April, 1601

Dr. Matthew Lister to Wilton
July, 1604

William Herbert born
April 8, 1580

Philip Herbert became Earl of Montgomery
May 4, 1605

Philip Herbert born
Oct 16, 1584

William became Lord Chamberlain
Dec 23, 1615

1585   1590   1595   1600   1605   1610   1615   1620

14 The Incomparable Brethren at Court

UP TO THIS POINT the focus in this book has been on Mary Sidney Herbert—her background and literary circle, her connections with the source materials, and the similarities between her life, the sonnets, and the plays. But if Mary Sidney is truly the author of the Shakespearean works, why didn't she publish the plays under her own name? It is difficult today to understand why the publication of these bawdy, licentious, and politically insurgent works would have destroyed the careers of both of her sons. A brief look at life in the royal court in the late 1500s and early 1600s will hopefully provide a better understanding of the situation and her dilemma.

It is the essence of a gentleman's character to bear the visible mark of no profession whatsoever.
Samuel Johnson
1709–1784

Getting Ahead at Court

It is important to understand that noblemen did not get "jobs"—they received preferments, grants, or offices. The Queen or King would reward a person with one of these "favors." A preferment rarely entailed actually working for a living—generally, one merely reaped the rewards. For instance, you might be granted the import duty on currants, silk, or sweet wine, which means you would get all of the duty fees. Of course, you'd hire a tradesman to actually do the *job* of collecting and recording the duty fees and that person would send you the money regularly.

Being granted a monopoly on the manufacture of such things as starch for collars, on gold and silver thread, or on clay for making tobacco pipes (which was owned for a time by Archie Armstrong, the King's fool) meant that everyone involved in that trade had to buy a license from you.

Two creative courtiers had lighthouses erected on the coast and charged a penny a ton on all ships that passed by. A courtier might receive lands out of the royal holdings, the dowry for a daughter's marriage, or a flat-out payment of cash—in 1611 Mary's younger son Philip received £6,000 from the King simply as royal "benevolence." A title such as "Earl of Pembroke" gives you the right to collect rents and other fees from every person in that particular shire (county), such as Pembrokeshire.

Don't Get on the Wrong Side

But, "Not everybody prospered at court. Some made the wrong alliances and secured powerful enemies. Some bankrupted themselves trying to keep up with the senseless extravagance of the court, and had to retire at last, impoverished. Some incurred the dire fate of the King's active displeasure. There was, for instance, the luckless soul who was so intent upon begging a suit [making his request heard] that he neglected to admire the King's handsome new saddle. When his friends asked the King why he had not granted the man's petition, James snorted, 'Shall a King give heed to a dirty paper, when a beggar noteth not his gilt stirrups?'"[1] It was a world of temperamental favors and volatile royal opinion.

Sir Walter Raleigh incurred the Queen's disfavor by impregnating one of her maids-of-honor, then marrying her secretly without the Queen's permission. Even though he had honorably married her, Raleigh and his new wife were both imprisoned in the Tower for several months and were not readmitted to court for many years. "Now that the Queen was no longer his friend, [Raleigh] found himself 'like a fish cast on dry land, gasping for breath, with lame legs and lamer lungs.'"[2]

There is a well-known story about an argument on a tennis court, probably at Greenwich Palace, between Philip Sidney (Mary's older brother) and Edward de Vere, the Earl of Oxford. Philip was playing tennis with friends when the ever-arrogant Earl of Oxford arrived and wanted the tennis court. Oxford, "born great, greater by alliance, and superlative in the [Queen's] favor," imperiously ordered Philip

---

1   G. P. V. Akrigg, *Jacobean Pageant, or The Court of King James I* (Cambridge: Harvard University Press, 1963), 173.

2   Katherine Duncan-Jones, *Sir Philip Sidney: Courtier Poet* (New Haven: Yale University Press, 1991), 165, quoting Fulke Greville's *Prose Works*, 39.

Sidney and his friends to leave. "On Sidney's calm refusal, Oxford grew heated, and 'commands them to depart the court. To this Sir Philip temperately answers that if his lordship had been pleased to express desire in milder characters, perchance he might have led out those that he should now find would not be driven out with any scourge of fury. This answer, like a bellows blowing up the sparks of excess already kindled, made my lord [of Oxford] scornfully call Sir Philip by the name of puppy.'"[3] The argument became "loud and shrill" on both sides until Sidney and his friends abruptly left the tennis court.

A knight (Sir) is far below the title of Earl. But at the time of this quarrel, Philip hadn't been knighted; he was merely an untitled commoner, born into the gentleman class. See page 312, Appendix C.

When Philip complained to Queen Elizabeth about being treated so poorly, the Queen lectured Philip on "the difference in degree between earls and gentlemen, the respect inferiors owed to their superiors, and the necessity in [Kings or Queens] to maintain their own creations [those they invested with a rank or title], as degrees descending between the people's licentiousness and the anointed sovereignty of crowns."[4] Essentially the Queen was reminding Philip that there is an order in the universe and Philip was of a lower order, an untitled gentleman, lower than the Earl of Oxford and therefore "inferior" to Oxford and so rightfully must abase himself before his "superior."

Queen Elizabeth seems to have had a relentless dislike of Philip, as mentioned in Chapter 2. Since blood relations are so important in the English social system, the Queen's dislike of Philip extended to his family: "The Queen's suspicion [of the growing popularity of Philip] seems to have extended to Robert [Philip's younger brother], with dismal effects on the younger brother's prospects. . . . All his requests for advancement were denied, his military achievements scorned or ignored, his personal initiative discouraged, and his aspirations frustrated. Although his ambitions were more personal and far less grandiose than Philip's, Elizabeth took no chances where Robert was concerned. She never raised him to the position at the court for which his inheritance and service qualified him."[5] This is a clear case of the reputation of one family member destroying the court opportunities for another.

---

3   Ibid., 165.
4   Millicent V. Hay, The *Life of Robert Sidney, Earl of Leicester (1563–1626)* (Washington: The Folger Shakespeare Library, 1984), 38–39.
5   Michael Brennan, *Literary Patronage in the English Renaissance: The Pembroke Family* (London, New York: Routledge, 1988), 16–17.

A further example is when the Queen finally learned that her "favorite," Robert Dudley, the Earl of Leicester (Mary and Philip's uncle, their mother's brother), had secretly married the Queen's cousin. Not only was the Queen furious with Dudley, but her sense of betrayal stretched to Mary's mother, the Queen's trusted lady-in-waiting. Court life as Dudley's sister finally became too difficult and she retired to Penshurst, another victim of the system of preferment and rank. Mary's mother was treated with disdain even though she had risked her life while nursing the Queen through smallpox years earlier. Mary's mother caught smallpox in the process and was so disfigured from the pustules that she rarely appeared again in public, and never without a veil. Yet even that sort of sacrifice didn't guarantee a place in court if any family member fell out of favor.

In 1601, William Herbert, twenty-one years old, had been at court for several years when he saw what happened to John Donne, the poet, who "did little better [at advancement at court]. An early mistake of marrying above his station without his patron's . . . permission removed him for years from the usual paths of advancement."[6] What was Donne's sin? Marrying above his station and without permission, for which he was thrown into the Fleet prison for several weeks, dismissed from his post as private secretary to the Lord Keeper of the Great Seal, and forced into church work because King James eventually declared that Donne could not be employed outside the church. In Donne's poem, "Satire 5," he "creates a relentless downward spiral of depression as he describes the vicissitudes and degradation of preferment-hunting at the royal court."[7]

Growing up, Mary's oldest son William Herbert would have been painfully attuned to these tacit threats toward his family and perfectly aware that status and advancement at court was dependent not only on a person's own reputation, but on the unsullied reputation of every other member of the family.

---

6   Alvin Kernan, *Shakespeare, the King's Playwright* (New Haven: Yale University Press, 1995), 173. After sixteen years of a fairly happy although financially unstable marriage, Donne's wife, 32-year-old Anne, died after the stillborn delivery of their twelfth child.
7   Anne Somerset, *Elizabeth I* (New York: St. Martin's Griffin, 1991), 499.

William Herbert's Troubles

Around 1601 William had his own troubles at court. He openly resented the time spent with his dying father at Wilton House, worried that his enemies at court were "taking this advantage of my absence when I could make no answer for myself." When his father died, William seemed to express no grief ("Old Earl of Pembroke dead" is all his letter states), more concerned to obtain "certain small offices that his father had held." [8]

As briefly touched on earlier, a week after his father's death in 1601 it was discovered that William's mistress, Mary Fitton, was "proud with child." This Mary, who also was a maid-of-honor to the Queen and two years older than William, would dress in men's clothes to meet him away from court. She was of a lower rank, her father being untitled. Although William admitted paternity, he refused to marry Fitton and Queen Elizabeth threw him into the Fleet prison for several months. Mary Fitton's baby boy died almost immediately after its birth. "His reason for refusing to marry Mary Fitton is not known, but he probably intended to make a more advantageous match, as he later did with Mary Talbot, daughter of the Earl of Shrewsbury."

William was released from the Fleet prison, but Queen Elizabeth banished him first to Baynards Castle in London and then to the country, to Wilton House, where he complained, "I have not yet been a day in the country, and I am as weary of it as if I had been prisoner there seven year." He asked permission to leave England "that the change of the climate may purge me of melancholy," but the Queen refused. William even had the gall to try to salvage his own reputation by asking the Queen to grant a patent to Mary Fitton's father as appeasement. "He was oblivious to the impropriety of asking the Queen for a grant to pacify the Fittons, thereby requesting that she pay for his irresponsibility, and he never considered paying Fitton out of his own vast wealth." [9] William was not released from his disgrace and allowed back at court until Queen Elizabeth died.

---

8   Both notes from Margaret Hannay, *Philip's Phoenix: Mary Sidney, Countess of Pembroke* (Oxford: Oxford University Press, 1990), 169.
9   All citations above from Hannay, *Philip's Phoenix*, 170–71.

The court of her successor King James grew to be even more divided and decadent than that of Queen Elizabeth—a hotbed of factions, favoritism, and intrigue. "In a court where men and women 'loved but from the teeth outwards,' the competition for favor and position was relentless and brutal. . . . In this desperate place, lone individuals had no chance, and faction was the means by which people sought to protect themselves from their enemies and further their own interests."[10]

And one had to keep an eye on one's own family. For instance, "The Earl of Suffolk [Thomas Howard] had become an object of suspicion on account of his daughter's scandalous behavior and would never again be as powerful as he had been."[11] Note that it's not the Earl of Suffolk himself who did anything scandalous, but his daughter—yet her behavior irreparably damaged his own reputation and power.[12]

William's Struggle for Rewards

The records show that as soon as William Herbert arrived at King James' royal court as a young man of twenty-three, he immediately began working toward advancement. "The state papers and parliamentary records show [for William] an immensely detailed and patient building up of political power over the first decade of James's reign."[13]

William's career started off well enough. King James awarded him the lucrative keepership of various lands and offices in the tin-mining districts. He was also appointed Lord Lieutenant of Cornwall and governor of Portsmouth.[14]

---

10 Kernan, *Shakespeare, the King's Playwright*, 115.
11 David Riggs, *Ben Jonson: A Life* (Cambridge, London: Harvard University Press, 1989), 219.
12 Akrigg, *Shakespeare and the Earl of Southampton*, 190–204. Well, Suffolk's daughter's "scandalous behavior" was pretty horrible: She had Sir Thomas Overbury murdered with a poisoned enema in the Tower of London. Though she and her husband, Robert Carr, were found guilty, they were pardoned—but they did lose their power at court, which was considered punishment enough for people of that social class. They lived in an apartment in the Tower of London for a couple of years, which Carr remodeled with part of the annual income of £4,000 that came from his "office." Then they were banished to an estate in the English countryside—the penance for murder if you're an aristocrat. The lower-class "inferiors" involved in the murder plot, however, such as the apothecary who was required to supply the poison, the dress designer/madame who was hired to deliver the poison to the prison, the elderly serving man who unwittingly handed the poisonous enema to Overbury, and even the kind-hearted Lieutenant who for months had substituted fresh food for the obviously poisoned food, were hanged.
13 Gary Waller, *Sidney Family Romance* (Detroit: Wayne State University Press, 1993), 87.
14 Brennan, *Literary Patronage in the English Renaissance*, 122.

But in 1607 the favored positions of both William and his younger brother Philip were jeopardized when the King fell in love with the minor Scottish courtier, Robert Carr. Over the next few years both brothers were involved in violent and acrimonious public quarrels with other courtiers, and proposals were put before the Commons to exclude all Scots from court. "By 1611 the ambitions of the various factions at court were becoming more polarized." [15]

William Herbert was prepared to go to great lengths to protect his position in court and advance himself. He particularly desired the job of Lord Chamberlain, the office in charge of the public theater, printing, and the court entertainments, a position held at the time by the King's favorite, Robert Carr. Carr was the Earl of Somerset and well entrenched in the opposing Howard faction. Henry Howard, Earl of Northampton, wrote a letter on his deathbed in 1614 to Somerset stating that William Herbert and Robert Sidney were his worst enemies and begged Somerset not to give them any of Howard's offices when he died. [16]

Having been passed over for several significant posts during the years, William at last recognized a window of opportunity through which he could change the power structure at court and gain for himself the position he coveted. "In 1614, seemingly resigned to a minor political role, Pembroke held one of the most significant factional supper meetings in British politics at Baynards Castle. Pembroke, [Archbishop of Canterbury] Abbott, [Sir Ralph] Winwood, and Sir Thomas Lake decided to provide James with a new favorite to supplant Carr. The bait was Sir George Villiers, a Lancashire knight—handsome, sparkling, and superficial." [17]

The plan was that George Villiers would catch the eye of King James, topple Carr, the King's current favorite on the Howard side, with the result that William and his faction would then be in power. [18] They coached George how to walk, talk, primp, curl his hair, tie his ribbons, and sweeten his breath to entice King James. [19] Because George was so poor, William Herbert loaned him appropriate clothes so George

---

15 Ibid., 123.
16 Michael G. Brennan and Noel J. Kinnamon, *A Sidney Chronology 1554–1654* (Basingstoke: Palgrave Macmillan, 2003), 209.
17 Waller, *Sidney Family Romance*, 88.
18 Ibid., 88–89.
19 Kernan, *Shakespeare, the King's Playwright*, 115.

would be allowed to appear in court. Ben Jonson wrote a masque specifically for the occasion, *The Golden Age Restored,* that included a dance so George could show off his dancing legs to the King.[20]

George Villiers and his famous dancing legs.

It worked. King James fell madly in love with George, and William Herbert became the Lord Chamberlain with the specific condition that the position be passed on to his brother Philip when William died. George Villiers eventually became the Duke of Buckingham.

Mary's son, William Herbert, the 3rd Earl of Pembroke, went on to become the wealthiest and most powerful man in England, second only to the King. In 1615, "His pension of £3,600 was supplemented by additional perquisites that brought it to nearly £5,000, one of the highest incomes of any royal official."[21] William was responsible for court activities; access of suitors and embassies to the king; the master of the revels, the court plays and musicians; and had direct supervision of almost two thousand people in the court system. In 1617 he became Chancellor of Oxford University.[22] Thus, "In matters of political preferment at Oxford, Pembroke predictably sought to exercise the power and influence invested in the Chancellorship directly to his own benefit."[23] Nor did he forget those who did him favors: In 1619 Ben Jonson was given an honorary degree from Oxford at the behest of William Herbert.[24] From 1618 to 1625 William served as the Grand Master of the Freemasons.[25]

Even William's marriage to Mary Talbot, daughter of the Earl of Shrewsbury, was arranged to further his wealth and status. Both William Herbert and Mary Wroth, his cousin and lover, "married for family aggrandizement: Pembroke to acquire money and lands,

---

20 Riggs, *Ben Jonson: A Life,* 215–18.

21 Waller, *Sidney Family Romance,* 89.

22 Brennan, *Literary Patronage in the English Renaissance,* 160. Pembroke College at Oxford was originally called Broadgates Hall but changed its name in 1624 in honor of William Herbert. This Pembroke College is not to be confused with Pembroke College at Cambridge, founded in 1347 by Mary de St. Pol, Countess of Pembroke from 1321. St. John's College at Cambridge was also founded by a woman in 1511—Lady Margaret Beaufort, mother of Henry 7. The statue in the courtyard of the Bodleian Library at Oxford is of William Herbert.

23 Ibid., 163.

24 Rosalind Miles, *Ben Jonson: His Life and Work* (London and New York: Routledge & Kegan Paul, 1986), 206.

25 Kenneth R. H. MacKenzie, *Royal Masonic Cyclopaedia,* vol. 1 (1877; reprint, Montana: Kessinger Publications, 2002), 285.

marrying a woman of apparently little physical attractiveness or social grace—who eventually went, or more likely was conveniently declared, insane, largely for the financial benefit of her husband's family."[26]

Maintaining the Reputation

William's machinations into power and his preoccupation with appearances was well noted at the time. This Earl of Pembroke was "Characterized by 'Justice, Religion, and Piety,' of 'a lofty mind,' delights in 'Magnanimity . . . Courteous and affable to his friends but Cannot bear Injury or Cross in his *reputation*.' He is 'bountiful to his friends . . . but because of his regard for honor and *reputation*,' he 'shall be very dainty in the choice out of jealousy and suspicion.'"[27] [emphasis added]

Reputation, reputation, reputation: O, I have lost my reputation. **I have lost the immortal part of myself,** *and what remains is bestial. My reputation, Iago, my reputation.*

Cassio in *Othello*, 2.3.256–259

Fully understanding how to manipulate the royal court system to achieve his goals and maintain his power, William did just that. "Clarendon likewise distinguished Pembroke from the bulk of Stuart nobles and statesmen in that he had 'fame and *reputation* with all men, being the most universally beloved and esteemed of any of that age, and despite having a great office in the Court, he made the Court itself better esteemed, and more reverenced in the country.'"[28] [emphasis added] William had a great deal to protect in his position at court, but Clarendon does go on to acknowledge that he also had his particular vices, such as indulging in excesses of all pleasures and being typically "immoderately given up to women."[29]

In this world of the royal court, one can see that if Mary Sidney had been known to be writing "inappropriate" literary work, such as ribald and seditious plays for the public theater, there would have been a scandal easily capable of impeding, or more likely, destroying William's career at court. Margaret Hannay explains, "The lives of these aristocratic women, although less restricted in many ways than those of women in the lower classes, were still tightly constrained by an emphasis on the virtues of chastity, silence, and obedience."[30]

---

26 Waller, *Sidney Family Romance*, 123.

27 Hannay, *Philip's Phoenix*, quoting "William Herbert's Nativity" (Bodleian Library, MS Ashmole 394, ff.76–81), 211.

28 Waller, *Sidney Family Romance*, 56.

29 Edward Hyde, the Earl of Clarendon, *History of the Rebellion*, ed. W. Dunn Macray (Oxford, 1888), 71–73, quoted in *An Introduction to Shakespeare's Sonnets for the Use of Historians and Others*, by John Dover Wilson (New York: Cambridge University Press, 1964), 108.

30 Margaret Hannay, ed., *Word: Tudor Women as Patrons, Translators, and Writers of Religious Works* (Ohio: Kent State University Press, 1985), 10.

Cerasano and Wynne-Davies agree: "As a female author/translator, not to mention a member of the nobility, Mary Sidney would have opened her *reputation* to considerable risk by involving herself in public theater."[31] [emphasis added] Any question of his mother's reputation would be valuable material for William's enemies.

Consider what other scholars have to say about women and writing in the early 1600s:

> In a world in which privilege was attached to coterie circulation and published words were associated with promiscuity, the female writer could become a "fallen" woman in a double sense: branded as a harlot or a member of the non-elite.[32]

> The English Renaissance lady lived quashed in a double bind. If her family was rich and powerful enough, she was encouraged to develop her mind, learn languages, absorb the best of ancient wisdom. . . . If her mind made use of what it had been given and created some lines of verse, the lady was thought charming. If by some chance she was taken seriously, she walked thump against a wall that would effectively stop even the most passionately creative soul. The wall was called *reputation.*[33] [emphasis added]

> Wisdom, discretion, a wise and religious heart, humility: in the name of these virtues, women were prevented from asserting their own intellectual competence in any secular and most religious spheres. To do so was to risk the charge, perhaps even by their own consciences, of being foolish, indiscrete, vain, and even irreligious, all attributes of "loose" women. No wonder educated women were on the defensive to show that their learning had accomplished no permanent damage to their character![34]

31 S. Cerasano and Marion Wynne-Davies, eds., *Renaissance Drama by Women: Texts and Documents* (London and New York: Routledge, 1996), 15.

32 Wendy Wall, *The Imprint of Gender: Authorship and Publication in the English Renaissance* (Ithaca and London: Cornell University Press, 1993), 281.

33 Louise Bernikow, ed., *The World Split Open: Four Centuries of Women Poets in England and America, 1552–1950* (New York: Random House, 1974), 19.

34 Mary Ellen Lamb, "The Cooke Sisters: Attitudes toward Learned Women in the Renaissance," in *Silent but for the Word*, 115.

Constrained by the norms of acceptable feminine behavior, women were specifically discouraged from tapping into the newly popular channel of print; to do so threatened the cornerstone of their moral and social well-being.[35]

When their work was published, it was often anonymous; if it was known to be by a woman, it was usually restricted to manuscripts in the family circle.[36]

Mary Sidney, of course, did write and even publish "appropriate" works that were within the sphere of acceptance, yet pushing the boundaries. But writing for the public theater?

If [Mary Sidney, the Countess of] Pembroke had boldly written more secular works, then her *reputation* might well have been soiled.[37] [emphasis added]

Women were not able to write works for production in a public theater, but they were allowed to write plays for performance within their own homes, the parts being read, and perhaps acted, by members of their family and close friends.[38]

These plays were called *closet dramas,* such as Mary's acknowledged and published work, *Antonie.*

If female courtiers could arouse suspicion regarding their sexual and moral virtue because of their speech, female writers were even more suspect, and the majority of women who published their works felt the need to justify their boldness. They often claimed that their works were really private, but that some external force had compelled their publication. For writers of religious works it was divine inspiration, of advice manuals their duty as mothers, of political pieces the special gravity of the situation. Poets and playwrights stressed pressures by male friends or the desire to correct pirated versions of their work published without their consent. Even women's works published posthumously, often by their husbands or other male relatives, included

35 Wall, *The Imprint of Gender,* 280.
36 Hannay, *Silent but for the Word,* 109.
37 Margaret Hannay, "'Bearing the livery of your name': The Countess of Pembroke's Agency in Print and Scribal Publication" in *Sidney Journal* (2000) 18:1, 7.
38 Cerasano and Wynne-Davies, *Renaissance Drama by Women,* 93.

such justifications and claims that the author had been a paragon of female modesty whose writing had been done only out of duty to God or her children and had never interfered with her household or marital duties.[39]

Mary Sidney was already testing the limits by presenting herself at court "as a woman of culture, and not as a wife and mother."[40] But writing bawdy and often politically subversive plays for the public theater was over the edge—even more so during the reign of the misogynist King James.

Lord Chamberlain Above All

Why did William Herbert want the position of Lord Chamberlain so desperately? "Once he became Lord Chamberlain, he was responsible for overseeing all the court's entertainment *as well as having final control of licensing the public theater.*"[41] [emphasis added] This would, of course, include making sure his mother's theatrical works would never be published under her own name.

In E. E. Willoughby's classic book on the printing of the First Folio of the Shakespeare plays, he notes that "no new edition of the plays of Shakespeare had appeared since 1615."[42] The year 1615 is the year William Herbert became Lord Chamberlain.

Did William Herbert spend most of his career at court maneuvering for the position of Lord Chamberlain out of fear that his mother would expose herself as an author of popular, licentious, politically explosive plays for the public theater? Only as Lord Chamberlain would he have absolute control over their publication.

39 Axel Erdman, *My Gracious Silence: Women in the Mirror of 16th Century Printing in Western Europe* (Luzern: Gilhofer & Ranschburg, Switzerland, 1999), xvii.

40 Cerasano and Wynne-Davies, *Renaissance Drama by Women*, 13.

41 Waller, *Sidney Family Romance*, 230.

42 E. E. Willoughby, *A Printer of Shakespeare* (London: Philip Allan & Co. Ltd, 1934), 166.

Philip Herbert at Court

William Herbert wasn't Mary's only child at the royal court—her younger son, Philip, was there as well. He gained his power at court, however, through a very different process from that of his older brother.

Being a younger son, Philip had no chance at a hereditary title. As Lawrence and Jeanne Stone explain in An Open Elite?, "A third distinctive feature of the English landed elite was the fact that their younger sons were downwardly mobile, with few career options . . . unless they should have the good fortune to marry an heiress. Because there were no special legal privileges or hereditary titles attached to them, younger sons had to make their own way in the world." [43] Nor did younger sons of the nobility have a history of accomplishing much: "They certainly had the opportunity of making large fortunes and buying their way back into the society into which they had been born, perhaps indeed at a higher level, but few of them seem to have made it." [44]

Perhaps it was this automatic strike against Philip that made him so different from his older brother. John Aubrey, a gossip whose voluminous notes have survived, describes William Herbert as "a good scholar" who "delighted in poetry." But Aubrey insists that Philip Herbert "did not delight in books, or poetry" and preferred outdoor pursuits rather than the company of poets and scholars.[45] Edward Hyde, Earl of Clarendon, a historian and politician of the time, confirms this opinion and represents William as having "a good proportion of learning," while Philip "pretended to no other qualifications than to understand horses and dogs very well." [46]

As Philip's second wife later remarked, "He was no Scholar at all to speak of for he was not past three or four months at the University of Oxford being taken away from thence by his friends, presently after his father's death . . . to follow the court, as judging himself fit for that kind of life when he was not passing 15 or 16 years old." She also complained that he was "extremely choleric by nature." [47]

43 Lawrence Stone and Jeanne C. Fawtier Stone, An Open Elite? England 1540–1880, abridged ed. (1986; reprint, Oxford: Clarendon Press, 2001), 165.

44 Ibid., 185.

45 John Aubrey, Brief Lives, ed. by Richard Barber (1997; reprint, Woodbridge, Suffolk: The Boydell Press, 1982), 143.

46 Brennan, Literary Patronage in the English Renaissance, 119.

47 Hannay, Philip's Phoenix, 212.

But Philip had other gifts. Clarendon remarks that Philip "had the good fortune, by the comeliness of his person, his skill, and indefatigable industry in hunting, to be the first who drew the King's eyes towards him with affection."[48]

Wilder and more handsome than William, "Philip Herbert was even more successful than his elder brother in catching the royal eye. Before James's coronation, he was appointed as a Gentleman of Queen Anne's bedchamber and made a Knight of the Bath. Gossip about the King's favor for Philip grew when late in 1603 he received, along with [two others], a grant for the transport of cloth, rumored to be worth not less than £10,000."[49]

"By the time of the coronation in July, [Philip] was familiar enough with the king to be able to get away with kissing him on the lips rather than the hand at the ceremony, and he had great influence with the king from the earliest days of the reign."[50] Philip was 19 years old.

Philip's Reward

On the first New Year's night of King James's court, 1603–1604, "Philip Herbert was exploiting to the full the effects which his physical charms were having upon the King. When [Philip] was asked for an interpretation of his [heraldic design], 'a fair horse colt in a fair green field,' Philip explained that it signified 'a colt of Bucephalus's race and had this virtue of his sire that none could mount him but one as great at least as Alexander.' Delighted by such innuendoes, James 'made himself merry with threatening to send this colt to the stable.'"[51]

Bucephalus was the huge and untamable horse belonging to Alexander the Great. It was high-spirited and difficult to control, but as a young boy Alexander was the only one able to ride it. At the spot where the horse later died in battle in India, Alexander founded the city of Bucephala.

In October of 1604, Philip married Susan de Vere, a match secretly arranged by the lovers themselves. She was the youngest daughter of Edward de Vere, the Earl of Oxford; six months after the Earl died, they arranged their marriage. On their first morning after the wedding, with great glee, "the King in his shirt and nightgown gave them a Reveille Matin before they were up and spent a good time in or upon the bed, choose which you will."[52]

---

48 Brennan, *Literary Patronage in the English Renaissance*, 119.

49 Ibid., 106.

50 Kernan, *Shakespeare, the King's Playwright*, 11.

51 Brennan, *Literary Patronage in the English Renaissance*, 107–09.

52 In a letter from Dudley Carleton to Winwood, quoted in Waller, *Sidney Family Romance* (Detroit: Wayne State University Press, 1993), 83.

Philip's relationship with the King progressed: "Robert Cecil's letters of 1605 are filled with references to Philip's intimacy with James."[53] Finally, the pay-off: "In May, 1605, King James granted Philip Herbert an earldom in his own right, even though he was a younger son."[54]

Alvin Kernan in *Shakespeare, the King's Playwright,* is more explicit: "Later James took up with [William] Herbert's younger brother, the even more handsome Philip, who as a result of this intimacy was made Earl of Montgomery in 1605."[55]

An earldom wasn't the only honor King James heaped upon Philip Herbert. He also presented the handsome young man with lands worth £1,200 a year in rents and tithes. The King "paid out of the royal purse the debts which the loose-living and extravagant young man had accumulated," created him a Knight of the Garter, the highest order of knighthood in England, and outright gave him £6,000 as a gift.[56]

Although William and Philip received their awards through different means, "By July 1616, when the Earl of Pembroke, as Lord Chamberlain, presided over the arrangements for the King's summer progress, the Herbert brothers were widely recognized as being among James' most intimate advisers and friends."[57]

With her only surviving children desperately clawing their way up the factious court ladder, how could Mary Sidney, as their mother, engage publicly in any potentially subversive literary activity?

A Bawd, a Whore, and a Matron

So Mary's sons became two of the wealthiest and most powerful men in the English court, and the self-proclaimed poet laureate Ben Jonson had a part in their success with his masque for George Villiers, the King's bait. Several years later, right before Mary dies, a collection of the Shakespearean plays goes to press in a book now called the First Folio, as discussed at length in Chapter 16. The First Folio is dedicated to Mary Sidney's two sons, and Ben Jonson writes a eulogy praising the author of the plays.

When King James died in 1625 at the age of 59, it was in the arms of Mary's son William Herbert, just as the young King Edward 6 (son of Henry 8) died in the arms of Mary's father.

53 Brennan, *Literary Patronage in the English Renaissance,* 106.
54 Hannay, *Philip's Phoenix,* 191.
55 Kernan, *Shakespeare, the King's Playwright,* 118.
56 Akrigg, *Shakespeare and the Earl of Southampton,* 52.
57 Brennan, *Literary Patronage in the English Renaissance,* 167.

One of the most compelling features of Jonson's poem is his own introduction to it. He complains that some people might pretend to praise someone, while actually trying to ruin a person. He says this is how a bawd (pimp) or a whore might treat an older gentlewoman:

> *Or crafty malice, might pretend this praise,*
> *And think to ruin, where it seemed to raise.*
> *These are, as some infamous Bawd, or Whore,*
> *Should praise a Matron. What could hurt her more?*

There has been no reasonable clarification as to why Ben Jonson mentions a bawd, a whore, and a matron in the introduction to the folio, which reads as a eulogy, "To the memory of my beloved, the AUTHOR." Jonson was a careful writer who enjoyed clear and specific language and symbolism; in fact, he derided other poets who used words lightly or inappropriately. It would be unthinkable for Jonson to use such loaded words as *bawd* and *whore* thoughtlessly. What do a bawd, a whore, and a matron have to do with William Shakespeare?

An explanation might lie in the fact that Jonson was a key player in William Herbert's plot to change the power structure in King James' court by providing the King with a new lover. In this plot, William essentially acts as a BAWD/pimp. And Jonson is well aware—as is everyone at court—that Mary's younger son, Philip Herbert, acts as WHORE in exchange for the title Earl of Montgomery and other favors. If Mary Sidney is the author of these plays, how could Jonson have made it any clearer?

> *This is the way a bawd (such as Mary's older son) or whore*
> *(such as Mary's younger son) might pretend to praise an older*
> *gentlewoman (Mary herself) while really planning to subvert*
> *or undermine her. What could hurt her more?*

The entire poem, published in 1623, is filled with other odd references. For instance, Jonson compares Shakespeare to Marlowe, Lyly, and Kyd, three writers he had previously disparaged and who had all been dead for two or three decades. Lyly wrote letters that complain of failure and neglect, he hadn't written anything since 1590, and had died in 1606; Kyd had been imprisoned and tortured for atheism and died in poverty in 1594; Marlowe was murdered in 1593. What is Jonson actually saying?

The following two pages include a paraphrase of the introduction. The full poem and a paraphrase are in Appendix B for those who might like to study the many odd ambiguities it includes.

To the memory of my beloved,
The AUTHOR

M R . W I L L I A M   S H A K E S P E A R E :

1   To draw no envy (Shakespeare) on thy name,

2   Am I thus ample to thy Book, and Fame:

3   While I confess thy writings to be such,

4   As neither Man, nor Muse, can praise too much.

5   'Tis true, and all men's suffrage. But these ways

6   Were not the paths I meant unto thy praise:

7   For seeliest Ignorance on these may light,

8   Which, when it sounds at best, but echoes right;

9   Or blind Affection, which doth ne'er advance

10 The truth, but gropes, and urgeth all by chance;

11 *Or crafty Malice, might pretend this praise,*

12 *And think to ruin, where it seem'd to raise.*

13 *These are, as some infamous Bawd, or Whore,*

14 *Should praise a Matron. What could hurt her more?*

15 But thou art proof against them, and indeed

16 Above th' ill fortune of them, or the need.

17 I, therefore will begin. Soul of the Age!

seel: sew a hawk's eyelids closed for training, or to close a person's eyes to prevent one from seeing or discovering something; to hoodwink.

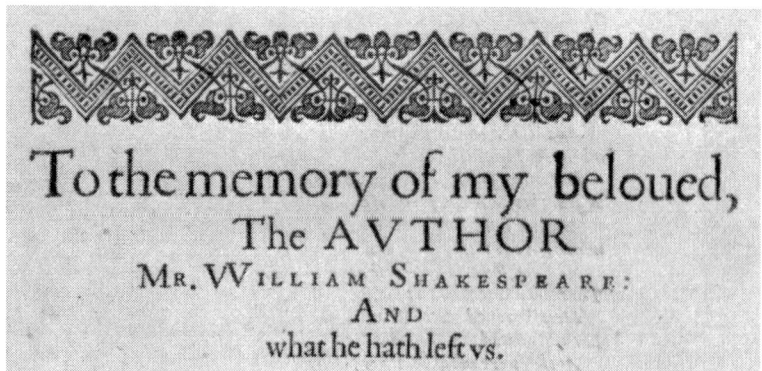

To the memory of my beloued,
The AVTHOR
MR. WILLIAM SHAKESPEARE:
AND
what he hath left vs.

[paraphrase]

1 To avoid attracting malice and spite (Shakespeare) to your "name,"
2 Is why I am consequently so unrestrained in the matter of this published book and your reputation.
3 At the same time that I acknowledge my belief that your writings are the kind
4 That neither Man nor Muse can commend them more than they deserve.
5 It's true, and is the consensus of all men. But this kind of praise
6 Is not the course of action I had in mind with which to honor you.
7 For the most blindly uninformed people may read these lines,
8 Which, at the time that their ignorance examines/proves these lines to be good, they are really only/merely imitations of what is true.
9 Or you might be praised with "blind affection"—people who have never actually seen you in person but love your works—which never gets any closer to or promotes
10 The truth, but only searches for it uncertainly and asserts what it does by accident (but not by honesty).
11 *Or with cunning ill will, some might use this praise as a pretext to elevate someone*
12 *But actually intend to destroy/demolish that person in a place (such as this eulogy) where it gives the appearance of putting someone in a higher position.*
13 *These are the sorts of tricks with which some notorious pimp or whore*
14 *Might praise a respectable elderly lady of the upper class. What could actually hurt her more?*
15 But you, my beloved author, are impervious to these tricks and, to be sure,
16 You are far above the unfortunate destiny they plan for you, or the necessity of it.
17 I, accordingly, will lay the true foundation: Soul of the Age!

Intriguingly, the soul is always feminine, including in the Shakespeare plays.

Within this wall of flesh
*There is a **soul** counts thee **her** creditor*
And with advantage means to pay thy love.
King John in *King John*, 3.3

DID A WOMAN WRITE SHAKESPEARE?

On to the Plays

More information about Ben Jonson, his poem, and his important contribution to the printed collection of Shakespearean works is in Chapter 16, "The Publication of the First Folio." But first, let's look at the publication of the plays themselves during Mary Sidney's and William Shakespeare's lifetimes.

Part Seven

The Publications

On writing poetry, Mary's brother wrote:

Thus doing, your name shall flourish
   in the printers' shops.
Thus doing, you shall be of kin
   to many a poetical preface.
Thus doing, you shall be most fair,
   most rich, most wise, most all;
   you shall dwell upon superlatives.

Philip Sidney,
The Defense of Poesie
published 1595

Plays in print during Shakespeare's lifetime

Queen Elizabeth died in March, 1603. Shakespeare died in April, 1616. Mary Sidney died in late September, 1621.

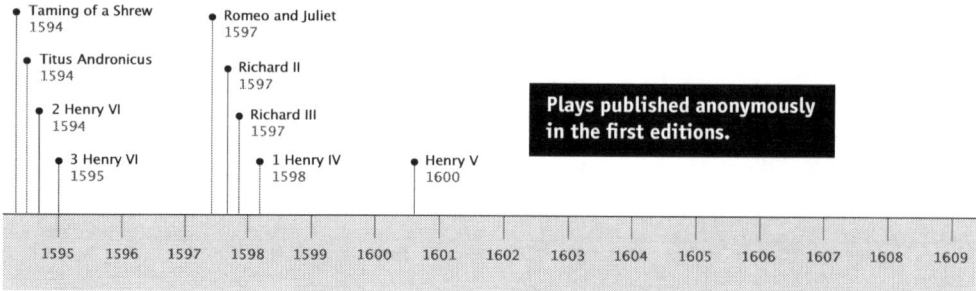

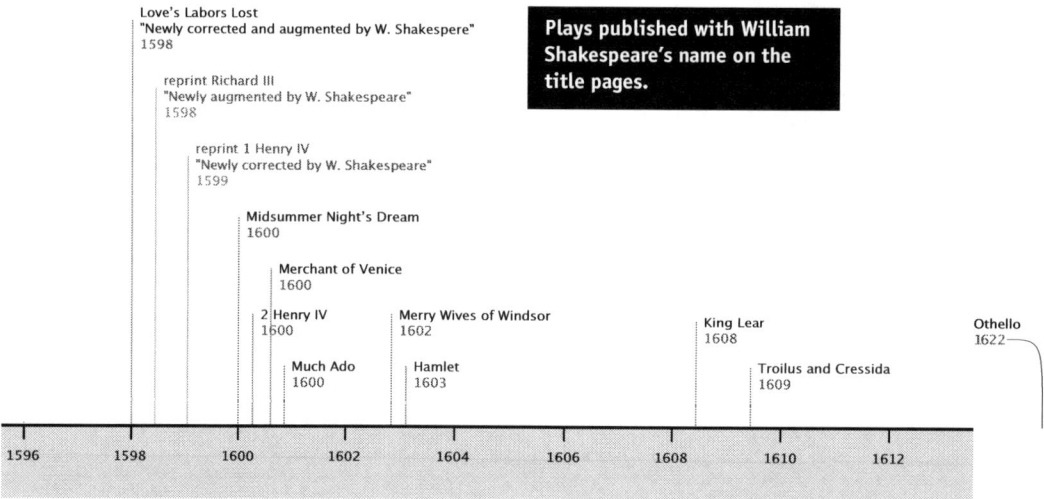

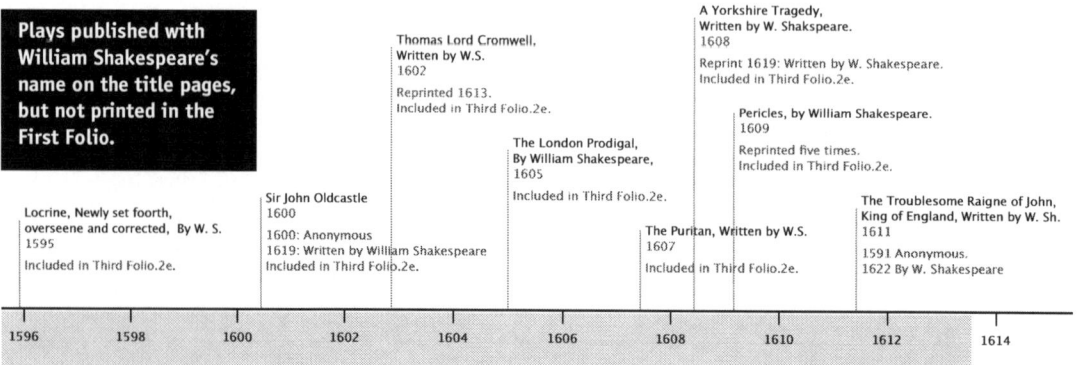

Plays published anonymously in the first editions.

- Taming of a Shrew
1594
- Titus Andronicus
1594
- 2 Henry VI
1594
- 3 Henry VI
1595
- Romeo and Juliet
1597
- Richard II
1597
- Richard III
1597
- 1 Henry IV
1598
- Henry V
1600

| 1595 | 1596 | 1597 | 1598 | 1599 | 1600 | 1601 | 1602 | 1603 | 1604 | 1605 | 1606 | 1607 | 1608 | 1609 |

Plays published with William Shakespeare's name on the title pages.

- Love's Labors Lost
"Newly corrected and augmented by W. Shakespere"
1598
- reprint Richard III
"Newly augmented by W. Shakespeare"
1598
- reprint 1 Henry IV
"Newly corrected by W. Shakespeare"
1599
- Midsummer Night's Dream
1600
- Merchant of Venice
1600
- 2 Henry IV
1600
- Much Ado
1600
- Merry Wives of Windsor
1602
- Hamlet
1603
- King Lear
1608
- Troilus and Cressida
1609
- Othello
1622

| 1596 | 1598 | 1600 | 1602 | 1604 | 1606 | 1608 | 1610 | 1612 |

Plays published with William Shakespeare's name on the title pages, but not printed in the First Folio.

- Locrine, Newly set foorth, overseene and corrected, By W. S.
1595
Included in Third Folio.2e.

- Sir John Oldcastle
1600
1600: Anonymous
1619: Written by William Shakespeare
Included in Third Folio.2e.

- Thomas Lord Cromwell,
Written by W.S.
1602
Reprinted 1613.
Included in Third Folio.2e.

- The London Prodigal,
By William Shakespeare,
1605
Included in Third Folio.2e.

- The Puritan, Written by W.S.
1607
Included in Third Folio.2e.

- A Yorkshire Tragedy,
Written by W. Shakspeare.
1608
Reprint 1619: Written by W. Shakespeare.
Included in Third Folio.2e.

- Pericles, by William Shakespeare.
1609
Reprinted five times.
Included in Third Folio.2e.

- The Troublesome Raigne of John,
King of England, Written by W. Sh.
1611
1591 Anonymous.
1622 By W. Shakespeare

| 1596 | 1598 | 1600 | 1602 | 1604 | 1606 | 1608 | 1610 | 1612 | 1614 |

15 The Publication of the Plays

AS IT IS IN LONDON TODAY, the theater during the English Renaissance was a vibrant and thriving enterprise. There were from five to nine theaters open at all times, holding from 1,500 to 3,000 people each. Plays were staged every day except Sunday, and often sold out.

Between 1610 and 1620, when the population of London is estimated to have been about 200,000, the attendance of theatergoers *daily* "finally settled down to a range of 8,000 or less to just over 10,000."[1] In 1595, the Admiral's Men and the Lord Chamberlain's Men "together averaged about 2,500 paying customers a day, or 15,000 a week."[2]

William Ingram claims there were more than a thousand professional actors in town.[3] Bentley tells us there were more than fifty professional dramatists.[4] And slightly more than 200 amateur play writers.[5]

In competition with theater performances were bearbaiting, bullbaiting, and cockfighting, with the most important matches held on Sundays. Rich and poor, commoners and nobility attended the theaters and the baitings. Queen Elizabeth was so fond of bearbaiting that for a time she had the theaters closed down two extra days a week so they wouldn't compete with the bears.[6]

Man's mind,
stretched to a new idea,
never goes back to its
original dimension.
Oliver Wendell Holmes
1809–1894

In bearbaiting, a bear was tied to a stake and set upon by a pack of mastiff dogs. The bear usually killed or maimed a couple of dogs, and when the dogs would hang back, new dogs were introduced until the bear was beaten or had maimed all of the dogs. Rarely was the bear killed by the dogs. Bull-baiting was similar.

---

1   Ann Jennalie Cook, *The Privileged Playgoers of Shakespeare's London, 1576–1642* (Princeton: Princeton University Press, 1981), 176.
2   David Riggs, *Ben Jonson: A Life* (Cambridge: Harvard University Press, 1989), 24.
3   William Ingram, "The Economics of Playing," in *A Companion to Shakespeare,* ed. David Scott Kastan (Oxford: Blackwell Publishers, 1999), 314.
4   Gerald Eades Bentley, *The Profession of Dramatist in Shakespeare's Time, 1590–1642* (Princeton: Princeton University Press, 1971), 25.
5   Ibid., 17.
6   Anne Somerset, *Elizabeth I* (New York: St. Martin's Griffin, 1991), 368.

Because theater was so popular, the acting companies constantly needed new material. "The urban audience included a substantial number of repeat visitors who required a continuously varied menu of dramatic entertainments. The typical life span of a new script . . . was about two weeks, with double admission prices on opening day. The very factor that made the new playhouses so lucrative—their sheer size—made a steady supply of new plays an economic imperative."[7]

Sir Peter Hall estimates that 800 new plays were performed between the mid-1580s and 1616, but admits that we do not know the half of it.[8] Bentley reports that we know the titles of about 1,500 plays from 1590 to 1642. We know nothing at all regarding the authorship of 370 others.[9] And in addition, "there probably were written as many as 500 plays of which we know not even the titles."[10]

It boils down to this conservative estimate: During the publication of the Shakespearean plays that spanned about 25 years (1590–1615), almost 3,000 plays were written and produced—that's more than two new plays every week. Although the only playwright of this time whom most people can name is "Shakespeare," there were actually fewer plays from this writer than from almost any other popular dramatist—only 36 of those 1,500 plays we know the titles of, as compared to 200 for Thomas Heywood, 69 for John Fletcher, and 64 for Thomas Dekker.[11] Henry Chettle had a hand in 52 plays in five years.[12]

The Anonymous Author

A careful look at the publication history of the Shakespearean plays shows a number of interesting things.

In the first printed collection of plays, called the First Folio (discussed at length in the following chapter), there are 36 plays, all of which are believed to be written by the same author. (Recent research indicates that several of the very early and very late plays might include additions from other authors.)

In the second edition of the Third Folio (the third printing of the Folio in 1664) and in the Fourth Folio (1685), seven plays attributed to

---

7   Riggs, *Ben Jonson: A Life*, 24.
8   Sir Peter Hall, *Cities in Civilization* (New York: Pantheon Books, 1998), 115.
9   Bentley, *The Profession of Dramatist in Shakespeare's Time*, 199.
10 Ibid., 16.
11 Hall, *Cities in Civilization*, 115.
12 Bentley, *The Profession of Dramatist in Shakespeare's Time*, 100.

Shakespeare were added: *Locrine, The Life of Sir John Oldcastle, The Puritan, A Yorkshire Tragedy, The London Prodigal, Thomas Lord Cromwell,* and *Pericles.* All of these were in print with Shakespeare's name or initials during his lifetime, as shown on page 258. Today, the only one of these seven that has been generally accepted as primarily authored by Shakespeare is *Pericles.*

There are a number of apocryphal plays that have been attributed to Shakespeare for one reason or another, including *The Two Noble Kinsmen, Edward 3,* and *Cardenio.*[13] But this chapter is concerned only with the 36 plays printed in the First Folio, plus those attributed to Shakespeare while he was alive.

The first eight Shakespearean plays that appeared in print were published anonymously:

> *Titus Andronicus* (1594)
> *The Taming of a Shrew* (1594)
> *2 Henry 6* (1594, 1600)
> *3 Henry 6* (1595, 1600)
> *Romeo and Juliet* (1597, 1599)
> *1 Henry 4* (1598)
> *Richard 2* (1597)
> *Richard 3* (1597)

Scholars are not in agreement over whether the anonymous printed version of *The Taming of a Shrew* is a source play for *The Taming of the Shrew* by someone else or a "bad quarto" of a Shakespearean play.

Provocatively, the title pages of *Titus Andronicus, The Taming of a Shrew,* and *3 Henry 6,* while listing no author, all state they had been played by the Earl of Pembroke's Men, the acting company sponsored by Mary Sidney and her husband. Scholars believe *2 Henry 6* was also played by Pembroke's Men, documenting that at least three (and probably four) of the early, anonymous Shakespearean plays were played by the acting company sponsored by Mary.[14]

Although scholars claim that Shakespeare was a member of Pembroke's Men, that is only an assumption—there is no record that the man named William Shakespeare was associated with this acting troupe.

The first play printed with Shakespeare's name on it, *Love's Labor's Lost,* does not appear until 1598. Its title page does not state, "By William Shakespeare"; it says: "Newly corrected and augmented By W. Shakespere."

---

13 Besides the six other plays published in the Third Folio, there are three plays that Humphrey Moseley entered in the Stationers' Register in 1660 as Shakespeare's: *Duke Humphrey, Iphis and Iantha,* and *King Stephen.* In the library of King Charles (reigned 1660–1685), there was a volume titled *Shakespeare Volume I* that includes *Mucedorus, Fair Em,* and *The Merry Devil of Edmonton.*

14 Oscar James Campbell, ed., *The Reader's Encyclopedia of Shakespeare* (New York: MJF Books, 1966), 621.

In fact, the first *three* plays with Shakespeare's name on the title pages are not categorically by Shakespeare—*his name is each time listed only as an augmenter or corrector.* Two of the previously anonymous plays were reprinted:

> The 1598 reprint (and succeeding ones) of *Richard 3* states, "Newly augmented by W. Shakespeare."

> The 1599 reprint of *1 Henry 6* states, "Newly corrected by W. Shakespeare." But regarding the notation that it is newly corrected, Oscar James Campbell writes, "This statement is not true, for there are only very small differences between the texts of the two quartos." [15]

The 1598 reprint of a third anonymous play, *Richard 2*, states for the first time, "By William Shake-speare."

A ninth play was printed anonymously in 1600, *Henry 5*, and reprinted anonymously in 1602. The next ten plays that were printed before Shakespeare's death, as shown on page 186, had Shakespeare's name on the title pages. Thus out of almost 3,000 plays that were produced during the 25 years of Shakespearean authorship, 36 plays are indisputably in the Shakespearean canon.

Of these 36 plays, only 12 titles appeared bearing William Shakespeare's name while he was alive—12 out of 3,000 plays over a period of 25 years.

And Who Wrote These?

Have you ever heard of the plays titled *Locrine, A Yorkshire Tragedy,* or *The London Prodigal?* These plays, among others, appeared in print while Shakespeare was alive with his name or initials on the title pages, and they appear in several of the Folios of Shakespearean plays. Scholars have created the mythology that Shakespeare's name appears on so many other plays because he was so popular as a dramatist. Supposedly, having his name on the written play would sell more copies of the play or make more people show up at the theater. But *The Tragedy of Locrine* (included in the 1664 Third Folio, second edition) was published "by W. S." in 1595, three years *before* the first play appeared with his name on it and before he had made a name for himself in the theater business. Interestingly, the title page of *Locrine* states that the play was "Newly set forth, overseen, and corrected by W. S." This attribution is remarkably similar to the title pages of three

---

15 Ibid., 313.

of the first four plays that carry Shakespeare's name, as mentioned on the previous page:

1598   *Love's Labor's Lost:* "Newly corrected and augmented By W. Shakespere."

1598   Reprint of *Richard 3:* "Newly augmented by W. Shakespeare."

1599   Reprint of *1 Henry 4:* "Newly corrected by W. Shakespeare."

Perhaps a more likely reason that Shakespeare's name appears on the title pages of those other plays is that the man named William Shakespeare also sold those other plays to printers, in addition to the twelve known Shakespearean plays. Diana Price, in her book *Shakespeare's Unorthodox Biography,* sets forth a clear case arguing that William Shaksper was a play broker.

In Shakespeare's time, the only people who would know a play's author are those very closely involved with the theater. And even of that small and close-knit group, no one personally mentions William Shakespeare as a *writer* of plays, although he was known to be an actor and a shareholder. Nor did anyone in this close-knit group record paying him for writing a play.

Pirates Ahead

Some of the plays that went into print individually were reproduced by means of what scholars have called "memorial reconstruction."[16] "According to the theory of memorial reconstruction, an actor (or actors) reconstructed the entire play from memory; evidence suggests that attempts at memorial reconstruction were usually made by actors who had had minor roles in the play."[17] For instance, Berryman believes that *2 Henry 6* was "constructed probably from memory by a minor actor with Pembroke's Men."[18] Although this theory of memorial reconstruction has been widely challenged, it is interesting that Clinton Heylin believes one of the most prolific of the transcriptionists was John Davies of Hereford, renowned for his speed-writing,

---

16   These plays have been thought by scholars to have been sold to a printer and reproduced through memorial reconstruction: *Richard 2, Henry 5, Merry Wives of Windsor, Romeo and Juliet, Hamlet, King Lear, Pericles.*

17   Campbell, *The Reader's Encyclopedia of Shakespeare,* 520.

18   John Berryman and John Haffenden, eds., *Berryman's Shakespeare* (New York: Farrar, Straus and Giroux, 1999), 36.

who then, according to Clinton, sold the plays to the press.[19] John Davies was Mary Sidney's secretary.

It is generally believed that the printed works attributed to Shakespeare are all unauthorized publications. Shakespeare's works, collectively, were by far the most frequently "pirated" (after "Anonymous"). Other authors were pirated, such as Francis Beaumont, John Fletcher, Robert Greene, Christopher Marlowe, and George Peele, but not more than two printings each.[20] As Diana Price explains, "Shakspere was a shrewd businessman, yet the flow of unauthorized editions went unchecked. Although copyright laws existed to serve licensing procedures and the stationers rather than to protect the author, it is not as though writers, even those who had less business savvy than Shakspere, had to tolerate unauthorized publications."[21] She describes the actions taken by Thomas Lodge, Samuel Daniel, George Chapman, Nicholas Breton, and Thomas Heywood when pirated editions of their work were published. "These writers protested, even if their protests came to naught. Shakspere did nothing."[22]

The long-held theory that theatrical companies did not want plays in print to prevent other acting companies from performing them has been effectively demolished by Roslyn Knutson and others, although the belief persists.[23] The canard that authors had no legal rights over their play texts after giving them to the acting company is also an inventive theory that has persisted as a supposed fact. Lukas Erne clarifies: "Unless a contract specifically forbade playwrights to have their plays published, what the acting company acquired from the author was the exclusive right to *perform* the play rather than a copyright in anything resembling its modern sense."[24] Nor is the theory credible that if a play was in print, it would prevent people from seeing the play: Peter Blayney states that there is "no evidence that any player ever feared that those who bought and read plays

---

19 Clinton Heylin, *So Long as Men Can Breathe: The Untold Story of Shakespeare's Sonnets* (New York: Da Capo Press, 2009), 188–266.

20 Diana Price, *Shakespeare's Unorthodox Biography: New Evidence of an Authorship Problem* (Westport: Greenwood Press, 2001), 130.

21 Ibid., 130.

22 Ibid., 131.

23 Roslyn L. Knutson, *The Repertory of Shakespeare's Company, 1594–1613* (Fayetteville, Arkansas: University of Arkansas Press, 1991).

24 Erne, *Shakespeare as Literary Dramatist*, 140n4.

would consequently lose interest in seeing them performed."[25] One has to wonder who was behind getting all these plays into print, and why did the author never complain?

"Never blotted out a line"

Writers would create a draft of a work, the theory goes, which was called the "foul papers." This draft was copied, often by a professional scribe, into a neat and clean version which was called the "fair papers." This is particularly interesting in light of comments about the manuscripts of the Shakespearean plays—it was recorded twice, after his death, that Shakespeare wrote so easily and fluidly that the players received manuscripts from him with not a single line blotted out. Ben Jonson mentions that the players told him this, and it's also mentioned by the actors who wrote an introduction in the First Folio.[26]

Few scholars believe even Shakespeare could write these complex, lengthy, and finely crafted plays so perfectly with no drafts at all, so it's a bit of a puzzlement why this bit of information has come down through history—twice—with so much certainty. Is it possible the acting companies never saw blotted lines because Shakespeare actually gave them, not his own "perfect" foul papers, but the fair papers from another author?

Documented Data

- The first eight plays in print were originally published anonymously.
- At least the first four published plays were performed by Pembroke's Men, the acting company sponsored by Mary Sidney, the Countess of Pembroke.
- The first three plays with Shakespeare's name on them claimed to be "newly corrected" by Shakespeare, but weren't.

25 Peter W. M. Blayney, "The Publication of Playbooks" in *A New History of Early English Drama* (New York: Columbia University Press, 1997), 386.

26 E. K. Chambers, *William Shakespeare: A Study of Facts and Problems*, vol. 2 (Oxford: Clarendon Press, 1930), 210. In Ben Jonson's papers called *Timber, or Discoveries*, he wrote, "I remember, the Players have often mentioned it as an honor to Shakespeare that in his writing (whatsoever he penned), he never blotted out a line. My answer hath been, would he had blotted a thousand. Which they thought a malevolent speech. I had not told posterity this, but for their ignorance, who choose that circumstance to commend their friend by, wherein he most faulted." In the First Folio, the epistle supposedly by Heminge and Condell states, "And what he thought, he uttered with that easiness, that we have scarce received from him a blot in his papers."

- It is theorized by traditional scholars that several of the plays were sold to printers by a bit actor or a transcriptionist.

- Several of the plays that were originally published anonymously were reprinted later with Shakespeare's name on the title pages. Scholars tell us all the printed plays were pirated—it was not Shakespeare who took them to press. Why, then, would a pirate assign a *reprint* to Shakespeare?

- In extant legal documents, William Shakespeare signed his name as Shakp, Shakspe, Shaksper, Shakspere, and Shakspear.[27] Yet on all but two printings of every play that bears his name over a thirty-year period, the plays are attributed to "Shakespeare."[28]

Was William Shakespeare the bit actor who intercepted these manuscripts and realized he could safely take credit for them in the playhouse? Did William Shakespeare take credit for the manuscripts and surreptitiously sell them to the printers? Was he, as Diana Price outlines, a play broker? The idea must be considered.

Fewer Plays but Most Published

Here's another odd thing: Although "Shakespeare" wrote fewer plays than many of the other playwrights, more Shakespearean plays were actually printed: Shakespeare "had become the best-published dramatist with far more title page ascriptions than any other English playwright dead or alive."[29]

The evidence that the Shakespearean plays were in print in a far greater number than any other contemporaneous plays indicates this author recognized the value of print for longevity. This is why the beliefs about Shakespeare that I find most untenable are 1) that Shakespeare was merely writing to put bread on the table, 2) that he did not realize he was a genius, and 3) that the plays meant little to him. This contradicts the author's own comments about the immortality of the printed work, lines such as, "When in eternal lines to time thou growest," or "Your monument shall be my gentle verse." Is any

---

27 The sixth signature is on his will and is illegible. It is assumed that it is spelled "Shakspere," as on the other page.

28 The anomalies: *Love's Labor's Lost* in 1598, "by W. Shakespere"; *King Lear* in 1608, "by William Shak-speare." Occasionally the name Shakespeare is hyphenated.

29 Lukas Erne, *Shakespeare as Literary Dramatist* (Cambridge: Cambridge University Press, 2013), 135.

genius of this level completely unaware that their work is better than others in their field? It is not the ephemerality of the stage that is going to guarantee a writer's immortality, but the perpetuity of print. As Lukas Erne states, "He could not help knowing that his plays were being read and reread, printed and reprinted, excerpted and anthologized as he was writing more plays."[30] This is a sign of an author who understands the value of their work.

We'll look next at the huge task of printing the entire collected works, known today as the First Folio.

---

30 Erne, *Shakespeare as Literary Dramatist,* 25.

Documented Data

- The first printed collection of Shakespearean plays is called the First Folio. It went to press five years after William Shakespeare died, and printing was completed two years later.

- There is no record of who paid for this large and expensive undertaking.

- The book is dedicated to Mary Sidney's two sons.

- Not a scrap of an original manuscript of a Shakespearean play or poem has ever been found.

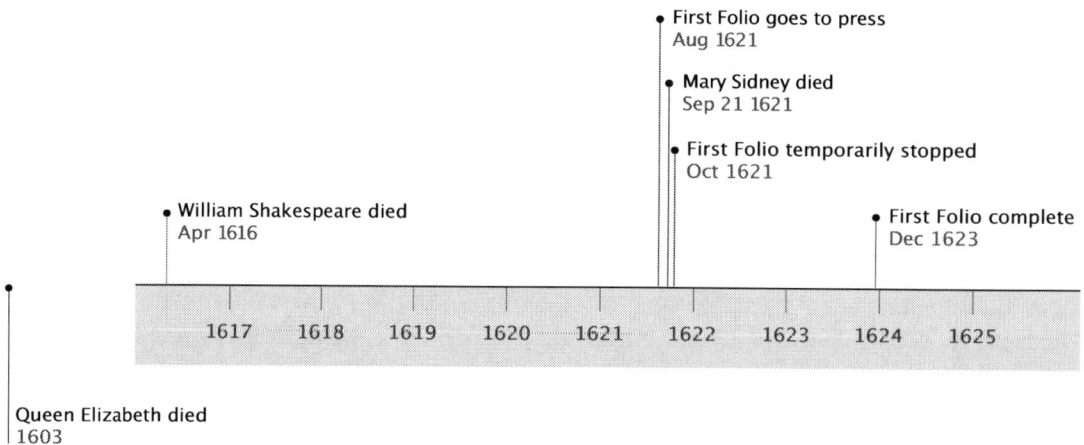

First Folio goes to press
Aug 1621

Mary Sidney died
Sep 21 1621

First Folio temporarily stopped
Oct 1621

William Shakespeare died
Apr 1616

First Folio complete
Dec 1623

1617 1618 1619 1620 1621 1622 1623 1624 1625

Queen Elizabeth died
1603

16 The Publication of the First Folio

IN 1623, THE PUBLICATION OF THE ENTIRE COLLECTION OF PLAYS was completed in what we now call the First Folio. Examining the publication history of this important book offers some interesting reflections on the possible author of the works.

The term "First Folio" is actually quite generic—it means this was the *first* time the plays were printed on large sizes of paper which were folded in half, called *folios,* and the final copies were hard bound. Shakespeare's First Folio is a book about 13 inches tall, 8.5 inches wide, 2 inches thick, and it weighs more than ten pounds. This is not a book that actors carry around on stage—it was printed to be *read,* as its epistle states: "for the Great Variety of Readers."

The First Folio is dedicated to Mary Sidney's two sons: William Herbert, the third Earl of Pembroke, and Philip Herbert, the first Earl of Montgomery. No personal or professional connection between Shakespeare and Mary's sons has ever been found. In fact, *The Reader's Encyclopedia of Shakespeare* muses that "[Philip] Herbert was a generous patron of the arts, but he was habitually in debt, a fact which makes his selection as a dedicatee of such an expensive volume as the folio somewhat unusual."[1]

By the time the dedication was written, William Shakespeare had been dead for seven years. The dedication is not from Shakespeare—it is from two actors in the King's Men (the acting company of which Shakespeare was a member) named John Heminges and Henry Condell. They are *assumed* to be the editors of the First Folio. The famous portrait of Shakespeare in the First Folio was engraved by

Time and trouble will tame an advanced young woman, but an advanced old woman is uncontrollable by any earthly force.
Dorothy L. Sayers
1893–1957

---

1   Oscar James Campbell, ed., *The Reader's Encyclopedia of Shakespeare* (New York: MJF Books, 1966), 620.

22-year-old Martin Droeshout, who was only 15 years old when Shakespeare died; there is no evidence that Droeshout ever knew William Shakespeare.

The Missing Manuscripts

As mentioned previously, the theory is that a writer's original draft is called the "foul papers"; when a draft is complete, the foul papers are neatly rewritten, often by a professional scribe, into the "fair papers" that would be sent to the print shop or playhouse. A "prompt book" is the authoritative playhouse copy of the entire script, sometimes broken down into acts, scenes, and stage directions. From the prompt book, each actor's part was written on a long paper scroll, or roll, from which comes our present term for an actor's "role."

Not one scrap of paper from any of the original handwritten Shakespearean manuscripts has ever been found. Not one piece—no plot outline, no foul papers, no fair papers. Thirty-six lengthy plays spanning a publishing period of more than twenty-five years (1594 to 1619), and not one word in the author's handwriting.[2]

Stratfordian scholars insist this means nothing, that once a play was in print, the original handwritten manuscripts were useless and the paper recycled—cooks would use it to wrap fish or line baking pans, or bookbinders would use it to attach hardbound covers.

Some will even tell you there are no original manuscripts of anyone else's plays either. But Thomas Middleton's play, *A Game at Chess*, was printed in three quarto editions within a year and a half, was hugely popular on stage, and yet survives in a number of manuscript copies. Fulke Greville wrote three tragedies between 1594 and 1601: *Antonie and Cleopatra*, *Mustapha*, and *Alaham*; "The first he himself destroyed; *the other two are extant in both manuscript and print*."[3] [emphasis added]

In *Dramatic Documents from the Elizabethan Playhouses*, Greg describes in great detail the original handwritten plots, actor's parts, prompt books, and manuscript plays from that era that are in museums and collections, and he doesn't even include the extant pages from early dramas, masques (elaborate performances at court or in aristocrats' homes), court entertainments, closet dramas, or academic plays. Greg's

2   *Othello* was registered in 1611 but not printed in quarto until 1622.

3   Gerald Eades Bentley, *The Profession of Dramatist in Shakespeare's Time, 1590–1642* (Princeton: Princeton University Press, 1971), 20.

oversized companion book, *Reproductions & Transcripts,* provides reproductions of many of the documents. There are handwritten manuscripts for plays by a number of Shakespeare's contemporaries, such as Munday, Massinger, Heywood, Suckling, Daborne, Fletcher, Beaumont, and others—many of which went to press.

Paul Werstine, in "Plays in Manuscript," complains that Greg's work was too limited, that he did not record the extensive holdings of the Folger Shakespeare Library in Washington, D.C., the Huntington Library in San Marino, California, or the Alnwick Castle library, north of Newcastle, England.[4] And just recently—within the past thirty years—dramatic manuscripts from the Elizabethan and Tudor eras have been found at the Warwickshire Record Office, Arbury Hall in Nuneaton, and Castle Ashby.[5] But even Werstine's more far-reaching scope has yet to find one page of a manuscript of a Shakespearean play or sonnet.

There are a great number of manuscript documents of other written work, besides plays, that also went to press. H. R. Woudhuysen in *Sir Philip Sidney and the Circulation of Manuscripts* tells us, "There are three such manuscripts of *Astrophel and Stella* and eleven of the *Old Arcadia* or parts of it.... One manuscript of the *New Arcadia* survives, two of *A Defense of Poetry,* and a dozen or so private miscellanies contain poems in texts not copied from the early prints."[6] All of these works went to press, yet we still have the manuscripts. Woudhuysen also states that, "Copies of individual shorter poems presented to specific patrons or friends also sometimes survive entirely in the author's hand."[7]

An "authorial" (handwritten by the author) manuscript by John Donne, "The Gunpowder Plot Sermon," was recently discovered to add to the sixteen other *manuscripts* of Donne's *printed* collection of sermons. There are also two manuscript copies of the first book printed in two colors in England, a book of falconry written by Dame Juliana Berners in 1486.

....

4   Paul Werstine, "Plays in Manuscript," in *A New History of Early English Drama,* eds. John D. Cox and David Scott Kastan (New York: Columbia University Press, 1997), 482.

5   Ibid., 493. Specifically, the Malone Society found *Tom A Lincoln* in 1992; six manuscripts were found at the Warwickshire Record Office and Arbury Hall "constituting the canon of the amateur playwright John Newdigate III"; in 1977 at Castle Ashby, William Williams found thirteen manuscript plays written by Cosmo Manuche, three of which were in multiple drafts.

6   H. R. Woudhuysen, *Sir Philip Sidney and the Circulation of Manuscripts, 1558–1640* (Oxford: Oxford University Press, 1996), 212.

7   Ibid., 92.

There are even extant preliminary *drafts* of works by various authors. "There are plenty of examples of Bacon's working drafts of his philosophical and scientific works, especially in Latin; Camden's autograph preliminary version of Edward Herbert, Lord Cherbury's prose works are preserved in the National Library of Wales. Autograph notes for *Of the lawes of ecclesiasticall politie* and a draft of one of Hooker's sermons are at Trinity College Dublin. . . . Several notebooks and sets of memorandums in Sir Walter Raleigh's hand are extant."[8]

Why are the manuscripts of these writers still available? Often it is because an author had a sense of his or her own importance and suspected the manuscript would always be valuable. It is bizarre to insist that the man named William Shakespeare, supposedly the most profound genius in literary history, did not understand and appreciate the value of his own work and thus simply tossed the original manuscripts of every single play and poem into the rubbish bin or gave them to the cook to use as liners in pastry dishes.

The First Folio itself belies the traditional excuse that there are no Shakespearean manuscripts because they were always destroyed as soon as a play was printed. As Charlton Hinman explains, "Some of the plays in the Folio apparently do reproduce Shakespeare's own 'foul papers' . . . and a number were set into type from combinations, part manuscript and part printed, or materials variously related to Shakespeare's original papers."[9]

Eighteen of the plays in the Folio had been printed in the previous thirty years, most of them in several editions, before the First Folio was compiled. Of these eighteen plays previously in print, scholars believe that the editors of the First Folio used original manuscripts or even foul papers (drafts) for at least five of the plays, and the prompt books for three others.[10] Each of these eight plays had been in print

---

8 Ibid., 95.

9 Charlton Hinman, *The Printing and Proof-Reading of the First Folio of Shakespeare*, vol. 1 (Oxford: Clarendon Press, 1963), 4.

10 According to *The Reader's Encyclopedia of Shakespeare* and E. K. Chambers, the following printed plays used original manuscripts for the First Folio: *Titus Andronicus*, originally printed in 1594, used the original manuscript in 1622, almost thirty years later. *The Taming of the Shrew*, originally printed in 1594, used the original manuscript almost thirty years later. *2 Henry 4*, originally printed in 1600, used the original manuscript. *Troilus and Cressida*, originally printed in 1609, was set in conjunction with the original manuscript. *Henry 5*, originally printed in 1600, used the draft or foul papers. *Hamlet*, originally printed in 1603, *The Merry Wives of Windsor*, originally printed in 1602, and *King Lear*, originally printed in 1608, apparently used prompt books.

between 1594 and 1609, yet the original manuscripts or at least the prompt books were still available in 1622, during the printing process. This indicates it was *not* a ubiquitous practice to destroy the manuscript after a play went to press.

Publishing Literary Works

Woudhuysen states that it was the posthumous publication of Philip Sidney's work, begun in the 1590s, that paved the way for writers like Shakespeare to print their own works:

> Sidney's sudden availability in print also had an important influence on the production of literature. It is too simple to suggest that writers thought that if his work could be exposed to the public view their own could be as well, but there may be an element of truth in this. . . . Sidney became a standard author, as Daniel . . . Spenser, Drayton, Jonson, Shakespeare, and eventually Greville were all to do within the next few years. In this way, it could be argued that the 1598 folio [of Philip's literary works] served as a model for later writers and promoted the idea of a predominantly print-based literary culture.[11]

Philip had died in 1586—*it was Mary Sidney who published Philip's collected works in folio in 1598 in the form and style appropriate to the writing, thus establishing a permanent place for him in the literary world.* It is Mary Sidney who promoted the idea of a print-based—as opposed to manuscript-based—literary culture. Mary also published her own writing, and her audacity thus paved the way for men—even noblemen—to publish their own work.

Ben Jonson, in 1616, set a precedent for considering dramatic works as enduring literary achievements by publishing his plays in *The Works of Benjamin Jonson.* Rosalind Miles states, "By his insistence that plays were worthy of the kind of formal treatment and attention that had previously been reserved for other literary productions, Jonson made an incalculable contribution to the raising of the drama's status in England."[12]

---

11 Woudhuysen, *Sir Philip Sidney and the Circulation of Manuscripts, 1558–1640*, 386–87.

12 Rosalind Miles, *Ben Jonson: His Life and Work* (London and New York: Routledge & Kegan Paul, 1986), 171.

It has often been said by Stratfordians, as an excuse to explain Shakespeare's odd reluctance to produce an authoritative collection of his own work while he was alive, that everyone laughed when Jonson published his plays. This aspersion is simply not true. For one thing, Jonson published his folio six months *after Shakespeare died;* obviously, William Shakespeare was not intimidated by the reaction to it. Jonson's own Folio "was ushered into the world with the support of laudatory verses from many of Jonson's friends," including John Selden, George Chapman, Francis Beaumont, Edward Hayward, and Abraham Holland. The portrait engraved for the book was printed and sold separately, "which gives some indication of Jonson's popularity and the public interest in him at this time."[13] David Riggs assures us that Jonson was "a man who outshone even Shakespeare and Donne in the eyes of his contemporaries."[14] Jonson's collected works did not ridicule the process—it legitimized plays as literature.

The one derogatory comment that Stratfordians refer to, if they even know the actual reference, is this, by an anonymous wit: "Pray tell me, Ben, where doth the mystery lurk, What others call a play you call a work." But this comment was made in 1640, almost twenty-five years after Shakespeare died. The comment was answered anonymously: "Ben's plays are works, when others' works are plays."[15] Please don't be misled into believing that Shakespeare didn't publish his works because Jonson was supposedly derided—this is simply one of the many unsupported anecdotes used to explain anomalies in Williams Shakespeare's supposed career.

Printing the First Folio

The entire collection of Shakespearean plays, half of them never printed before and few documented as being performed on stage, was first taken to the press in August of 1621.[16] William Shakespeare had been dead for five years. Did Mary Sidney begin the printing process?

The First Folio went to press without being licensed—not an extremely rare occurrence, but it is unusual.[17] "Before a play could be printed, it had to be licensed. The licensing agent responsible for

---

13 Ibid., 172.
14 David Riggs, *Ben Jonson: A Life* (Cambridge, London: Harvard Univ. Press, 1989), 3.
15 W. David Kay, *Ben Jonson, A Literary Life* (New York: St. Martin's Press, 1995), 141.
16 E. E. Willoughby, *The Printing of the First Folio of Shakespeare* (Great Britain: Oxford University Press, 1932), 28. Hinman's challenge to Willoughby's timeline is not convincing.
17 E. E. Willoughby, *A Printer of Shakespeare* (London: Philip Allan & Co. Ltd, 1934), 21.

printed matter was a panel of London clergymen . . . operating under the authority of the Privy Council, the Bishop of London, the Archbishop of Canterbury, and the Lord Chamberlain."[18] Who was the Lord Chamberlain in 1621? Mary's oldest son, William Herbert. "Once he became Lord Chamberlain . . . he was responsible for overseeing all the court's entertainment as well as having final control of licensing the public theater."[19]

Is it possible Mary Sidney had to circumvent licensing a book that would have threatened the reputation of the Lord Chamberlain, a book she didn't even want her son to know she was publishing?

The title page of the First Folio falsely states, "Published According to the True Original Copies." The first four plays in the Folio were printed from copies made by a professional scribe; the others are cobbled together from a variety of sources, as explained in the previous pages.[20] "If the editors had planned to continue this practice [of using true original copies] throughout the volume, however, they abandoned it after the fourth play and turned instead to a variety of sorts of copy."[21]

Did Mary provide the printer with these first four plays, planning to supply the others as the project progressed? We know that in July of 1621 she entertained King James at Houghton House in Ampthill, where the King's Men, the acting company to which Shakespeare and Richard Burbage belonged, acted before the court—possibly a performance of As You Like It.[22] But in August of 1621 she was back in her London home on Aldersgate Street, just a block or two from Jaggard's printshop where the First Folio was printed. Did she come into London for the specific purpose of finally publishing her own work?

The printer begins production of the book in August, 1621.[23] Production of the book stops in October. Where was Mary Sidney? Between the onset of publication and the stopping of the press, she died.

18 David Bevington, ed., The Complete Works of Shakespeare, 6th ed. (New York: Pearson Longman, 2009), xcv.
19 Gary Waller, Sidney Family Romance (Detroit: Wayne State University Press, 1993), 230.
20 The first four plays are The Tempest, Two Gentlemen of Verona, The Merry Wives of Windsor, and Measure for Measure. (Perhaps also The Winter's Tale and Cymbeline.)
21 Bevington, Complete Works of Shakespeare, xcvii.
22 Michael G. Brennan and Noel J. Kinnamon, A Sidney Chronology 1554–1654 (New York: Palgrave Macmillan, 2003), 176.
23 Willoughby, A Printer of Shakespeare, 166. Also W. W. Greg, The Shakespeare First Folio: Its Bibliographic and Textual History (Oxford: Clarendon Press, 1955), 4.

Her funeral was held at St. Paul's in London; her tomb is under the choir steps of Salisbury Cathedral, directly on the Avon River, near her Wilton home. The parish records of Salisbury Cathedral state only that she was buried, but John Chamberlain (a gentleman and scholar in the court of King James) gossiped in a letter from London, "The old Countess of Pembroke died here some ten days since of the smallpox, and on Wednesday night was carried with a great store of coaches [probably no less than a hundred] and torchlight toward Wilton where she is to be buried."[24] It is said that no will was found, which is extremely odd for a woman of her age and with her assets. Mary's lover, Dr. Matthew Lister, received £120 to £140 a year (close to $25,000 today) for the rest of his life—how did that happen without a will? And why?

But back to the press: Printing eventually resumed for the First Folio and the project was completed in December, 1623—seven and a half years after William Shakespeare died. The expense must have been enormous. William Prynne, a Puritan leader, was incensed that this book of plays was "printed in the best Crown paper, far better than most Bibles."[25]

In *Who Wrote Shakespeare?*, John Michell remarks on the finished folio:

> The editors of the First Folio hinted by two or three phrases that the author was the man buried at Stratford-upon-Avon, but they never openly stated it. There were no biographical notes on the great dramatist, nor any indications of where and when the plays were written. On the question of how they acquired authentic copies and the rights to plays previously published, the editors were secretive and mendacious. The originals from which they worked have never been seen since.[26]

The traditional theory of the publication of the First Folio contradicts standard scholarship that once a play was bought by an acting company, it was owned by the acting company.

24 Margaret Hannay, *Philip's Phoenix: Mary Sidney, Countess of Pembroke* (Oxford: Oxford University Press, 1990), 205.
25 Quoted in Anthony James West, *The Shakespeare First Folio: The History of the Book* (Oxford: Oxford University Press, 2001), 7.
26 John Michell, *Who Wrote Shakespeare?* (London: Thames and Hudson, 1996), 80.

[This theory] does not tell us why the King's Men would let two of their members appropriate so valuable a property and dispose of it on their own—for there is no suggestion that the company itself had any hand in publishing the plays. It does not tell us how two actors would have raised the small fortune such a publishing venture would have called for or why anyone putting up the funds would have left the immensely important task of editing the thirty-six plays and preparing them for the printer to two undistinguished stage-players with no experience to fit them for the work, one of them to turn grocer. If we seek answers to the crucial questions the First Folio raises, I think we shall be forced to accept the indications that those primarily responsible for the publication were the Herbert brothers.[27]

Shakespeare had been an actor with the King's Men.

The Herbert brothers, of course, are Mary's sons.

If Mary Sidney is the author, where are *her* manuscripts of these plays? It is possible that her son William Herbert destroyed any manuscripts he came across, as he is known to have destroyed documents about his illegitimate children. It is possible that manuscripts are yet to be found; perhaps we've been looking in the wrong places. If Mary Sidney is the author, would she have hidden the manuscripts from her son? With extensive libraries, several estates, and the ability to travel freely, where might a brilliant woman safely leave her writing? And what happened to her will?

---

27 Charlton Ogburn, *The Mysterious William Shakespeare: The Myth and the Reality* (McLean, Virginia: Dodd, Mead & Co./EPM Publications, Inc., 1984), 219. Also, as shown at the end of the previous chapter in this book, this theory of ownership has been proven to be false.

Ben Jonson's Poem to "the AUTHOR"

*Ben Jonson,
self-proclaimed poet
laureate of England.*

Ben Jonson wrote a poem for the First Folio that is rather puzzling. In 1618, two years after William Shakespeare died, Jonson specifically told the poet Sir William Drummond that Shakespeare "wanted art," meaning he lacked study in the art and craft of writing. Yet in the First Folio poem, Jonson praises the author for studying the craft of writing and for the meticulous fine-tuning. "This well-known poem is not merely a conventional tribute. The deep sincerity of Jonson's admiration and his true love for the dead Shakespeare are everywhere apparent. He salutes Shakespeare as 'Soul of the Age!' He places him above all contemporary poets; he is the one genius with which Britain may rival the classical writers of old, and Jonson envisages him transported to heaven to reign as a 'star of poets' to inspire his successors." [28]

David Riggs, one of Jonson's foremost biographers, is more critical: "Much of what Jonson has to say in this poem is strikingly at odds with his previous references to Shakespeare. . . . Heretofore, [Jonson] had always championed the cause of art and had repeatedly chastised the popular playwrights of his day for relying on their own raw talent; now Jonson turned the tables and praised Shakespeare for the very qualities he had derided in the past. . . . But his willingness to grant that Shakespeare actually satisfied this criterion comes as a surprise and has even prompted critics to question his sincerity." [29]

For all of Jonson's acclamation in the First Folio in 1623, on Shakespeare's death in 1616, Jonson never wrote a word. Nor did he later acknowledge Shakespeare as one of the great writers. In his prose piece *Timber, or Discoveries* (printed in 1641 but written earlier), Jonson recommends, "And as it is fit to read the best authors to youth first, so let them be of the openest and clearest. As Livy before Sallust, *Sidney* before Donne; and beware of letting them taste Gower or Chaucer at first." [emphasis added] He also recommends that students read Edmund Spenser.

To which **Sidney** does Jonson refer?

But no Shakespeare.

Ben Jonson had long been closely associated with Mary and her Wilton Circle, her sons, and her younger brother Robert. In 1616, the year Shakespeare died, Jonson wrote a poem about Mary's childhood home, Penshurst, where Robert continued to live as an adult. "Sir Robert Sidney . . . despite his own insoluble financial difficulties,

---

28 Campbell, *Reader's Encyclopedia of Shakespeare*, 407.
29 Riggs, *Ben Jonson: A Life*, 277–78.

offered Jonson both patronage and hospitality at his country house Penshurst in Kent, which Jonson came to love dearly."[30]

One reason for his love is that the Sidneys and Herberts treated Jonson with warmth and respect, seating and conversing with him at the same supper table and serving him the same beer and bread—treatment he was not accorded in other noble households. William Herbert gave Ben Jonson £20 every New Year's Day to buy books. When Ben copied out sonnets written by Lady Mary Wroth (Mary Sidney's niece, Robert's daughter), he claimed that he became "a better lover and much better poet."[31] Jonson wrote numerous poems and epigrams to and about members of the family. "Jonson consistently portrays the Sidneys and the Herberts as members of a self-contained aristocratic community that is answerable only to its own ancestral traditions."[32]

Understanding how the generally cantankerous Ben Jonson admired and respected the Sidney and Herbert families, is it possible, after Mary Sidney died and the First Folio was on the press, that William Herbert confided to Ben Jonson that his mother was the author of these plays? Was Jonson the editor? Or is it the other way around—did Jonson tell William Herbert that the author was his mother?

It might explain why Jonson, who had previously spoken poorly of William Shakespeare, in the First Folio eulogy calls "my beloved, the AUTHOR" the *Star of Poets* and the *Sweet Swan of Avon*.

It is *assumed* that Heminges and Condell, two actors with the King's Men, were the editors of the First Folio. But in *The Reader's Encyclopedia of Shakespeare*, Oscar James Campbell observes, "The text was obviously edited by someone familiar with the plays who would be responsible for eliminating profanity, making acting divisions, and other details. It is doubtful that Heminges and Condell would be qualified for this exacting work."[33]

Riggs believes that Jonson may well have been one of the editors. He notes that whoever prepared the Folio "remade Shakespeare in Jonson's image" and describes how the prefatory letters and poems in the book "transform Shakespeare into a specifically literary figure

---

30 Miles, *Ben Jonson: His Life and Work*, 87–88.
31 Kay, *Ben Jonson, A Literary Life*, 117.
32 Riggs, *Ben Jonson: A Life*, 180.
33 Campbell, *Reader's Encyclopedia of Shakespeare*, 229–30.

whose works have achieved the status of modern classics; the closest analogue to these tributes are the poems prefixed to Jonson's 1616 folio."[34] Riggs explains how the First Folio follows the same method of punctuation that Jonson used in his own *Works* instead of that used in the previously published editions of the Shakespearean plays. And the "extensive use of parentheses, semicolons, and end-stopped lines in the 1623 [Shakespearean First Folio] owes more to Jonson's example than to Shakespeare's habits of composition."[35] A line in *Julius Caesar* that Jonson had derided as ridiculous appears in the First Folio as corrected and logical—is this Jonson's edit?[36]

The Possibility

If Mary Sidney began the printing process in 1621, is it possible that after she died, the printer contacted her son the Lord Chamberlain about the unfinished project—and payment?

As mentioned in Chapter 4, Mary Sidney and William Herbert had been estranged for at least ten years, beginning about 1604. The cause of the estrangement is not clear; was it her relationship with the lower-class doctor—or did William discover his mother was writing plays for the public theater? Up until this time, William Herbert might have been the only person aware that Mary Sidney was the author. But now, to finish the project and attribute the plays to William Shakespeare for posterity, Herbert would have needed help—did he at this point call on Ben Jonson? Or as mentioned earlier, did Ben Jonson call on William Herbert? And why did Jonson call the author of the plays the "Sweet Swan of Avon"?

---

34 Riggs, *Ben Jonson: A Life*, 276.

35 Ibid., 276.

36 In Jonson's *Timber, or Discoveries*, published posthumously in 1641, he wrote this of "Shakespeare": "Many times he fell into those things, could not escape laughter: As when he said in the person of Caesar, one speaking to him; Caesar, thou dost me wrong. He replyed: Caesar did never wrong, but with just cause: and such like; which were ridiculous." The line in the First Folio has been changed to the logical "Caesar doth not wrong, nor without cause will he be satisfied."

17 The Sweet Swan of Avon

SPECIFICALLY WRITTEN FOR THE PUBLICATION of the First Folio, the poem by Ben Jonson calls the author of the plays his "Beloved" and the "Sweet Swan of Avon":

> Sweet Swan of Avon! what a sight it were
> To see thee in our waters yet appear,
> And make those flights upon the banks of Thames,
> That so did take Eliza [Queen Elizabeth] and our [King] James!

What did thy song bode, lady? Hark, canst thou hear me? I will play the swan, And die in music. "Willow, willow, willow."
Emilia in *Othello*, 5.2.255–257

Why would Ben Jonson call a great writer a "Sweet Swan"? No one on record refers to William Shakespeare as a swan.

A good writer uses symbols to enrich phrases and to capture all of the connotations of an image into a succinct impression. Ben Jonson was no exception; throughout his life he insisted on the importance of correct speech. He rebuked careless writers who used "such impropriety of phrase, such plenty of solecisms, such dearth of sense, so bold prolepses, so racked metaphors."[1] To Jonson, literary sloppiness was a sign of intellectual weakness.

Why does Jonson call the author a swan? A swan is sometimes called the Bird of Return. White swans are famous for their beauty, but more importantly and pertinently, white swans are mute until their dying breath.

> 'Tis strange that Death should sing.
> I am the cygnet to this pale faint swan
> Who chants a doleful hymn to his own death,
> And from the organ-pipe of frailty sings
> His soul and body to their lasting rest.
> Prince Henry, to his dying father in *King John*, 5.7.20–24

A cygnet is a baby swan. The "organ-pipe of frailty" is the long neck of the swan, through which her dying gasp creates a sort of song.

---

1 David Riggs, *Ben Jonson: A Life* (Cambridge, London: Harvard University Press, 1989), 13 (spelling modernized).

The traditional assumption of "Sweet Swan of Avon" is that Jonson refers to William Shakespeare who lived in the village of Stratford, situated on the Avon River—which still doesn't explain the swan or the swan making flights on the banks of the Thames river.

Was Jonson really referring to Shakespeare? His entire eulogy to "my beloved the AUTHOR" is suspect in that he seemingly idolizes a man for whom he is on record as having disliked and whom he later ignored.[2]

There are several rivers in England named Avon, and Ben Jonson never mentions Stratford in any reference to Shakespeare. Mary Sidney, however, lived on an estate encompassing 14,000 acres at the time, or 22 square miles. The Wiltshire Avon ran through her property. A tributary of the Avon, called the Wylye, flows right past Wilton House, as does the River Nadder. She is buried in Salisbury Cathedral, located three miles from Wilton House and directly on the Avon River.

Mary chose to be known by her maiden name, Sidney. We know that her brother, Philip Sidney, because of his name, was referred to as a swan by his French friends: "So his French admirers made play with the similarity of sound between *Sidney* and *cygne* [French for swan] and made puns about swans."[3] A portrait of Philip printed in a French translation of *Arcadia* is topped with swans.[4] Philip was immortalized by poets as a swan, as in this example by the French poet Du Bartas:

> And (World-mourn'd) Sidney, warbling to the Thames
> His Swan-like tunes, so courts her coy proud streams . . . [5]

Perhaps it was the French influence of *Sidney/cygne* that encouraged Mary to take the swan as her own personal emblem, or perhaps it was a memorial to Philip after his death. In one of this playwright's favorite books, *Metamorphoses*, Ovid tells of three persons named Cygnus, each of whom gets transformed into an actual swan.

In 1592, Samuel Daniel, an important writer of the era and a close friend of hers, writes of Mary in his sonnet sequence titled *Delia*, Sonnet 48. Delia, according to every Sidneian scholar, refers to Mary Sidney:[6]

---

2   Ibid., 277.
3   John Buxton, *Sir Philip Sidney and the English Renaissance* (New York and London: St. Martin's Press, 1966), 106n1.
4   Ibid., frontispiece.
5   Quoted in Buxton, *Sir Philip Sidney*, 48.
6   Christopher Marlowe also refers to Mary as Delia: In a dedication to "Mary Countess of Pembroke," Marlowe begins, "Delia born of a laurel-crowned race, true sister of Sidney the bard of Apollo . . . ."

> *But Avon, rich in fame, though poor in waters*
> *Shall have my song, where Delia hath her seat.*
> *Avon shall be my Thames, and she my song;*
> *I'll sound her name the river all along.*

Of this phrase in the sonnet, Margaret Hannay remarks, "In fact, Wilton [the house itself] is not far from the Avon, which runs through Salisbury, but a more plausible reference is to Mary Sidney's seat at Ivychurch, a few miles southeast of Wilton on the Avon." [7]

The writer Michael Drayton, a contemporary of Mary's who is honored with burial in Poets' Corner in Westminster Abbey, refers to Mary in 1593 as a swan on the Thames in his poem "Shepherd's Garland":

> *The lofty subject of a heavenly tale,*
> *Thames' fairest Swan, our summer's Nightingale.* [8]

In a portrait of Mary when she was 57 years old, shown on the following page, she poses wearing a large, lace collar and wrist-cuffs embroidered with a motif of swans. Swan wings connect the bottom of the oval frame. The portrait is surrounded by two large, feather pens in ink wells—a female swan is called a "pen." She is noted to have used white swan quill pens for her writing; swan quills were the most expensive and last the longest. Was Mary's swan motif a poignant message of her anonymous writing?

In the portrait, she is shown holding one of the books she wrote, *David's Psalms,* and the image is topped with a poet's laurel wreath above the Sidney spearhead. This is the image of a woman who wants to be remembered as a writer and as a Sidney.

As mentioned, Ben Jonson refers to the author of the First Folio as the "Sweet Swan of Avon." Five lines later, Jonson declares that the author is a constellation:

> *But stay, I see thee in the Hemisphere*
> *Advanc'd, and made a constellation there!*

The constellation Jonson refers to is probably Cygnus, the swan, since he just mentioned the swan.

---

7   Margaret Hannay, *Philip's Phoenix: Mary Sidney, Countess of Pembroke* (Oxford: Oxford University Press, 1990), 117. Today the Wilton House estate encompasses only twenty-one acres. However, when Mary Sidney lived at Wilton House with its 14,000 acres, the Avon River ran through her property.

8   Quoted in Frances Berkeley Young, *Mary Sidney, Countess of Pembroke* (London: David Nutt, 1912), 175–76.

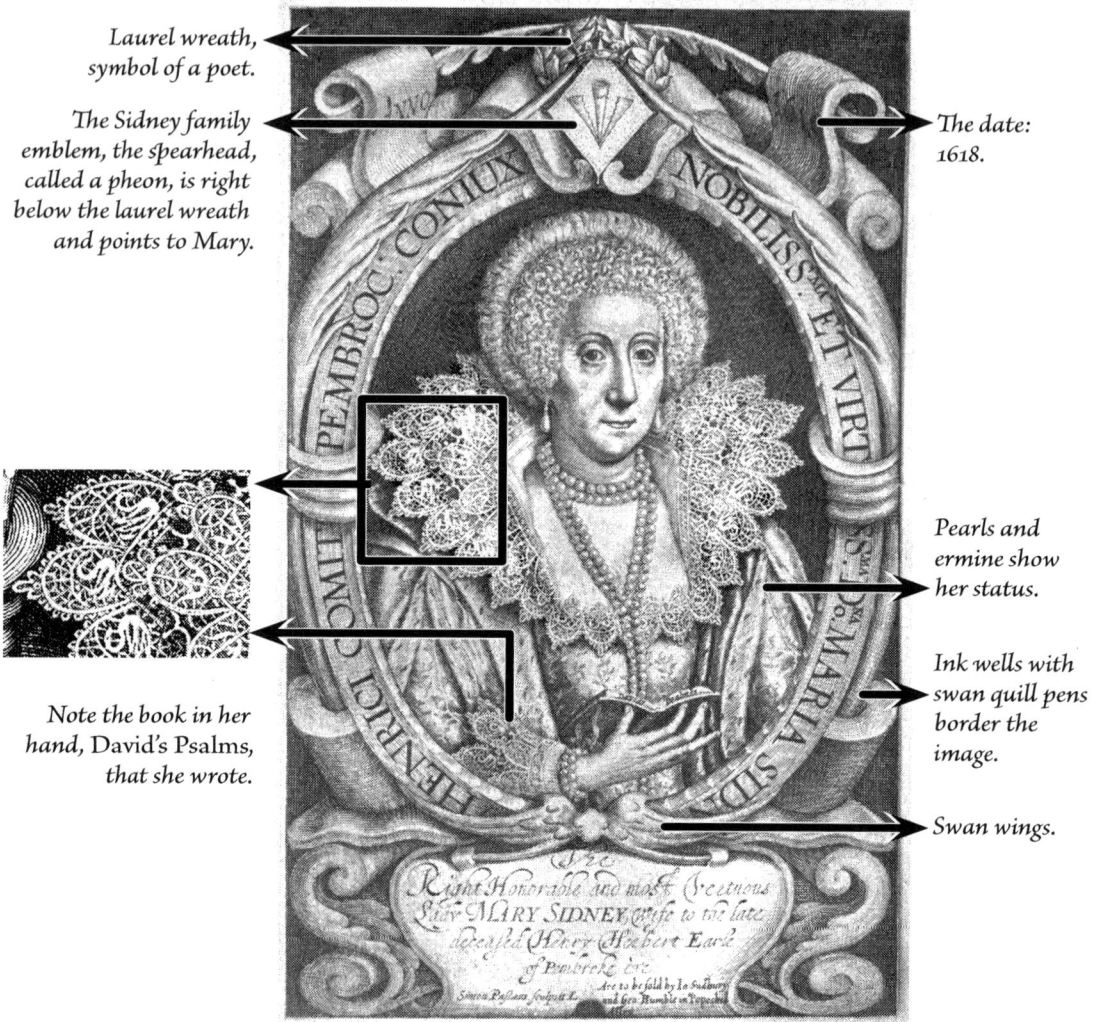

Laurel wreath, symbol of a poet.

The Sidney family emblem, the spearhead, called a pheon, is right below the laurel wreath and points to Mary.

The date: 1618.

Pearls and ermine show her status.

Ink wells with swan quill pens border the image.

Note the book in her hand, David's Psalms, that she wrote.

Swan wings.

This inscription refers to her as "Mary Sidney," her maiden name, and not as Mary Herbert.

Knowing that this brilliant writer adopted the swan as her personal symbol, combined with the tangible Avon associations—contemporary poets call her a swan; the name she prefers to be known by is, in French, essentially "Swan"; the Avon River ran through her estate; she is buried on the Avon River—is it possible that Ben Jonson is referring to Mary Sidney as the *Sweet Swan of Avon*?

Part Eight

The Possibility

*All truths are easy to understand
once they are discovered—
the trick is to discover them.*

Galileo, 1564–1642, 78 years old

It has become fashionable in recent literary criticism . . . to deny the relevance of the author . . . . Whatever justification our personal interest in Shakespeare may have, I can only say that I feel no need to apologize for it. Our curiosity is too natural and too common to be blushed at. Like millions of others, I am interested in who Shakespeare was as a simple matter of historical fact, and if the doctors of literature condemn our inquiry, we can appeal to the historian.

Joseph Sobran in *Alias Shakespeare*

18 Mary Sidney, alias Shakespeare

THE FOLLOWING IS A WHAT-IF STORY that involves the known facts about the lives of William Shakespeare and Mary Sidney. In the story, all of the statements are documented facts *except for the italicized phrases,* which are suggestions based on my research. This exercise shows us how little it would take to acknowledge her authorship.

First they ignore you, then they ridicule you, then they fight you, then you win.
Mahatma Ghandi

IN 1561, MARY SIDNEY, born into the aristocracy, is invited by Queen Elizabeth to be a maid-of-honor in the royal court after the deaths of both of her sisters. She is thirteen years old. Her first experience at court is the nineteen-day extravaganza held at Kenilworth Castle, home of her uncle Robert Dudley, the Queen's favorite. Mary, at 13, is acknowledged in writing for her intelligence.

Robert Dudley arranges a politically motivated marriage for Mary, age 15, with a 43-year-old nobleman, the widowed Welsh Earl of Pembroke. Within a year after the wedding Mary leaves Elizabeth's court to preside over her own "court" at Wilton House, her husband's estate.

Mary's beloved older brother, Philip Sidney, spends most of his time at Wilton after returning from his European tour. Philip nurtures their mission to create great works of literature in the English language. He and Mary study, write, and develop a literary salon at Wilton House. While Philip writes his sonnet sequence that will inspire the sonnet craze in England, Mary writes *seventeen "procreation" sonnets for Philip because* he is almost thirty years old, is the only heir to two powerful Earls, and he is yet unmarried.

Tragedy strikes: Mary's cherished and spirited three-year-old daughter dies the day Mary gives birth to her second son. Within the year Mary's father dies. Three months later her mother dies.

Devastated, Mary herself takes ill and almost dies. Two months later Mary's beloved brother Philip dies while fighting a war for the Queen. Mary is barely 25 years old.

Mary writes *Sonnet 18* ("Shall I compare thee to a summer's day") *as a goodbye letter to Philip,* but is not allowed to participate in the public eulogies at his funeral because she is a woman. She publishes several elegies to her brother in other works over the next few years.

She spends two years in mourning, *writes Titus Andronicus,* and at the end of this period literally marches triumphantly into London in a grand and brilliant procession. Mary takes the literary mantle from her brother—her mentor—and carries on his work. She is 27 years old.

While Mary Sidney marries, then births and buries her children and other close family members, William Shakespeare, 18 years old, takes a license to marry young Anne Whateley of Temple Grafton. But the next day he is hauled off by two older men, friends of Ann Hathaway's dead father, to marry Ann Hathaway of Stratford—half-again as old as Shakespeare and three months pregnant. Ann gives birth to a girl, then two years later, twins (a boy and a girl). Shakespeare moves to London without his family.

Mary publishes her brother's works and zealously strives to keep his memory alive as a poet. While her children grow up, Mary writes. "For almost two decades Mary Sidney and her household at Wilton become one of the most dynamic cultural influences in late Elizabethan England, and at the center of Wilton's life were her writings."[1]

Members of the Wilton Circle, however, do not know that Mary *writes plays for the public theater.* Mary publishes the works of her own that are considered "appropriate" for women—direct translations and religious works—to the critical acclaim of contemporaries.

Titus Andronicus is acted by Pembroke's Men, the troupe sponsored by Mary Sidney and her husband, and printed anonymously. *The Turning of a Shrew* and *3 Henry 6* are also acted by Pembroke's Men and printed anonymously.

Meanwhile, Shakespeare becomes a member of the Lord Chamberlain's Men, an acting company.

In 1592, Mary Sidney publishes a lengthy meditative work, *A Discourse of Life and Death,* a translation from French.

---

1   Margaret Hannay, et al., eds., *The Collected Works of Mary Sidney Herbert, Countess of Pembroke,* vol. 1 (Oxford: Clarendon Press, 1998), 49.

In 1596, Shakespeare's son Hamnet, eleven years old, dies in Stratford. There is no extant poem, sonnet, or note written by William Shakespeare about the death of his only son.

The following year, 1597, *Shakespeare, a play broker, sells three plays to the printer.* Shakespeare pays £60 cash for the deed to the second-largest house in Stratford. He still spends most of his time in London. This year he also defaults on taxes of 5 shillings.

Shakespeare, *who has been claiming authorship of and selling Mary's plays, as well as plays by other writers,* now begins to attach his name to the printed works. He sells a load of stone to Mr. Chamberlin. In 1599 he defaults on his taxes of 13 shillings 4 pence. In 1601 a shepherd's will claims Shakespeare and his wife still owe him 40 shillings (£2)—in the prime of his popularity, Shakespeare hadn't paid back the money he borrowed from a shepherd.

In 1601, Mary's husband dies and with him most of her power and influence. Over the next several years she is abandoned by almost all who had previously sought her patronage. She is in court over jewel thieves and the murder of her servant. Her house and servants are attacked; she struggles to maintain control of her holdings for her ungrateful son. This same son, William Herbert, is imprisoned for impregnating a maid-of-honor to the Queen, whom he abandons; the baby dies.

Around this time in 1601, William Herbert inherits his father's title and estates, *and Shakespeare makes a deal with Mary or her son William Herbert (is it blackmail? is John Davies of Hereford a go-between?).* In 1602 Shakespeare pays £320 cash for 107 acres near Stratford and also buys a cottage. In 1604 he sues an apothecary in Stratford for 35 shillings. In 1605, Shakespeare pays £440 for a share in the lease of tithes in Stratford; at a yield of £60/year, it will be more than seven years before he starts making a return on his investment.

Struggling after her husband's death, in 1604 Mary falls deeply in love with Dr. Matthew Lister, who is far beneath her social status. Interrupting their lifetime of devotion to each other, there is a period of profound emotional distress when she thinks her adored niece and goddaughter, Mary Wroth, is having an affair with Lister, but it turns out this isn't true—Wroth is actually having an affair with Mary's oldest son, Will Herbert, while both are married to other people.

Mary expresses the powerful and conflicting emotions in the turmoil of these relationships *in the form of sonnets.*

Besides running Wilton House with its 200 servants, Mary was also responsible for several other family estates: Baynards Castle in London; Cardiff Castle in Cardiff, Wales; Ludlow Castle in Wales; Ivychurch, near Wilton, on the Avon River; and Ramsbury, a smaller estate in northern Wiltshire. The family lived in Wales each summer.

Mary suffers a devastating loss in 1606 when her 23-year-old daughter dies of a recurring illness (or perhaps leaves for the New World with her Puritan husband).

In 1607, Mary and Dr. Lister cross the Channel and travel to Spa in Belgium where they stay for a short time.

In 1608 Shakespeare sues a John Addenbrooke in Stratford for £6.

Mary's son William turns against her when he discovers that not only is she is writing *dramatic productions for the public theater that threaten his career in the royal court,* but she has taken a younger, lower-class physician as a lover. William doesn't speak to his mother for ten years.

In 1609, John Davies of Hereford (Mary's secretary) *takes her sonnet collection to press and has it printed in Shakespeare's name,* including his own poem at the end of the book. The sonnets are dedicated from the publisher to "Mr. W. H.," perhaps William Herbert.

Shakespeare *discovers that* most of the sonnets published in his name are love poems to a man and *demands that William Herbert suppress the book.*

In 1613, Shakespeare buys a share in the Blackfriars gatehouse; £80 of this is in cash. The elaborate arrangements of the deal effectively deprive Shakespeare's widow of her dower right to a share for life in this part of his estate.

Meanwhile, Mary's oldest son William Herbert has been constantly involved in machinations for advancement at court.

Mary's younger, wilder, and more handsome son, Philip Herbert, acts as whore to King James and in exchange is rewarded with his own earldom and enormous cash gifts.

Around 1614, William Herbert plots to change the power structure at court to become Lord Chamberlain. In that position he can control the publication of *his mother's* plays. Included in the plan is the family friend Ben Jonson, as well as several noblemen and the Archbishop of Canterbury. The scheme is successful in providing King James with a new boyfriend; George Villiers becomes the King's favorite lover and eventually the Duke of Buckingham; and William Herbert gets the job of Lord Chamberlain with the condition that when he dies, his younger brother takes over the position. In 1619 Herbert contrives an honorary degree from Oxford University for Jonson. Herbert is extremely protective of his hard-won power and wealth.

Shakespeare retires to Stratford. He apparently stops writing plays.

Mary builds Houghton House in England with her lover.

In 1611 Mary leaves to spend three years on the Continent with her lover, Dr. Lister, where she hosts a literary salon, entertains, dances, smokes, shoots pistols, and continues to write.

William Herbert fathers two illegitimate children with his first cousin, Mary Wroth, shortly after Mary Wroth's husband dies in 1614. William covers up all references to this union and issue (an event discovered in 1935), to the extent of destroying pertinent documents.

No Shakespearean plays are legitimately published after 1615— William Herbert, as Lord Chamberlain, prevents any plays with Shakespeare's name on them from getting into print.[2]

Shakespeare's younger daughter, Judith, is now 31 years old and still unmarried. She runs off and marries the village ne'er-do-well, Thomas Quiney, 23 years old. Because Thomas already has another woman pregnant, Judith and Thomas marry in a hurry without a license and are excommunicated. Shakespeare immediately changes his will. The young woman Thomas impregnated and her baby both die (conveniently for Thomas) in childbirth.

Shakespeare, in 1616, dies near his 52nd birthday, one month after he changes his will. Judith's rascal husband eventually abandons her, and all of their children die.

Five years after Shakespeare dies, Mary approaches her sixtieth birthday. *She takes the manuscripts of four plays to the printer and* publication begins on what is now called the First Folio, a collection of all the plays believed to be written by "William Shakespeare." The works are not licensed before printing begins, even though it's required by law—the license would need to come from the Lord Chamberlain, Mary's son, William Herbert.

Fair copies of four of the plays are taken to the printer. *Mary plans to bring fair copies of the others as the printing progresses.* She lives in London on Aldersgate Street at the time, just a few blocks from the printer. But Mary dies in her London home, allegedly of smallpox, one month after printing of the First Folio begins, and one month before her sixtieth birthday. She is buried on an evening in a grand torchlight procession.

---

2   E. E. Willoughby, *A Printer of Shakespeare* (London: Philip Allan & Co. Ltd, 1934), 166.

Her will is never found, although Dr. Matthew Lister receives about £140 a year for the rest of his life.[3] It is not clear why he receives this money or where it comes from.

The printer halts the printing of the collection of plays *and contacts the Lord Chamberlain. William confides in Ben Jonson, or vice versa, one of whom was unaware of the true authorship of the plays until now. Jonson helps gather copies of the rest of the plays and acts as editor. William wants to perpetuate the attribution of his mother's plays to William Shakespeare.*

Jonson writes a poem titled "To the Memory of my Beloved, the AUTHOR" to include in the publication. In its introduction he complains how a pimp/bawd and a whore pretend to praise someone when they're really trying to ruin an old gentlewoman. Jonson calls the author the "Sweet Swan of Avon." The books and manuscripts in Jonson's library are burned just weeks after the publication of the First Folio, devastating Jonson. William Herbert arranges for Ben Jonson to receive £20 every New Year for books.

The printer continues production of the First Folio. The book is licensed the day before it comes off the press, seven and a half years after Shakespeare died. It is dedicated to the two Herbert brothers, the Earl of Pembroke and the Earl of Montgomery.

No one has ever found a single page of any original manuscript of the plays or the sonnets.

Consider the Question

Until a pertinent letter or an original manuscript of any play or sonnet is found that provides conclusive evidence of one author or another, the Authorship Question will remain alive as a vital inquiry. With rigorous documentation, the profiles of contenders may become more realistic. Ironically, of the candidates brought forward, William Shakespeare presents the weakest documentation.

---

3   "[William Herbert, Earl of] Pembroke showed considerable generosity in settling his mother's estate, avoiding the sibling quarrels that so often occur when a parent dies intestate: 'the Lord Chamberlain [William Herbert] hath given the earl of Montgomery [Philip Herbert] all her personal estate, contenting himself with her jointure, for she died without [a] will.'" Margaret Hannay, *Philip's Phoenix: Mary Sidney, Countess of Pembroke* (Oxford: Oxford University Press, 1990), 206. Did William Herbert hope to avoid anyone poking into her death and assets?

Mary Sidney Herbert, the Countess of Pembroke, may very well be the most logical and compelling choice for authorship of the plays and sonnets. With her extensive education, knowledge of languages and music and law, leadership of the most important literary circle in English history, interest in metaphysical ideas, published work of her own, connections with the material known to be used as sources for the plays, involvement in the world about which the plays were written, documented evidence of her life reflected in the story of the sonnets, and as a forward-thinking, courageous woman working steadily despite the strictures in a man's world—is it possible to imagine her in yet another role—unacknowledged author of the most influential literature written in English?

What could she have done, as a noble woman of the late sixteenth/ early seventeenth centuries, when publishing the plays under her own name would have destroyed the careers of her two sons in the royal court? What recourse would there be for her?

Mary Sidney Herbert, the Countess of Pembroke, is a literary enigma, a demonstrable force in Elizabethan literature, richly deserving modern recognition. She is also the strongest candidate for the curious Authorship Question.

Or I shall live your epitaph to make,
Or you survive when I in earth am rotten;
From hence your memory death cannot take,
Although in me each part will be forgotten.

Your name from hence immortal life shall have,
Though I, once gone, to all the world must die:
The earth can yield me but a common grave,
When you entombed in men's eyes shall lie.

Your monument shall be my gentle verse;
Which eyes not yet created shall o'er-read,
And tongues to be your being shall rehearse
When all the breathers of this world are dead;

You still shall live—such virtue hath my pen—
Where breath most breathes, even in the mouths of men.

SONNET 81

THE MOST DISPIRITING TRAIT of the professional scholars is not their consensus about Shakespeare's identity, but their refusal to admit that there can be any room for doubt. Realizing very well how little is known about Mr. Shakspere of Stratford, they should at least allow for an agnostic middle ground. It is one thing to say that the testimony in favor of Mr. Shakspere's authorship remains, on balance, more satisfying than all the arguments made against it. It's quite another matter to concede nothing to dissent, or even uncertainty.

In the writing of orthodox scholars on the anti-Stratfordian* heresies, it is rare to find a concessive note. Animadversions, often vituperative, are the rule. It is almost never admitted that any of the heretics has ever raised a point worth taking into account.

The impulse to scold the dissenter; the inability to acknowledge even the possibility of reasonable doubt; suspicion even of the non-committal; the denial of ambiguities in our imperfect records of the past; intense frustration with anything less than unanimity; the conviction that dissent reveals a moral or psychological defect— these are the marks of the brittle belief systems we call cults or ideologies, as opposed to the balanced judgment that tries to come to terms with all the available evidence.

Joseph Sobran
"The Authorship Debate" in *The QPB Companion to Shakespeare*

Part Nine

The Appendices

It is not the fashion to see the Lady the
epilogue; but it is no more unhandsome
than to see the Lord the prologue.

Rosalind in *As You Like It*, Epilogue, 1–3

Appendix A
Old School Sexism

In 1924, Alexander Witherspoon wrote about the Wilton Circle in *The Influence of Robert Garnier on Elizabethan Drama.* In this book Witherspoon interprets Mary's importance to literature by stating that "from a pure sense of duty" to her brother to reform English drama, Mary "went about the task with the executive ability of a good housewife."[1] He doesn't seem to believe that a woman might actually enjoy writing literature or have a talent for it. Witherspoon claims that Mary's intent with her group of writers was to combat the "uncouth and unlearned" plays on the popular stage, such as the Shakespearean ones. Unfortunately, there are scholars today who still parrot this unfounded presentation of Mary Sidney. But Margaret Hannay, a modern biographer of Mary Sidney, retorts:

> Rather than portraying the countess as the leader of a campaign to destroy the native dramatic tradition, we can characterize her as among the first to bring the continental genre of historical tragedy to England, making her a precursor, certainly not an antagonist, of "the man Shakespeare" and of Jacobean political drama.[2]

Hannay also states:

> Nor can the countess possibly be combating Shakespeare in her *Antonius* for he had only recently begun his career by the time she completed her translation in 1590. . . . Given the Dudley/ Sidney family's long tradition of support for the popular drama and the Earl of Pembroke's nominal sponsorship of a dramatic

---

1   Alexander Maclaren Witherspoon, *The Influence of Robert Garnier on Elizabethan Drama* (New York: Phaeton Press, 1968), 182.
2   Margaret Hannay, *Philip's Phoenix: Mary Sidney, Countess of Pembroke* (Oxford: Oxford University Press, 1990), 129.

troupe during the early 1590s, it is more likely that the countess would have encouraged the work of the rising dramatist than opposed him.[3]

This view is supported by other scholars. "Mary Sidney could hardly have been attacking the 'popular melodrama' of Shakespeare, since he had written very little by 1590. On the contrary, she should be acknowledged as one of the earliest contributors to politicized historical drama."[4]

As mentioned earlier, Mary was involved with the theater all of her life, as was her entire family. Under her influence, Ludlow Castle became a center of cultural activity. She grew up watching and participating in theater; she and her husband sponsored an acting troupe; her uncle sponsored a troupe; she acted in plays at the royal court; two of the most famous comic actors, Will Kempe and Richard Tarlton, were both on her uncle Robert Dudley's staff; her brother Philip acted as godfather to Richard Tarlton's son.[5]

An odd irony

Considering the possibility that Mary Sidney wrote the works attributed to a man, it's ironically predictable to discover that several men have assumed that a man must have really written Mary Sidney's works. Regarding her *Psalms* versification, during her lifetime Sir John Harington (1561–1612) suggested that Mary had surely needed her Bishop, Gervase Babington, to advise her because "it was more than a woman's skill to express the sense so right as she hath done in her verse, and more than the English or Latin translation could have given her."[6]

About the ballad, "The Doleful Lay of Clorinda," that Mary Sidney wrote for her brother Philip on his death, Margaret Hannay points

---

3   Margaret Hannay, et al., eds., *The Collected Works of Mary Sidney Herbert, Countess of Pembroke*, vol. 1 (Oxford: Clarendon Press, 1998), 36–37.

4   S. Cerasano and Marion Wynne-Davies, eds., *Renaissance Drama by Women: Texts and Documents* (London and New York: Routledge, 1996), 16.

5   Katherine Duncan-Jones, *Sir Philip Sidney, Courtier Poet* (New Haven: Yale University Press, 1991), 148.

6   Sir John Harington, *Nugae Antiquae*, ed. Henry Harington (London: Vernon and Hood, 1804), 1:173; quoted in Margaret Hannay, *Philip's Phoenix: Mary Sidney, Countess of Pembroke* (Oxford: Oxford University Press, 1990), 134. It is unclear whether Hannay is actually referring to Sir John Harington (Mary's contemporary, 1561–1612) as the author of the quote or to Henry Harington, the editor in 1804, since Hannay simply refers to "Harington." Spelling is modernized.

out that "Spenser's statement that the countess wrote 'The Doleful Lay of Clorinda' was generally accepted until Ernest de Selincourt suggested in 1912 that 'Spenser wrote it in her name.'"[7] Since then, says Hannay, the debate has been tedious, and the discussion "often turns on assumptions about gender."[8]

These are not antiquated sexist statements. Consider a question from as late as 1978:

> J. Max Patrick has even gone so far as to suggest that the Countess did not write her best works, asking whether we "could account for the high excellence of the poetry attributed to the Countess of Pembroke by giving the credit for it to others? . . . Was she putting her name on work composed by [the male] members of the Wilton Circle such as Breton, Fraunce, Lok, Daniel, and Greville, or on her own work radically improved by them?"[9]

To which Gary Waller appropriately responds, "What we know of Breton's, Fraunce's, and Lok's work suggest they might have benefited more from the Countess than she from them!"[10]

In her final portrait, Mary chose to present herself holding one of her works, the *Psalms*. The portrait is framed by ink wells and pens and is crowned with a laurel wreath, the traditional symbol of a writer/poet. This deliberate visual statement graphically reinforces the literary focus of Mary Sidney's life—this is a woman who wants to go down in history as a writer.

7 Hannay, *Philip's Phoenix*, 64–65.
8 Ibid., 65.
9 Gary F. Waller, *Mary Sidney, Countess of Pembroke: A Critical Study of Her Writings and Literary Milieu* (Salzburg: Universität Salzburg, 1979), 267.
10 Ibid., 267.

As Margaret Cavendish, the Duchess of Newcastle-upon-Tyne wrote in 1622:

> *A woman write a Play!*
> *Out upon it, out upon it, for it cannot be good . . . .*
> *If it be good, they will think she did not write it . . .*
> *for men will not allow women to have wit.*

From the introduction to a collection of hers called *Playes.*

Appendix *B*
Jonson's Eulogy

The full text of Ben Jonson's poem to the "AUTHOR" follows, with a corresponding line-by-line paraphrase on the facing page.

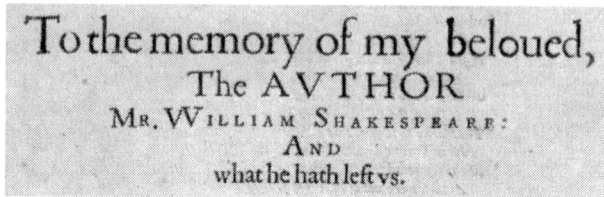

> To the memory of my beloued,
> The AVTHOR
> Mr. William Shakespeare:
> And
> what he hath left vs.

1. To draw no envy (Shakespeare) on thy name,

2. Am I thus ample to thy Book, and Fame:

3. While I confess thy writings to be such,

4. As neither Man, nor Muse, can praise too much.

5. 'Tis true, and all men's suffrage. But these ways

6. Were not the paths I meant unto thy praise:

7. For *seeliest* Ignorance on these may light,

8. Which, when it sounds at best, but echoes right;

9. Or blind Affection, which doth ne'er advance

10. The truth, but gropes, and urgeth all by chance;

11. Or crafty Malice, might pretend this praise,

12. And think to ruin, where it seem'd to raise.

13. These are, as some infamous Bawd, or Whore,

14. Should praise a Matron. What could hurt her more?

15. But thou art proof against them, and indeed

16. Above th' ill fortune of them, or the need.

17. I, therefore will begin. Soul of the Age!

To the memory of my beloved, The AUTHOR

Mr. William Shakespeare:

And

what he hath left us.

[paraphrase]

1. To avoid attracting malice and spite (Shakespeare) to your "name,"

2. Is why I am consequently so unrestrained in the matter of this published book and your reputation.

3. At the same time that I acknowledge my belief that your writings are the kind

4. That neither Man nor Muse can commend more than they deserve.

5. It's true, and is the opinion of all men. But this kind of praise

6. Is not the course of action I had in mind with which to honor you.

7. For the most blindly unknowing people may read these lines,

> **Seely** *means Pitiable, deserving of sympathy; poor, miserable.*
> *Trifling, insignificant; silly, foolish.*
> **Seely** *also means a person's eyes are closed. Also, figuratively,*
> *to make blind, to prevent from seeing, hoodwink. It comes from*
> **seel,** *which is to sew shut the eyelids of a hawk while in training.*

8. Which, at the time that their ignorance examines/proves these lines to be good, they are really only/merely imitations of what is true.

9. Or you might be praised with "blind affection"—people who have never actually seen you in person but love your works—which never gets any closer to or promotes

10. The truth, but only searches for it uncertainly and asserts what it does by accident (but not by honesty).

11. Or with cunning ill will, some might use this praise as a pretext to elevate someone

12. But actually intend to destroy/demolish that person in a place (such as this eulogy) where it gives the appearance of putting someone in a higher position.

13. These are the sorts of tricks with which some notorious pimp or whore

14. Might praise a respectable elderly lady of the upper class. What could actually hurt her more?

15. But you are impervious to these tricks and, to be sure,

16. You are far above the unfortunate destiny they plan for you, or the necessity of it.

17. I, accordingly, will lay the true foundation: Soul of the Age!

Would Ben Jonson really call William Shakespeare his "beloved"? If Shakespeare is his beloved, why did Jonson not write a word upon Shakespeare's death seven years earlier?

Blind affection follows up **seely ignorance** in line 7.

The **Soul** is always feminine.

18. The applause! delight! the wonder of our Stage!

19. My Shakespeare rise; I will not lodge thee by

20. Chaucer, or Spenser, or bid Beaumont lie

21. A little further, to make thee a room:[1]

22. Thou art a Monument, without a tomb,

23. And are alive still, while thy Book doth live,

24. And we have wits to read, and praise to give.

25. That I not mix thee so, my brain excuses,

26. I mean with great, but disproportion'd Muses

27. For, if I thought my judgment were of years,

28. I should commit thee surely with thy peers,

29. And tell, how far thou didst our Lily outshine,

18. You are the acclaimed, the source of pleasure, and the prodigy/ astonishment of our theaters!

19. My "Shakespeare," ascend from the grave; I will not have you dwell at the side of

20. Geoffrey Chaucer *(writer, about 1343–1400, d. 57 y.o.)* or Edmund Spenser *(poet, about 1552–1599, d. 47 y.o.)*, nor will I request that Francis Beaumont *(playwright, about 1584–1616, d. 32 y.o.)*

21. Scoot over a little in their graves to make room for you in Westminster Abbey.[1] *(Each of the men in line 20 is buried in Poets Corner in Westminster Abbey, but not William Shakespeare.)*

22. You yourself are an enduring edifice, enduring beyond and outside of any tomb,

23. And you are in the world still, as long as your written works are in print,

24. And as long as the rest of us have the intellectual/creative capacity to understand/learn/discover/guess/perceive your work and have the glorification to attribute/bestow on it.

25. In as much as I should not mingle you with such company as mentioned above, my thoughts ask pardon/have justification because

26. I have in mind to place you in the same company as other powerful Muses, even though you are disproportionately greater

27. Because, if I considered that my opinion here was only to last these few years (rather than for all time)

28. I would be inclined to ensconce you undoubtedly/certainly with your fellow writers here in England

29. And explain to what degree you surpassed our playwright John Lyly *(c.1554–1606, d. 60 y.o.; he did not write after 1590; his letters complain of failure and neglect; most of his plays are written for child actors or select audiences with Queen Elizabeth)*

The nine **Muses** are all women. Mary was several times suggested, by other writers, to be the tenth Muse.

In 1623, why does Jonson compare the author to these three playwrights in lines 29–30, each of whom was either murdered, tortured, or neglected, and who were not contemporaries of "Shakespeare's" greatest works, but had all been dead for quite a while, and none had written anything since 1594 at the latest?

1 E. K. Chambers, *William Shakespeare: A Study of Facts and Problems*, vol. 2 (Oxford: Clarendon Press, 1930), 226. In a book of John Donne's titled *Poems*, published in 1633, is a short poem that begins:

    Renownèd Spencer, lie a thought more nigh
    To learnèd Chaucer, and rare Beaumont lie
    A little nearer Spenser to make room
    For Shakespeare in your threefold fourfold Tomb.

This poem was later ascribed to William Basse. This poem is often used to prove that someone noticed that Shakespeare had died, but there is no date on the poem and it wasn't in print until 1633, almost two decades after Shakespeare's death; thus we cannot say that this poem came *before* this eulogy from Jonson—it is easily possible that Basse (or whoever wrote it) took the names and idea from Jonson's poem instead of the other way around.

Intriguingly, William Basse wrote of Mary Sidney in his "Eclogue V" and in correspondence.

30. Or sporting Kid, or Marlowe's mighty line.

Line 31 has been intentionally misinterpreted for centuries because it fits the mythology of Shakespeare to have a reference to his genius despite a lack of education. But as you can see here in context, Jonson actually refers to the lack of *works* in Latin and Greek with which to compare the author. Jonson compares the poet to the English writers, and then compares the poet to the Greek and Roman writers, even though "Shakespeare" has few or no works in those languages with which to compare.

31. And though thou hadst small Latin, and less Greek,

32. From thence to honour thee, I would not seek

33. For names; but call forth thund'ring Æschilus,

34. Euripides, and Sophocles to us,

35. Pacuvius, Accius, him of Cordova, dead,

36. To life again, to hear thy Buskin tread,

37. And shake a Stage: Or, when thy Socks were on,

38. Leave thee alone, for the comparison

39. Of all, that insolent Greece, or haughty Rome

40. Sent forth, or since did from their ashes come.

41. Triumph, my Britain, thou hast one to show,

42. To whom all Scenes of Europe homage owe.

43. He was not of an age, but for all time!

44. And all the Muses still were in their prime,

30. Or the amusing/contemptuous/mocking playwright Thomas Kyd
    (*1558–1594, d. 36 y.o.; imprisoned for supposed atheism, tortured; died
    broken, forlorn, and in poverty shortly thereafter*)

    or playwright Christopher Marlowe's illustrious/potent/powerful
    written works (*1564–1593, d. 29 y.o.; murdered supposedly over a bar tab*)

31. And even though you wrote few works in Latin and even fewer
    in Greek

32. For which we can honor you, I do not need to solicit

33. Names for comparison, but summon powerful Aeschylus
    (*c.525–456 BC, d. 69 y.o., playwright known as "the father of Greek
    Tragedy"*),

34. Euripedes (*c.480–406 BC, d. 74 y.o., Greek tragic playwright*)

    and Sophocles to us, (*c.495–406 BC, d. 91 y.o., Greek tragic playwright*)

35. Marcus Pacuvius (*c.130–220, d. 90 y.o., painter, playwright, greatest of the
    Roman tragic poets*)

    and Lucius Accius (*170–c.86 BC, d. 84 y.o., Roman poet, playwright,
    and scholar*)

    and Lucius Annaeus Seneca (*the Younger*), him of Cordova
    (*about 3 BC–65 AD; a Roman born in Cordova, Spain; tutor to Nero;
    poet, tragedian, philosopher; forced by Nero to commit suicide at
    about 68 years old*)

    Mary Sidney led the
    Senecan movement
    in England.

    all these who are dead,

36. I would like to bring them all to life again so they could hear your
    tragedies (*tragic actors wore heavy-soled half boots called buskins*)

37. And see how you inspire the acting profession. Or, when your
    comedies are played (*comic actors wore soft slippers called socks*)

38. They would realize you are so far above them as to be alone, compared

39. With everything that the arrogant Greek playwrights or the proud
    Roman playwrights

40. Have ever written or anything that has been discovered from there
    since the destruction of their civilizations.

41. Exult, Britain, for you have one writer to brag of

42. To whom all the theaters of Europe owe respect and reverence.

43. This writer was not limited to this one short time period in history,
    but will endure forever.

44. It is as if all the female Muses even yet were at their heights of
    perfection,

45. When like Apollo he came forth to warm

46. Our ears, or like a Mercury to charm!

47. Nature herself was proud of his designs,

48. And joy'd to wear the dressing of his lines!

49. Which were so richly spun, and woven so fit,

50. As, since, she will vouchsafe no other Wit.

51. The merry Greek, tart Aristophanes,

45. At the same time that, resembling/in the manner of Apollo (*Greek god who loved poetry and music; his weapon a bow, his plant the laurel*) who provided instruction and lessons, OR

46. In the manner of Mercury to charm us (*"charm" meant a magic spell, bewitchment, pretending one thing over another*). It is fascinating that Ben Jonson connects Mercury to Shakespeare:

    > *Mercury's primary function is the protection of thieves and businessmen, travelers, athletes, miscreants, harlots, and old crones, the god of intrigue and covert reasoning, a psychopomp and messenger between the gods, although he is also (on the side) the patron of enigmatic writing and poetry, astrology, and alchemy. Mercury's gift to Pandora was seductive words and lies. "He presides over eloquence and persuasion, skills employed by those under his patronage: heralds, merchants, thieves, and con men. He is the god of crafty thoughts and wiles, and the use of persuasive deception and trickery."* [2]

    > *"On any view, his cult was old, and it had close links with shop-keepers and transporters of goods, notably grain . . . . Mediator between gods and mortals, between the dead and the living, and always in motion, Mercury is also a deceiver, since he moves on the boundaries and the intervening space; he is patron of the shop-keeper as much as the trader, the traveller as well as the brigand."* [3]

47. Nature—the creative power herself—had a high opinion of the author's enterprises

48. And delighted to bear/carry/have/own the costumes of his poetry,

49. Which were created so abundantly and appropriately

50. That, ever since Nature has known your work, she will not condescend to participate in the works of any other intellectual power.

51. The merry Greek Menander (*c.342–292 BCE, drowned when 50 y.o., wrote more than a hundred comedies in the New Comedy style— and was accused of plagiarism*)

    . . . cynical and sharp Aristophanes (*c.448–386 BCE, d. 62 y.o., master of ancient Greek comedy in the Old Comedy style*)

---

2 http://www.theoi.com/Olympios/HermesGod.html #Language

3 Simon Hornblower and Antony Spawforth, eds., *The Oxford Classical Dictionary*, 3rd ed. (Oxford: Oxford University Press, 1996), 962.

52. Neat Terence, witty Plautus, now not please;

53. But antiquated, and deserted lie

54. As they were not of Nature's family.

55. Yet must I not give Nature all: Thy Art,

56. My gentle Shakespeare, must enjoy a part.

57. For though the Poets' matter, Nature be,

58. His Art doth give the fashion. And, that he,

59. Who casts to write a living line, must sweat,

60. (such as thine are) and strike the second heat

61. Upon the Muse's anvil: turn the same,

62. (And himself with it) that he thinks to frame;

52. Precise and pithy Terence *(c.189–159 BCE, a freed slave and Roman playwright who is said to have put his name on works written by noblemen)*

>*"It is commonly said that Scipio [Scipio Africanus the Younger, a Roman aristocrat] and Laelius [Caius Laelius Sapiens, tribune, legate, governor, c.138 CE] assisted the author in his plays; and indeed, Terence himself increased that suspicion by the little pains he took to refute it. . . . To wipe off the aspersion of plagiarism," Terence took a boat to Greece and was never heard from again. "Some ancient writers relate that he died at sea." He was 25 or 30 years old.*[4]

. . . clever and amusing Titus Maccius Plautus *(c.254–184 BCE, d. 70 y.o., comic playwright)*

don't even please us anymore,

53. Their works only rest here quietly, obsolete and abandoned

54. As if they were not in the same category of natural creative power.

55. But I must not give natural creativity (raw talent or genius) all the credit. Your skill, as the result of study and practice . . .

>*Jonson "had always championed the cause of art [study] and had repeatedly chastised the popular playwrights of his day for relying on their own raw talent."[5] Here he emphasizes that this author, his beloved, has spent a good deal of time studying and practicing.*

56. My well-born author, must possess a share of the credit

>*Jonson was the first person ever to call Shakespeare "gentle," seven years after he died. "Gentle" almost always (at the time) means upper class, which Shakespeare wasn't.*

57. Even though the subject/substance/theme for Poets is Nature,

58. It is a writer's learned skill that shows/proclaims/publishes/represents the shape and form of literature. In addition, it is true that he

59. Who casts or forms in a mold (as for bronzing) and attempts to compose a line of poetry that is full of life and animation, must toil and labor *(pun on sweating in a blacksmith's shop)*

60. (Of the same sort as the lines you have written) and work again and edit (strike the second heat)

61. Upon the Muse's anvil: shape the lines, transform/work with the words in a different way

62. (And himself he must reshape/think through again) that which he plans to develop, shape, and direct,

This is the third reference to the author either being a **Muse** or working closely with.

4 Alfred Bates, *The Drama, Its History, Literature, and Influence on Civilization*, vol. 2 (London: Historical Publishing Company, 1906), 205–07, all cited material in this paragraph.

5 David Riggs, *Ben Jonson: A Life* (Cambridge, London: Harvard University Press, 1989), 277.

63. Or for the laurel, he may gain a scorn,

64. For a good Poet's made, as well as born.

65. And such wert thou. Look how the father's face

66. Lives in his issue, even so, the race

67. Of Shakspeare's mind, and manners brightly shines

68. In his well turned, and true filed lines:

69. In each of which, he seems to shake a Lance,

70. As brandish't at the eyes of Ignorance.

71. Sweet Swan of Avon! what a sight it were

72. To see thee in our waters yet appear,

73. And make those flights upon the banks of Thames,

74. That so did take Eliza, and our James!

75. But stay, I see thee in the Hemisphere

76. Advanc'd, and made a Constellation there!

77. Shine forth, thou Star of Poets, and with rage,

78. Or influence, chide, or cheer the drooping Stage;

79. Which, since thy flight from hence, hath mourn'd like night,

80. And despairs day, but for thy Volume's light.

Ben: Jonson 1623

63. Or if he doesn't strive to improve his Art, he may receive scorn instead of the honor of the poet's laurel wreath

    Or: he will be scorned for wearing the laurel wreath and pretending to be a poet,

64. For a good Poet is made—by hard work and study—as well as having been born naturally gifted.

65. And such a good Poet are you, my beloved Author—both born gifted and a student of the craft. Notice how the features in a father's face

66. Appear in the face of his son; even in this manner, the natural disposition

67. Of the author's intellect and behavior can be clearly seen

68. In his well-shaped and formed and finely polished lines.

69. In each of which, he seems to contemptuously shake a spear

70. As if threatening the people who don't understand/are ignorant/ lack any culture of the mind *or* who lack experience, skill, and/or knowledge of what is going on.

71. Fragrant/pleasing/delightful/lovely/kind/meek/mild/dear/ endearing Swan of Avon!

72. To see your plays still appear in London

73. And create/beget those soaring excursions of imagination along the banks of the Thames (in our playhouses and the court)

74. That so captivated/delighted Queen Elizabeth and King James!

75. But wait, you have been promoted to the heavens

76. And designated there as a constellation! (*Cygnus, the Swan*)

77. Illuminate into the open, you Star of Poets, and with headline passion/intensity

78. Or with divine force and the power to affect the mind, either rebuke or comfort the languishing theater world

79. Which, since that time when you hastily departed (*flight = secret departure*) from here, has been as gloomy as night is dark

80. And hopeless in the day, if it wasn't for the brilliance of this collection of your Work.

After death, the souls of illustrious persons appear as new **stars** in the heavens. A star has the power to influence human affairs.

Benjamin Jonson 1623

Appendix C
English Peerage

Below is the order of the British peerage (those holding a hereditary or honorary title). A Duke is the highest peer next to a King or Queen. These are *not* titles of royalty. One is *born* into royalty; a title can be *acquired* (if you're born in the right circles).

When George Villiers was made Duke of Buckingham in 1623, there had been no Dukes since the Duke of Norfolk had his head chopped off in 1572. Villiers was assassinated in 1628 during the reign of King James' son, Charles 1.

Duke and Duchess

Marquess (*MAR kwess*) **and Marchioness** (*MAR shuh ness*)

Earl and Countess

Viscount (*VIE count,* rhymes with *PIE count*) **and Viscountess**

Baron and Baroness

Knight is not a peerage title, and in Mary Sidney's time, you could be given the honor of Knight by titled peers without the Queen's or King's permission.

If your father had no peer title, you were a **commoner.** Philip Sidney was a commoner. The Mother of Queen Elizabeth 2 was called a commoner, even though she was descended from kings and grew up in Glamis Castle; she was a commoner because at the time she married, her father did not have a title (he later became Earl of Strathmore and Kinghorne).

To distinguish "commoners" such as the Queen Mother or Winston Churchill (born in Blenheim Palace) from the rest of us, we are called **baseborn,** mean, of low birth or origin, as opposed to **highborn** people who are born into the ruling class or aristocracy. In Mary Sidney's time, it was believed that God ordained you to be born into a particular class, just as He ordained some creatures to be snails and some lions.

Appendix *D*
The History Plays

The following is the rest of the data from Mary Sidney's genealogy and the history plays. For the other plays, please see Chapter 11.

Richard 2, 1 and 2 Henry 4, and Henry 5

Character	Relation to Mary Sidney
King Richard 2	1C 7R
Queen Isabel	— *(by marriage)*
John of Gaunt	6G Grandfather
Eleanor de Bohun, Duchess of Gloucester	7G Aunt
Edmund of Langley, 1st Duke of York	7G Uncle
Duchess of York, mother of Aumerle	7G Aunt
Edward of Norwich, Duke of Aumerle	1C 7R
Henry Bolingbroke, Duke of Hereford, afterward King Henry 4	6G Uncle (half)
Thomas Mowbray, 1st Duke of Norfolk	5G Grandfather
Thomas Holland, Duke of Surrey	2C 5R
John Montacute, 3rd Earl of Salisbury	*his son married Mary's 2C 5R*
Thomas Lord Berkeley	6G Grandfather
Sir Henry Green	4G Uncle
Sir John Bushy	—
Sir William (or John) Bagot	—
Henry Percy, 1st Earl of Northumberland	7G Uncle
Henry Percy, called Hotspur	1C 7R
William Lord Ross	*married to 1C 7R*
William, 5th Baron Willoughby de Ersby	6G Uncle
Walter Lord Fitzwater	*very distantly related*
Thomas Marke, Bishop of Carlisle	—
William de Colchester, Abbot of Westminster	—
Thomas Holland, Lord Marshall	2C 5R
Sir Stephen Scroop (Scrope)	*unclear*
Henry, Prince of Wales (Prince Hal), afterwards King Henry 5	1C 6R (half)
Prince John of Lancaster, Duke of Bedford	1C 6R (half)
Ralph Neville, 1st Earl of Westmorland	5G Grandfather
Sir Walter Blunt	7G Grandfather
Lady Percy, wife of Hotspur	2C 6R
Thomas Percy, Earl of Worcester	1C 7R
Edmund Mortimer	2C 6R
Lady Mortimer (Glendower's daughter)	*married to 2C 6R*
Richard Scroop (Scrope), Archbishop of York	*distant relation*

Archibald, 4th Earl of Douglas	—
Owen Glendower	*his daughter married Mary's 2C 6R*
King Henry 5	1C 6R (half)
Thomas Beaufort, Duke of Exeter	5G Uncle
Edward of Norwich, 2nd Duke of York	1C 7R
Thomas Montacute, 4th Earl of Salisbury	*married to Mary's 2C 5R*
Richard Plantagenet, Earl of Cambridge	1C 7R
Henry Chichele, Archbishop of Canterbury	—
John Fordham, Bishop of Ely	—
Henry of Masham, 3rd Baron Scrope	*married to 2C 5R*
Sir Thomas Grey	1C 6R
Captain Fluellen (Welsh)	*based on Davy Gam*
Captain Jamy (Scottish)	*probably a reference to King James 1 of Scotland who went to France with Henry 5*
Sir Thomas Erpingham	—
Philip the Good, Duke of Burgundy	*distant relation*
Sir Richard Vernon	—
Thomas Plantagenet, Duke of Clarence	1C 6R (half)
Humphrey Plantagenet, Duke of Gloucester and Earl of Pembroke	1C 6R (half)
Richard Beauchamp, 13th Earl of Warwick	5G Grandfather
Thomas Fitzalan, 5th Earl of Surrey and 11th Earl of Arundel	6G Uncle
Sir Thomas Harcourt (probably)	—
Sir John Blunt	6G Uncle
Lord Chief Justice, Sir William Gascoigne	*very distant*
Margaret Neville, Lady Northumberland	7G Aunt
Thomas Lord Mowbray	4G Uncle
Thomas Lord Bardolph	—
Sir John Coleville	—
Sir John Falstaff	—

mentioned in the plays:

Straight out of Holinshed:	
Sir Thomas Blount of Belton	—
Sir Bennet Seely	—
Sir John Norberry	—
Reginald, 2nd Lord Cobham	—
Francis Quoint (or Point)	—
Sir Walter Blunt	7G Grandfather
William le Scrope, Earl of Wiltshire	*unclear*
Thomas of Woodstock, Duke of Gloucester	7G Uncle
Owen Glendower	*his daughter married Mary's 2C 6R*
Davy Gam	*7G Grandfather of Mary's husband. His daughter became the mother of William Herbert, 1st Earl of Pembroke in the Herbert house.*
Michael de la Pole, 3rd Earl of Suffolk	2C 6R
Gilbert Talbot	5G Uncle
Sir Richard Ketley	—
John Holland, Earl of Huntingdon	1C 6R (half)

Three parts of Henry 6, plus Richard 3

Character	Relation to Mary Sidney
King Henry 6	2C 5R (half)
Queen Margaret of Anjou	— (by marriage)
Humphrey Plantagenet, Duke of Gloucester and Earl of Pembroke	1C 6R (half)
Prince John of Lancaster, Duke of Bedford	1C 6R (half)
Thomas Beaufort, Duke of Exeter	6G Uncle
Henry Beaufort, Bishop then Cardinal of Winchester	6G Uncle
John Beaufort, 3rd Earl of Somerset	1C 6R
Richard Plantagenet, 3rd Duke of York	5G Uncle
Cecily Neville, Duchess of York	5G Aunt
Edmund Plantagenet, Earl of Rutland	1C 5R
Richard Beauchamp, 13th Earl of Warwick	5G Grandfather
Thomas Montacute, 4th Earl of Salisbury	married to Mary's 2C 5R
William de la Pole, 4th Earl of Suffolk, later 1st Duke of Suffolk	2C 6R
John Lord Talbot, 1st Earl of Shrewsbury	4G Grandfather
John Talbot (son of above), Viscount and 1st Baron Lisle	3G Grandfather
Edmund Mortimer, 5th Earl of March	3C 4R
Edmund Beaufort, 2nd Duke of Somerset	5G Uncle
Edward Plantagenet, 3rd Earl of March (to become King Edward 4)	1C 5R
Humphrey Stafford, Duke of Buckingham	5G Grandfather
Richard Neville, 5th Earl of Salisbury	5G Uncle
Richard Neville, 16th Earl of Warwick, the Kingmaker	1C 5R
Thomas Lord Clifford	unclear
John, Young Clifford, later Lord Clifford	unclear; there is a John Lord Clifford in her genealogy, but it's a mistake
Edward, Prince of Wales (son of Henry 6)	3C 4R (half)
(Henry &) Edmund Beaufort, (3rd &) 4th Dukes of Somerset	1C 5R
Henry Holland, 2nd Duke of Exeter	2C 5R (half)
Henry Percy, 3rd Earl of Northumberland	1C 5R
Ralph Neville, 2nd Earl of Westmorland	1C 5R
George Plantagenet, Duke of Clarence	1C 5R
Richard Plantagenet, Duke of Gloucester (afterwards Richard 3)	1C 5R
Elizabeth Woodville, Lady Grey (afterwards Queen to Edward 4)	GG Aunt
John Neville, Marquess of Montague	1C 5R
William Herbert, Earl of Pembroke (non-speaking part)	Mary's husband's 5G Grandfather
William Lord Hastings	married to 1C 5R
John de Vere, 13th Earl of Oxford	distantly related
Edward Plantagenet, Prince of Wales, afterward King Edward 5	2C 4R
Richard Plantagenet, Duke of York (prince in the Tower)	2C 4R
Margaret, Countess of Salisbury ("Girl")	2C 4R

Edward Plantagenet, Earl of Warwick ("Boy")	2C 4R
Lady Anne Neville	2C 4R
Cardinal Thomas Bourchier	2C 6R
Thomas Scott Rotherham, Archbishop of York	—
Henry Stafford, 2nd Duke of Buckingham	2C 4R
John Howard, Duke of Norfolk (grandson of Mowbray in Richard 2)	1C 5R
Thomas Howard, Earl of Surrey (and 2nd Duke of Norfolk, son of above)	2C 4R
John Mowbray, 3rd Duke of Norfolk	1C 5R
Sir Thomas Grey, 1st Marquess of Dorset	1C 3R
Sir Thomas Stanley, 1st Earl of Derby	*married to 1C 5R*
Sir Thomas Vaughan	—
Francis, 12th Lord Lovel	2C 4R (his great-grandfather was Mary's 5G grandfather)
Sir Richard Radcliffe	*distantly related*
Sir William Catesby	*distantly related*
Sir James Blunt, grandson of Walter Blunt	5G Uncle
Sir Walter Herbert	her husband's 5G Uncle
Sir William Brandon	—
Sir Robert Brakenbury, Keeper of the Tower	*— he served under Mary's 2C 4R*
Sir Christopher Urswick, priest	*— he was personal agent and messenger for Margaret Beaufort, Mary's 1C 5R*
Henry Long of Wrexall, Sheriff of Wiltshire	—
Humphrey Lord Stafford (non-speaking part)	*distant relation*
Sir John Mortimer	*unclear; there are lots of Mortimers in her genealogy*
Sir Hugh Mortimer (non-speaking)	*unclear*
Henry Tudor, Earl of Richmond, afterwards Henry 7	3C 4R
Anthony Woodville, 2nd Earl of Rivers	*brother to Mary's GG Aunt*
William Neville, Lord Falconbridge and Earl of Kent	5G Uncle
Sir Thomas Stanley, 1st Earl of Derby (non-speaking part)	*married 1C 5R*
Sir John (Thomas) Montgomery	2C 3R
Thomas Lord Scales	3C 5R
James Fiennes, Lord Say	*— (there are other Fiennes and a Sir John Say in Mary's genealogy, but not this one)*
Sir John Stanley	—
Sir William Vaux	—
Matthew Goffe (Gough)	—
Alexander Iden of Kent	—

mentioned in the plays:

Sir Walter Blunt	7G Grandfather
Sir John Blunt	7G Uncle
Lord Walter Hungerford	5G Grandfather
Thomas de Scales, Lord Scales	3C 5R
Lionel of Antwerp, Duke of Clarence	7G Uncle
James Butler, Earl of Wiltshire and 5th Earl of Ormonde	2C 5R

Lord Clifford	*unclear*
Roger Mortimer, 4th Earl of March	2C 6R
Edmund/Edward Brooke, Lord Cobham of Kent	2C 4R
Lord Richard Grey, 8th Baron Ferrers of Groby	4C 3R *(error for Sir John Grey, first husband of QE Woodville)*
George Stanley	2C 4R
Sir John Guildford	3G Grandfather
Sir Richard Guildford	2G Grandfather
Sir Gilbert Talbot	1C 4R (half)
Sir William Stanley (brother to Thomas)	4C 2R
Jasper Tudor, Earl of Pembroke, "redoubted Pembroke"	—
Rhys ap Thomas	—
Henry Percy, (melancholy) Lord Northumberland	1C 5R
Walter Devereux, Lord Ferrers	—
Sir John Fastolf	—
Philip the Good, Duke of Burgundy	*distant relation*
Richard Woodville, Lieutenant of the Tower	*distant relation*
Sir Edward Courtenay	—
Bishop of Exeter	—
Sir William Lucy	*distant relation*
Sir William Glansdale	—
Sir Thomas Gargrave	—
Sir Richard Vernon	—

Henry 8

Character	Relation to Mary Sidney
King Henry 8	3C 3R
Queen Catharine of Aragon	—
Anne Boleyn, Marchioness of Pembroke	4C 2R
Thomas Howard, 2nd Duke of Norfolk	2C 4R
Charles Brandon, Duke of Suffolk	—
Edward Stafford, 3rd Duke of Buckingham	3C 3R
Charles Somerset, Lord Chamberlain	Great Grandfather
Sir Thomas More, Lord Chancellor	—
Stephen Gardiner, Bishop of Winchester	—
John Longland, Bishop of Lincoln	—
George Neville, Lord Abergavenny	1C 4R
Lord Sandys, Sir William Sandys	*distantly related*
Sir Henry Guildford	Great Uncle (half)
Sir Thomas Lovel	—
Sir Anthony Denny	—
Sir Nicholas Vaux	*his sister is Mary's 2G Grandmother*
Cardinal Wolsey	—
Cardinal Campeius	—
Thomas Cranmer, Archbishop of Canterbury	—
Thomas Cromwell	—

Appendix E
Real Money

The following is a list of the approximate equivalents in money values from the Elizabethan/Jacobean eras. I have used the formula developed by John J. McCusker based on the composite commodity price indices in Great Britain from 1600 to 2001.[1]

Below, the price in pounds is an approximation of the value in 2001; the price in U.S. dollars is what that price translates to in 2012.

One pound = £1 (1*l*)
£1 = 20 shillings (20*s*)
1*s* = 12 pence (12*d*)
£1 = 240 shillings

Year	Item	Amount	Today
1565*	Schoolmaster at Stratford school annual wages	£20	£2,675
1585*	London journeyman annual wages, plus meat and drink[2]	£4	£535 US $835
1585*	London journeyman wages, not including meat and drink	£8	£1,070 US $1,669
1597*	Shakespeare paid for the deed to his house, New Place	£60	£8,026 US $12,519
1600	Typical wage earner	£2 per year	£268 US $417
1600	Price paid to a playwright for a play	£5	£669 US $1,043
1602	Shakespeare paid cash for land	£320	£41,618 US $64,911
1605	Shakespeare paid cash for a share of the tithes in Stratford	£440	£60,591 US $94,503
1610	Price paid to a playwright for a play	£10	£1,232 US $1,922
1613	Shakespeare's share of buying the Blackfriars gatehouse	£140 altogether	£15,607 US $24,342
		£80 of it in cash	£8,918 US $13,910

*Although these are for the years 1585 and 1597, the nearest I could get was 1600 using McCusker's price indices.

---

1   John J. McCusker, *How Much Is That in Real Money? A Historical Commodity Price Index for Use as a Deflator of Money Values in the Economy of the United States*, 2nd ed., Revised and Enlarged (Worcester: American Antiquarian Society, 2001), Table D-1: "Commodity Price Indexes, Great Britain, 1600–2000," 93–106.

2   William Ingram, "The Economics of Playing," in *A Companion to Shakespeare*, ed. David Scott Kastan, (Oxford: Blackwell Publishers, 1999), 314.

"Working six days a week, a journeyman [or player] near the top end of the scale with an £8 yearly wage would find his pay amounting to something under sixpence per day. In a world of annual wages where the bottom range was £3 to £4, a worker earning £8 to £10 a year should have been able to live quite adequately, perhaps even comfortably."[3]

Included below, as a comparison, are some of the monetary amounts in the world of the Herbert boys, Mary's sons.

Year	Item	Amount	Today
1616	Money given away in Shakespeare's will	£210	£22,866 US $35,663
1621	Annual payment to Dr. Matthew Lister, Mary's lover	£140	£15,607 US $24,342
1623	Assumed price of the finished First Folio	£2 each	£208 US $325
1603	Philip Herbert and two others given a grant for transport of cloth	£10,000 per year	£1,377,059 US $2,147,785
1604	England's gift of a jewel to their new King (William Herbert is part of presentation)	£40,000	£6,041,290 US $9,422,541
1605	Philip Herbert's income from lands given to him by King James	£1,200 per year	£165,247 US $257,734
1610	William Herbert's gift to Ben Jonson every New Year's Day	£20	£2,464 US $3,843
1611	Gift to Philip Herbert from King James	£6,000	£802,629 US $1,251,8512
1615	William Herbert's annual income	£5,000	£544,419 US $849,124
1626	William Herbert's annual income	£22,000 per year	£2,452,476 US $3,825,103
1640	Philip Herbert's annual income	£30,000 per year	£3,344,286 US $5,216,049
1640	Philip spent on hunting annually	£18,000	£2,006,571 US $3,129,630

3   Ibid., 314; information about a player earning the same wage as a journeyman is on 320.

Index

A

Abbot, Archbishop, 243
Abuses Stript and Whipt, 41
academy of Navarre, 192–193
Accius, Lucius, 305
actors
in London at the time, 259
role, source of term, 270
Acts and Monuments of Martyrs, 152
Aeschylus, 305
Aggas, Edward, *A Discourse of Life and Death,* 83–84
Akrigg, G.P.V., 44
alchemy
elements of, 167
imagery
in *King Lear,* 167
in the plays, 21
invisible ink recipe, 92–93
Mary Sidney's interest in, 64, 167
Aldersey family papers and Ben Jonson, 105
Alençon, Duke of, 67
All is True **play,** 47–48
All's Well that Ends Well
source material for, 166
Alnwick Castle, manuscripts in, 271
Ampthill, Bedfordshire
appears in plays, 163
Mary built Houghton House in, 104
The Annals of England, 153
All is True, not *Henry 8,* 47–48
An Open Elite? 249
Antonie, Antonius
discussion of and excerpts from, 78–79
used as a source for *Antony and Cleopatra,* 151, 181
Antony and Cleopatra
source material for, 149, 151, 160
source materials were changed, 180
Aphra Behn, 126
apocryphal plays, 258, 261
Arbury Hall in Nuneaton, manuscripts found in, 271
Arcadia. *See The Countess of Pembroke's Arcadia*
Archbishop of Canterbury, 243, 275
Aretino, pornographic Italian writer, 165
Ariosto, Ludovico, 154
aristocracy vs. royalty, 312

Aristophanes, 307
Armstrong, Archie, the King's fool, 237
Astrea, 90
Astrophel, by Edmund Spenser, 77
Astrophel and Stella
influenced *Romeo and Juliet,* 149
line from, re Muse, 175
popularized the sonnet form, 68, 129
As You Like It
animal sports imagery in, 233–234
motley coat, Jacques, 60
possible performance at Wilton House, 275
source changes, 175–176
source material for, 158
Wilton House, possibly performed at, 56
Aubrey, John
Arcadia written by a woman, 148
chemistry interest of Mary's, 167
library of Mary Sidney, 65
Wilton House as an academy, 193
Authorship Question, why it is an issue, 33–56
Avon River runs through Salisbury, 282

B

babes and childbirth, 222–223
Babington, Gervase, Bishop, 297
Bacon, Lady Ann, 62
Bacon, Sir Francis
Anne Cooke, his mother, 61
gay, known to be, 115
major figure of his day, 41
manuscripts extant, 271
Bandello, Matteo, 153
Barlemont, Countess of, 104
Barnfield, Richard, 114
Barton, Anne
As You Like It, 175
Taming of the Shrew, 176
women in general in the plays, 206
baseborn
Shakespeare, 120
what is baseborn? 312
Bate, Jonathan, 47

D

G

H

Biographies and other books about Mary Sidney:

Margaret Hannay, *Philip's Phoenix: Mary Sidney, Countess of Pembroke* (Oxford: Oxford University Press, 1990).

Gary F. Waller, *Mary Sidney, Countess of Pembroke: A Critical Study of Her Writings and Literary Milieu* (Salzburg: Universität Salzburg, 1979).

Frances Berkeley Young, *Mary Sidney, Countess of Pembroke* (London: David Nutt, 1912).

Margaret Hannay, et al., eds., *The Collected Works of Mary Sidney Herbert, Countess of Pembroke*, vols. 1 and 2 (Oxford: Clarendon Press, 1998).

Michael G. Brennan and Noel J. Kinnamon, *A Sidney Chronology, 1554–1654* (Basingstoke and New York: Palgrave Macmillan, 2003).

Margaret P. Hannay, Michael G. Brennan and Mary Ellen Lamb, eds., *The Ashgate Companion to The Sidneys, 1500–1700; Volume 1: Lives, Volume 2: Literature* (Farnham, Surrey: Ashgate, 2015).

Brian O'Farrell, *Shakespeare's Patron: William Herbert, Third Earl of Pembroke, 1580–1630: Politics, Patronage and Power* (London: Bloomsbury Academic, 2011).

Germain Warkentin, Joseph L. Black, and William R. Bowen, *The Library of the Sidneys of Penshurst Place, circa 1665* (Toronto: University of Toronto Press, 2013).

Michael Brennan, *Literary Patronage in the English Renaissance: The Pembroke Family* (London, New York: Routledge, 1988).

....

Printed in Great Britain
by Amazon

51970100R00190